Hana-Kimi

For You in Full Blossom

15

story and art by
HISAYA NAKAJO

HANA-KIMI
For You in Full Blossom
VOLUME 15

STORY & ART BY HISAYA NAKAJO

Translation & English Adaptation/David Ury
Touch-Up Art & Lettering/Primary Graphix
Design/Izumi Evers
Editor/Jason Thompson

Managing Editor/Megan Bates
Editorial Director/Elizabeth Kawasaki
Editor in Chief/Alvin Lu
Sr. Director of Acquisitions/Rika Inouye
Senior VP of Marketing/Liza Coppola
Exec. VP of Sales & Marketing/John Easum
Publisher/Hyoe Narita

Published by VIZ Media, LLC, P.O. Box 77010, San Francisco, CA 94107

Shôjo Edition
10 9 8 7 6 5 4 3 2 1
First printing, December 2006

T 251174

www.viz.com
store.viz.com

PARENTAL ADVISORY
HANA-KIMI is rated T+ for Older Teen and is recom-
mended for ages 16 and up. Contains strong lan-
guage, sexual themes and alcohol and tobacco usage.

CONTENTS

ook ook

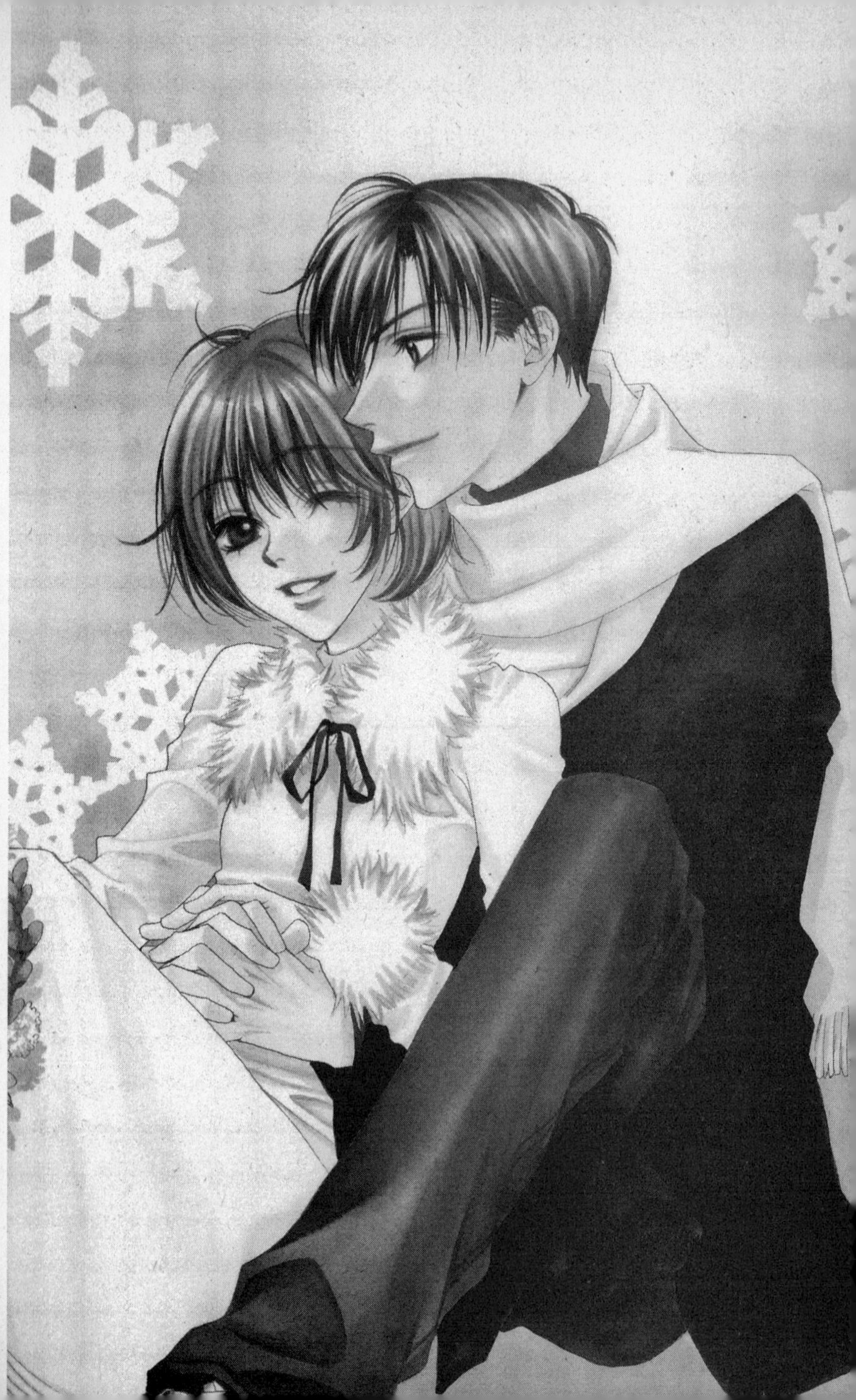

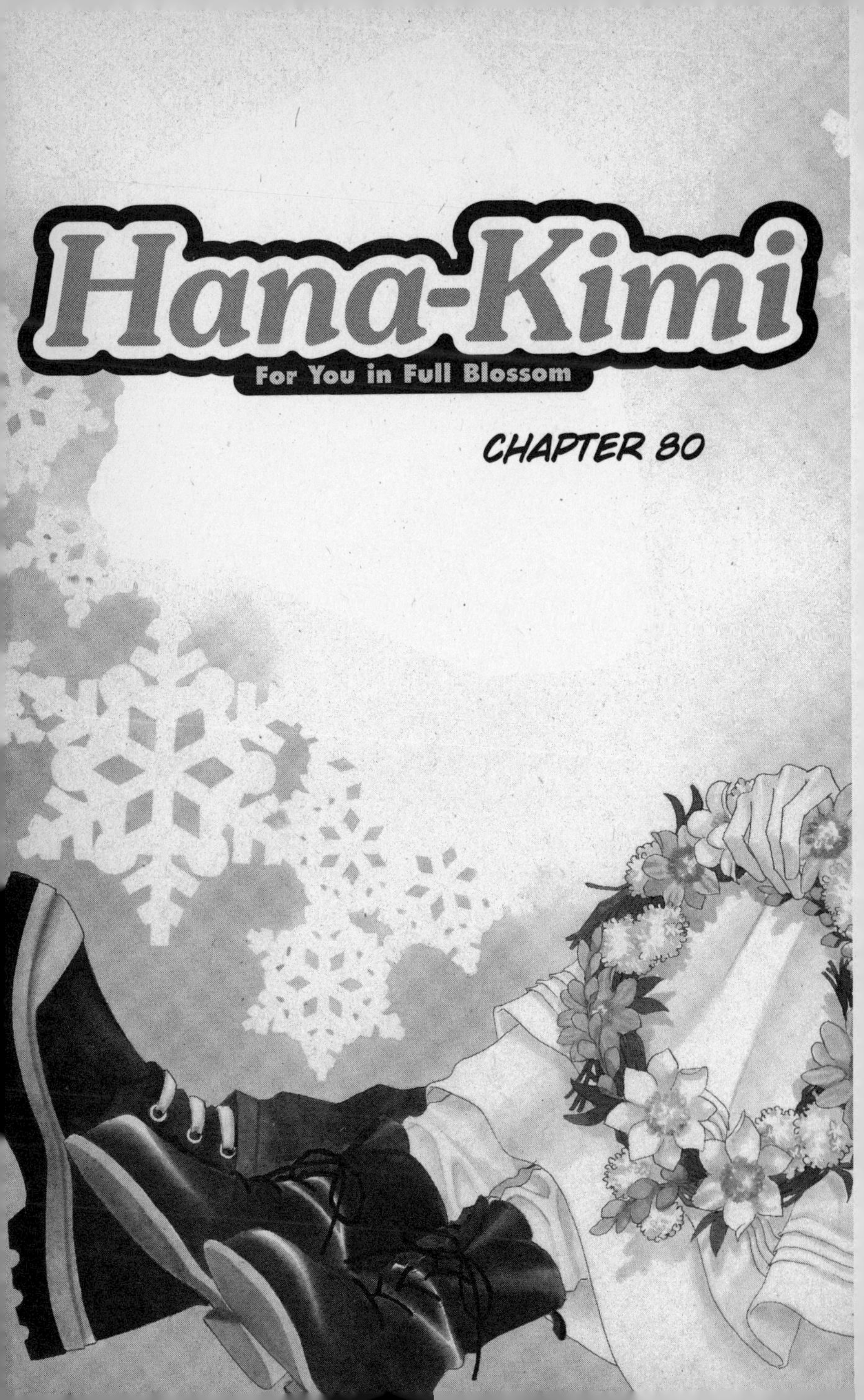
Hana-Kimi
For You in Full Blossom
CHAPTER 80

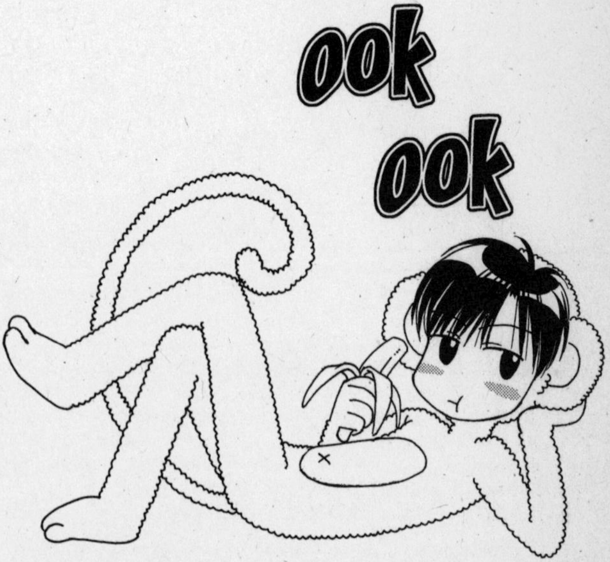
ook
ook

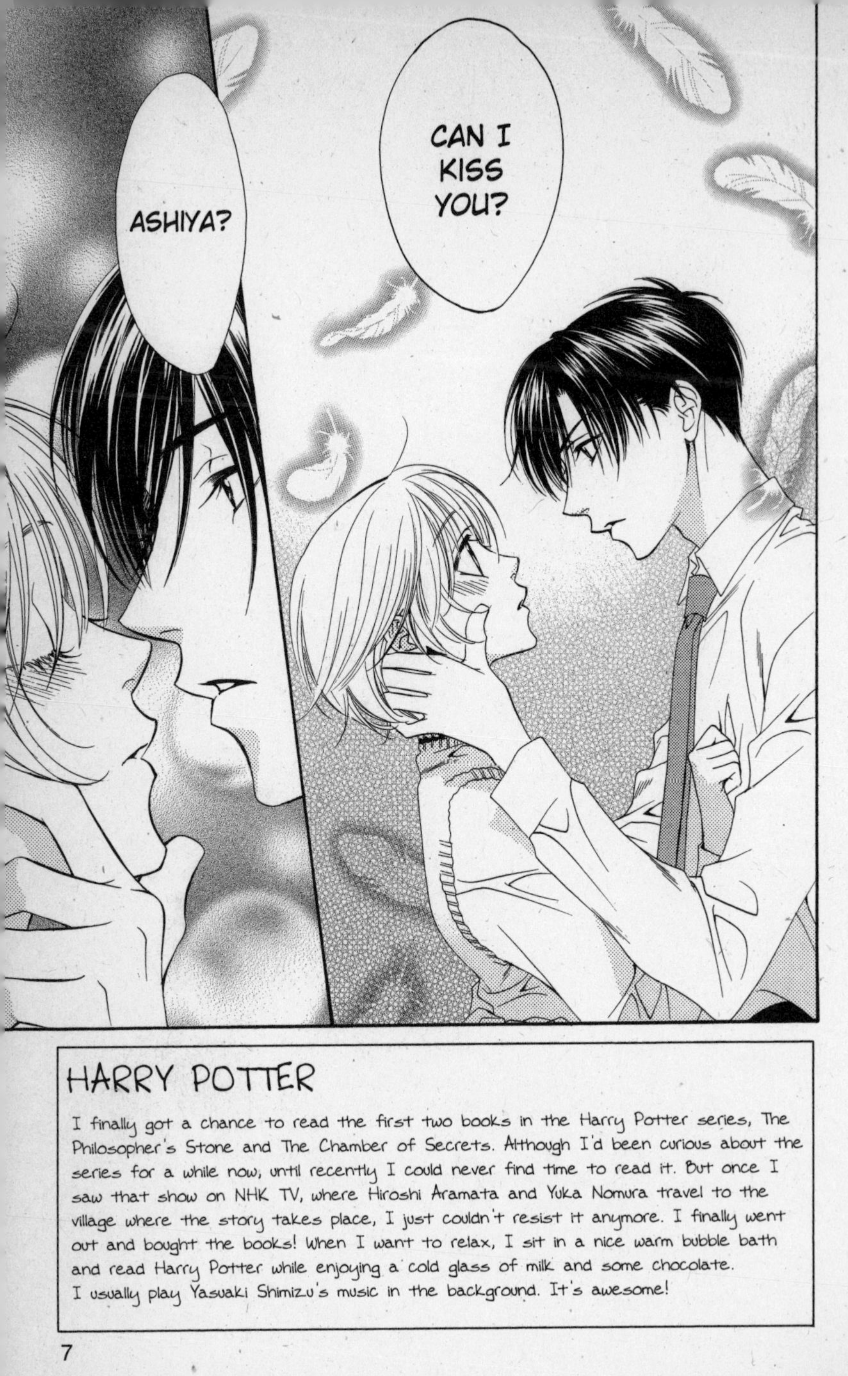
CAN I KISS YOU?
ASHIYA?

HARRY POTTER

I finally got a chance to read the first two books in the Harry Potter series, The Philosopher's Stone and The Chamber of Secrets. Although I'd been curious about the series for a while now, until recently I could never find time to read it. But once I saw that show on NHK TV, where Hiroshi Aramata and Yuka Nomura travel to the village where the story takes place, I just couldn't resist it anymore. I finally went out and bought the books! When I want to relax, I sit in a nice warm bubble bath and read Harry Potter while enjoying a cold glass of milk and some chocolate. I usually play Yasuaki Shimizu's music in the background. It's awesome!

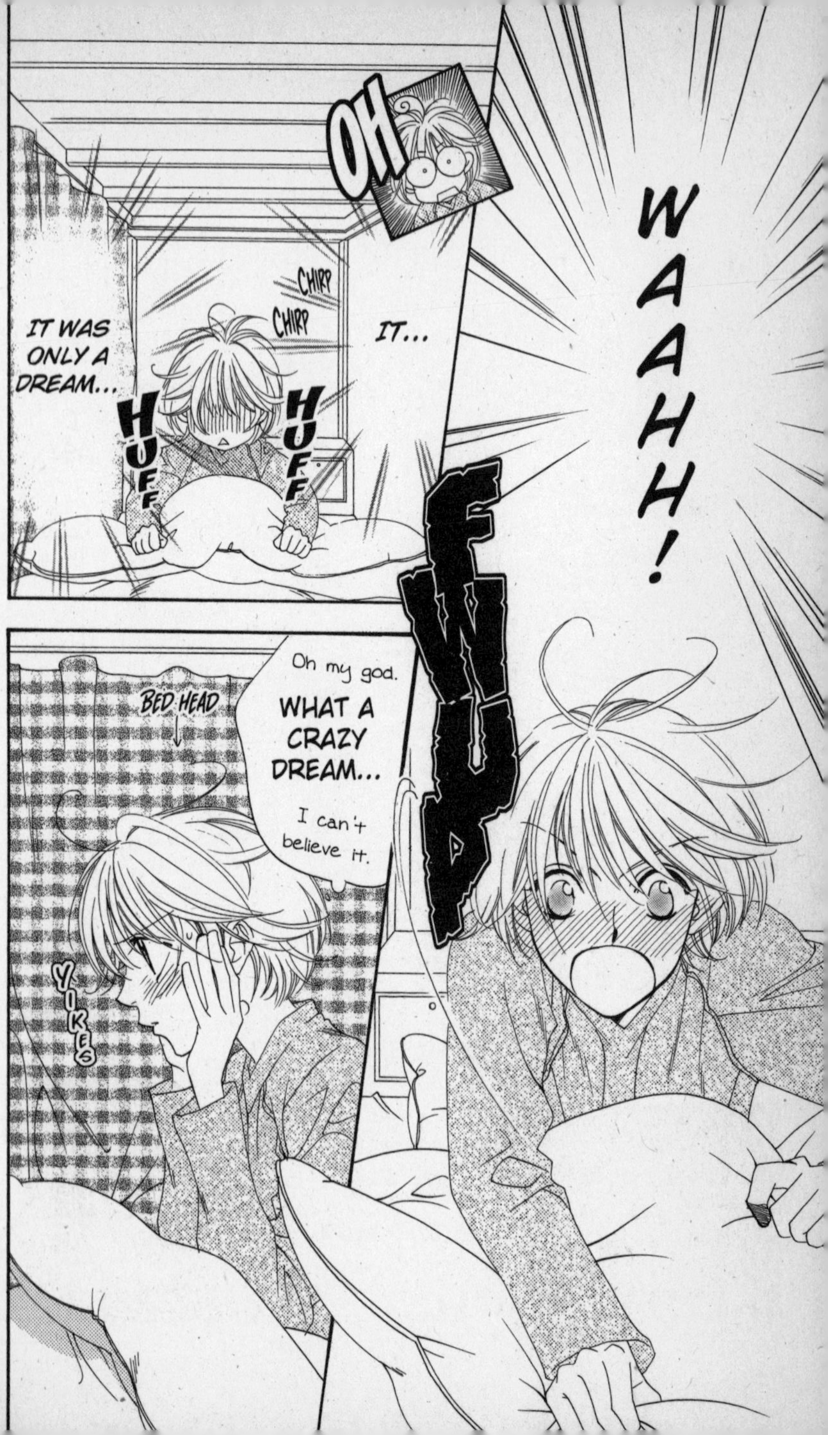
WAAHH!
FWUP
OH
IT...
CHIRP
CHIRP
IT WAS ONLY A DREAM...
HUFF
HUFF
Oh my god.
WHAT A CRAZY DREAM...
I can't believe it.
BED HEAD
YIKES

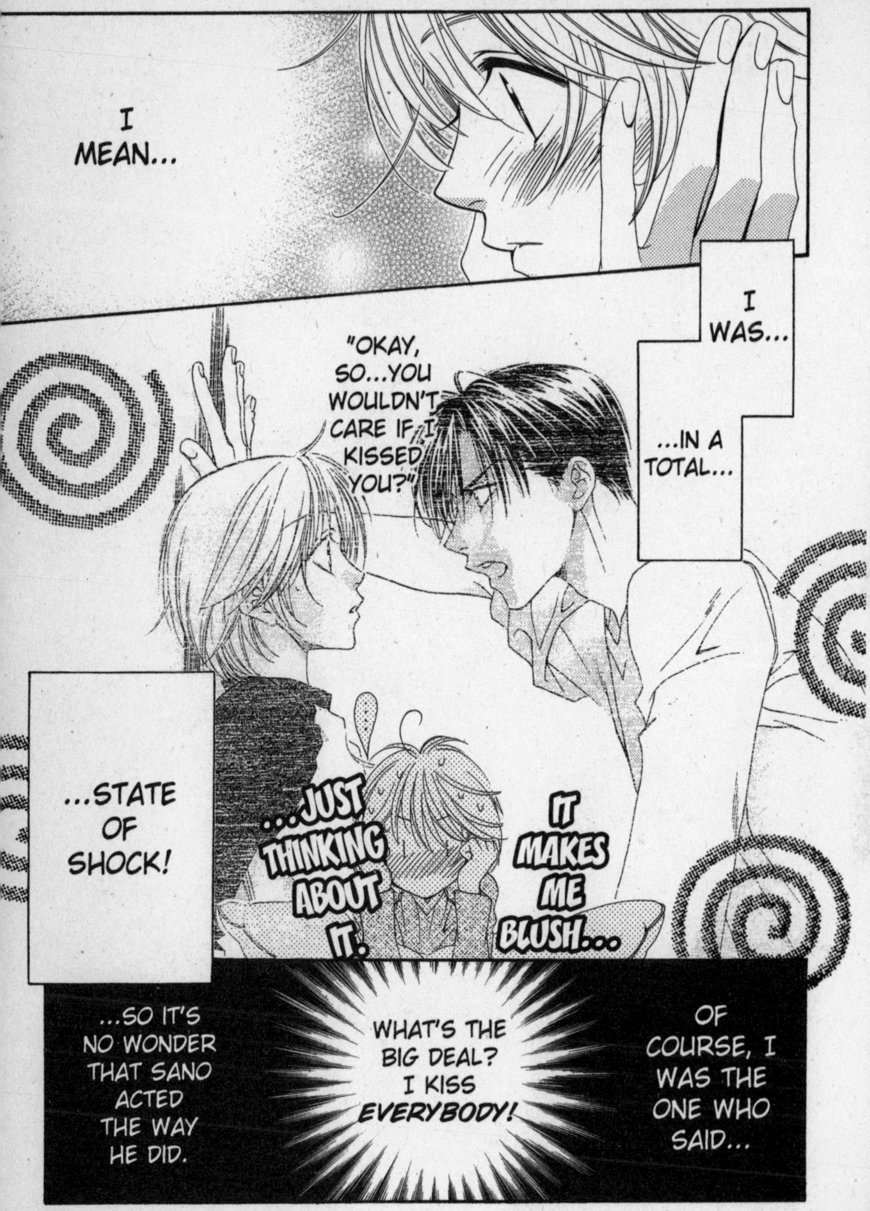
I MEAN...
I WAS...
...IN A TOTAL...
"OKAY, SO...YOU WOULDN'T CARE IF I KISSED YOU?"
...STATE OF SHOCK!
IT MAKES ME BLUSH...
...JUST THINKING ABOUT IT.
OF COURSE, I WAS THE ONE WHO SAID...
WHAT'S THE BIG DEAL? I KISS *EVERYBODY!*
...SO IT'S NO WONDER THAT SANO ACTED THE WAY HE DID.

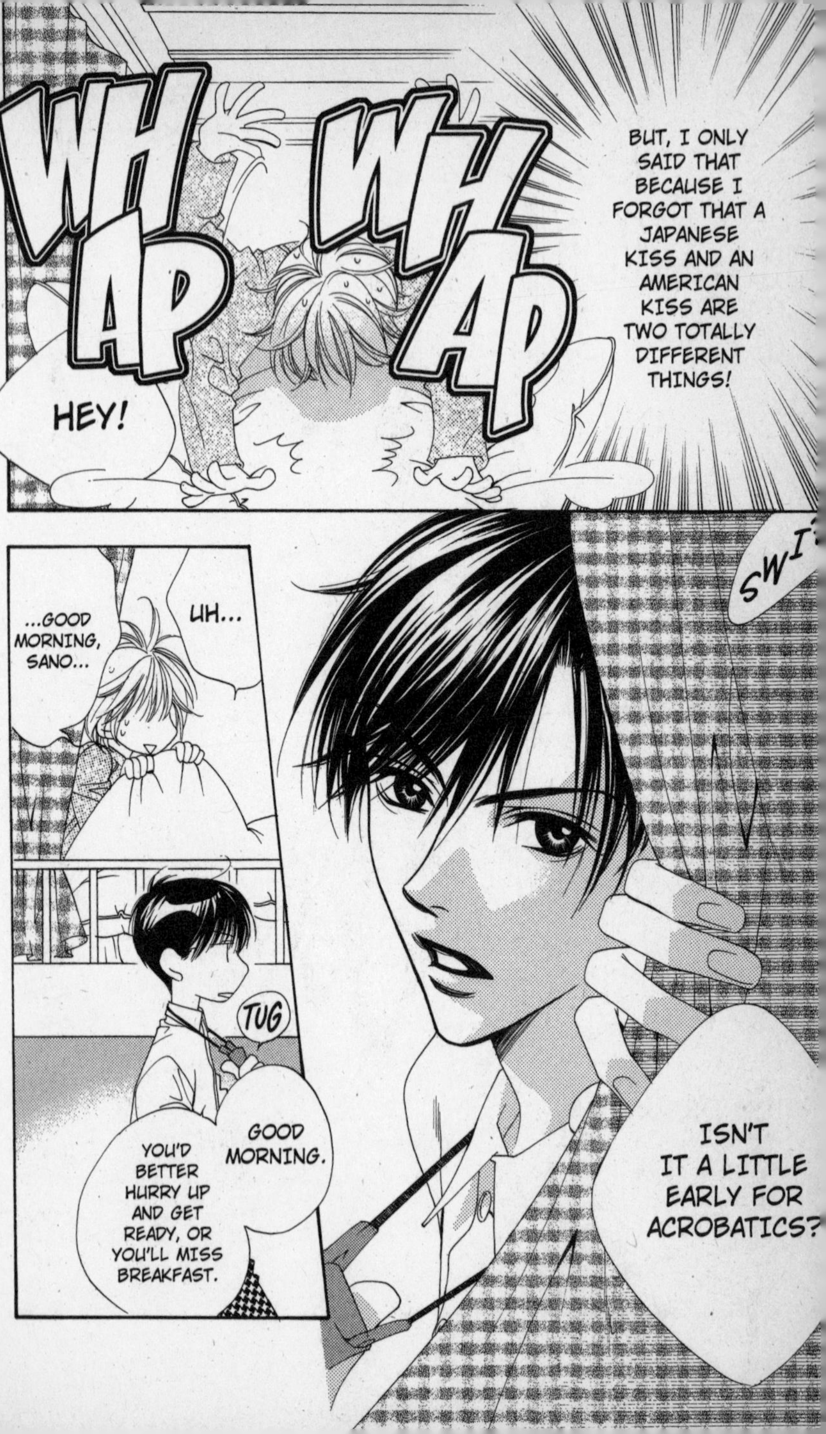
BUT, I ONLY SAID THAT BECAUSE I FORGOT THAT A JAPANESE KISS AND AN AMERICAN KISS ARE TWO TOTALLY DIFFERENT THINGS!
WHAP
WHAP
HEY!
SWI
ISN'T IT A LITTLE EARLY FOR ACROBATICS?
UH...
...GOOD MORNING, SANO...
TUG
GOOD MORNING.
YOU'D BETTER HURRY UP AND GET READY, OR YOU'LL MISS BREAKFAST.

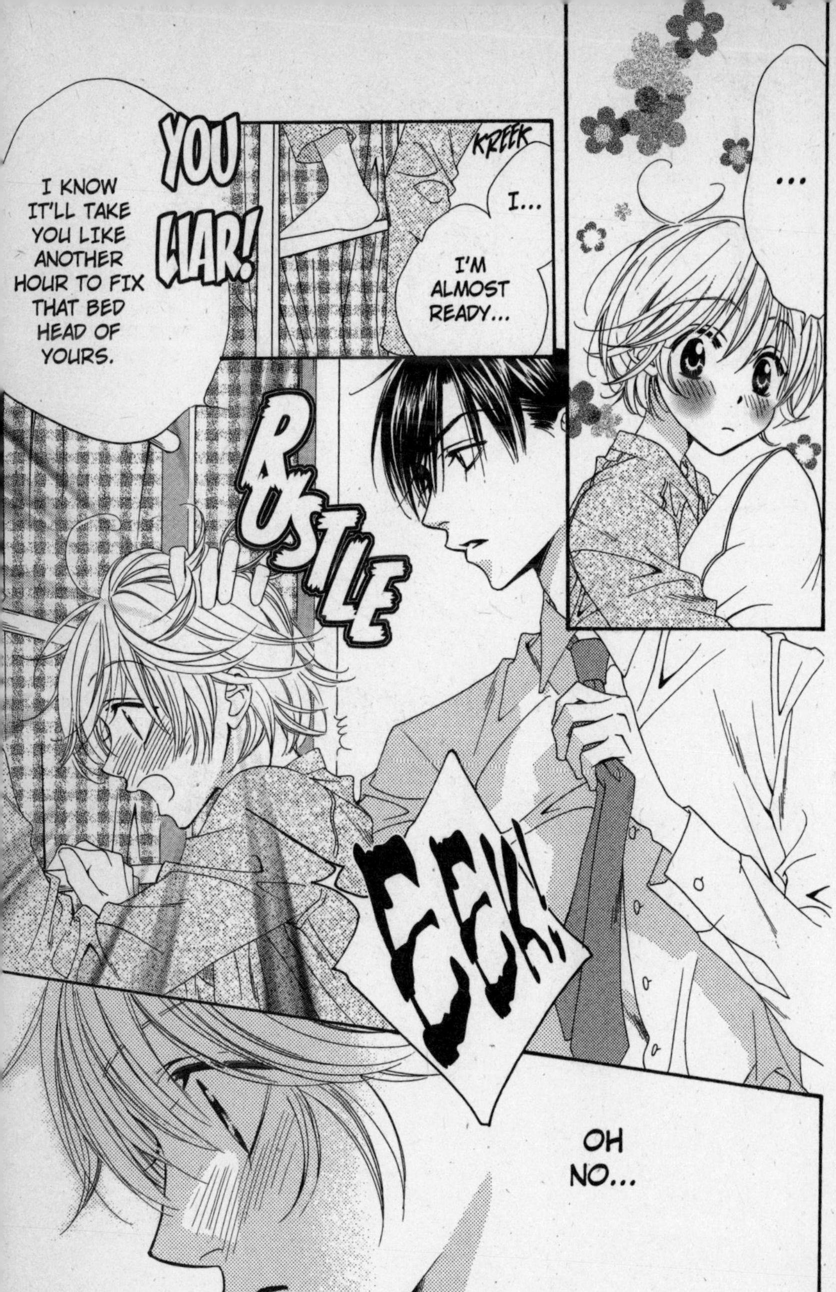
...
KREEK
I...
I'M ALMOST READY...
YOU LIAR!
I KNOW IT'LL TAKE YOU LIKE ANOTHER HOUR TO FIX THAT BED HEAD OF YOURS.
RUSTLE
EEK!!
OH NO...

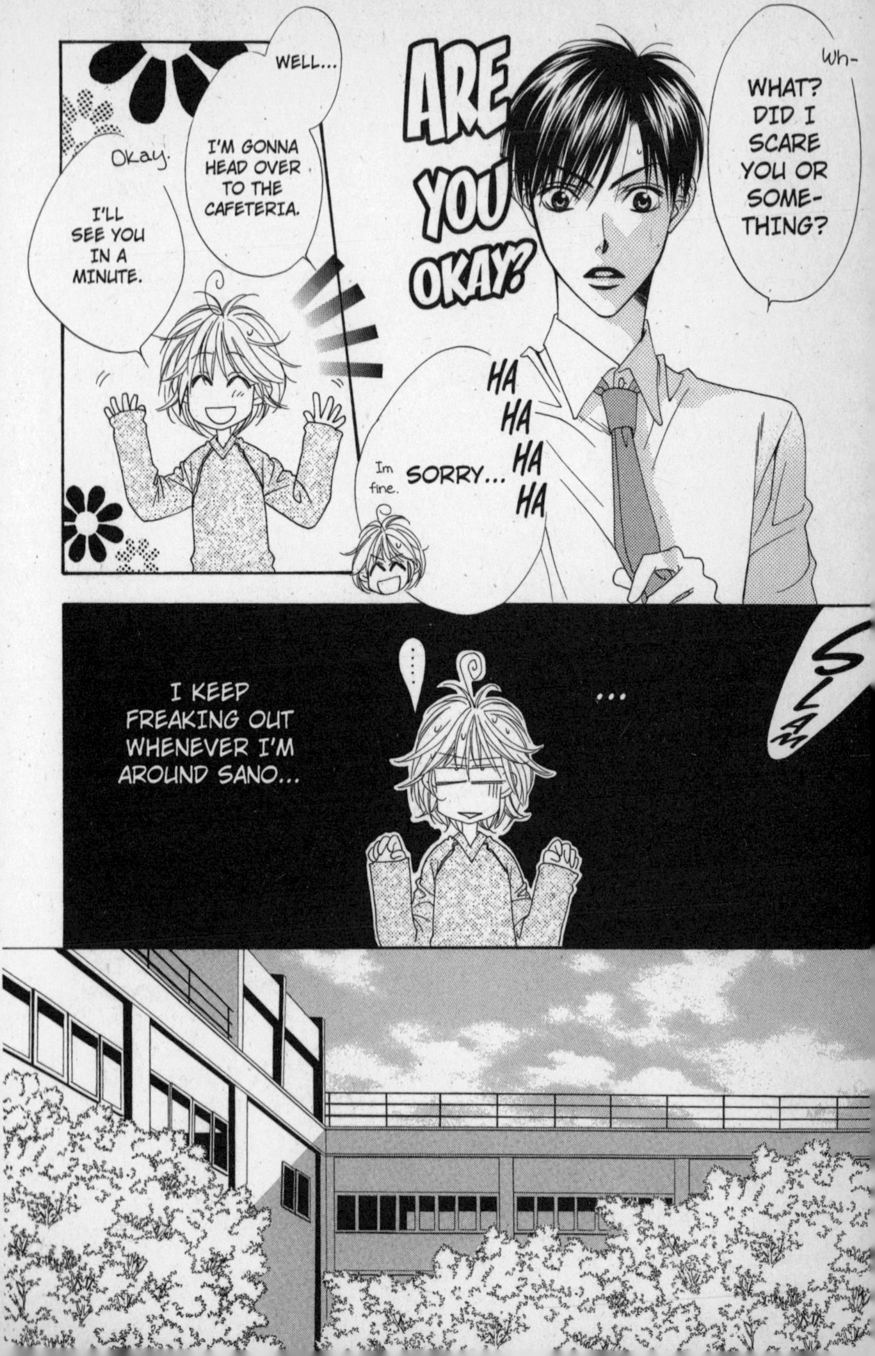
Wh-
WHAT? DID I SCARE YOU OR SOMETHING?
ARE YOU OKAY?
HA HA HA HA
SORRY...
Im fine.
WELL...
I'M GONNA HEAD OVER TO THE CAFETERIA.
Okay.
I'LL SEE YOU IN A MINUTE.
SLAM
...
!...
I KEEP FREAKING OUT WHENEVER I'M AROUND SANO...

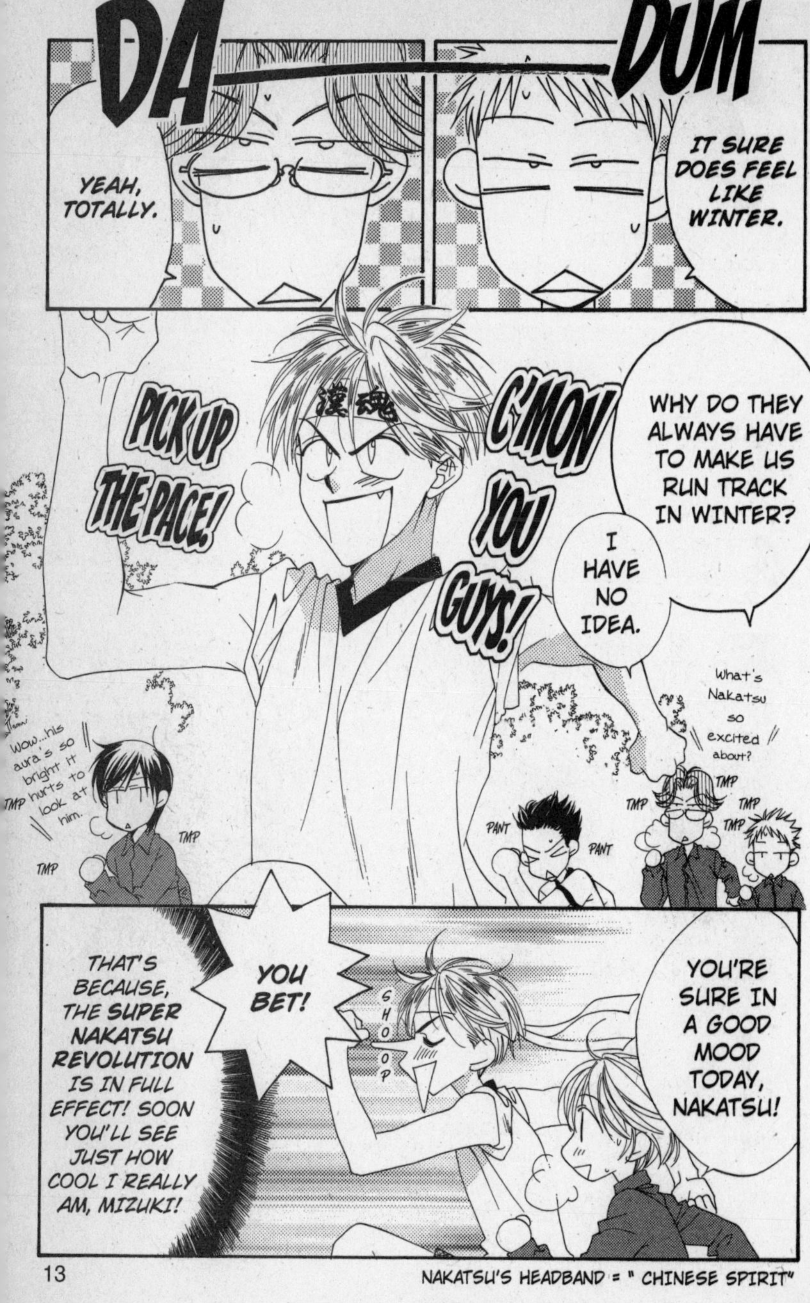
DA—DUM
IT SURE DOES FEEL LIKE WINTER.
YEAH, TOTALLY.
WHY DO THEY ALWAYS HAVE TO MAKE US RUN TRACK IN WINTER?
I HAVE NO IDEA.
C'MON YOU GUYS!
PICK UP THE PACE!
What's Nakatsu so excited about?
TMP
TMP
TMP
TMP
PANT
PANT
Wow...his aura's so bright it hurts to look at him.
TMP
TMP
TMP
YOU'RE SURE IN A GOOD MOOD TODAY, NAKATSU!
SHOOOP
YOU BET!
THAT'S BECAUSE, THE SUPER NAKATSU REVOLUTION IS IN FULL EFFECT! SOON YOU'LL SEE JUST HOW COOL I REALLY AM, MIZUKI!

NAKATSU'S HEADBAND = "CHINESE SPIRIT"

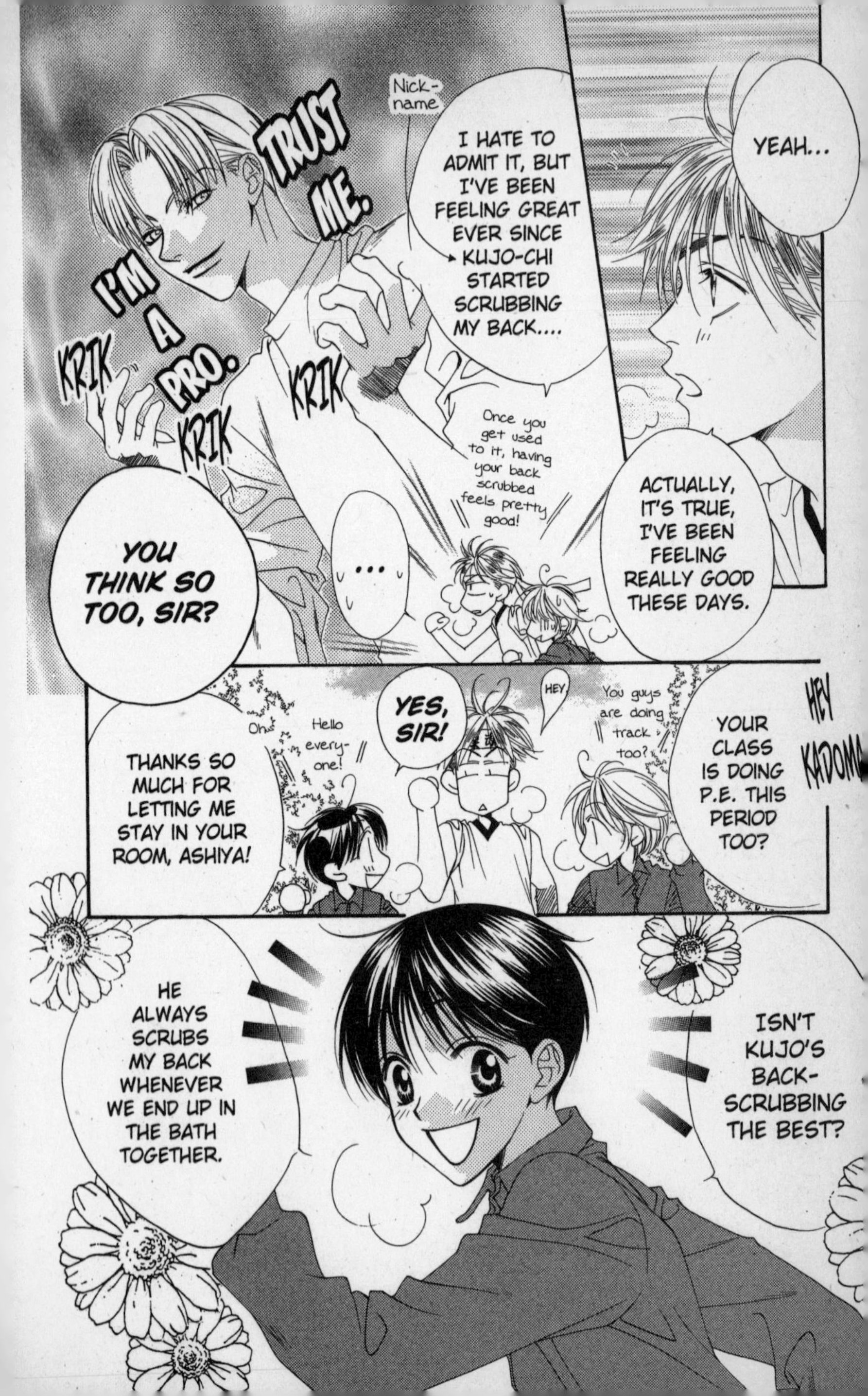
YEAH...
ACTUALLY, IT'S TRUE, I'VE BEEN FEELING REALLY GOOD THESE DAYS.
Nick-name
I HATE TO ADMIT IT, BUT I'VE BEEN FEELING GREAT EVER SINCE KUJO-CHI STARTED SCRUBBING MY BACK....
TRUST ME.
I'M A PRO.
KRIK
KRIK
KRIK
Once you get used to it, having your back scrubbed feels pretty good!
...
YOU THINK SO TOO, SIR?
HEY KADOM
YOUR CLASS IS DOING P.E. THIS PERIOD TOO?
HEY
You guys are doing track too?
YES, SIR!
Hello every-one!
Oh
THANKS SO MUCH FOR LETTING ME STAY IN YOUR ROOM, ASHIYA!
ISN'T KUJO'S BACK-SCRUBBING THE BEST?
HE ALWAYS SCRUBS MY BACK WHENEVER WE END UP IN THE BATH TOGETHER.

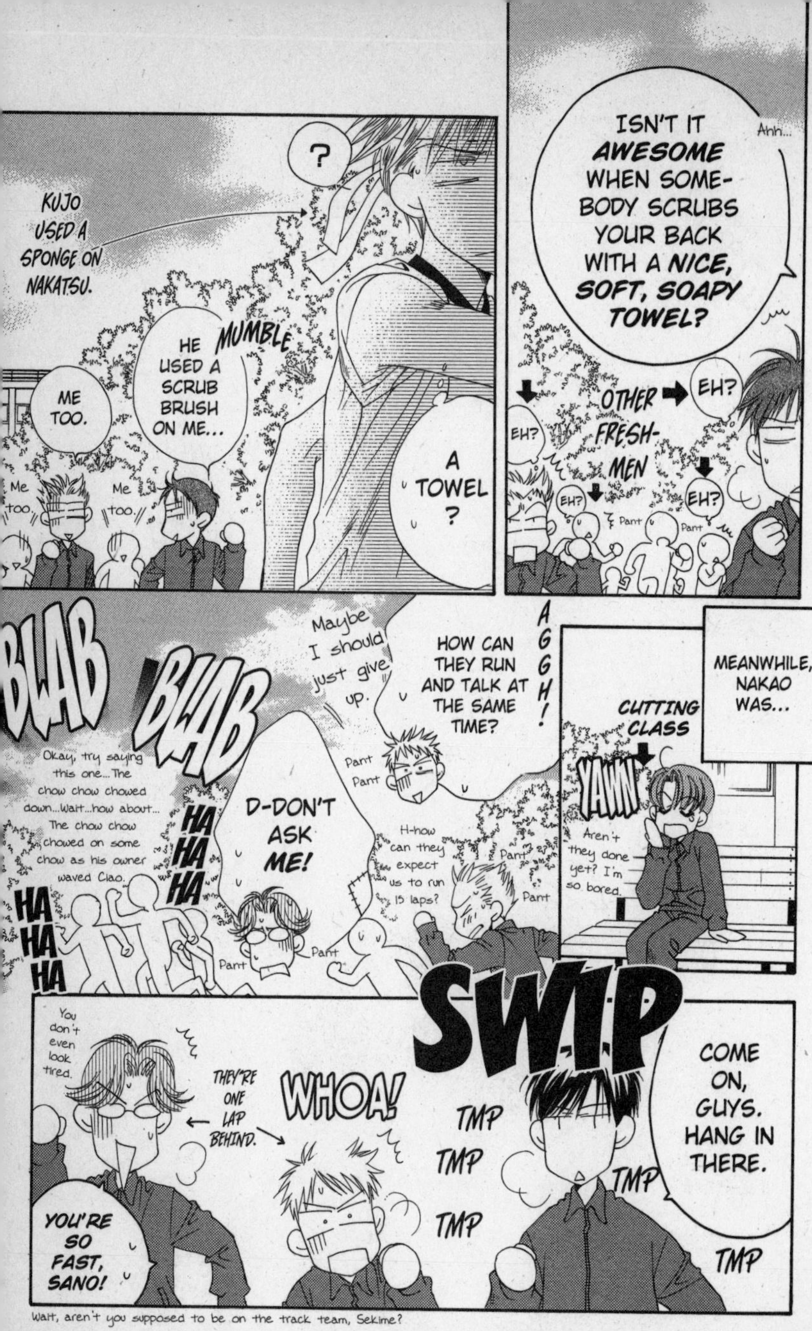
Anh...
ISN'T IT AWESOME WHEN SOMEBODY SCRUBS YOUR BACK WITH A NICE, SOFT, SOAPY TOWEL?
EH?
OTHER FRESHMEN
EH?
EH?
EH?
Pant
Pant
?
KUJO USED A SPONGE ON NAKATSU.
A TOWEL?
MUMBLE
HE USED A SCRUB BRUSH ON ME...
ME TOO.
Me too.
Me too.
MEANWHILE, NAKAO WAS...
CUTTING CLASS
YAWN
Aren't they done yet? I'm so bored.
AGGGH!
HOW CAN THEY RUN AND TALK AT THE SAME TIME?
Maybe I should just give up.
Pant Pant
Pant
Pant
H-how can they expect us to run 15 laps?
D-DON'T ASK ME!
Pant
Pant
BLAB
BLAB
Okay, try saying this one... The chow chow chowed down... Wait... how about... The chow chow chowed on some chow as his owner waved Ciao.
HA HA HA
HA HA HA
SWIP
COME ON, GUYS. HANG IN THERE.
TMP
TMP
TMP
TMP
TMP
WHOA!
THEY'RE ONE LAP BEHIND.
You don't even look tired.
YOU'RE SO FAST, SANO!

Wait, aren't you supposed to be on the track team, Sekime?

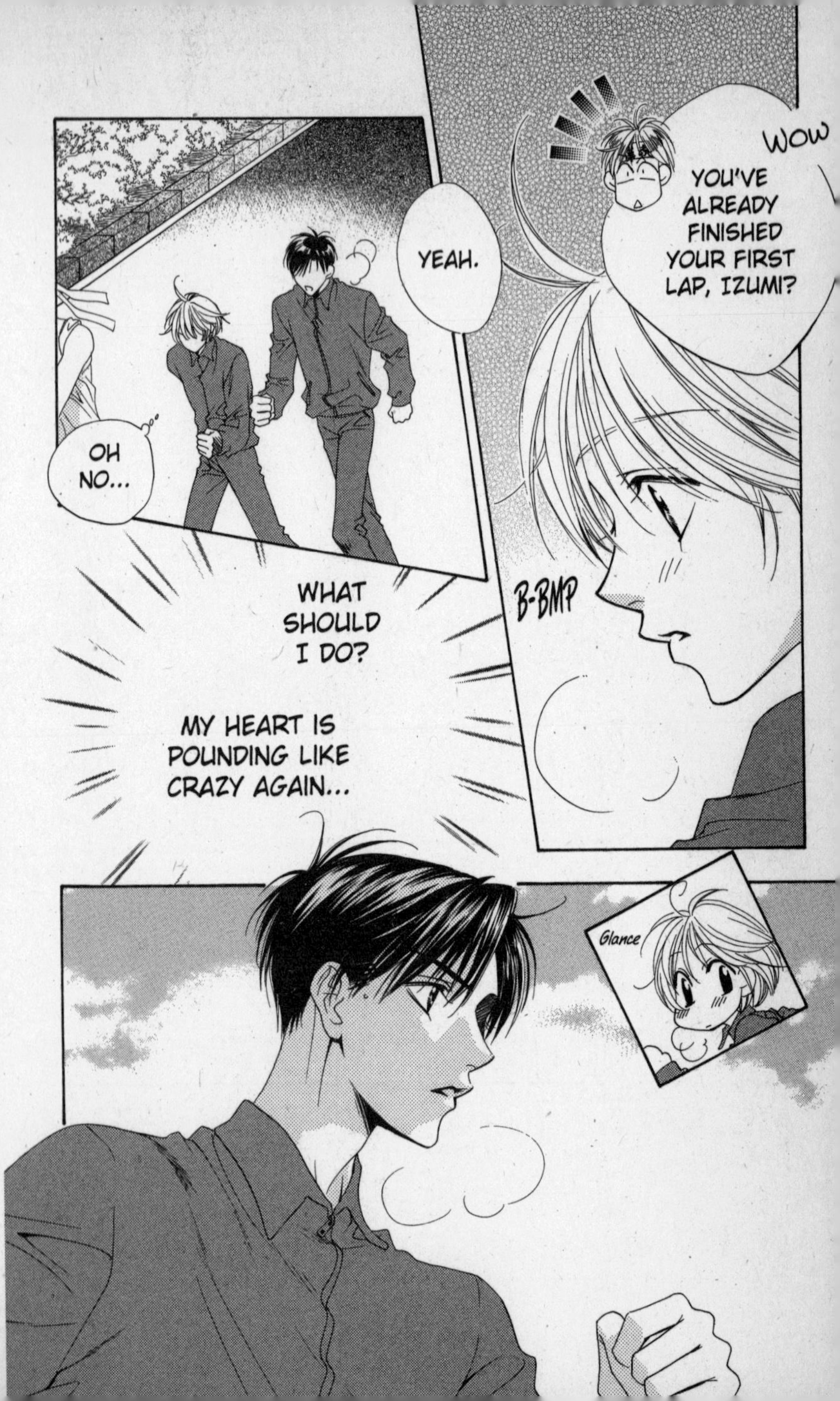
WOW
YOU'VE ALREADY FINISHED YOUR FIRST LAP, IZUMI?
YEAH.
B-BMP
OH NO...
WHAT SHOULD I DO?
MY HEART IS POUNDING LIKE CRAZY AGAIN...
Glance

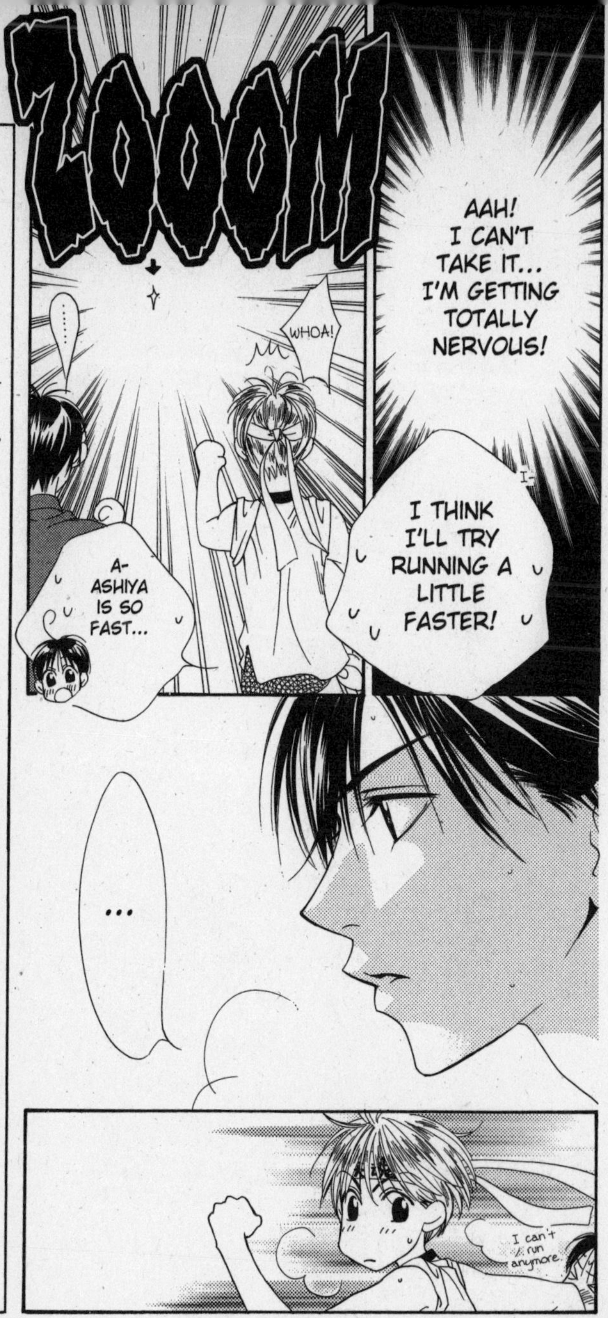
AAH! I CAN'T TAKE IT... I'M GETTING TOTALLY NERVOUS!
I-
I THINK I'LL TRY RUNNING A LITTLE FASTER!
ZOOOM
......
WHOA!
A- ASHIYA IS SO FAST...
...
I can't run anymore.

15

Hello! It's Hana-Kimi volume 15! Sano & Nakatsu are on the cover. I've heard that a lot of you guys are always trying to guess who's gonna be on the next cover. Did you get it right this time? Actually, I've been getting requests lately (ha ha)! One of the readers wrote in saying, "Please make sure Sano is on the cover of volume 15!" And a certain passionate Nakao fan keeps saying, "Please put Nakao on the cover someday!" (ha ha)...Will Nakao ever make it on the cover? See you in volume 16! (Da-da-dum!)

15

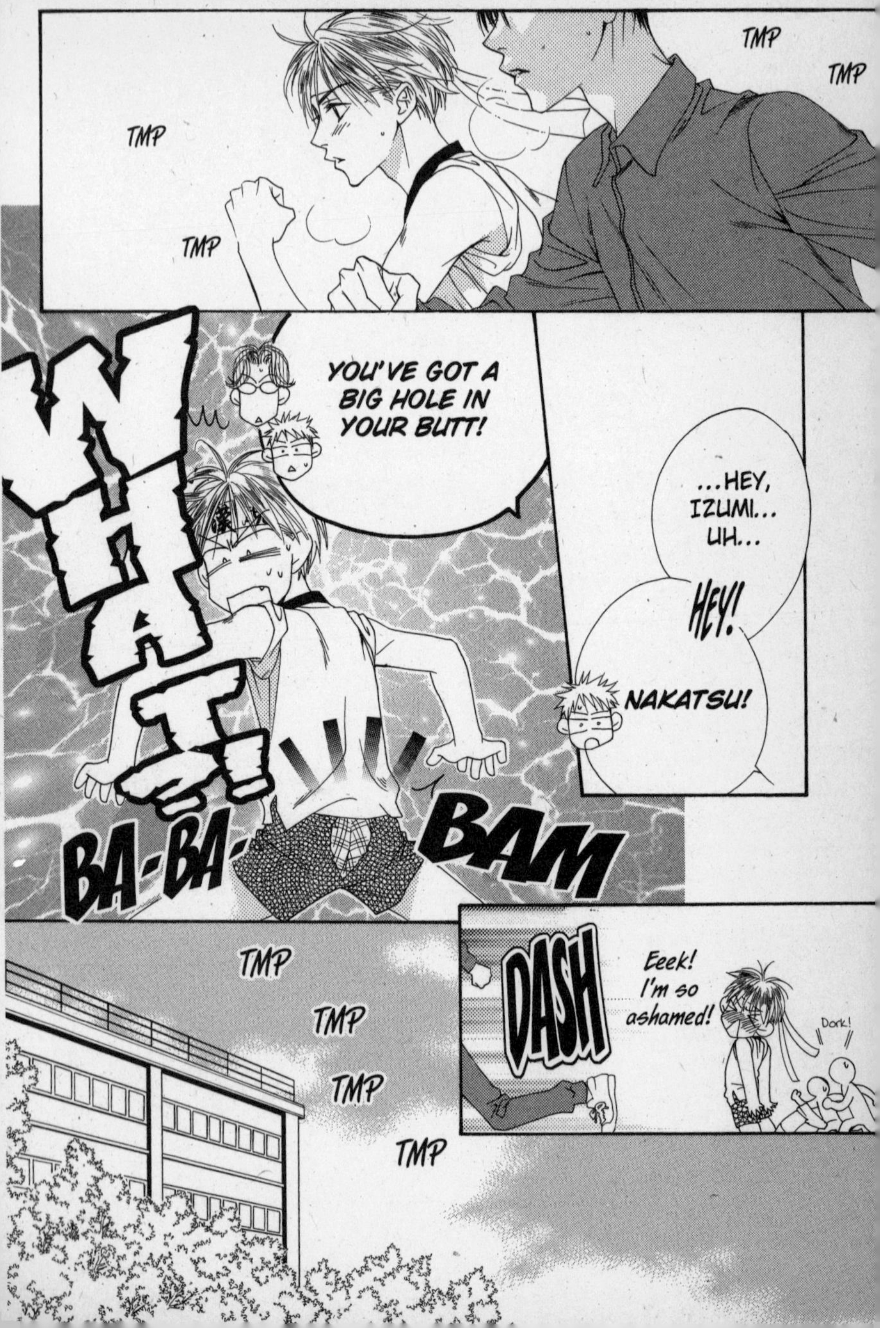
TMP
TMP
TMP
TMP
...HEY, IZUMI... UH...
HEY!
NAKATSU!
YOU'VE GOT A BIG HOLE IN YOUR BUTT!
WHAT
BA-BA-BAM
DASH
Eeek! I'm so ashamed!
Dork!
TMP
TMP
TMP
TMP

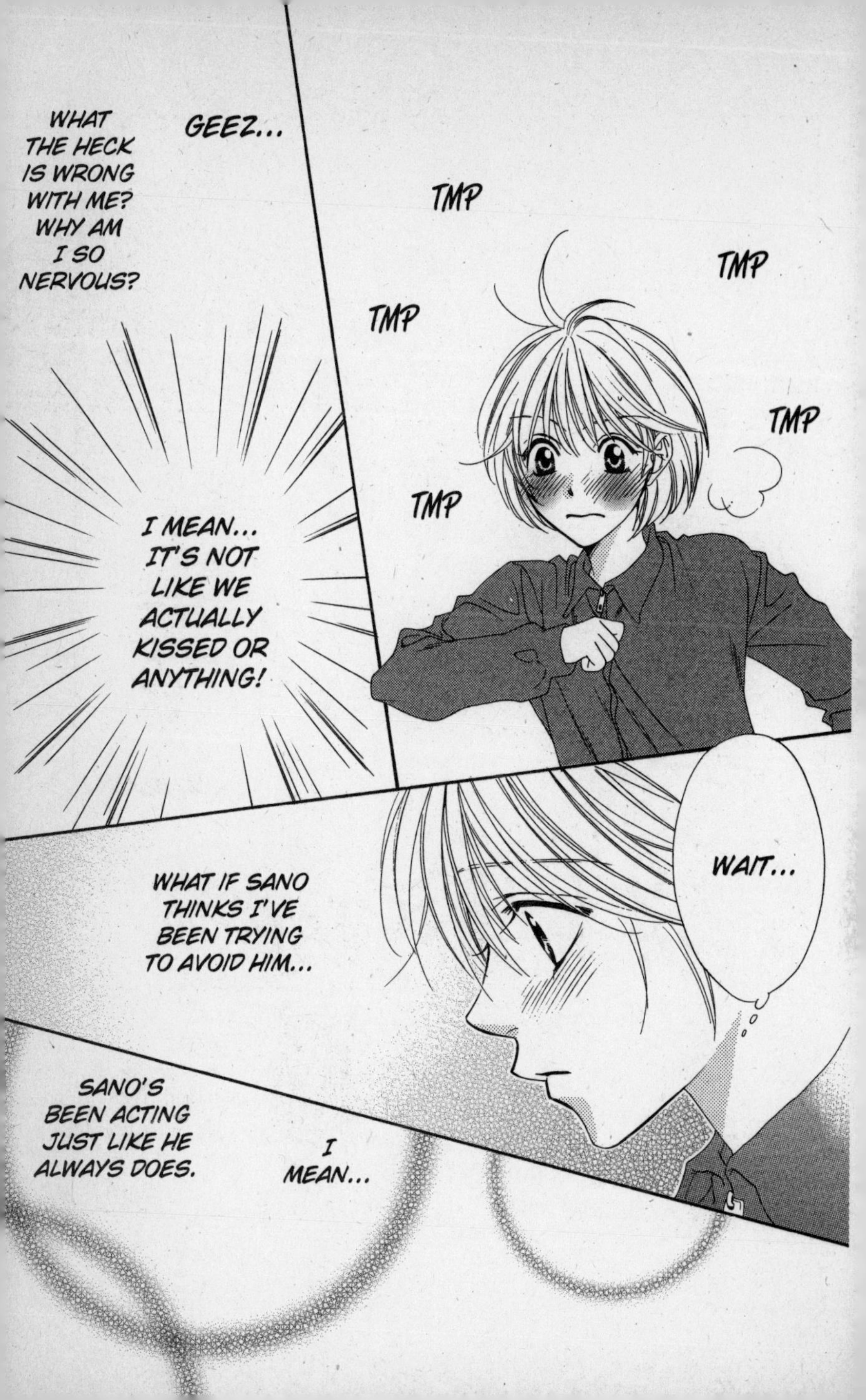
TMP
TMP
TMP
TMP
TMP
GEEZ...
WHAT THE HECK IS WRONG WITH ME? WHY AM I SO NERVOUS?
I MEAN... IT'S NOT LIKE WE ACTUALLY KISSED OR ANYTHING!
WAIT...
WHAT IF SANO THINKS I'VE BEEN TRYING TO AVOID HIM...
I MEAN...
SANO'S BEEN ACTING JUST LIKE HE ALWAYS DOES.

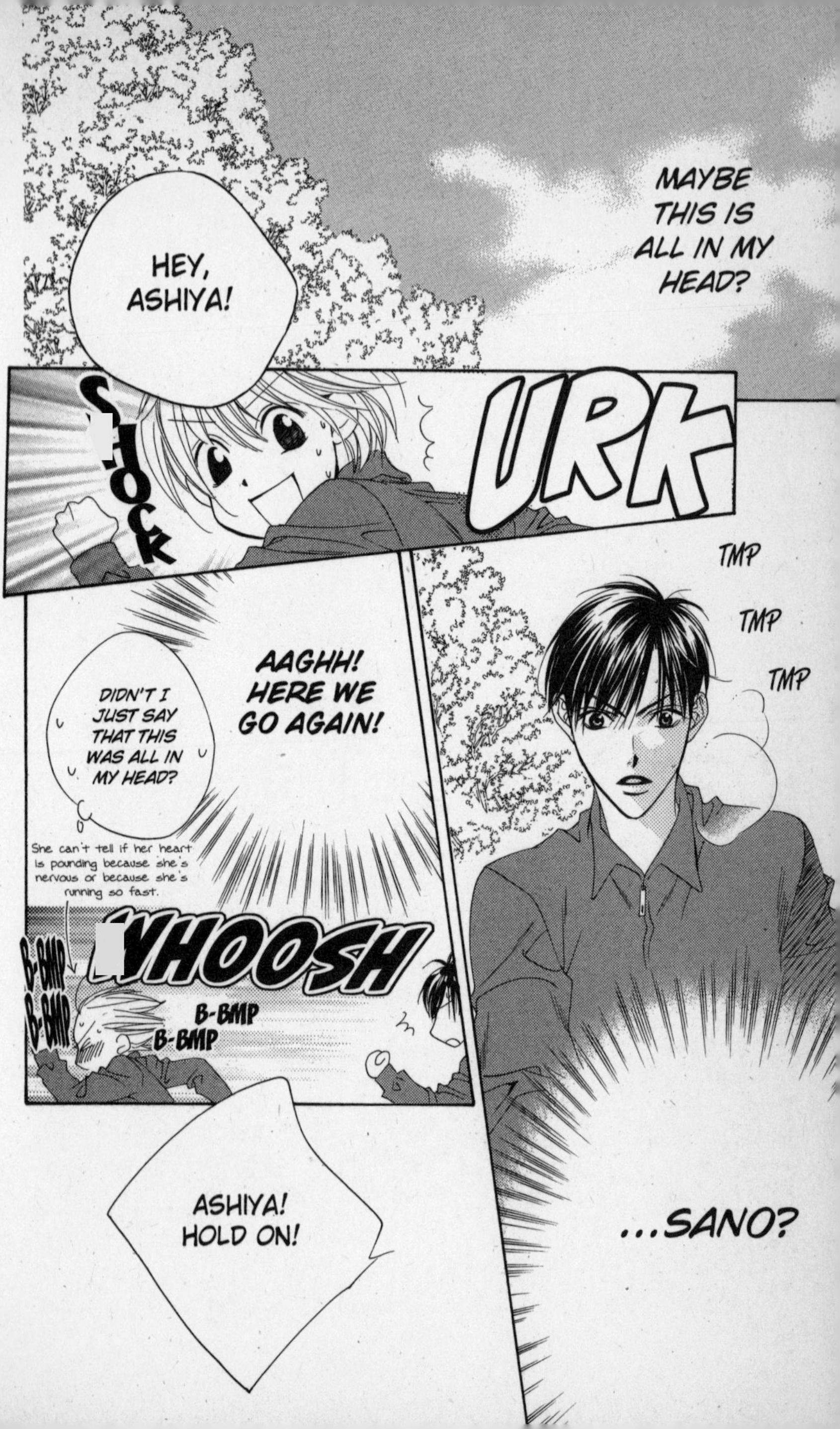
MAYBE THIS IS ALL IN MY HEAD?
HEY, ASHIYA!
URK
SHOCK
TMP
TMP
TMP
...SANO?
AAGHH! HERE WE GO AGAIN!
DIDN'T I JUST SAY THAT THIS WAS ALL IN MY HEAD?
She can't tell if her heart is pounding because she's nervous or because she's running so fast.
WHOOSH
B-BMP B-BMP
B-BMP B-BMP
ASHIYA! HOLD ON!

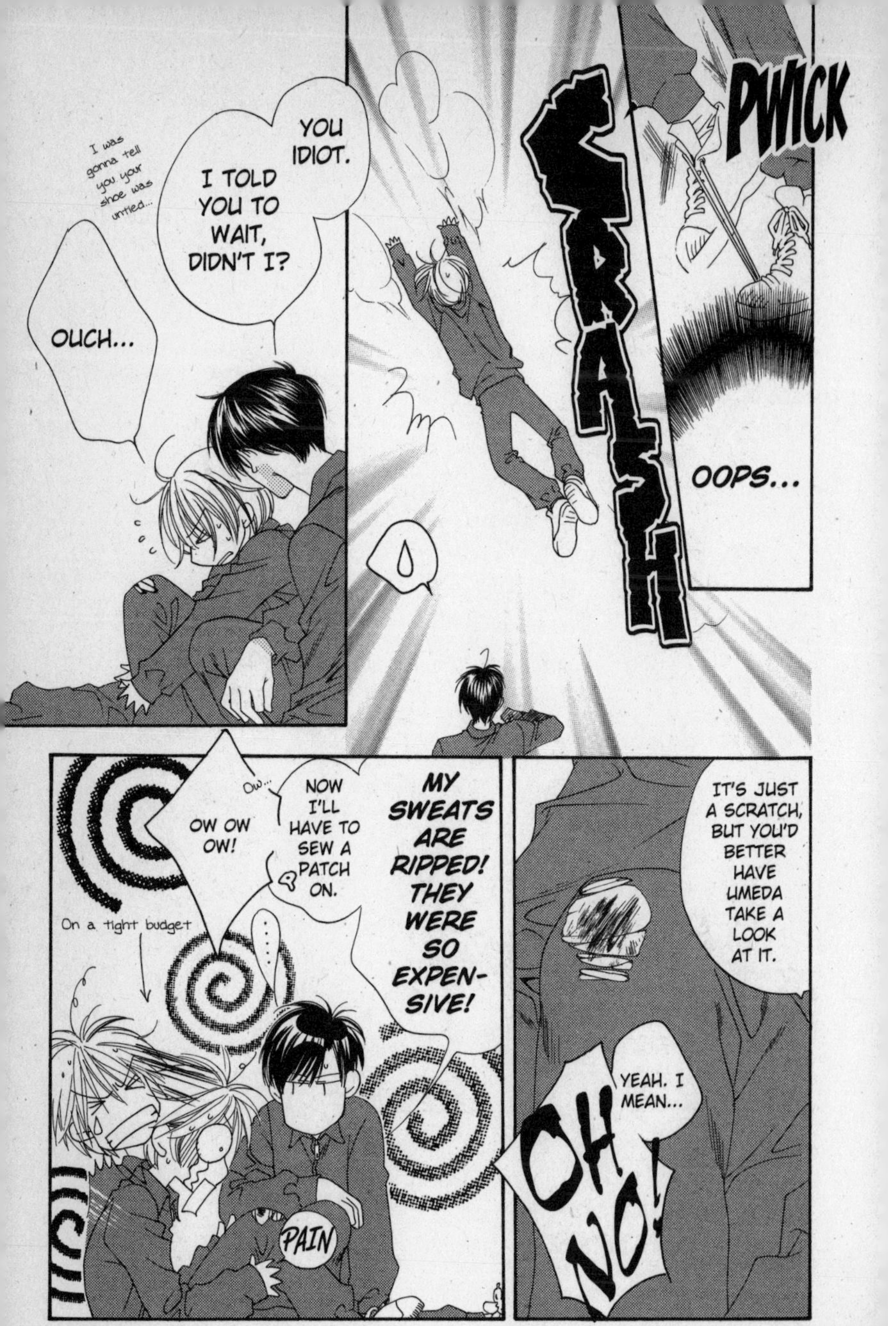
PWICK
OOPS...
CRASH
YOU IDIOT.
I TOLD YOU TO WAIT, DIDN'T I?
I was gonna tell you your shoe was untied...
OUCH...
IT'S JUST A SCRATCH, BUT YOU'D BETTER HAVE UMEDA TAKE A LOOK AT IT.
YEAH. I MEAN...
OH NO!
MY SWEATS ARE RIPPED! THEY WERE SO EXPEN-SIVE!
NOW I'LL HAVE TO SEW A PATCH ON.
Ow...
OW OW OW!
On a tight budget
PAIN

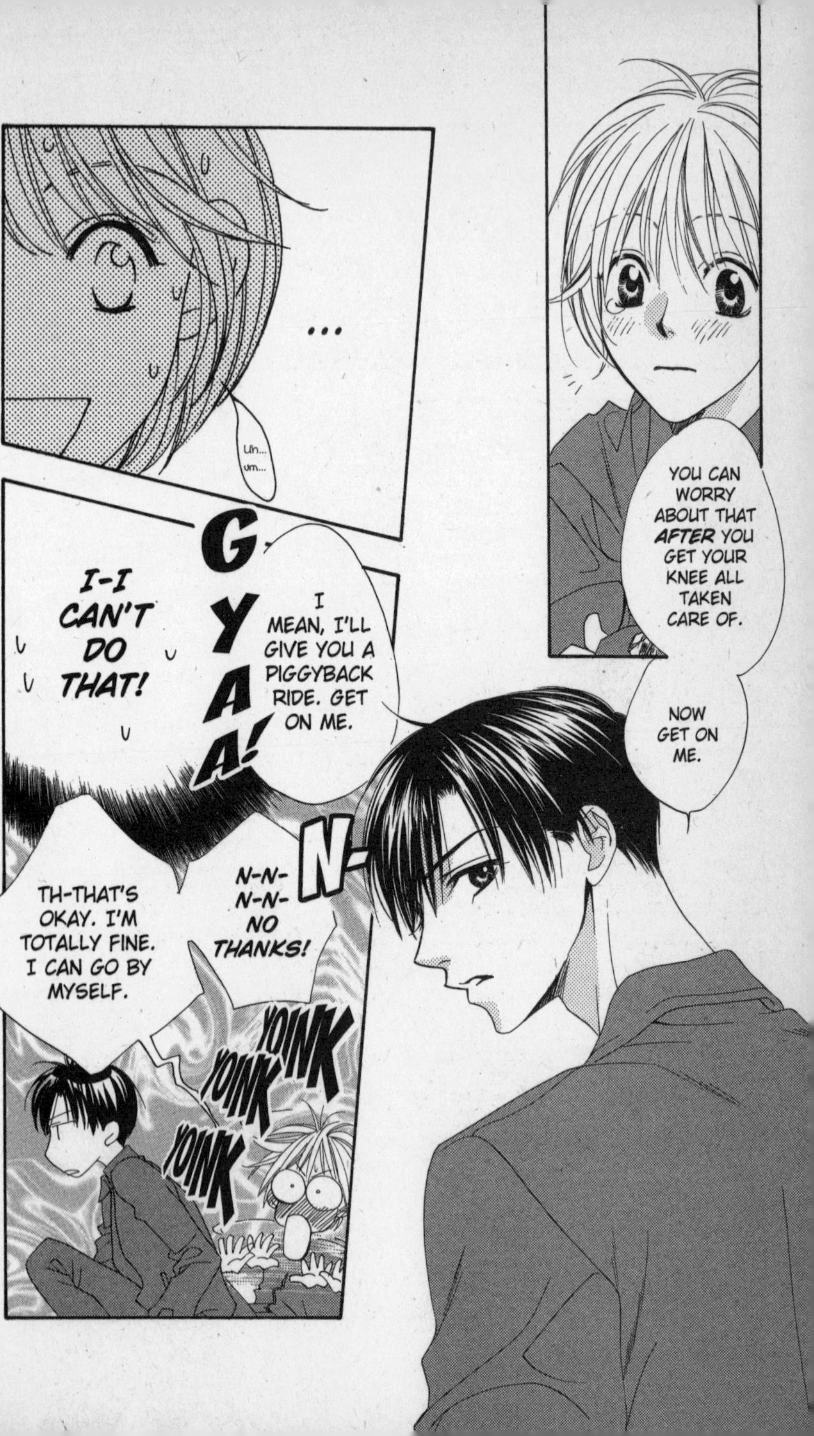
YOU CAN WORRY ABOUT THAT AFTER YOU GET YOUR KNEE ALL TAKEN CARE OF.
...
Uh... um...
NOW GET ON ME.
I MEAN, I'LL GIVE YOU A PIGGYBACK RIDE. GET ON ME.
GYAA!
I-I CAN'T DO THAT!
N-
N-N-N-N-NO THANKS!
TH-THAT'S OKAY. I'M TOTALLY FINE. I CAN GO BY MYSELF.
YOINK YOINK YOINK YOINK

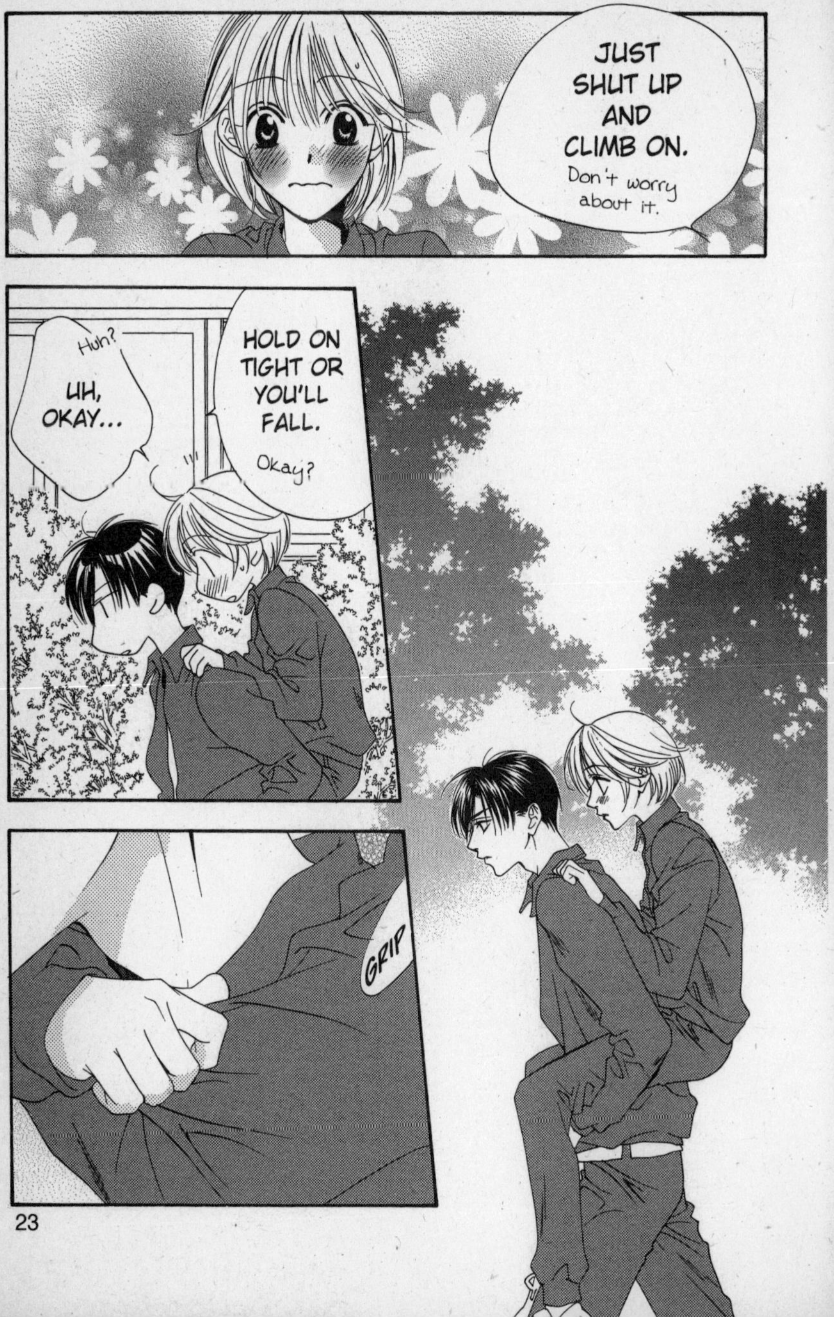
JUST SHUT UP AND CLIMB ON.
Don't worry about it.
HOLD ON TIGHT OR YOU'LL FALL.
Okay?
Huh?
UH, OKAY...
GRIP

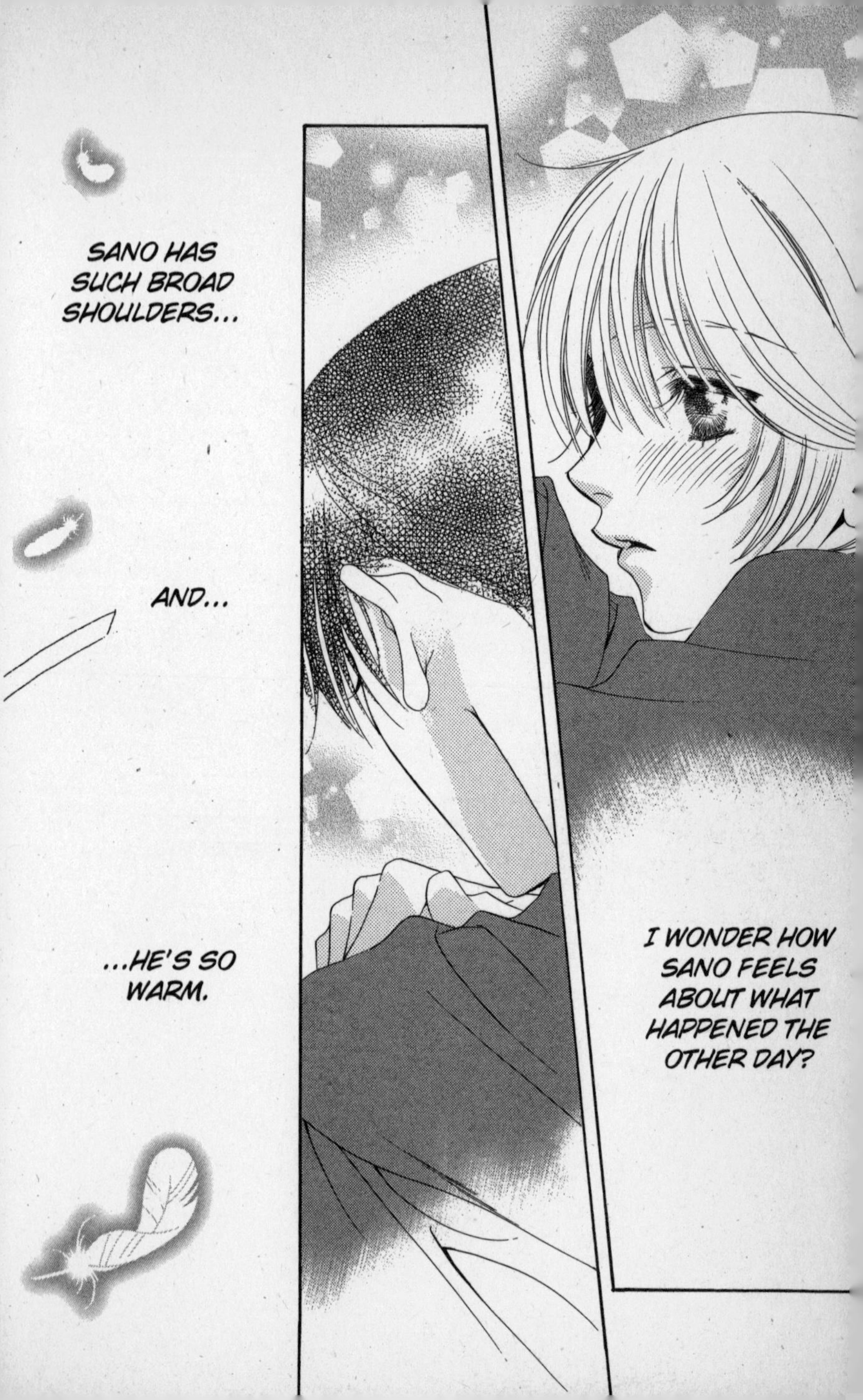
I WONDER HOW SANO FEELS ABOUT WHAT HAPPENED THE OTHER DAY?
SANO HAS SUCH BROAD SHOULDERS...
AND...
...HE'S SO WARM.

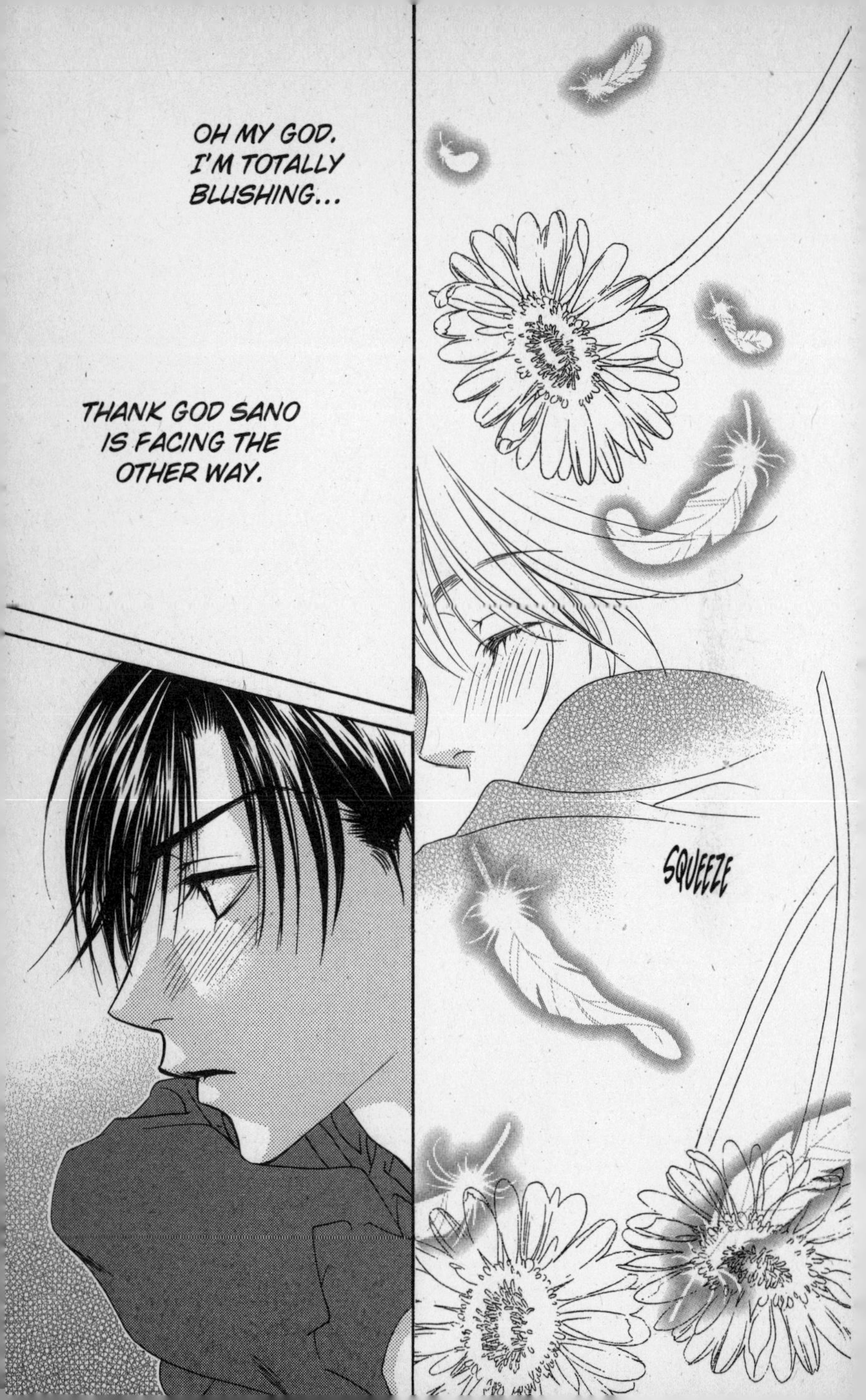
SQUEEZE
OH MY GOD. I'M TOTALLY BLUSHING...
THANK GOD SANO IS FACING THE OTHER WAY.

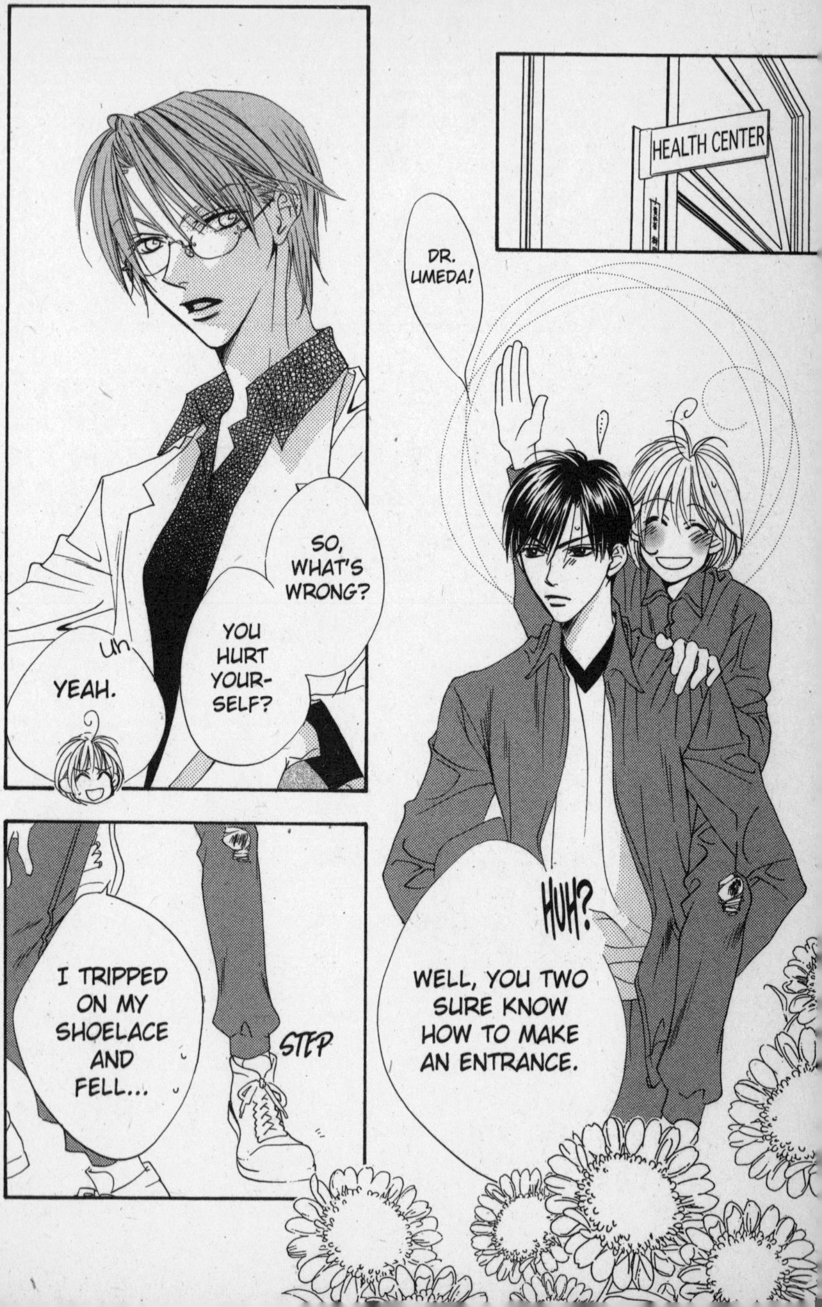
HEALTH CENTER
DR. UMEDA!
HUH?
WELL, YOU TWO SURE KNOW HOW TO MAKE AN ENTRANCE.
SO, WHAT'S WRONG?
YOU HURT YOURSELF?
Uh
YEAH.
I TRIPPED ON MY SHOELACE AND FELL...
STEP

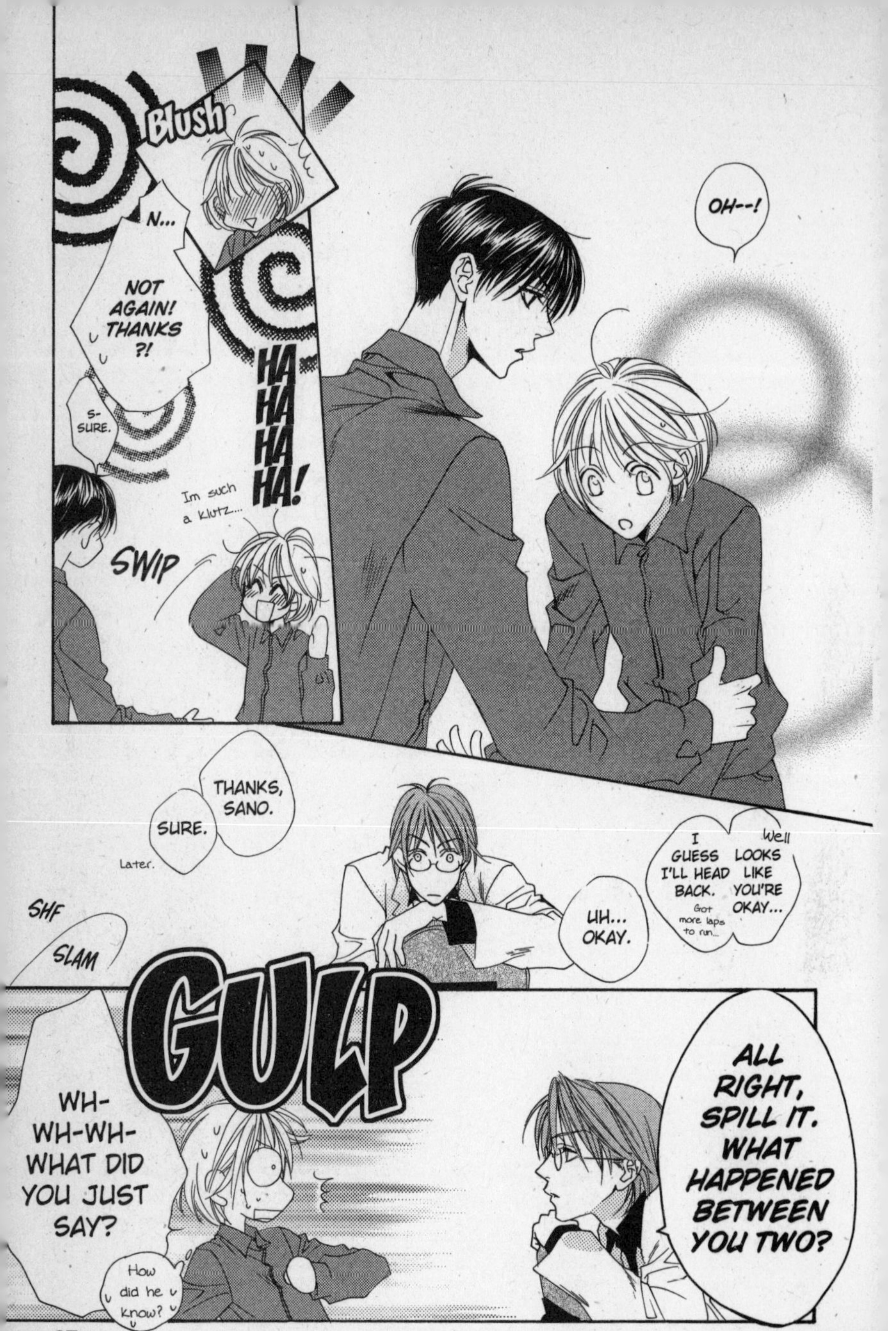
OH--!
Blush
N...
NOT AGAIN! THANKS?!
HA HA HA HA HA!
S-SURE.
Im such a klutz...
SWIP
Well LOOKS LIKE YOU'RE OKAY...
I GUESS I'LL HEAD BACK.
Got more laps to run...
UH... OKAY.
THANKS, SANO.
SURE.
Later.
SHF
SLAM
ALL RIGHT, SPILL IT. WHAT HAPPENED BETWEEN YOU TWO?
GULP
WH-WH-WH-WHAT DID YOU JUST SAY?
How did he know?

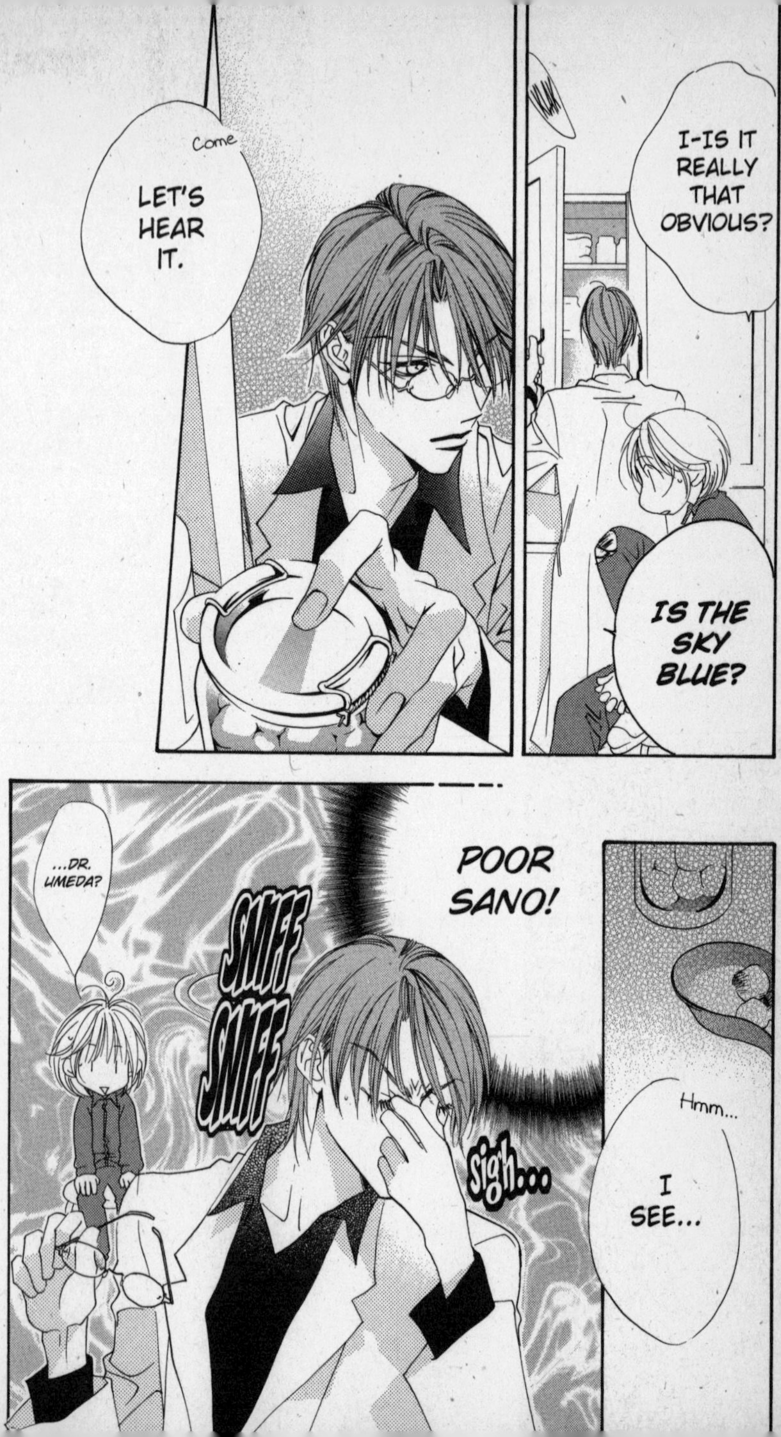
I-IS IT REALLY THAT OBVIOUS?
IS THE SKY BLUE?
Come
LET'S HEAR IT.
Hmm...
I SEE...
POOR SANO!
SNIFF SNIFF
sigh...
...DR. UMEDA?

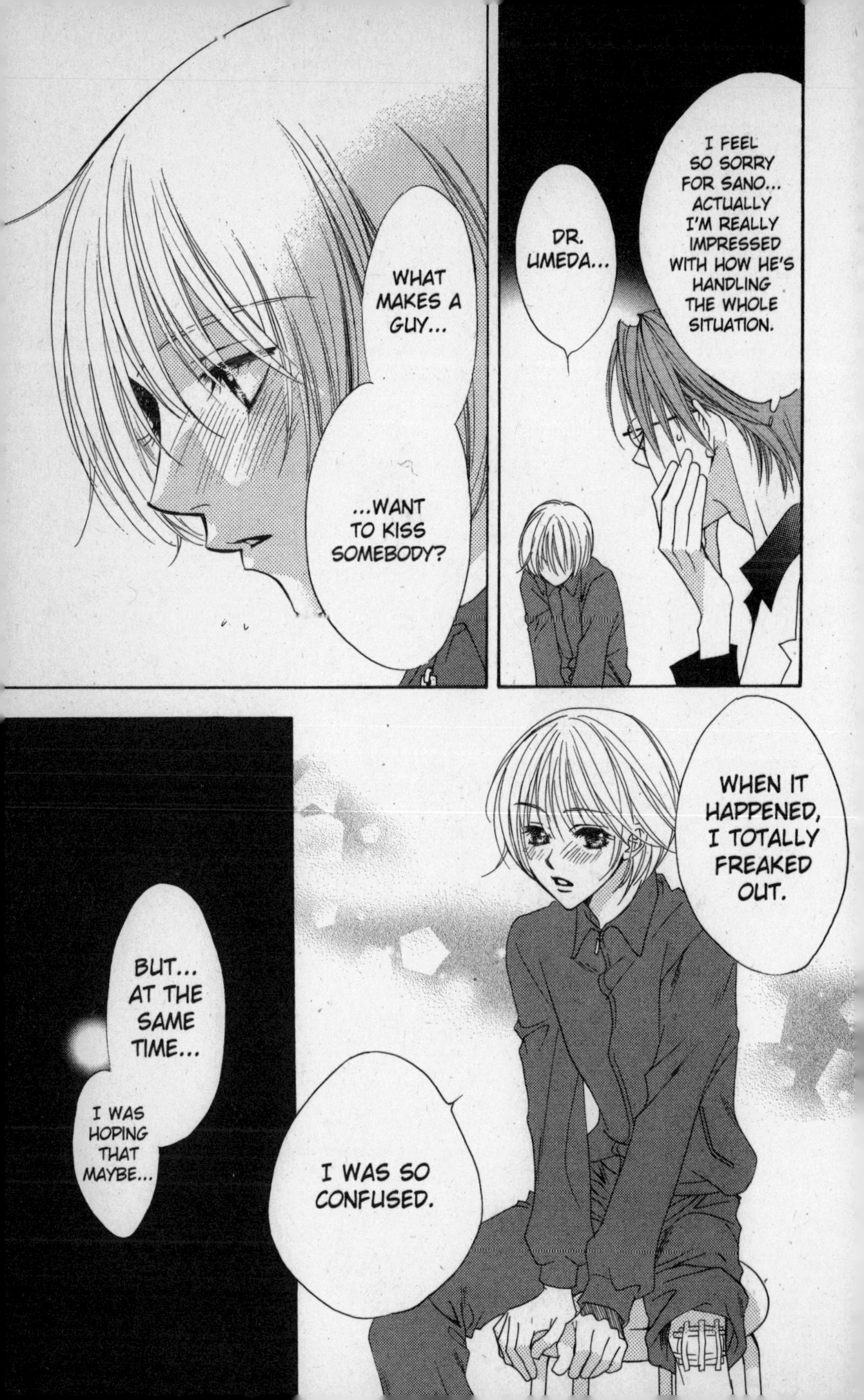
I FEEL SO SORRY FOR SANO... ACTUALLY I'M REALLY IMPRESSED WITH HOW HE'S HANDLING THE WHOLE SITUATION.
DR. UMEDA...
WHAT MAKES A GUY...
...WANT TO KISS SOMEBODY?
WHEN IT HAPPENED, I TOTALLY FREAKED OUT.
I WAS SO CONFUSED.
BUT... AT THE SAME TIME...
I WAS HOPING THAT MAYBE...

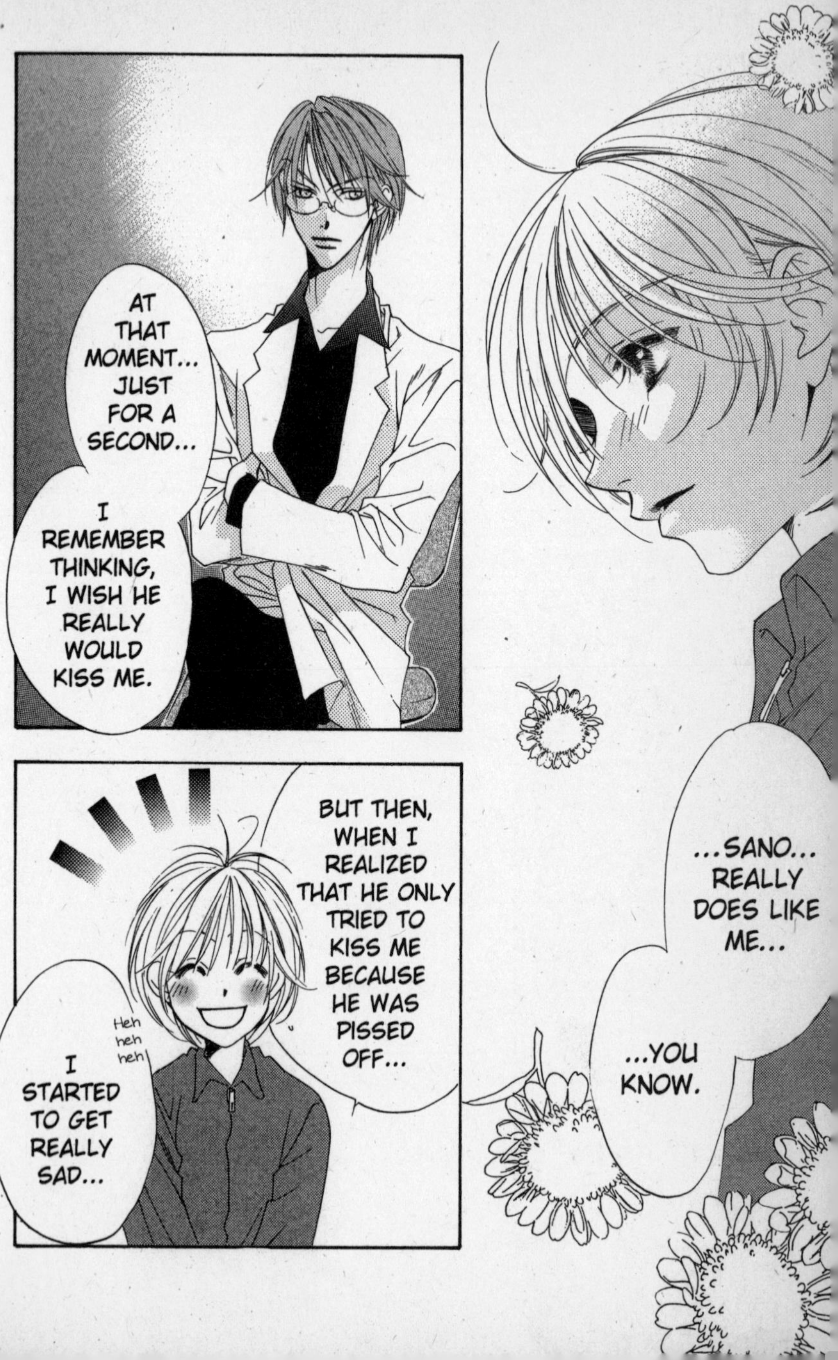
...SANO... REALLY DOES LIKE ME...
...YOU KNOW.
AT THAT MOMENT... JUST FOR A SECOND...
I REMEMBER THINKING, I WISH HE REALLY WOULD KISS ME.
BUT THEN, WHEN I REALIZED THAT HE ONLY TRIED TO KISS ME BECAUSE HE WAS PISSED OFF...
Heh heh heh
I STARTED TO GET REALLY SAD...

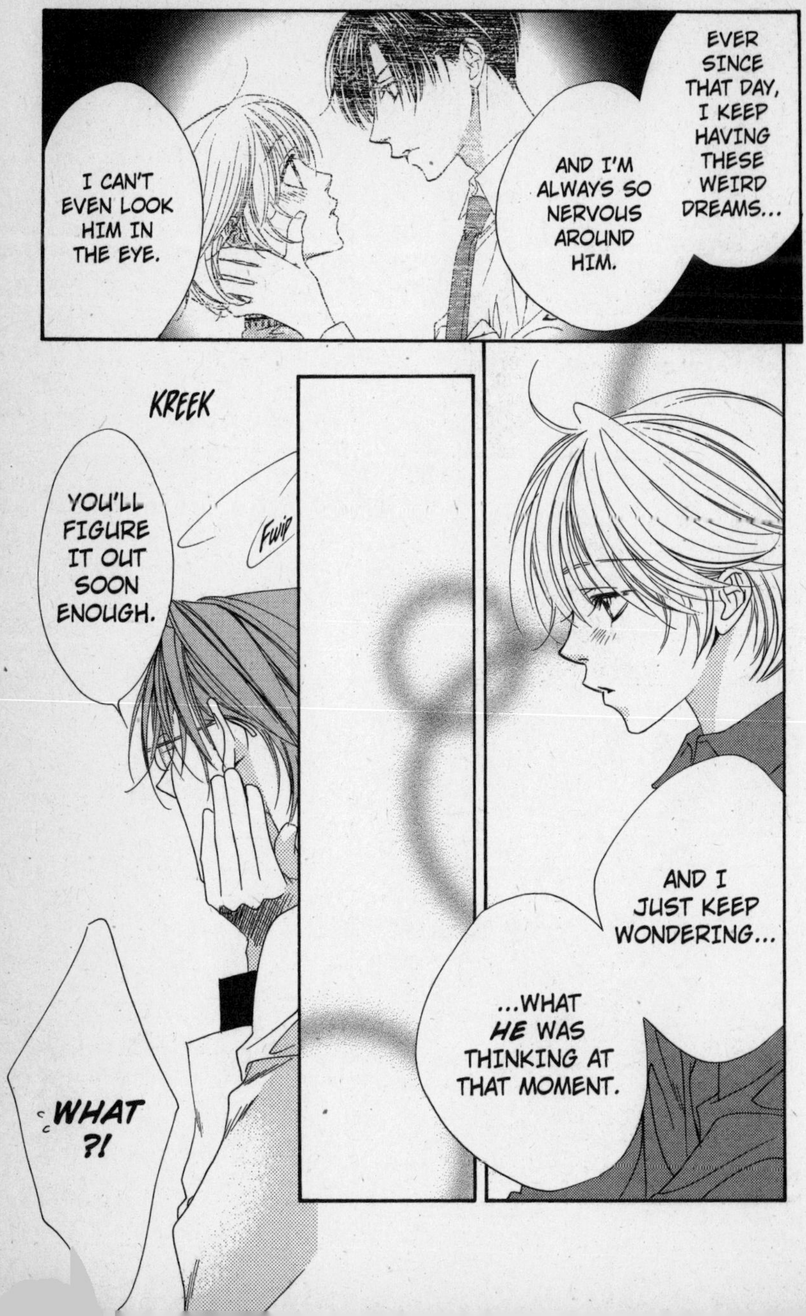
EVER SINCE THAT DAY, I KEEP HAVING THESE WEIRD DREAMS...
AND I'M ALWAYS SO NERVOUS AROUND HIM.
I CAN'T EVEN LOOK HIM IN THE EYE.
AND I JUST KEEP WONDERING...
...WHAT *HE* WAS THINKING AT THAT MOMENT.
KREEK
YOU'LL FIGURE IT OUT SOON ENOUGH.
Fwip
WHAT?!

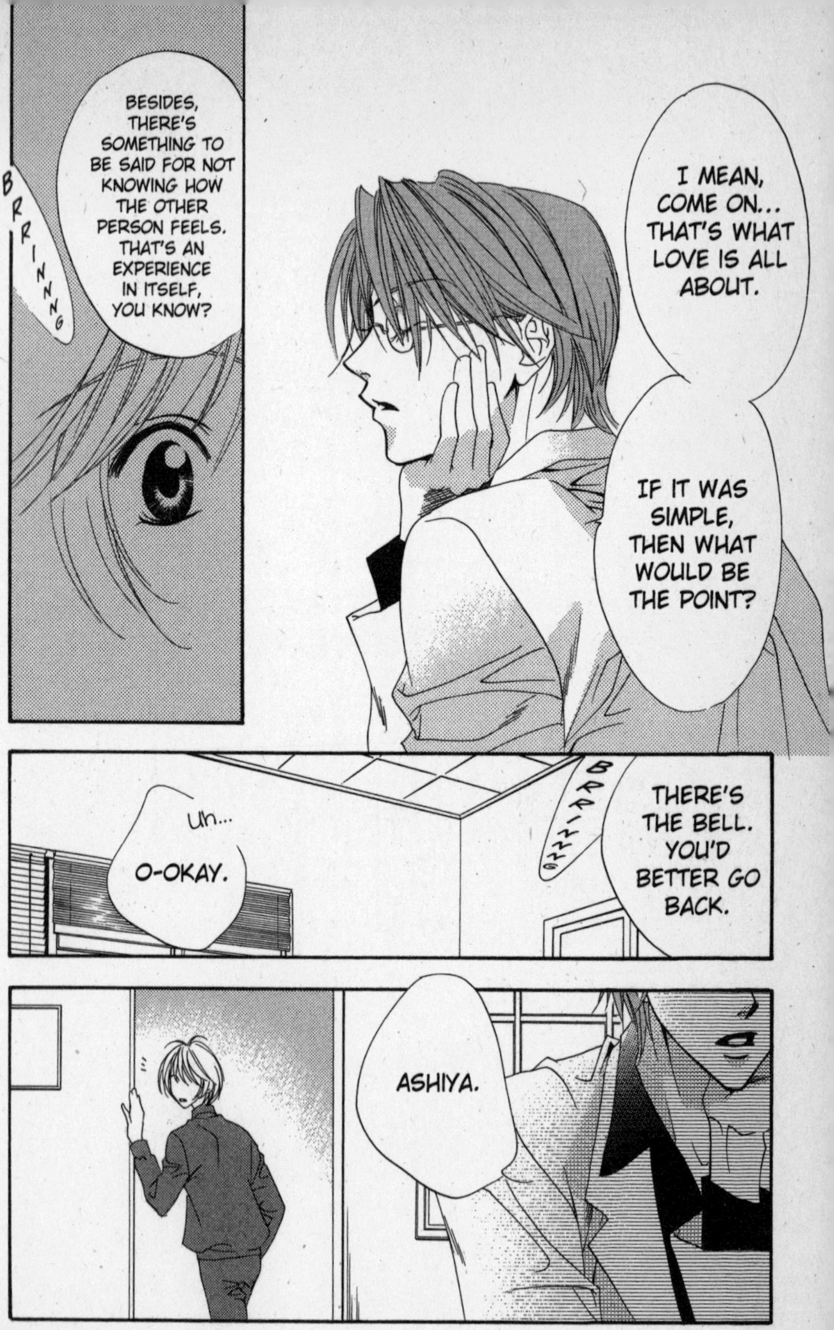
I MEAN, COME ON... THAT'S WHAT LOVE IS ALL ABOUT.
IF IT WAS SIMPLE, THEN WHAT WOULD BE THE POINT?
BESIDES, THERE'S SOMETHING TO BE SAID FOR NOT KNOWING HOW THE OTHER PERSON FEELS. THAT'S AN EXPERIENCE IN ITSELF, YOU KNOW?
BRRINNNG
THERE'S THE BELL. YOU'D BETTER GO BACK.
BRRINNNG
Uh...
O-OKAY.
ASHIYA.

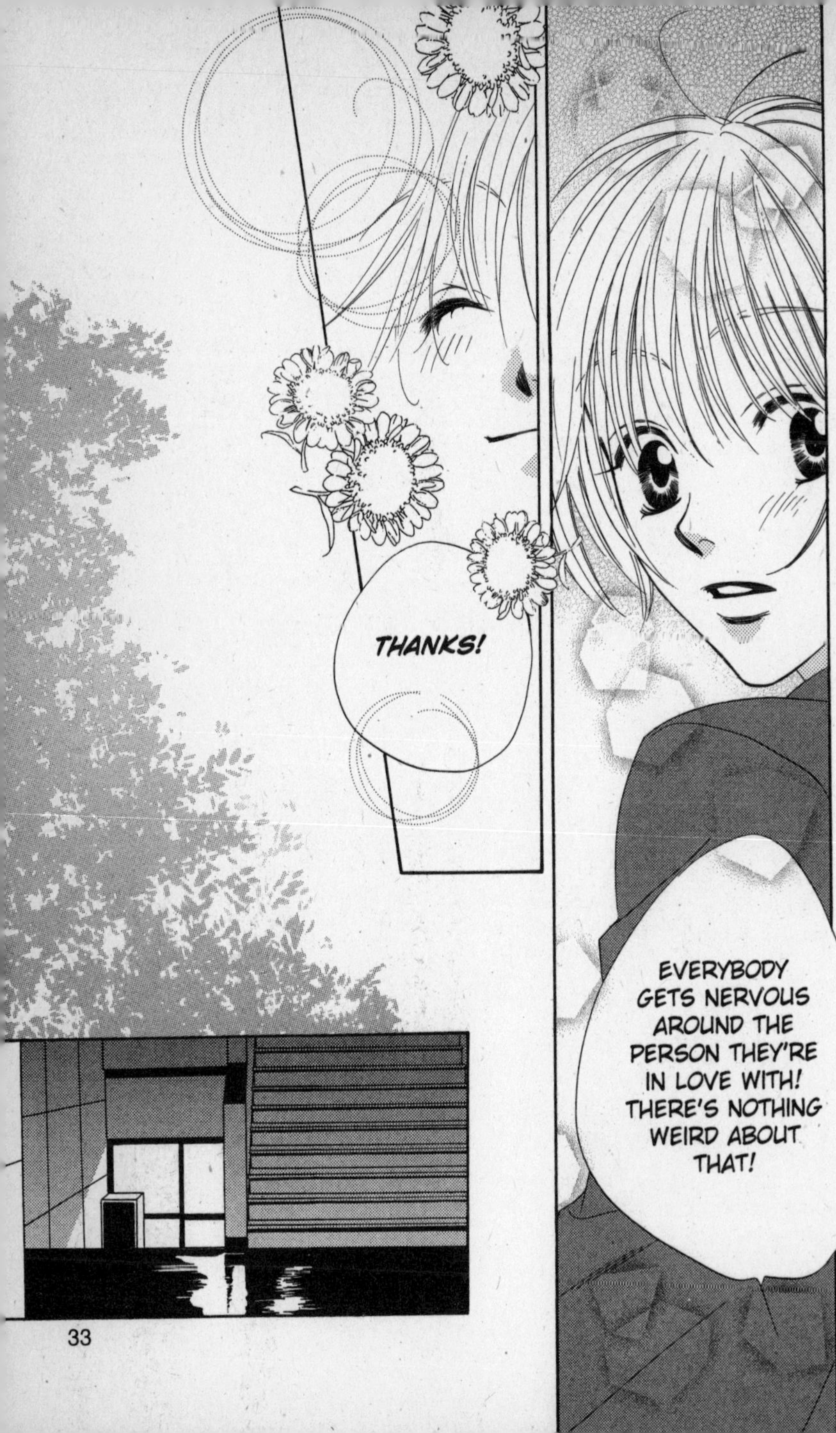
EVERYBODY GETS NERVOUS AROUND THE PERSON THEY'RE IN LOVE WITH! THERE'S NOTHING WEIRD ABOUT THAT!
THANKS!

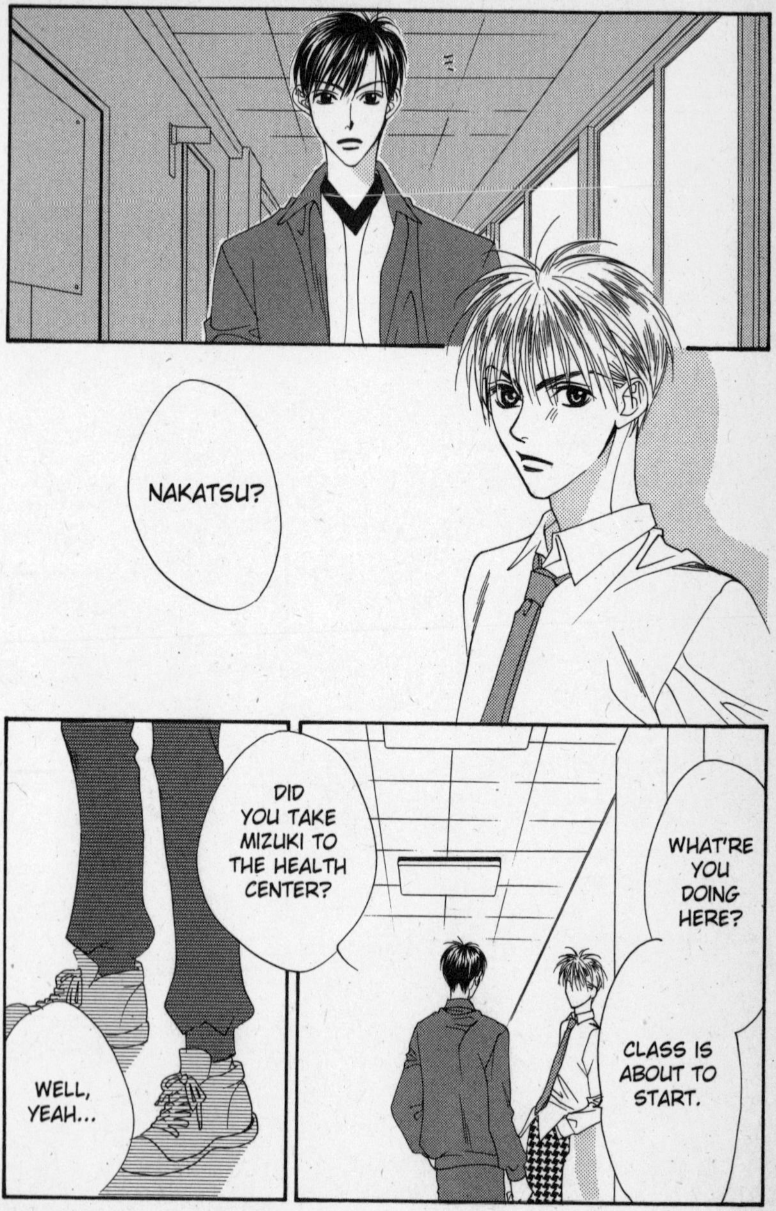
NAKATSU?
WHAT'RE YOU DOING HERE?
CLASS IS ABOUT TO START.
DID YOU TAKE MIZUKI TO THE HEALTH CENTER?
WELL, YEAH...

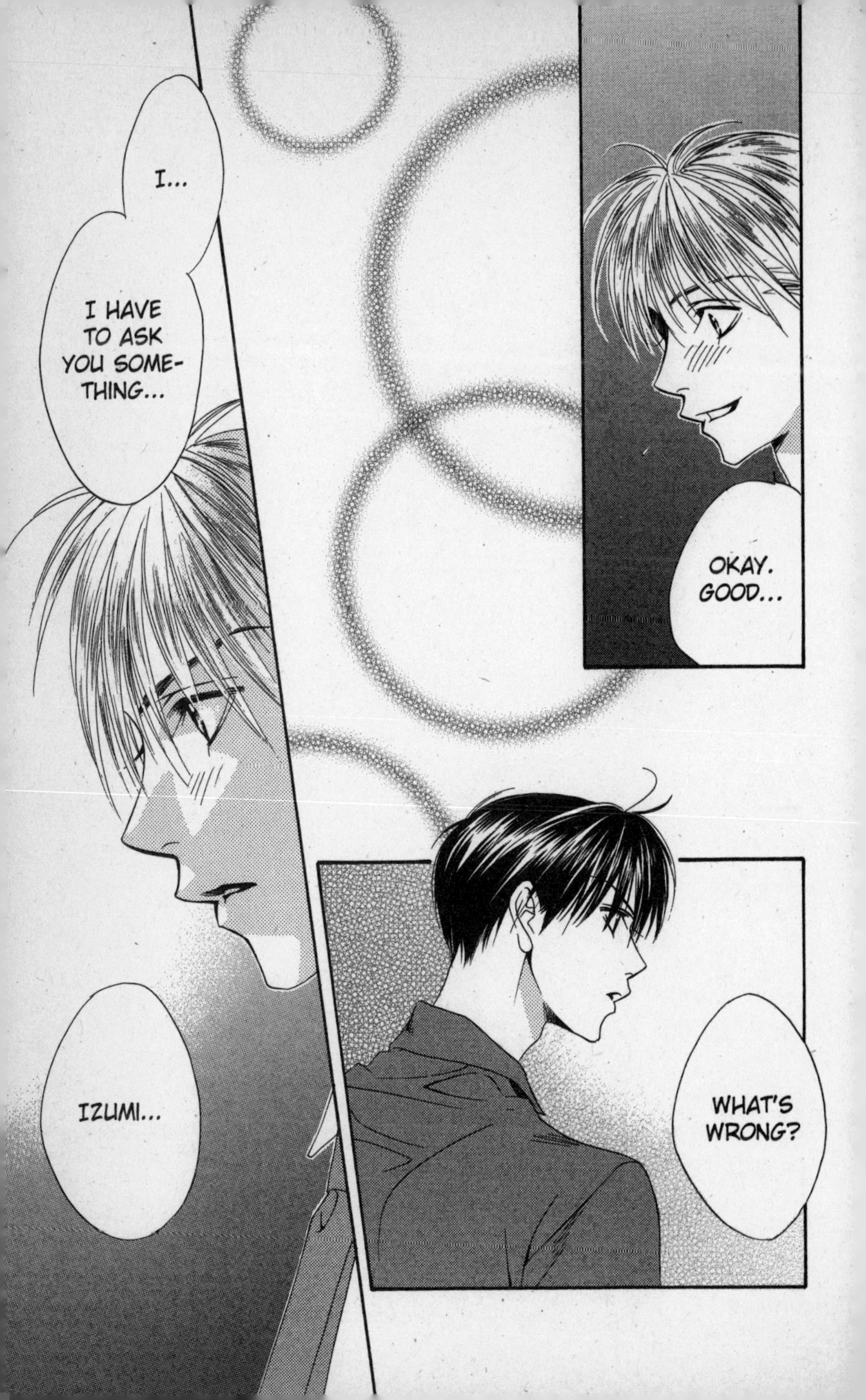
OKAY. GOOD...
WHAT'S WRONG?
I...
I HAVE TO ASK YOU SOME-THING...
IZUMI...

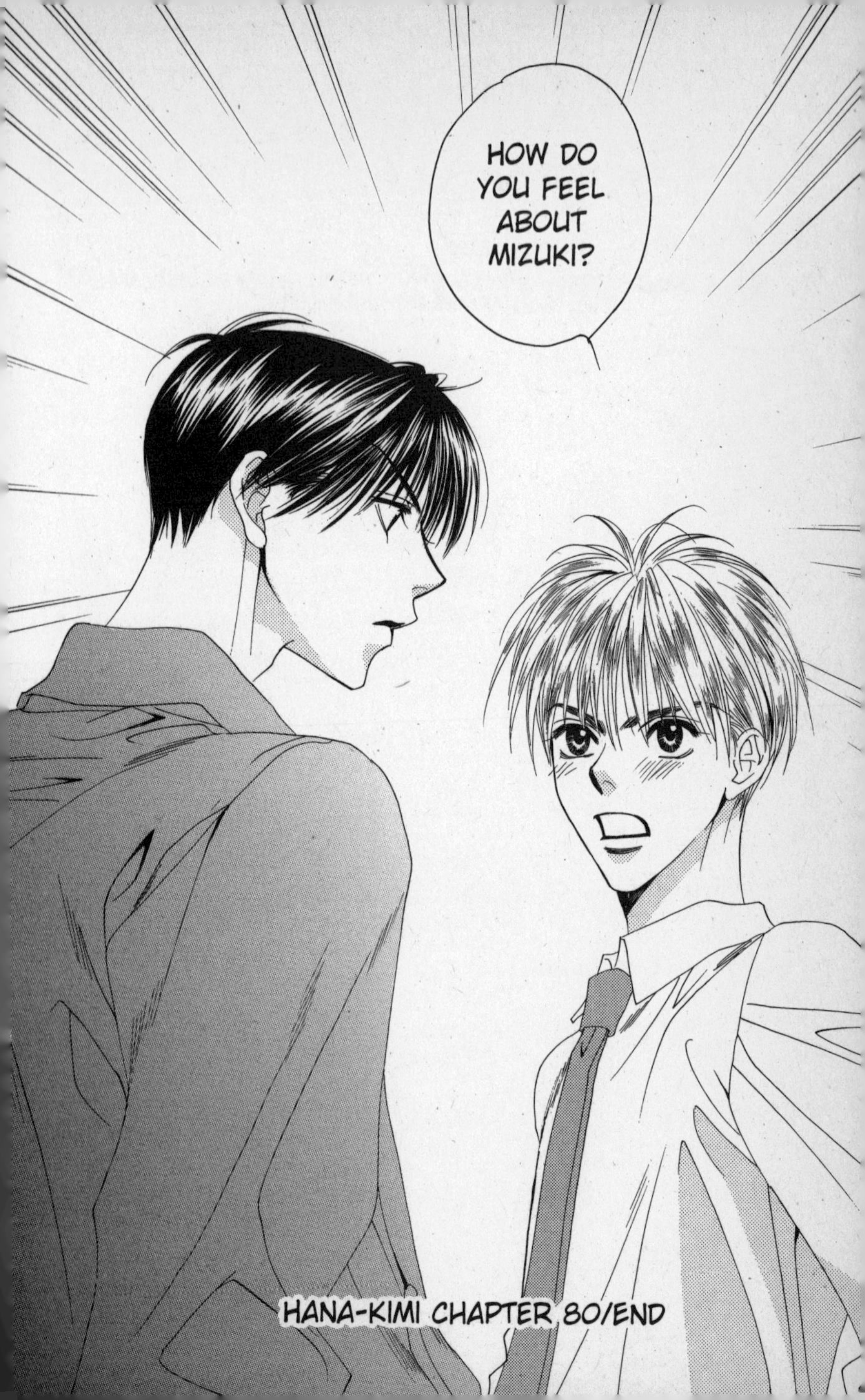
HOW DO YOU FEEL ABOUT MIZUKI?
HANA-KIMI CHAPTER 80/END

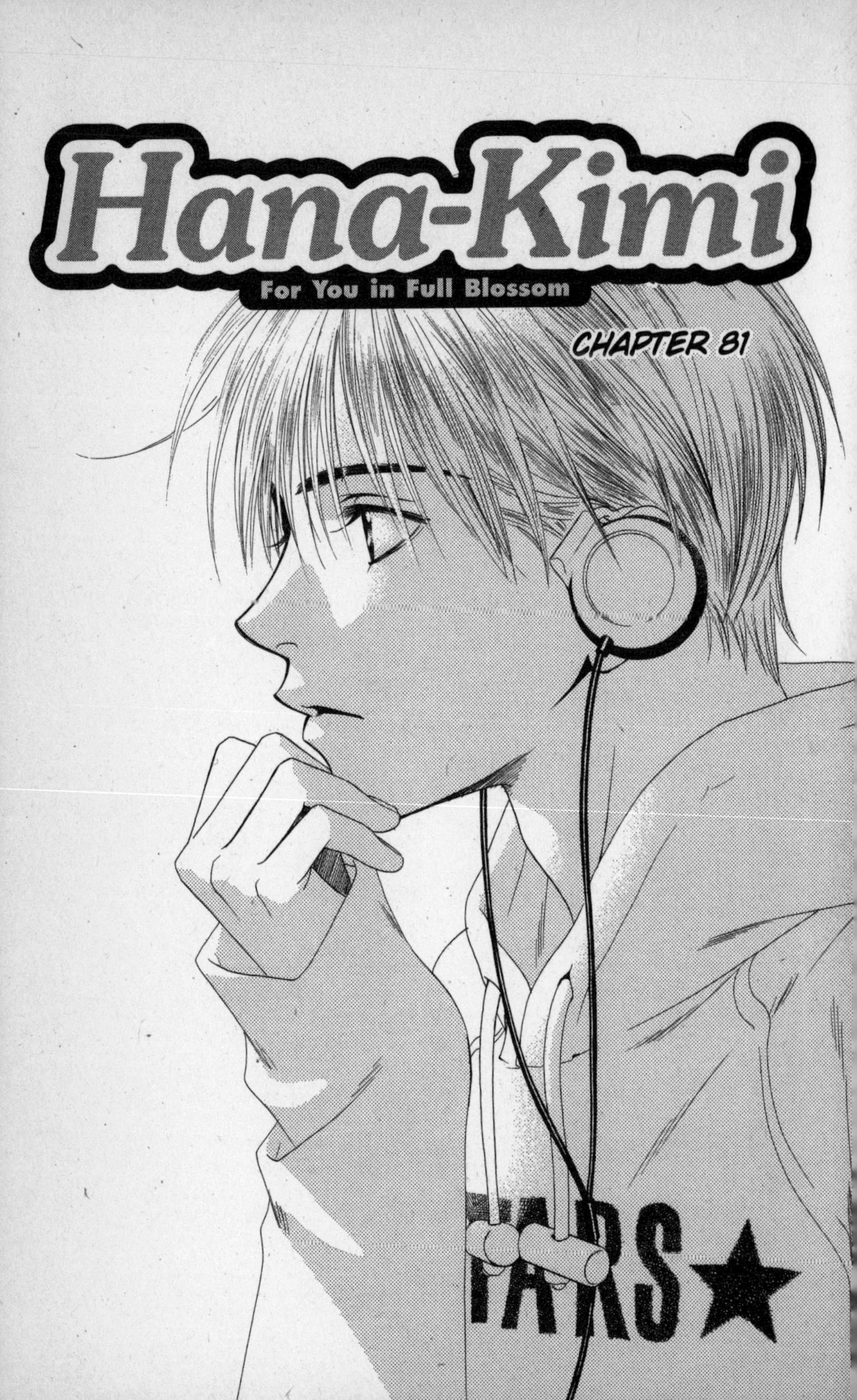
Hana-Kimi
For You in Full Blossom
CHAPTER 81

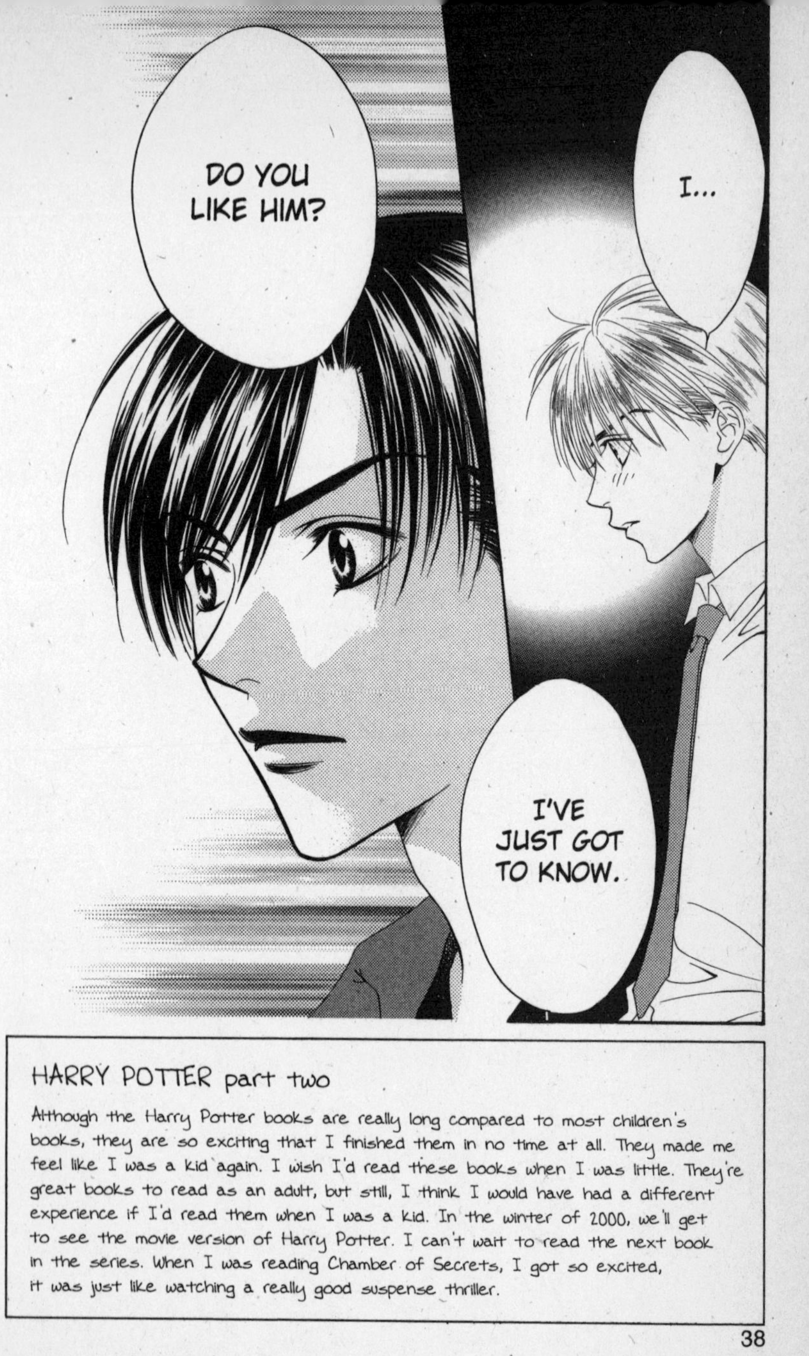
DO YOU LIKE HIM?
I...
I'VE JUST GOT TO KNOW.

HARRY POTTER part two

Although the Harry Potter books are really long compared to most children's books, they are so exciting that I finished them in no time at all. They made me feel like I was a kid again. I wish I'd read these books when I was little. They're great books to read as an adult, but still, I think I would have had a different experience if I'd read them when I was a kid. In the winter of 2000, we'll get to see the movie version of Harry Potter. I can't wait to read the next book in the series. When I was reading Chamber of Secrets, I got so excited, it was just like watching a really good suspense thriller.

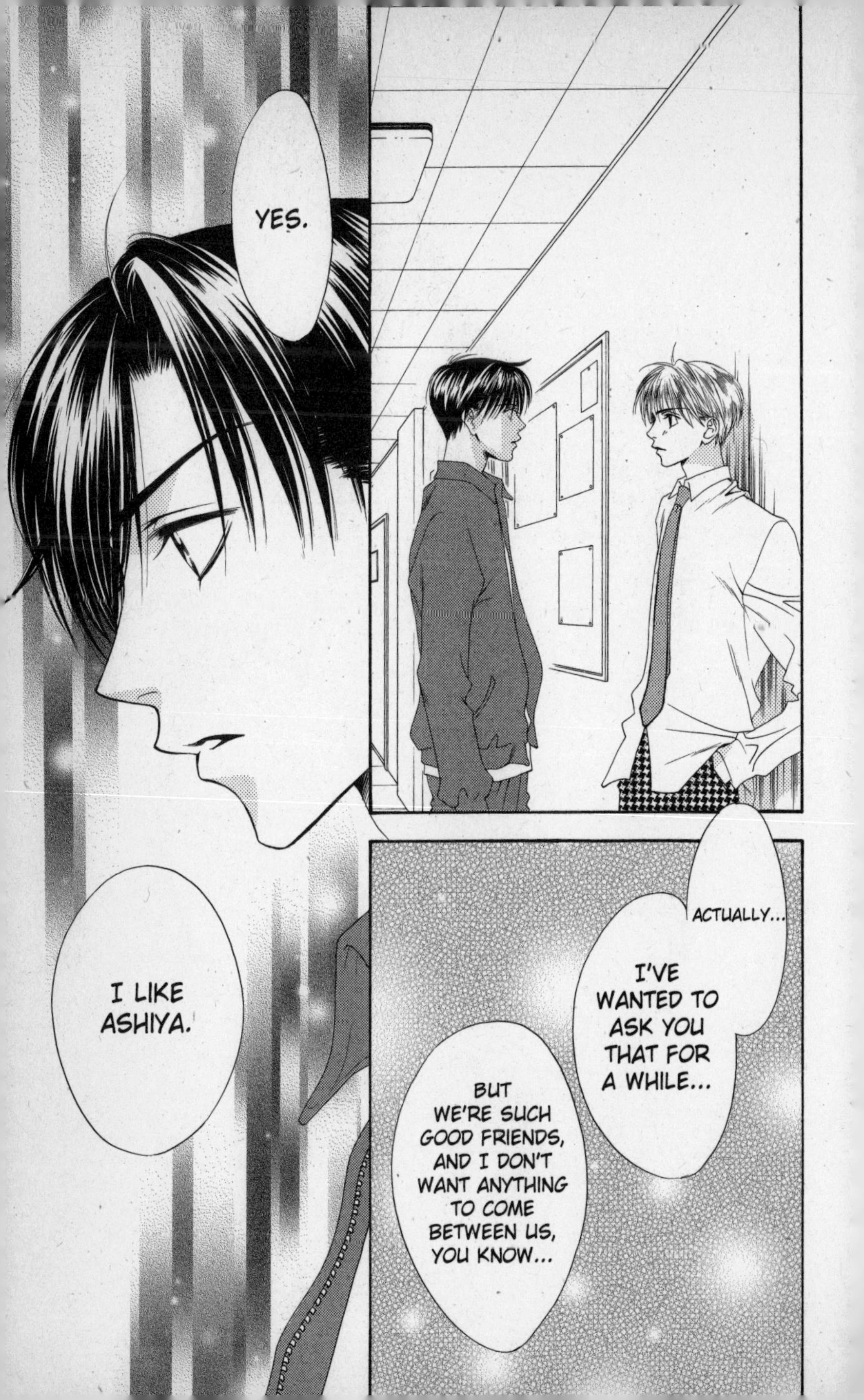
ACTUALLY...
I'VE WANTED TO ASK YOU THAT FOR A WHILE...
BUT WE'RE SUCH GOOD FRIENDS, AND I DON'T WANT ANYTHING TO COME BETWEEN US, YOU KNOW...
YES.
I LIKE ASHIYA.

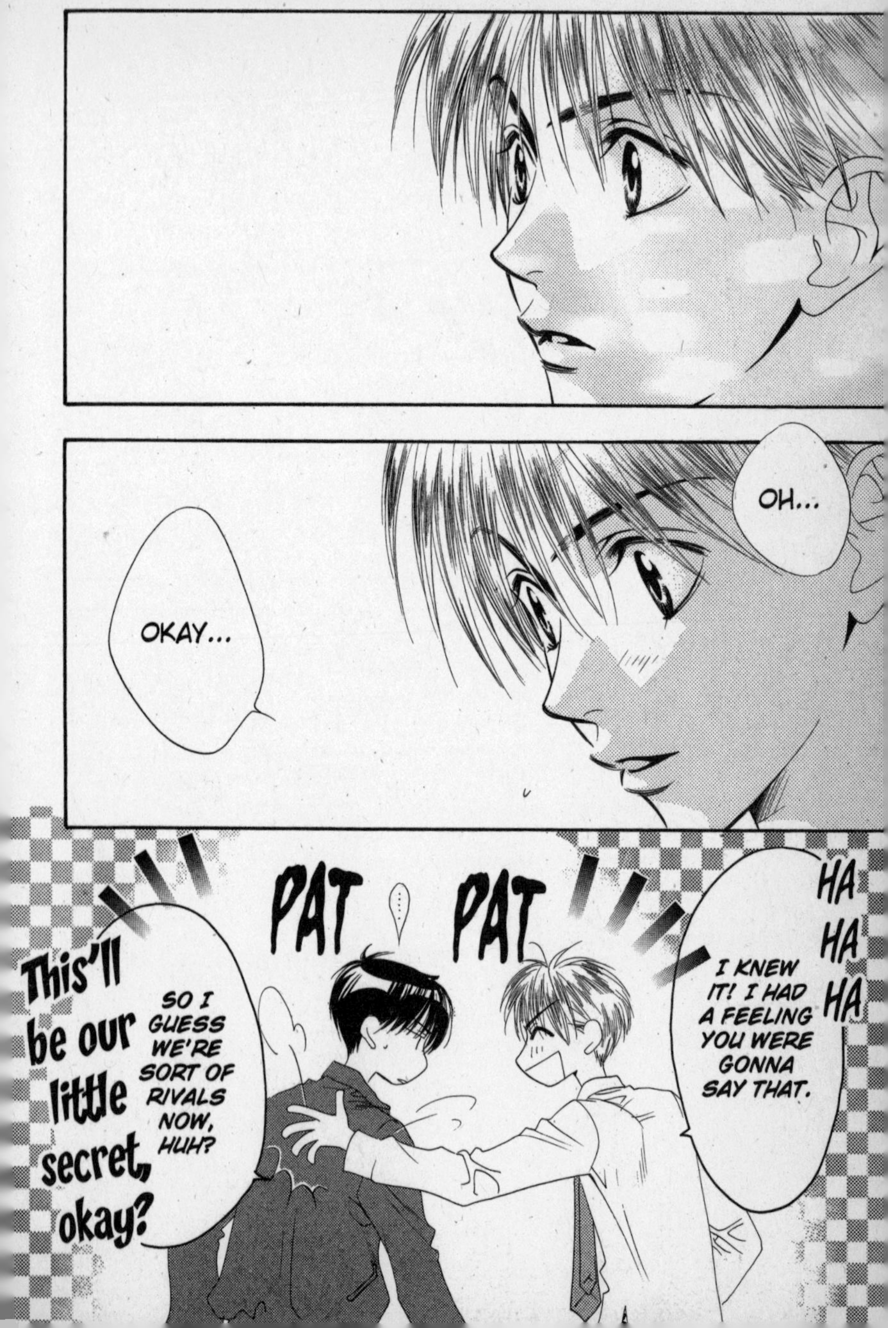
OH...
OKAY...
HA HA HA
I KNEW IT! I HAD A FEELING YOU WERE GONNA SAY THAT.
PAT PAT
SO I GUESS WE'RE SORT OF RIVALS NOW, HUH?
This'll be our little secret, okay?

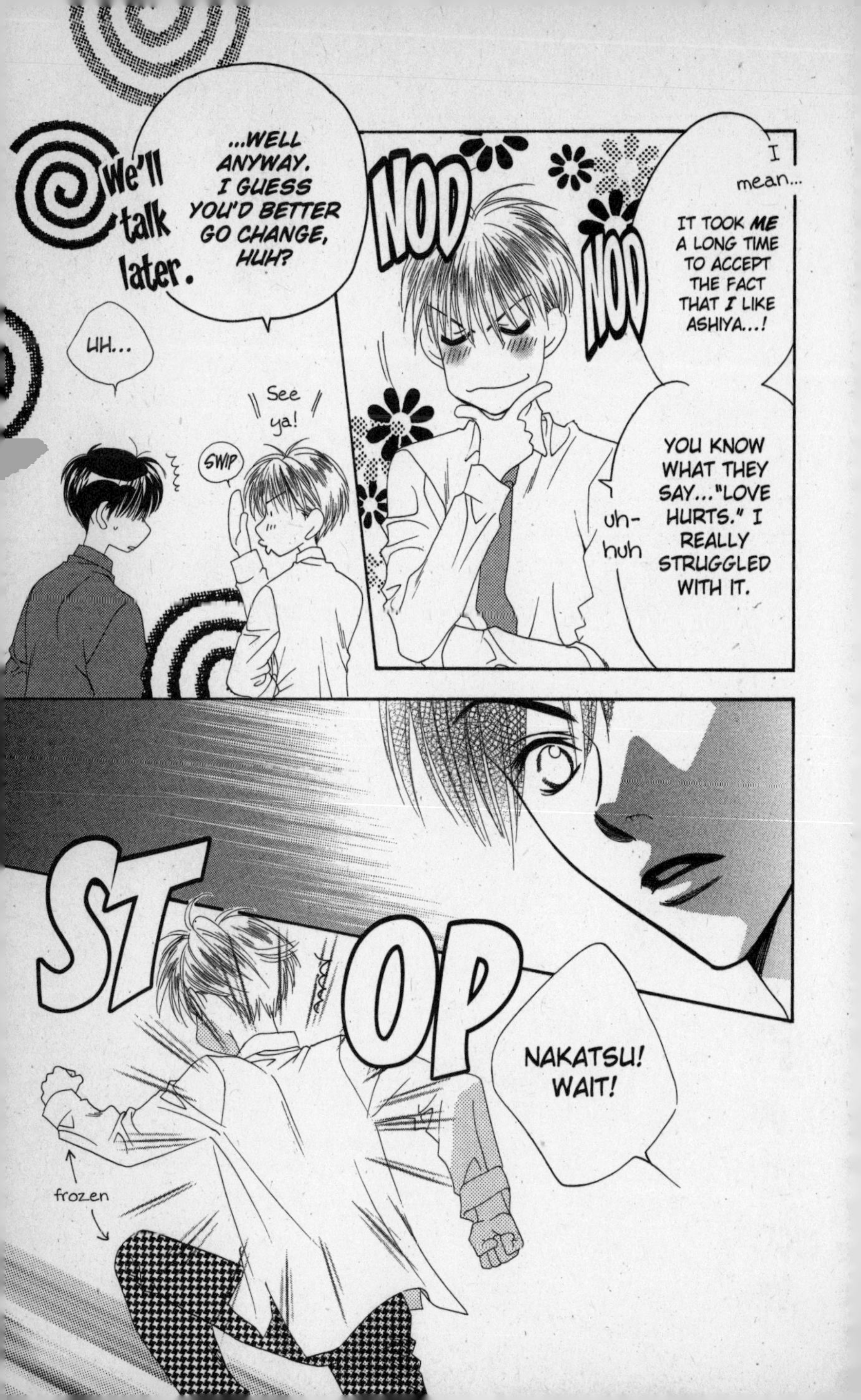
I mean...
IT TOOK ME A LONG TIME TO ACCEPT THE FACT THAT I LIKE ASHIYA...!
NOD
NOD
YOU KNOW WHAT THEY SAY..."LOVE HURTS." I REALLY STRUGGLED WITH IT.
uh-huh
...WELL ANYWAY. I GUESS YOU'D BETTER GO CHANGE, HUH?
We'll talk later.
UH...
See ya!
SWIP
NAKATSU! WAIT!
STOP
frozen

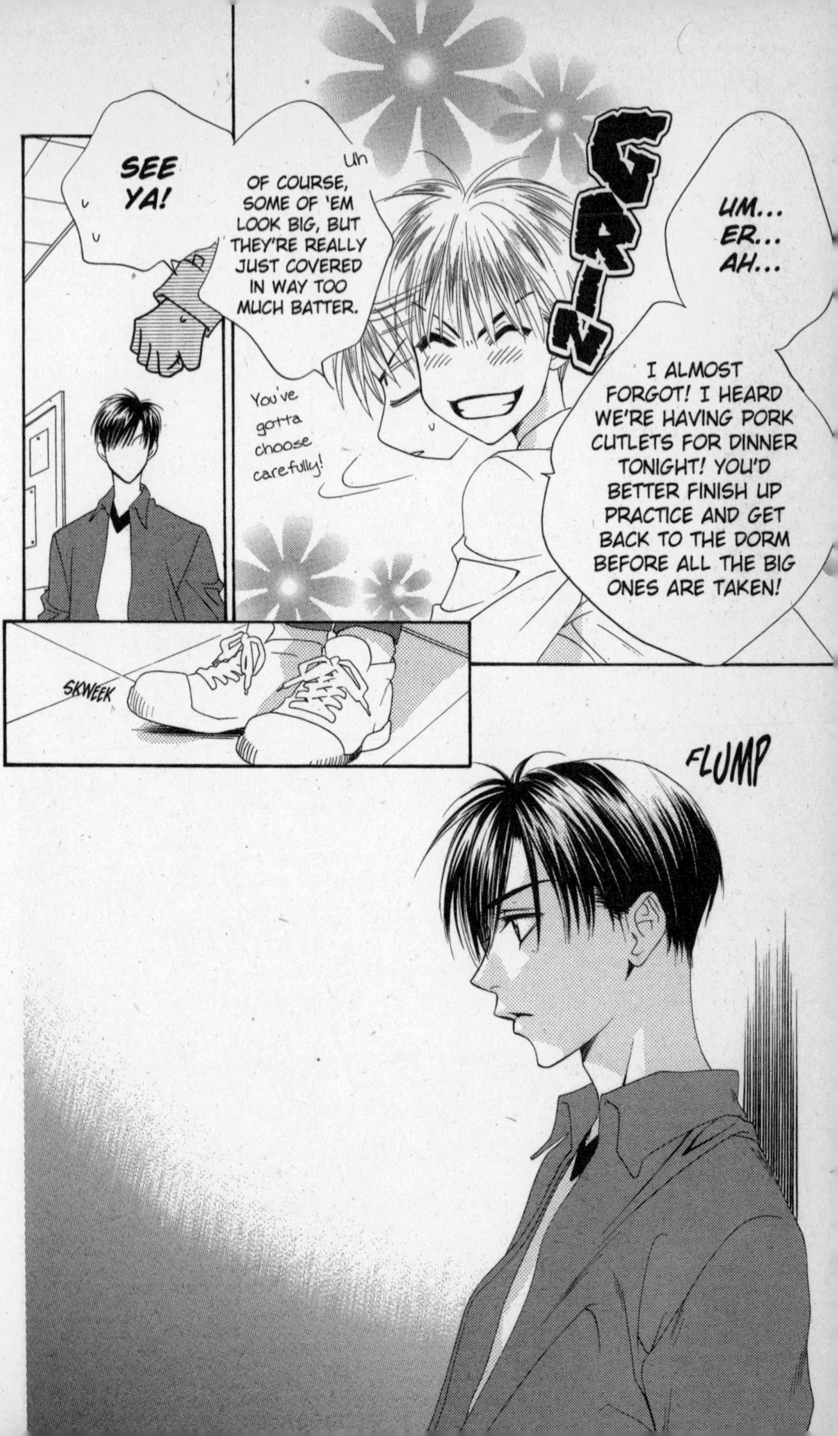
UM... ER... AH...
GRIN
I ALMOST FORGOT! I HEARD WE'RE HAVING PORK CUTLETS FOR DINNER TONIGHT! YOU'D BETTER FINISH UP PRACTICE AND GET BACK TO THE DORM BEFORE ALL THE BIG ONES ARE TAKEN!
Uh
OF COURSE, SOME OF 'EM LOOK BIG, BUT THEY'RE REALLY JUST COVERED IN WAY TOO MUCH BATTER.
You've gotta choose carefully!
SEE YA!
SKWEEK
FLUMP

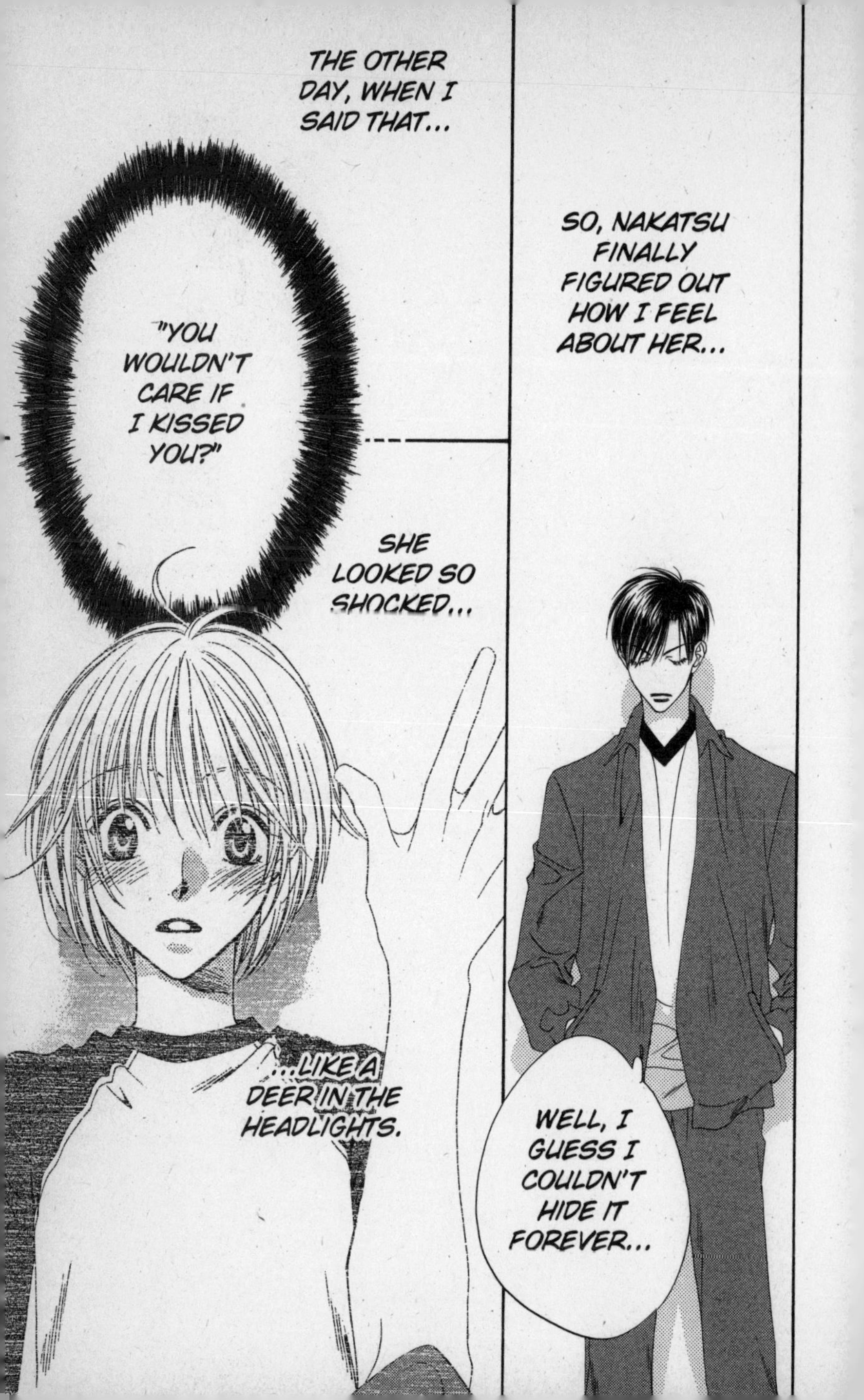
SO, NAKATSU FINALLY FIGURED OUT HOW I FEEL ABOUT HER...
WELL, I GUESS I COULDN'T HIDE IT FOREVER...
THE OTHER DAY, WHEN I SAID THAT...
"YOU WOULDN'T CARE IF I KISSED YOU?"
SHE LOOKED SO SHOCKED...
...LIKE A DEER IN THE HEADLIGHTS.

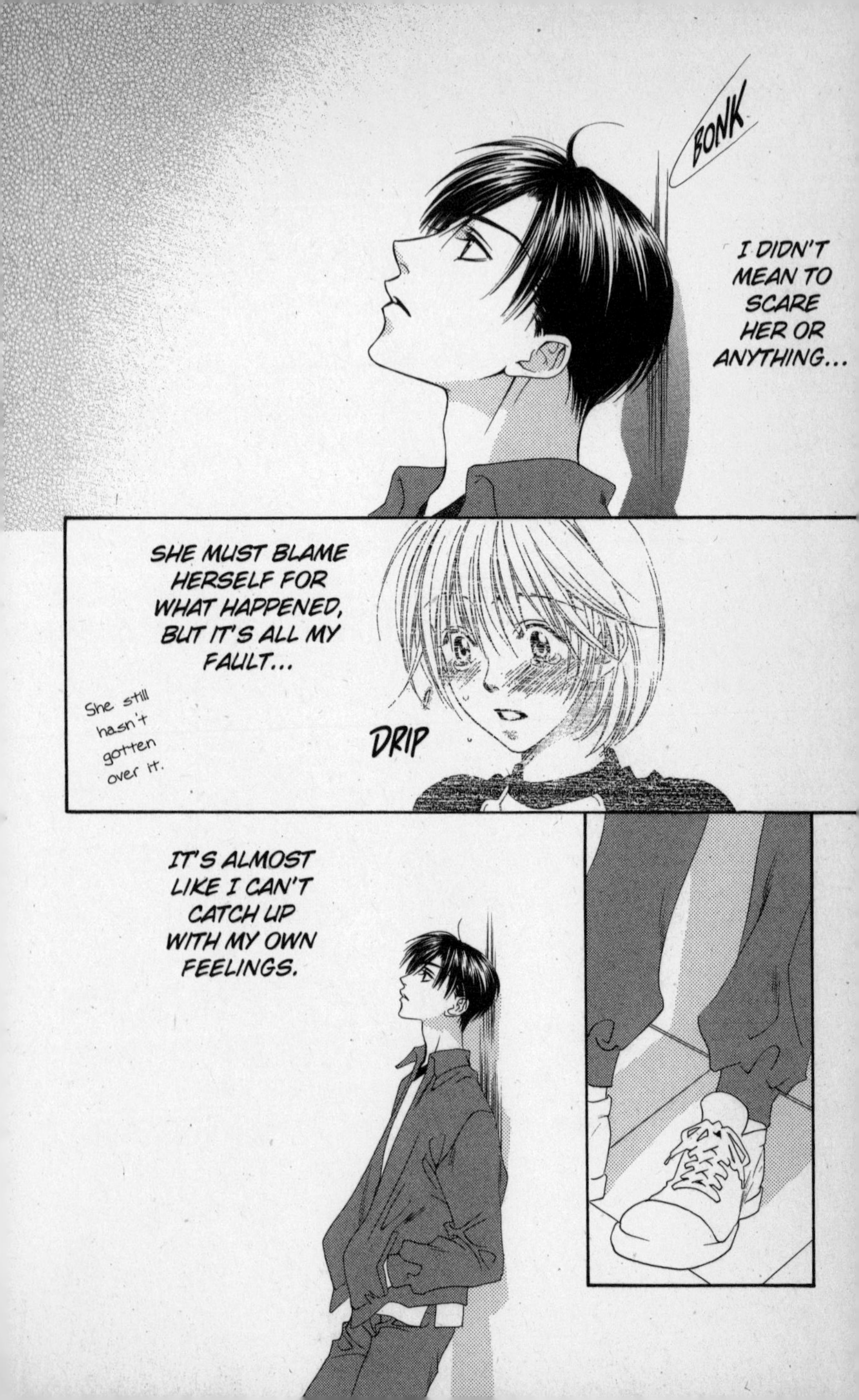
BONK
I DIDN'T MEAN TO SCARE HER OR ANYTHING...
SHE MUST BLAME HERSELF FOR WHAT HAPPENED, BUT IT'S ALL MY FAULT...
DRIP
She still hasn't gotten over it.
IT'S ALMOST LIKE I CAN'T CATCH UP WITH MY OWN FEELINGS.

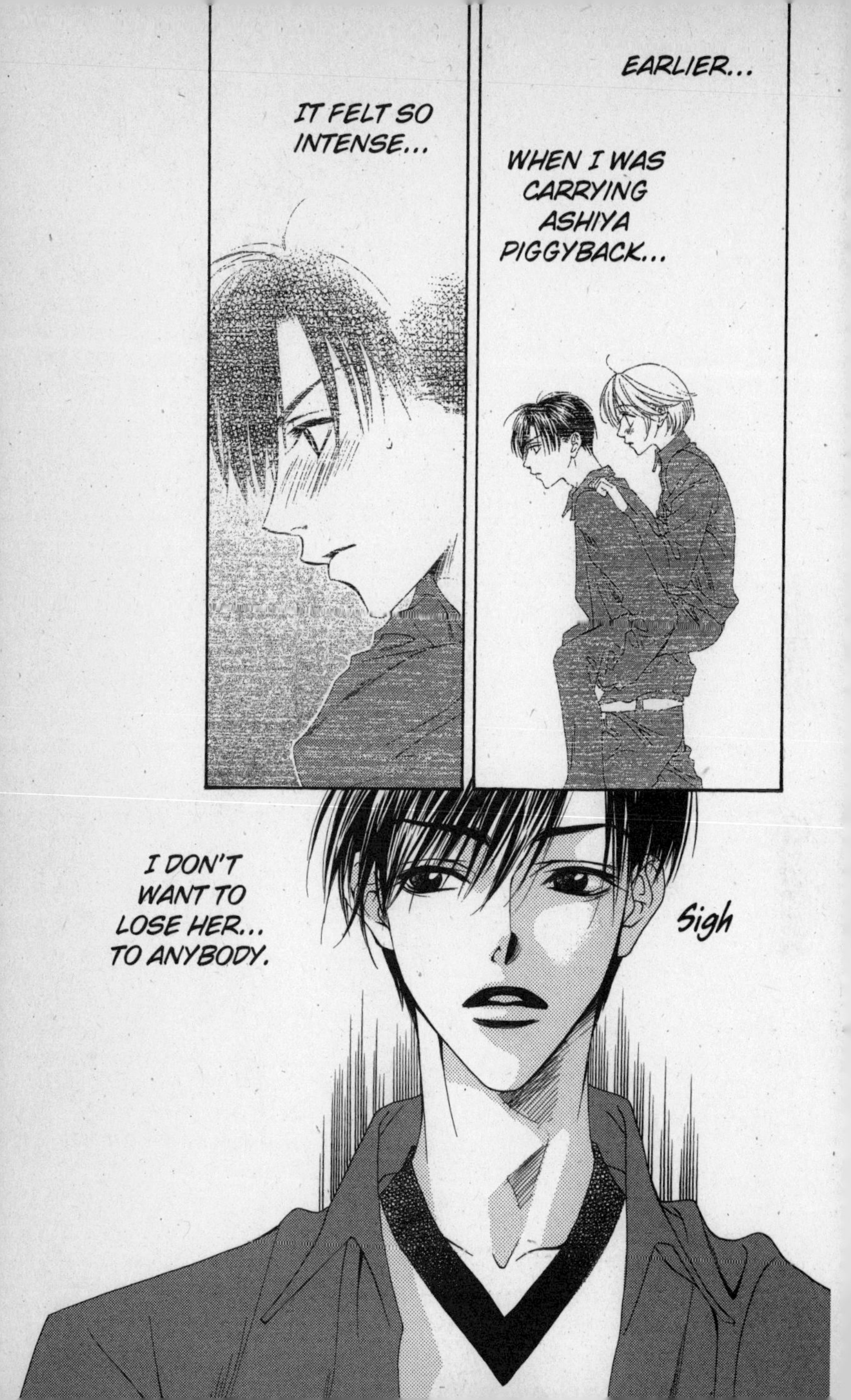
EARLIER...
WHEN I WAS CARRYING ASHIYA PIGGYBACK...
IT FELT SO INTENSE...
Sigh
I DON'T WANT TO LOSE HER... TO ANYBODY.

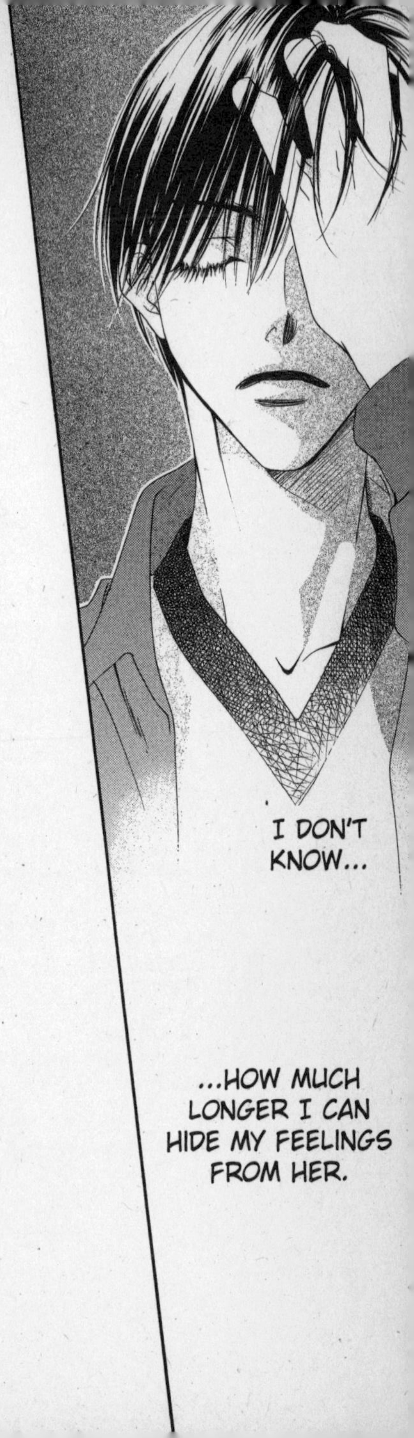
I DON'T KNOW...
...HOW MUCH LONGER I CAN HIDE MY FEELINGS FROM HER.

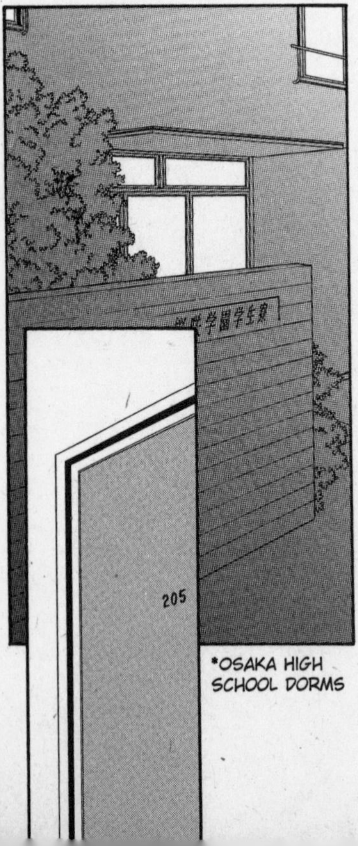
205
*OSAKA HIGH SCHOOL DORMS

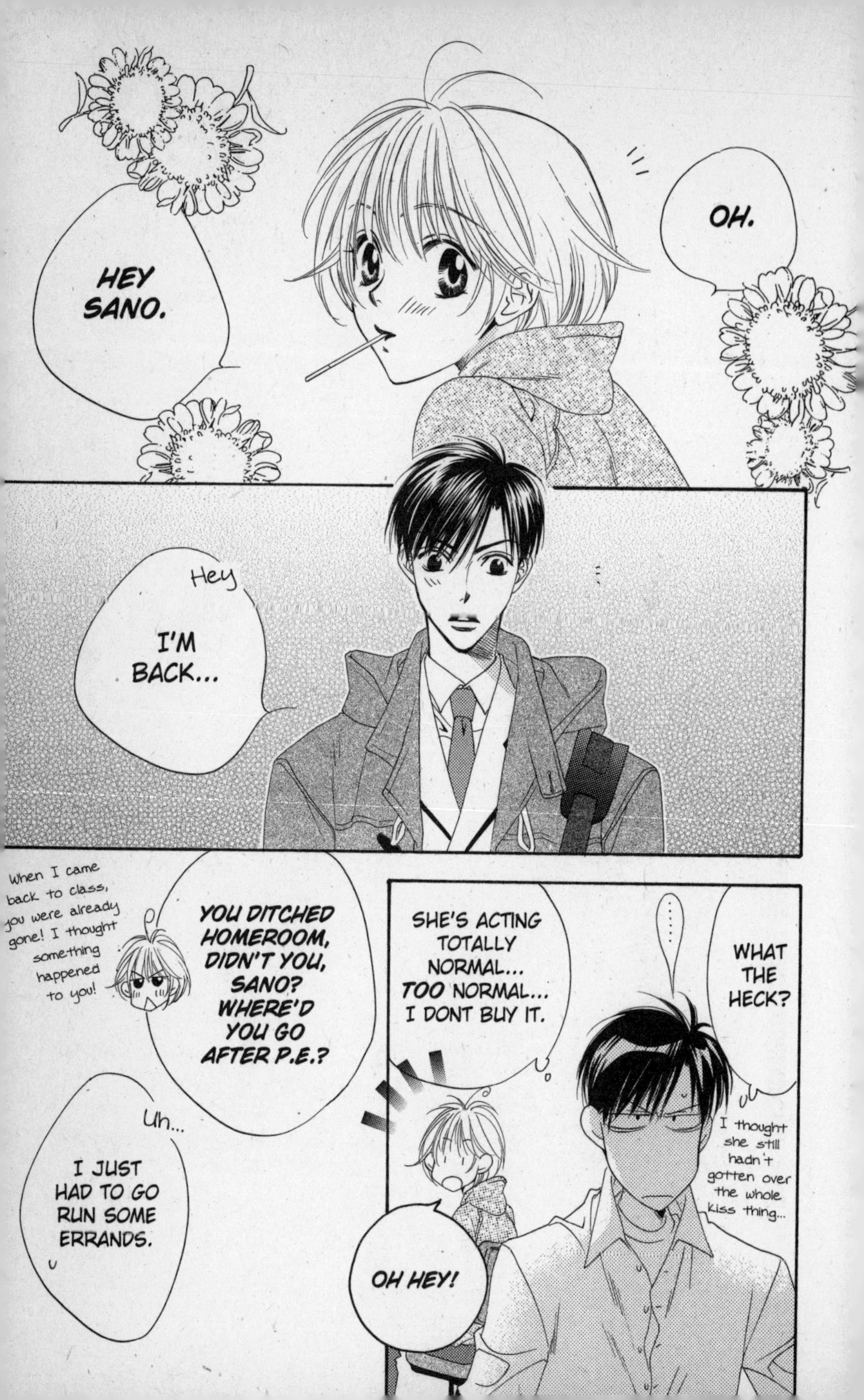
OH.
HEY SANO.
Hey
I'M BACK...
WHAT THE HECK?
......
SHE'S ACTING TOTALLY NORMAL... TOO NORMAL... I DONT BUY IT.
I thought she still hadn't gotten over the whole kiss thing...
OH HEY!
YOU DITCHED HOMEROOM, DIDN'T YOU, SANO? WHERE'D YOU GO AFTER P.E.?
When I came back to class, you were already gone! I thought something happened to you!
Uh...
I JUST HAD TO GO RUN SOME ERRANDS.

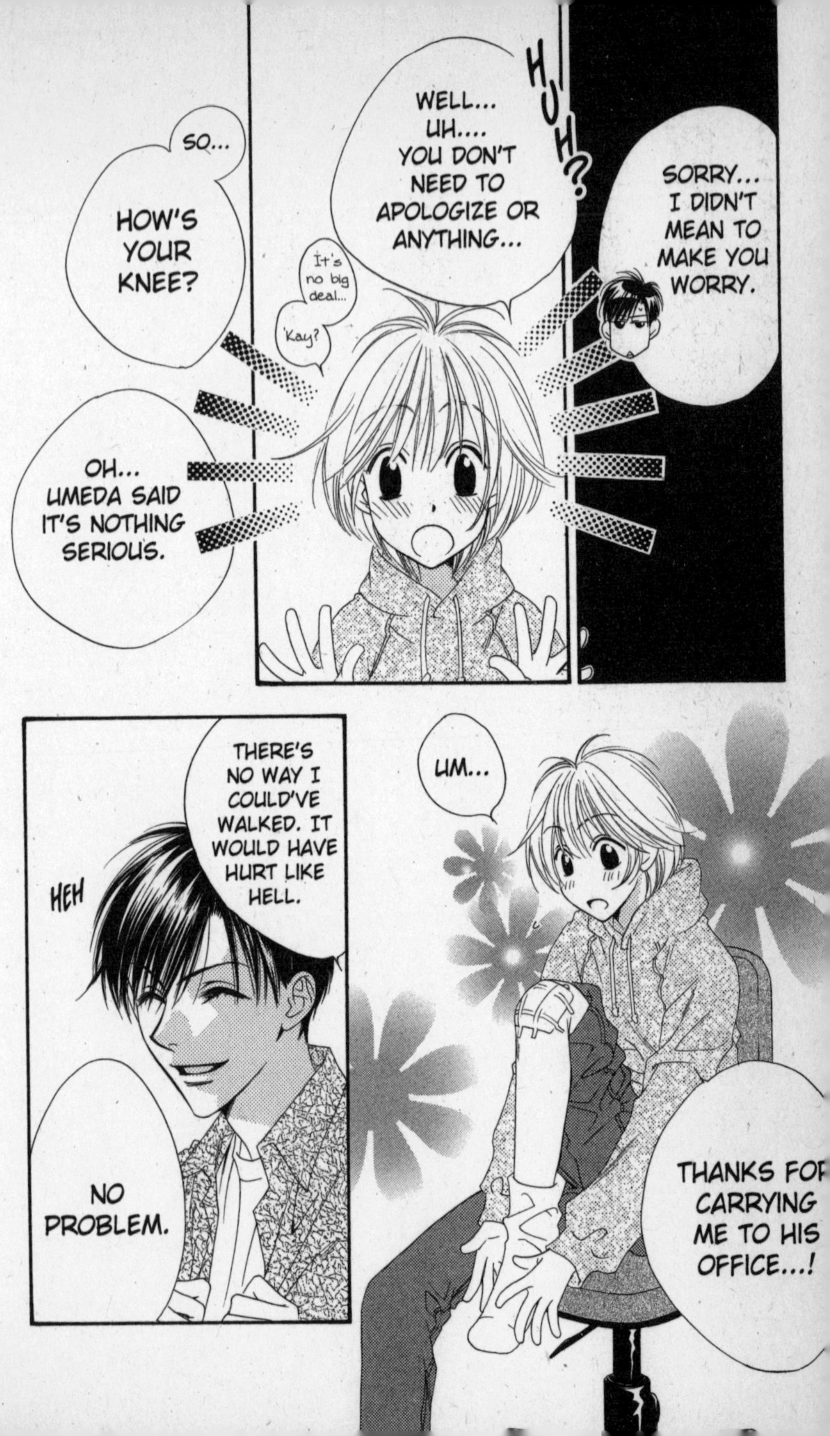
HUH?
SORRY... I DIDN'T MEAN TO MAKE YOU WORRY.
WELL... UH.... YOU DON'T NEED TO APOLOGIZE OR ANYTHING...
It's no big deal...
'Kay?
SO...
HOW'S YOUR KNEE?
OH... UMEDA SAID IT'S NOTHING SERIOUS.
UM...
THANKS FOR CARRYING ME TO HIS OFFICE...!
THERE'S NO WAY I COULD'VE WALKED. IT WOULD HAVE HURT LIKE HELL.
HEH
NO PROBLEM.

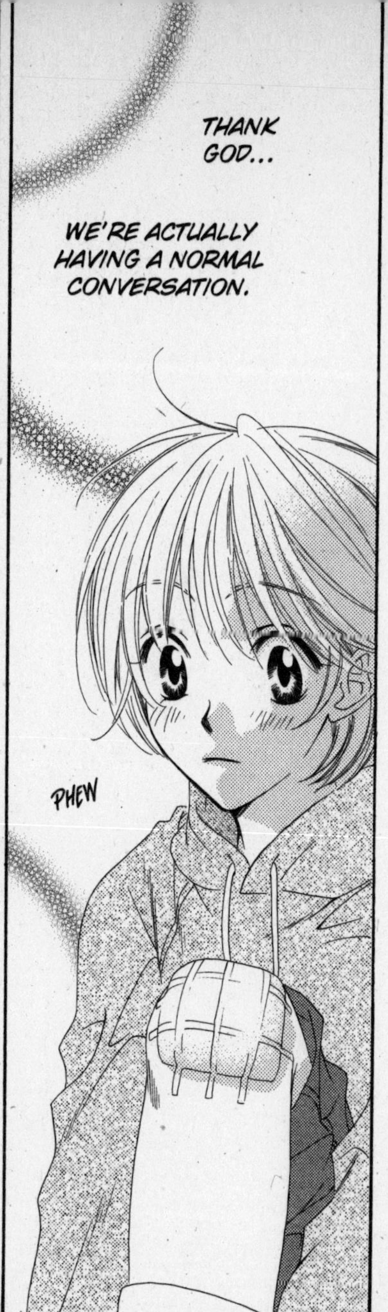
THANK GOD...
WE'RE ACTUALLY HAVING A NORMAL CONVERSATION.
PHEW

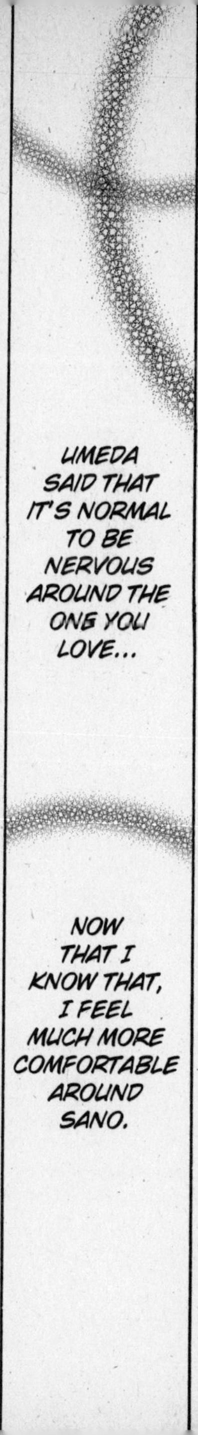
UMEDA SAID THAT IT'S NORMAL TO BE NERVOUS AROUND THE ONE YOU LOVE...
NOW THAT I KNOW THAT, I FEEL MUCH MORE COMFORTABLE AROUND SANO.

RADIO SHOW 2

...So, I made a guest appearance on a radio show again. It was for a show on Bunka Broadcasting called "Hana Yume Chikku ni LaLa Shimasho", hosted by voice actors Takehito Koyasu and Atsushi Kisaichi. I was asked to give Koyasu a Happy Birthday message during the show that aired on May 5th... Actually, I didn't go to the studio, they just put me on the air over the phone. I only had a few minutes before I went on air (maybe 2-3 minutes) because I didnt call them early enough... I was so nervous right before I went on.

→ To be continued.

On the Hana-Kimi CD, Koyasu played Sano, and Kisaichi played Himejima.

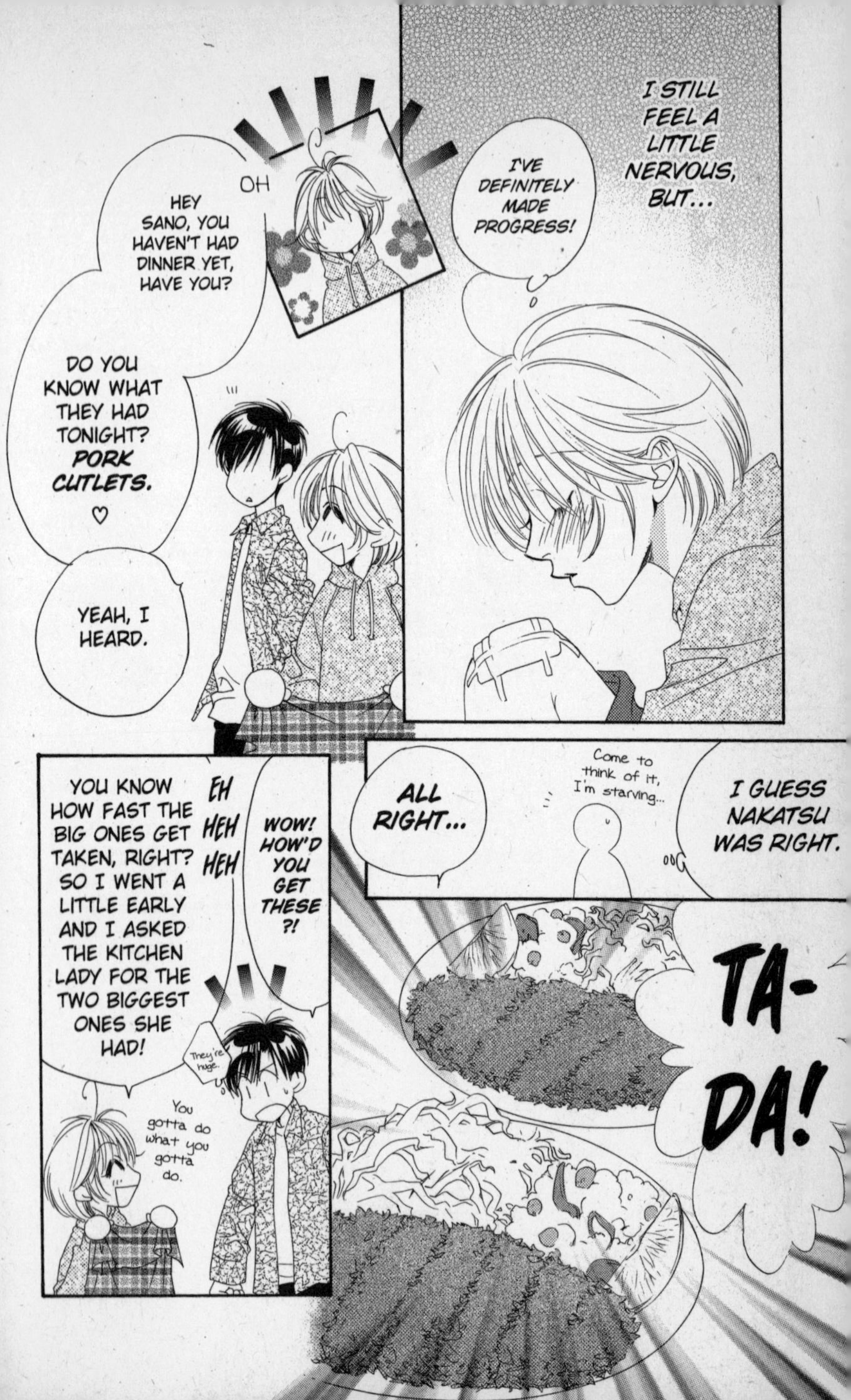
I STILL FEEL A LITTLE NERVOUS, BUT...
I'VE DEFINITELY MADE PROGRESS!
OH
HEY SANO, YOU HAVEN'T HAD DINNER YET, HAVE YOU?
DO YOU KNOW WHAT THEY HAD TONIGHT? PORK CUTLETS. ♡
YEAH, I HEARD.
I GUESS NAKATSU WAS RIGHT.
Come to think of it, I'm starving...
ALL RIGHT...
TA-DA!
WOW! HOW'D YOU GET THESE?!
EH HEH HEH
YOU KNOW HOW FAST THE BIG ONES GET TAKEN, RIGHT? SO I WENT A LITTLE EARLY AND I ASKED THE KITCHEN LADY FOR THE TWO BIGGEST ONES SHE HAD!
They're huge.
You gotta do what you gotta do.

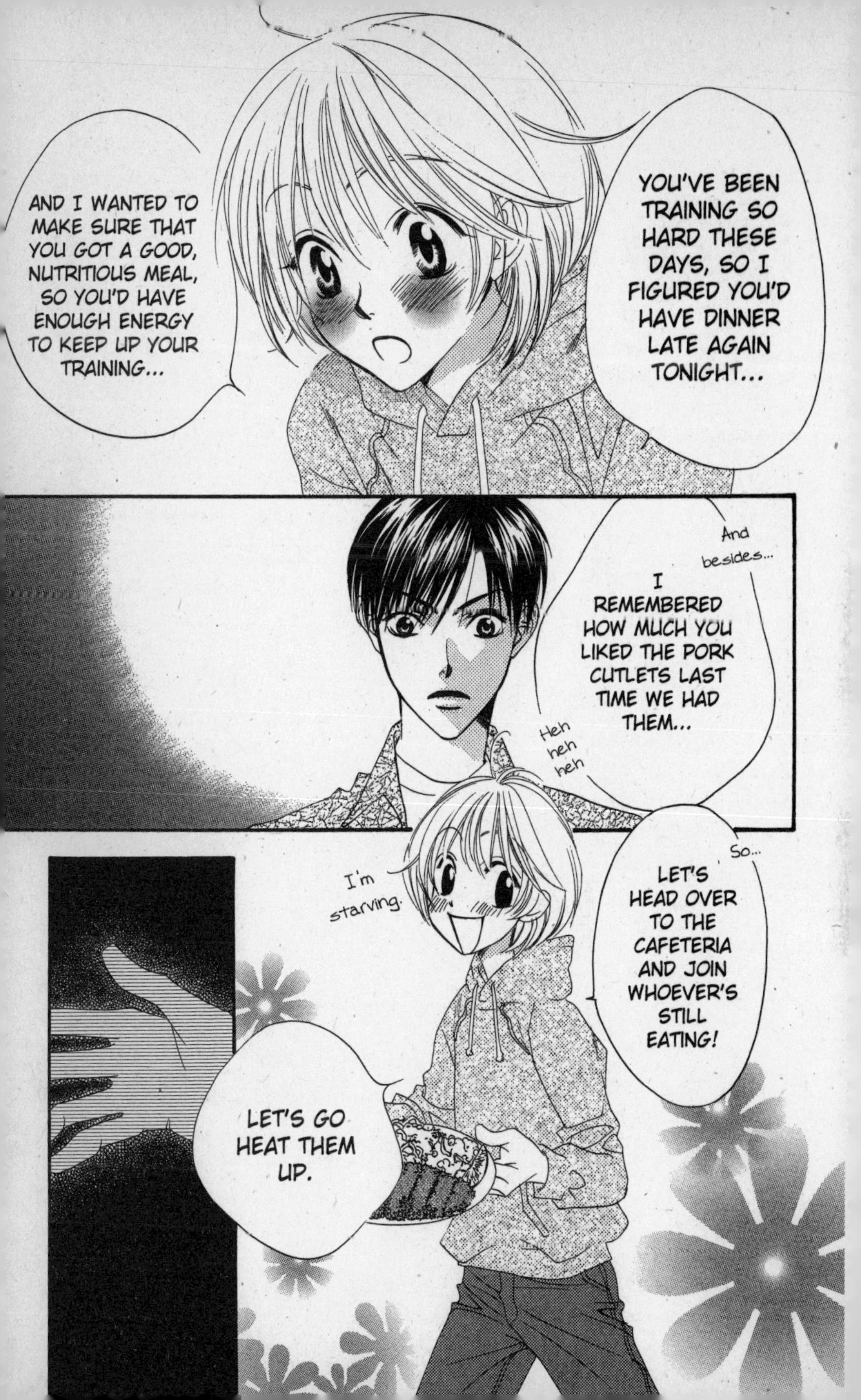
YOU'VE BEEN TRAINING SO HARD THESE DAYS, SO I FIGURED YOU'D HAVE DINNER LATE AGAIN TONIGHT...
AND I WANTED TO MAKE SURE THAT YOU GOT A GOOD, NUTRITIOUS MEAL, SO YOU'D HAVE ENOUGH ENERGY TO KEEP UP YOUR TRAINING...
And besides...
I REMEMBERED HOW MUCH YOU LIKED THE PORK CUTLETS LAST TIME WE HAD THEM...
Heh heh heh
So...
LET'S HEAD OVER TO THE CAFETERIA AND JOIN WHOEVER'S STILL EATING!
I'm starving.
LET'S GO HEAT THEM UP.

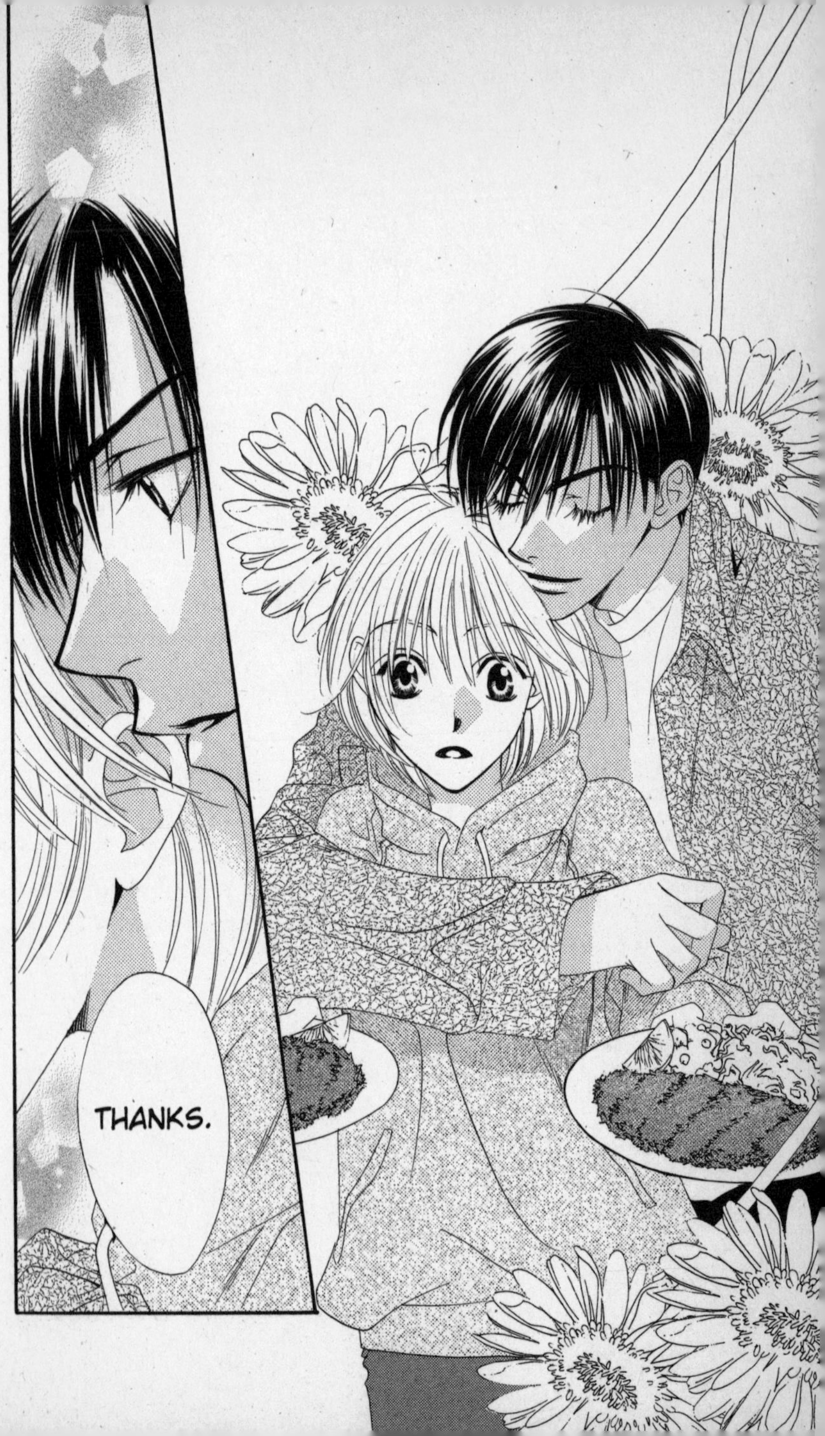
THANKS.

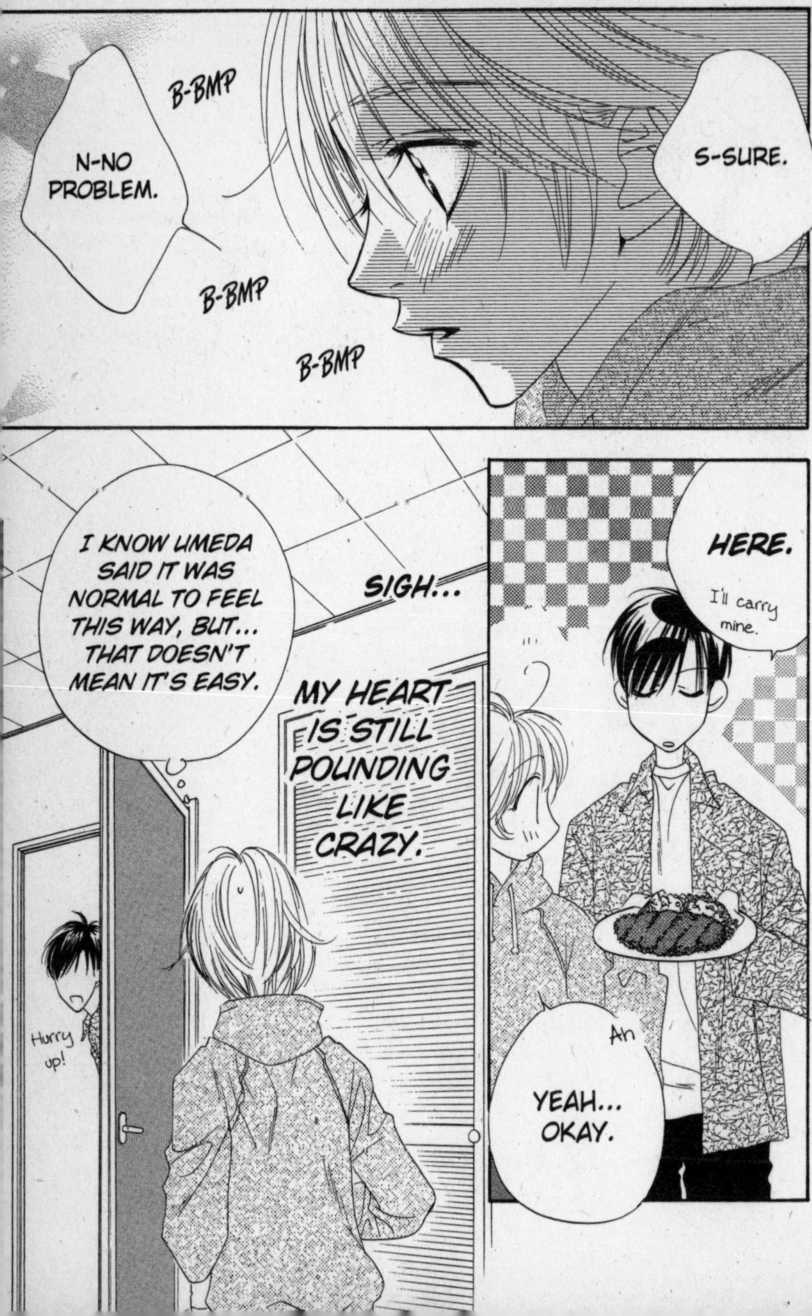
S-SURE.
B-BMP
N-NO PROBLEM.
B-BMP
B-BMP
HERE.
I'll carry mine.
An
YEAH... OKAY.
SIGH...
I KNOW UMEDA SAID IT WAS NORMAL TO FEEL THIS WAY, BUT... THAT DOESN'T MEAN IT'S EASY.
MY HEART IS STILL POUNDING LIKE CRAZY.
Hurry up!

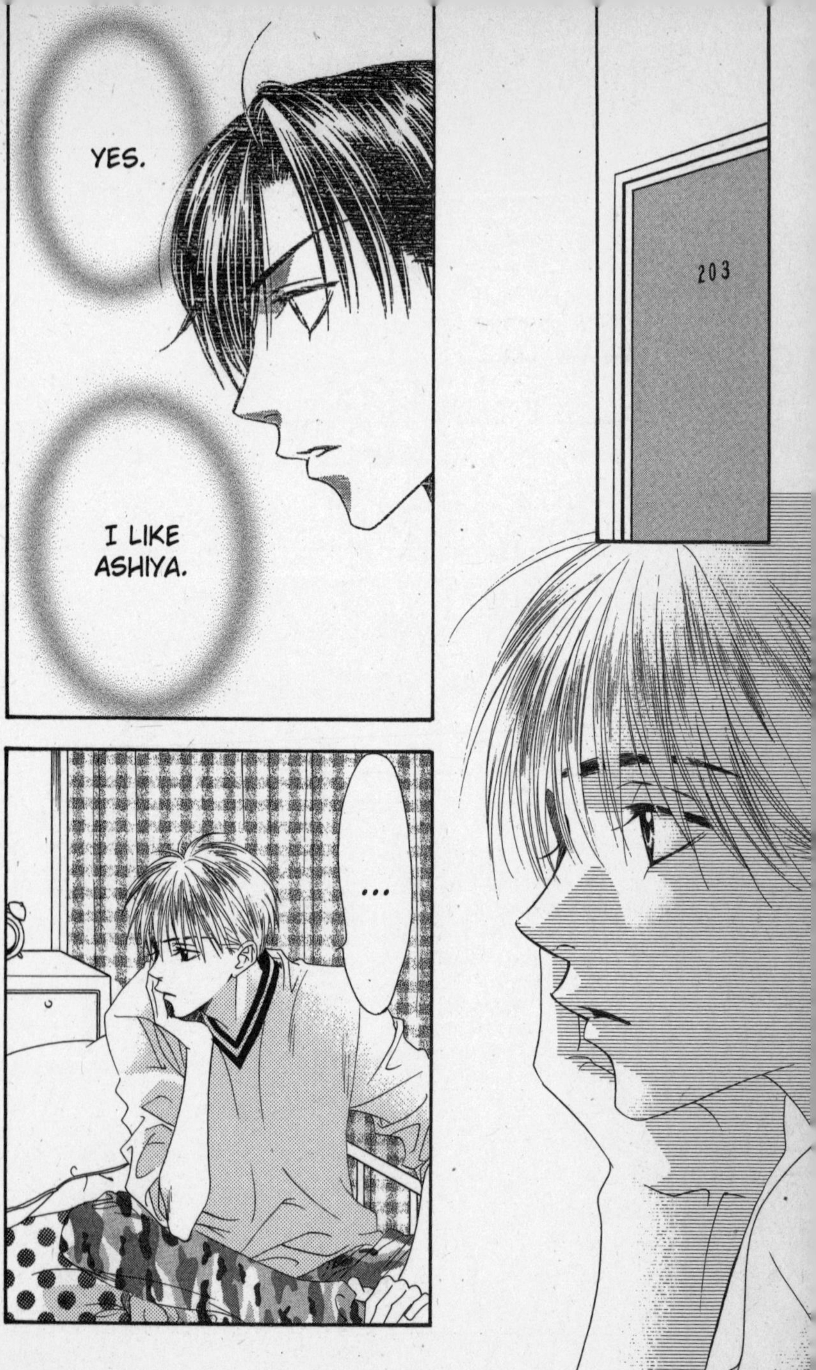
203
YES.
I LIKE ASHIYA.
...

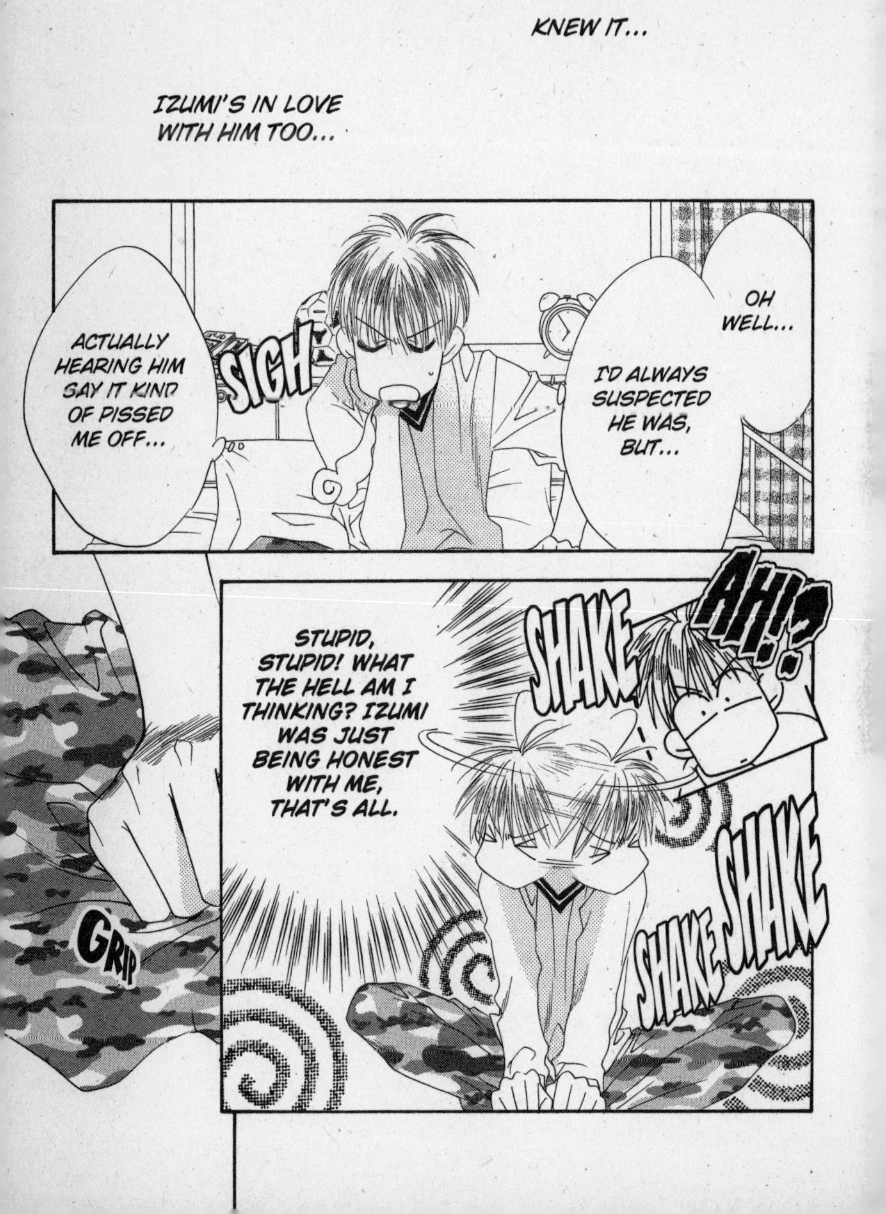
KNEW IT...
IZUMI'S IN LOVE WITH HIM TOO...
OH WELL...
I'D ALWAYS SUSPECTED HE WAS, BUT...
SIGH
ACTUALLY HEARING HIM SAY IT KIND OF PISSED ME OFF...
AH!?
SHAKE
STUPID, STUPID! WHAT THE HELL AM I THINKING? IZUMI WAS JUST BEING HONEST WITH ME, THAT'S ALL.
SHAKE SHAKE
GRIP

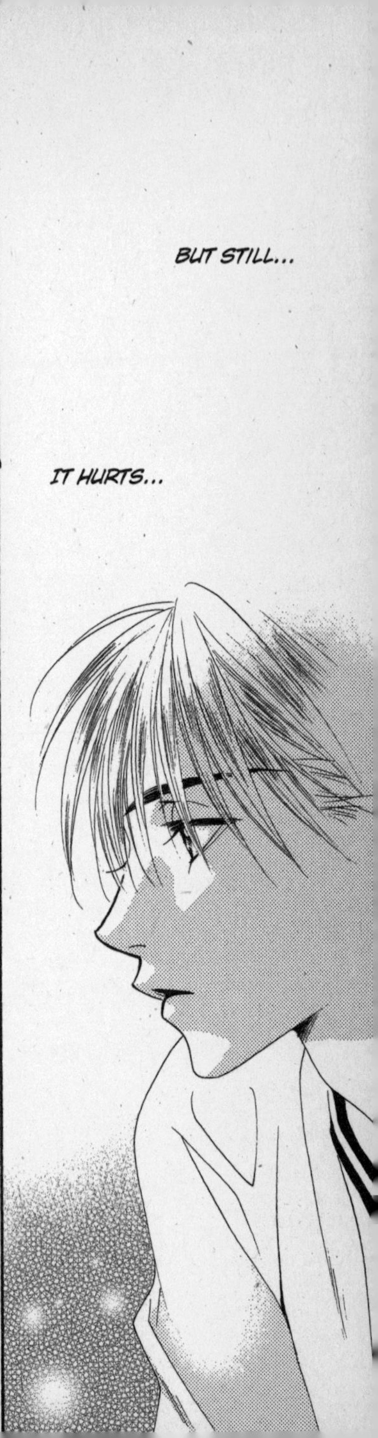
BUT STILL...
IT HURTS...

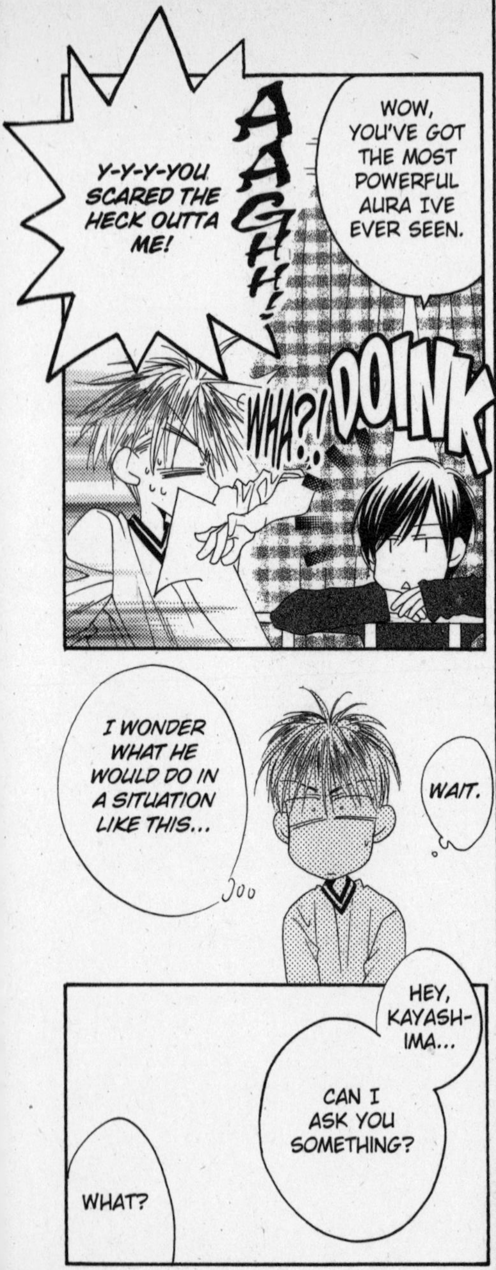
WOW, YOU'VE GOT THE MOST POWERFUL AURA IVE EVER SEEN.
AAGHH!!
Y-Y-Y-YOU SCARED THE HECK OUTTA ME!
DOINK
WHA?!
WAIT.
I WONDER WHAT HE WOULD DO IN A SITUATION LIKE THIS...
HEY, KAYASH-IMA...
CAN I ASK YOU SOMETHING?
WHAT?

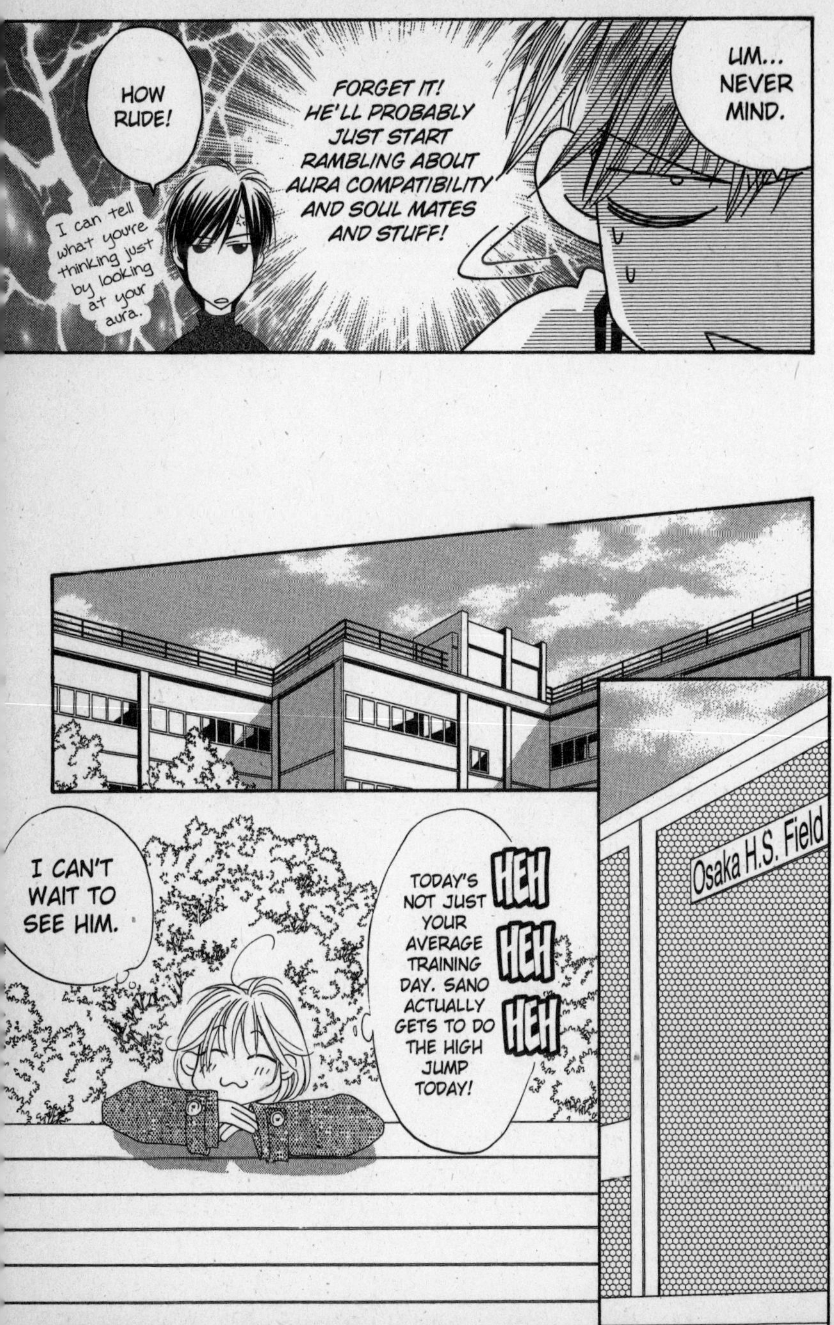
UM... NEVER MIND.
FORGET IT! HE'LL PROBABLY JUST START RAMBLING ABOUT AURA COMPATIBILITY AND SOUL MATES AND STUFF!
HOW RUDE!
I can tell what you're thinking just by looking at your aura.
Osaka H.S. Field
HEH HEH HEH
TODAY'S NOT JUST YOUR AVERAGE TRAINING DAY. SANO ACTUALLY GETS TO DO THE HIGH JUMP TODAY!
I CAN'T WAIT TO SEE HIM.

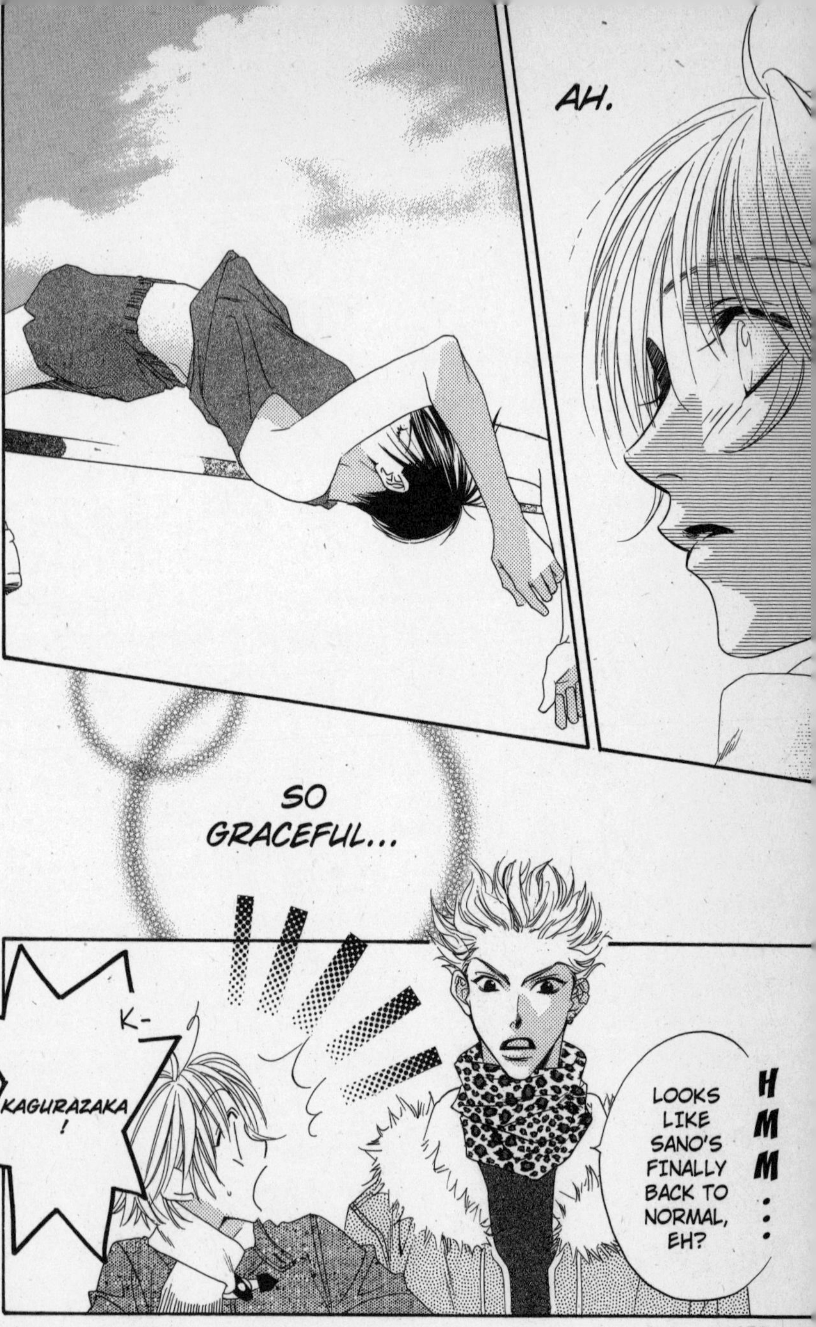
AH.
SO GRACEFUL...
HMM...
LOOKS LIKE SANO'S FINALLY BACK TO NORMAL, EH?
K-
KAGURAZAKA!

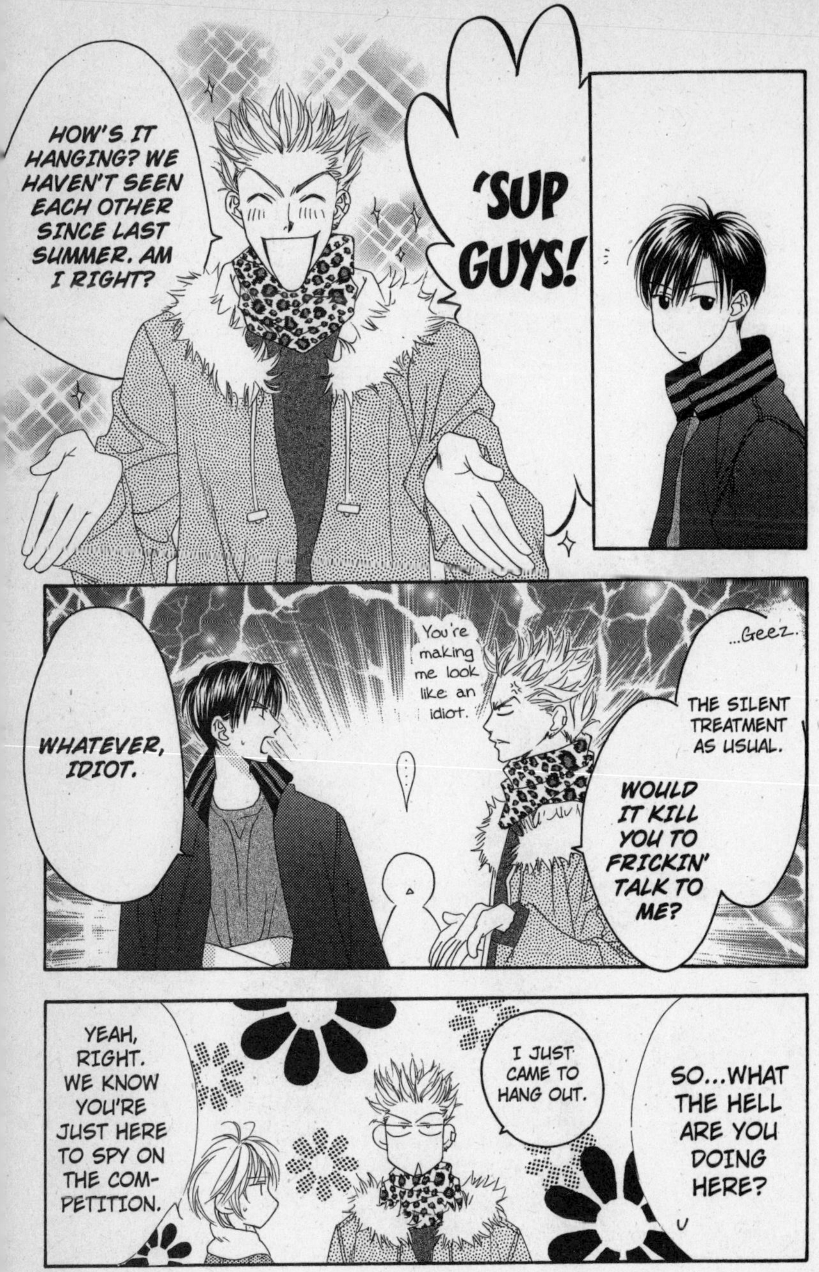
'SUP GUYS!
HOW'S IT HANGING? WE HAVEN'T SEEN EACH OTHER SINCE LAST SUMMER. AM I RIGHT?
...Geez.
THE SILENT TREATMENT AS USUAL.
WOULD IT KILL YOU TO FRICKIN' TALK TO ME?
You're making me look like an idiot.
WHATEVER, IDIOT.
SO...WHAT THE HELL ARE YOU DOING HERE?
I JUST CAME TO HANG OUT.
YEAH, RIGHT. WE KNOW YOU'RE JUST HERE TO SPY ON THE COM-PETITION.

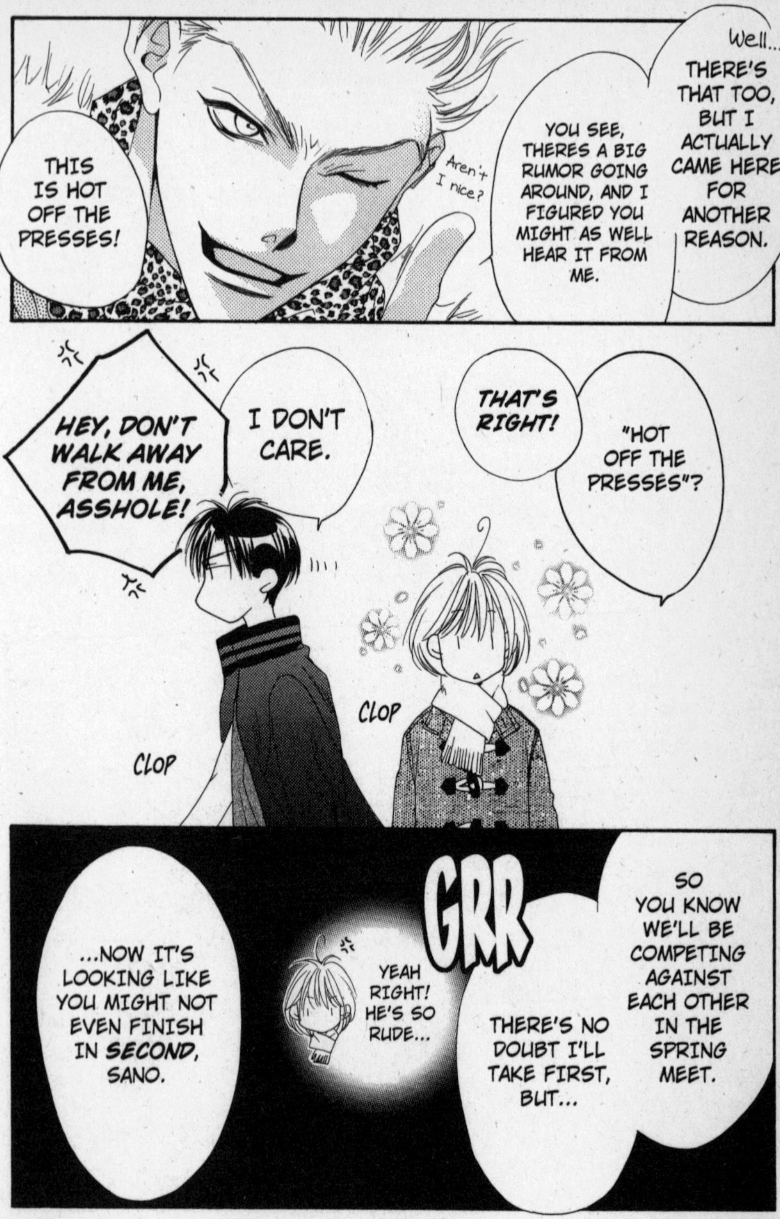
Well...
THERE'S THAT TOO, BUT I ACTUALLY CAME HERE FOR ANOTHER REASON.
YOU SEE, THERES A BIG RUMOR GOING AROUND, AND I FIGURED YOU MIGHT AS WELL HEAR IT FROM ME.
Aren't I nice?
THIS IS HOT OFF THE PRESSES!
"HOT OFF THE PRESSES"?
THAT'S RIGHT!
I DON'T CARE.
HEY, DON'T WALK AWAY FROM ME, ASSHOLE!
CLOP
CLOP
SO YOU KNOW WE'LL BE COMPETING AGAINST EACH OTHER IN THE SPRING MEET.
GRR
THERE'S NO DOUBT I'LL TAKE FIRST, BUT...
YEAH RIGHT! HE'S SO RUDE...
...NOW IT'S LOOKING LIKE YOU MIGHT NOT EVEN FINISH IN SECOND, SANO.

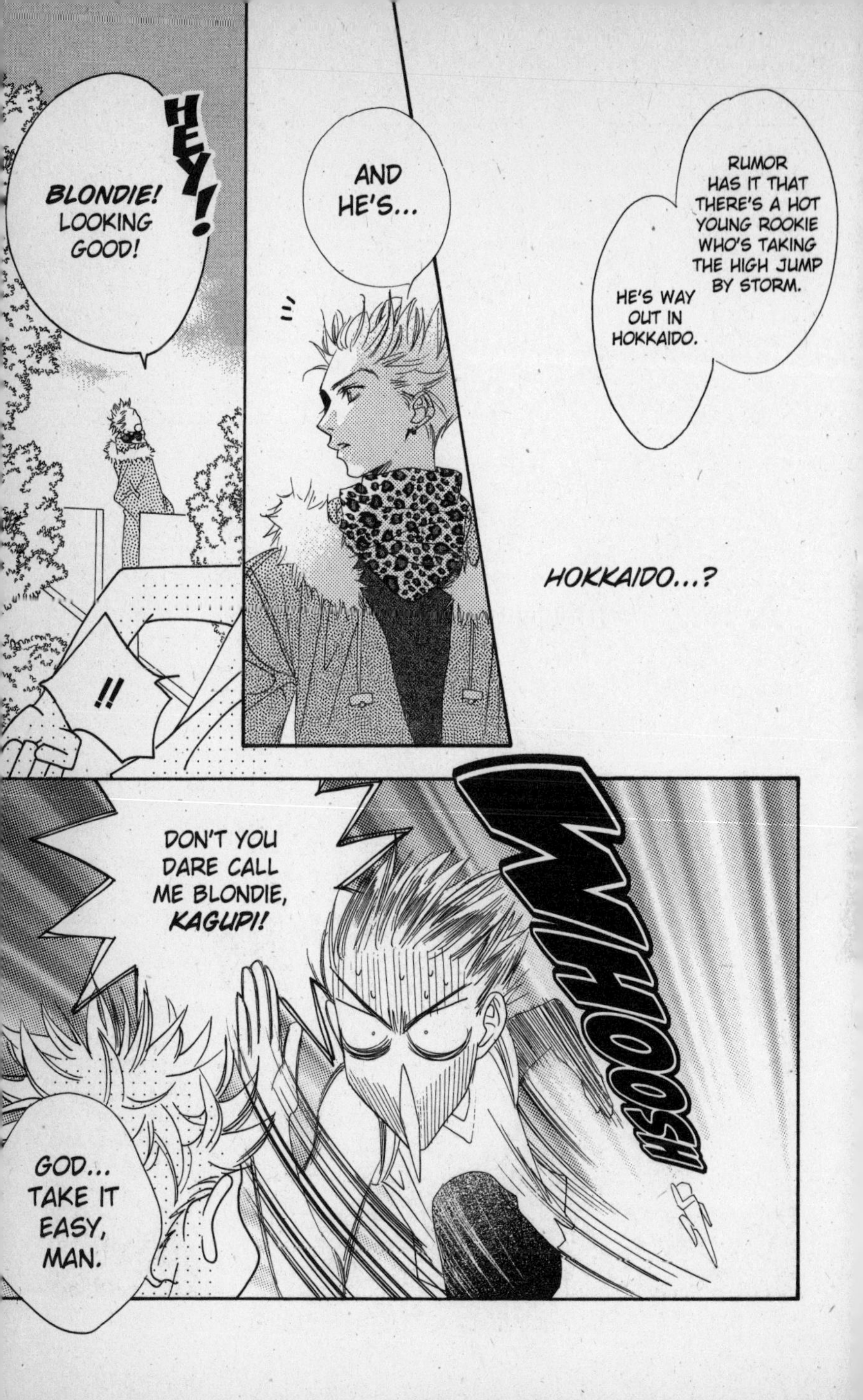
RUMOR HAS IT THAT THERE'S A HOT YOUNG ROOKIE WHO'S TAKING THE HIGH JUMP BY STORM.
HE'S WAY OUT IN HOKKAIDO.
HOKKAIDO...?
AND HE'S...
HEY!
BLONDIE! LOOKING GOOD!
!!
WHOOSH!
DON'T YOU DARE CALL ME BLONDIE, KAGUPI!
GOD... TAKE IT EASY, MAN.

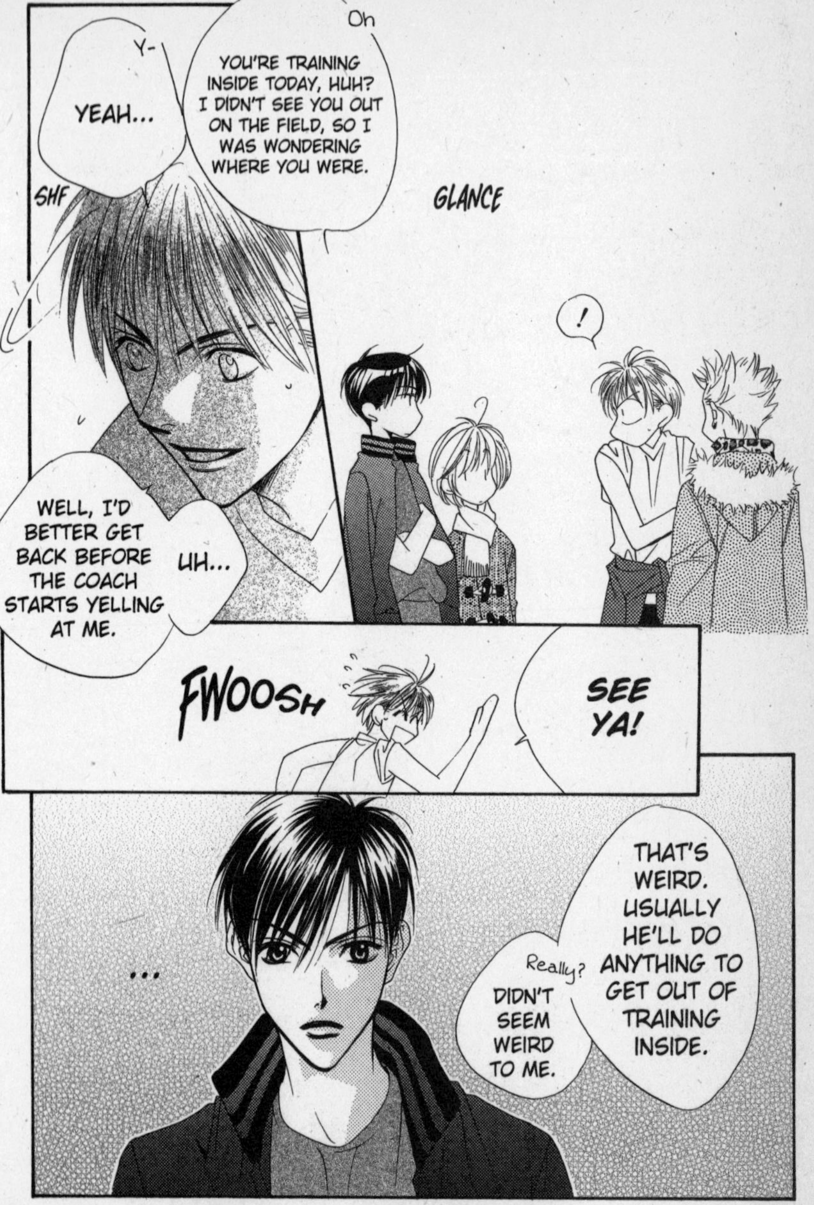
Oh
YOU'RE TRAINING INSIDE TODAY, HUH? I DIDN'T SEE YOU OUT ON THE FIELD, SO I WAS WONDERING WHERE YOU WERE.
GLANCE
!
Y-
YEAH...
SHF
UH...
WELL, I'D BETTER GET BACK BEFORE THE COACH STARTS YELLING AT ME.
SEE YA!
FWOOSH
THAT'S WEIRD. USUALLY HE'LL DO ANYTHING TO GET OUT OF TRAINING INSIDE.
Really?
DIDN'T SEEM WEIRD TO ME.
...

HANA-KIMI CHAPTER 81/END

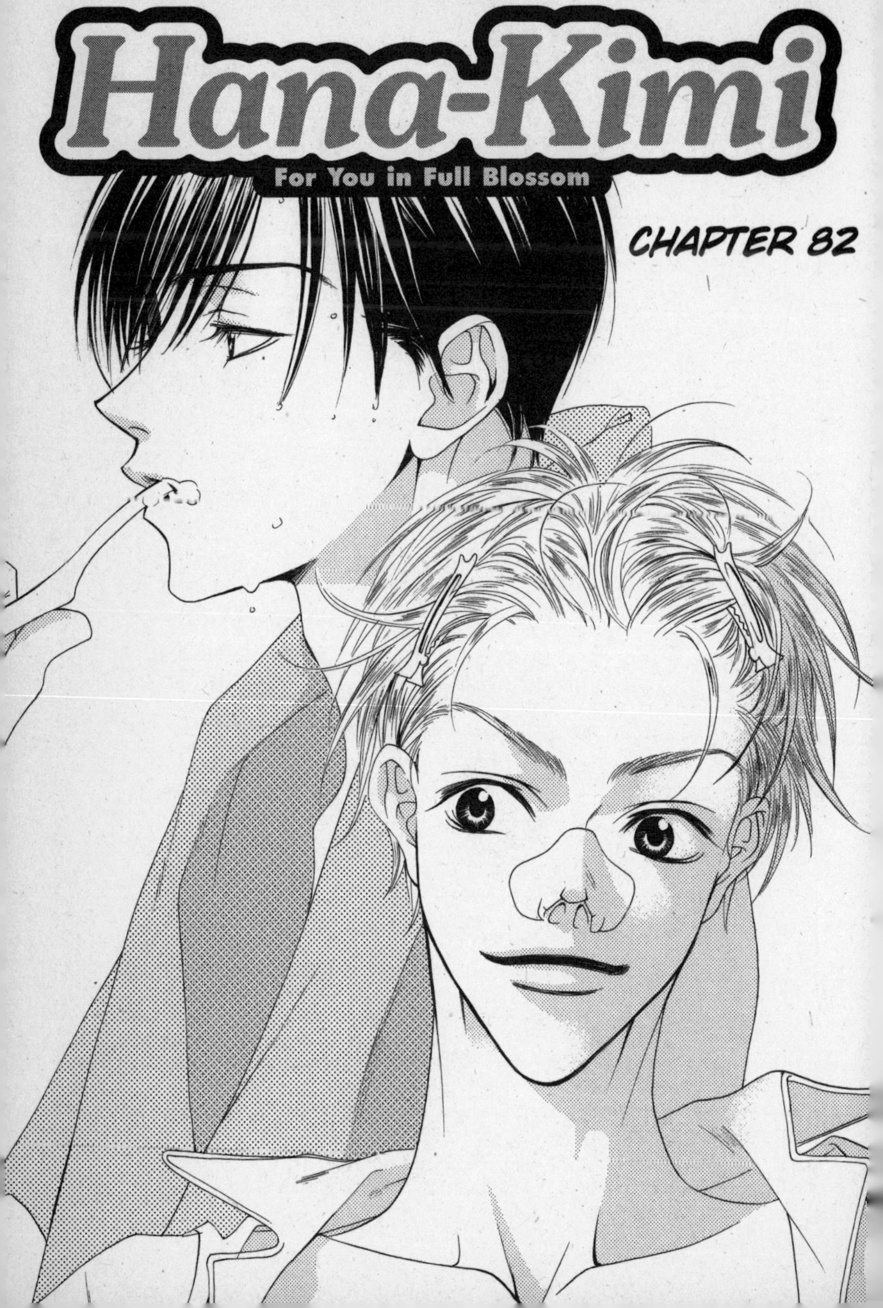
Hana-Kimi
For You in Full Blossom
CHAPTER 82

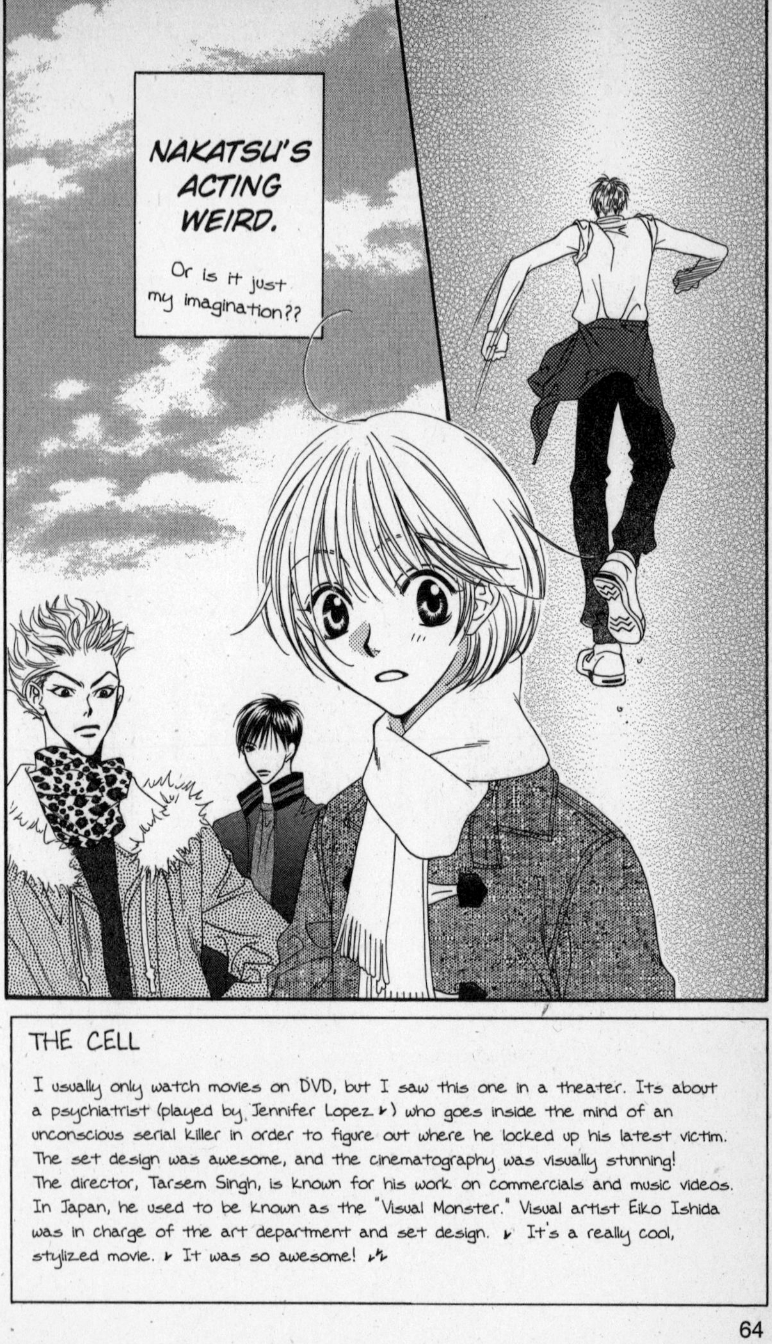
NAKATSU'S ACTING WEIRD.
Or is it just my imagination??

THE CELL

I usually only watch movies on DVD, but I saw this one in a theater. Its about a psychiatrist (played by Jennifer Lopez ♥) who goes inside the mind of an unconscious serial killer in order to figure out where he locked up his latest victim. The set design was awesome, and the cinematography was visually stunning! The director, Tarsem Singh, is known for his work on commercials and music videos. In Japan, he used to be known as the "Visual Monster." Visual artist Eiko Ishida was in charge of the art department and set design. ♥ It's a really cool, stylized movie. ♥ It was so awesome! ♥

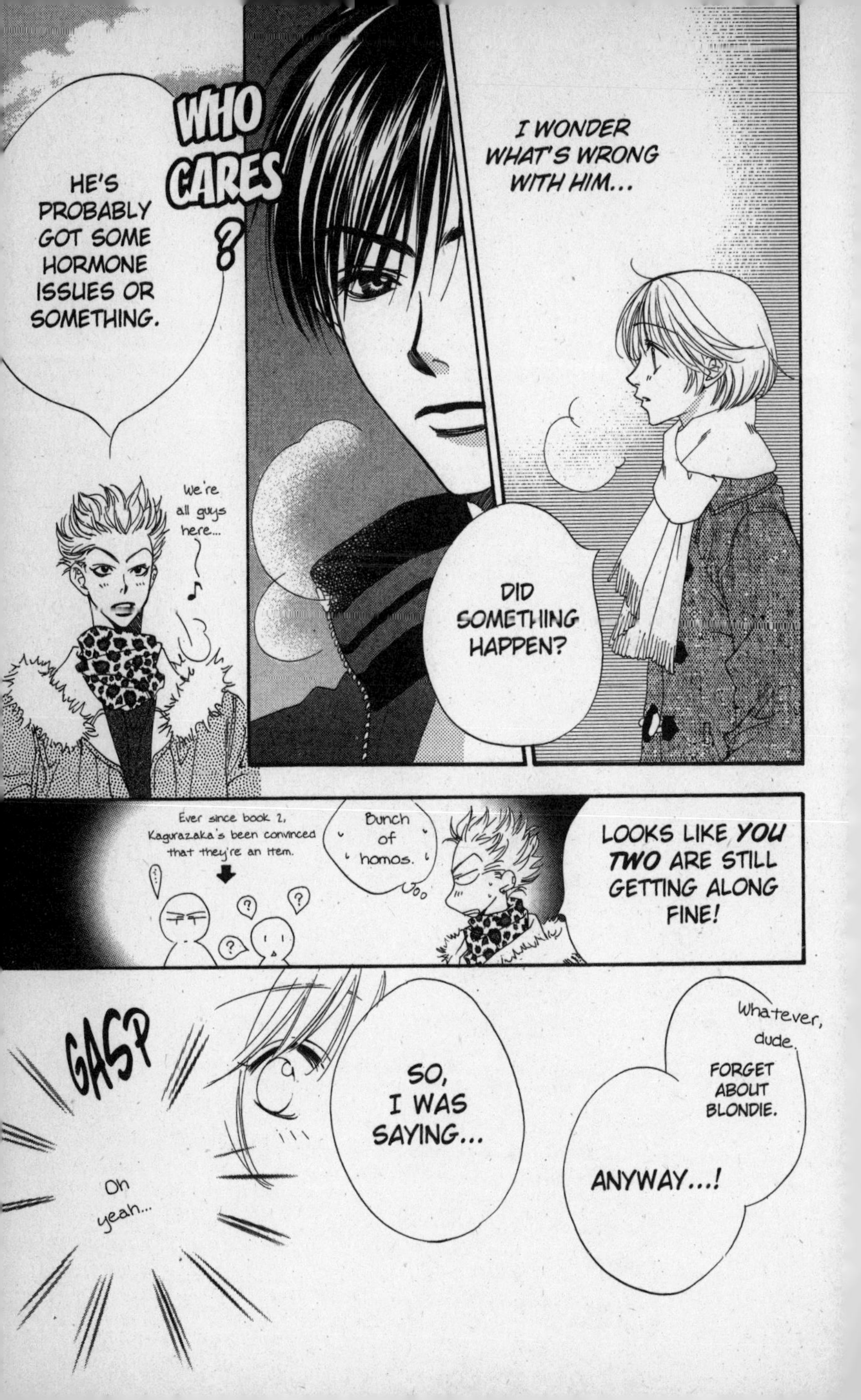
I WONDER WHAT'S WRONG WITH HIM...
DID SOMETHING HAPPEN?
WHO CARES?
HE'S PROBABLY GOT SOME HORMONE ISSUES OR SOMETHING.
We're all guys here...
LOOKS LIKE YOU TWO ARE STILL GETTING ALONG FINE!
Bunch of homos.
Ever since book 2, Kagurazaka's been convinced that they're an item.
Whatever, dude. FORGET ABOUT BLONDIE.
ANYWAY...!
SO, I WAS SAYING...
GASP
Oh yeah...

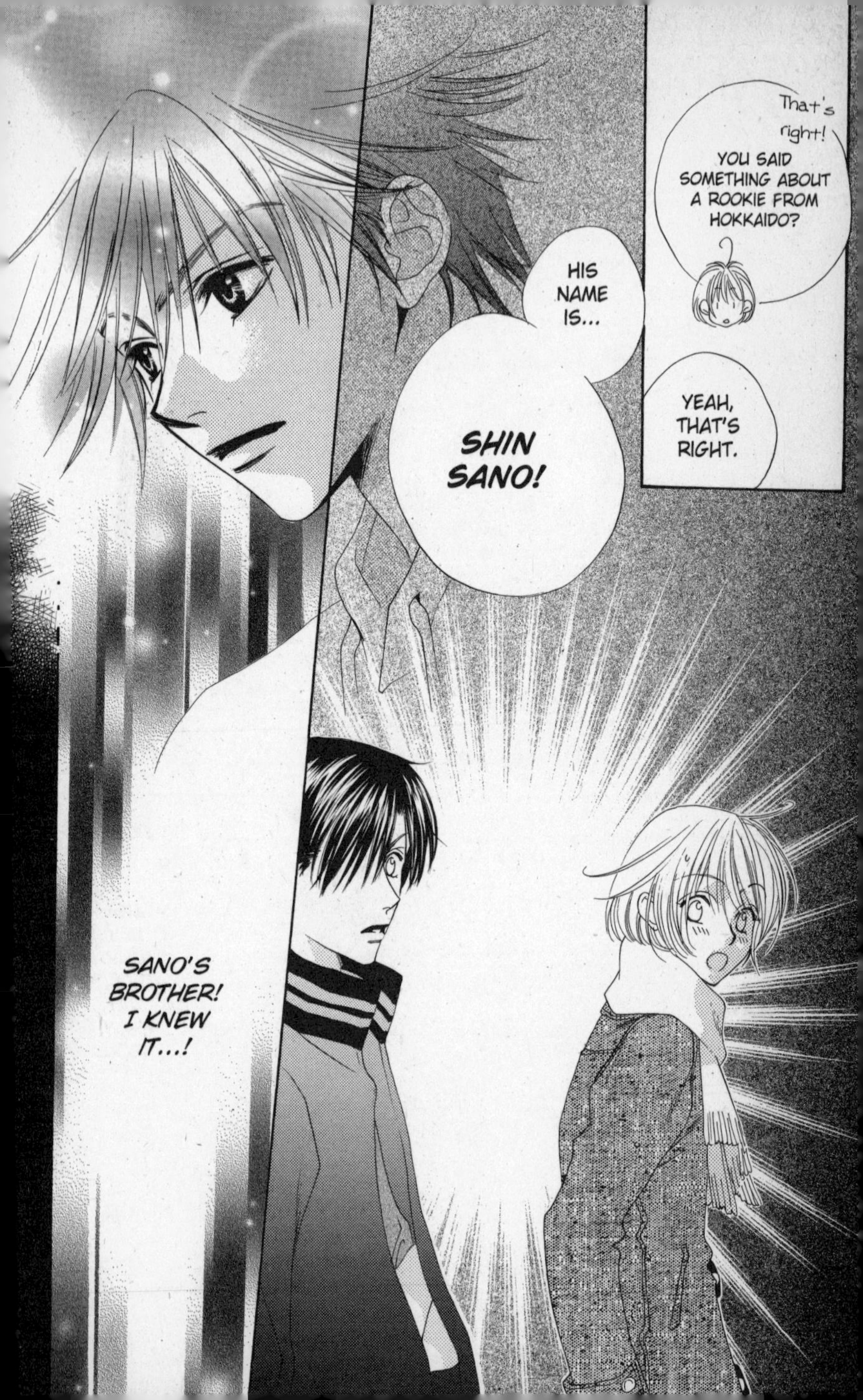
That's right!
YOU SAID SOMETHING ABOUT A ROOKIE FROM HOKKAIDO?
YEAH, THAT'S RIGHT.
HIS NAME IS...
SHIN SANO!
SANO'S BROTHER! I KNEW IT...!

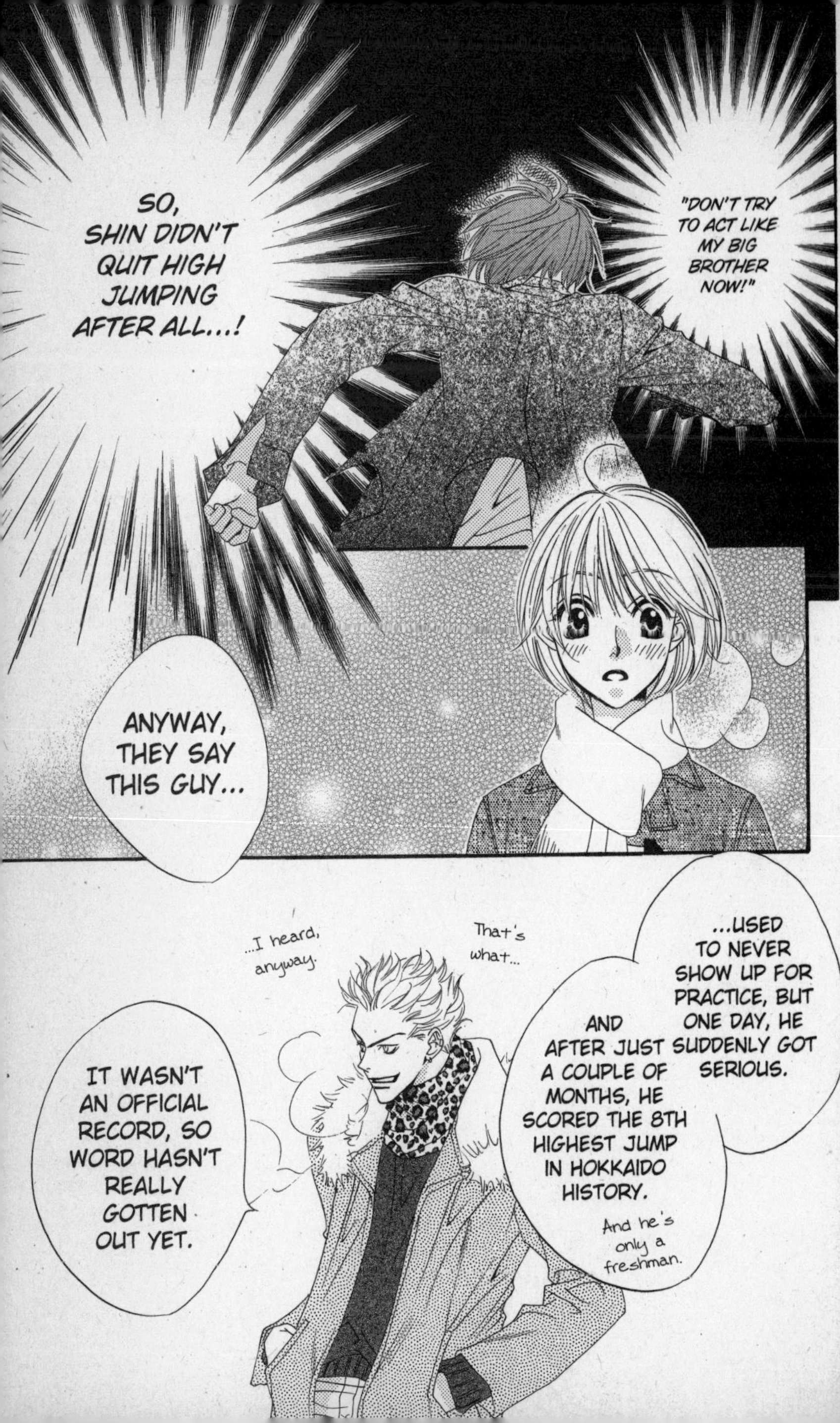
"DON'T TRY TO ACT LIKE MY BIG BROTHER NOW!"
SO, SHIN DIDN'T QUIT HIGH JUMPING AFTER ALL...!
ANYWAY, THEY SAY THIS GUY...
...USED TO NEVER SHOW UP FOR PRACTICE, BUT ONE DAY, HE SUDDENLY GOT SERIOUS.
AND AFTER JUST A COUPLE OF MONTHS, HE SCORED THE 8TH HIGHEST JUMP IN HOKKAIDO HISTORY.
And he's only a freshman.
That's what...
...I heard, anyway.
IT WASN'T AN OFFICIAL RECORD, SO WORD HASN'T REALLY GOTTEN OUT YET.

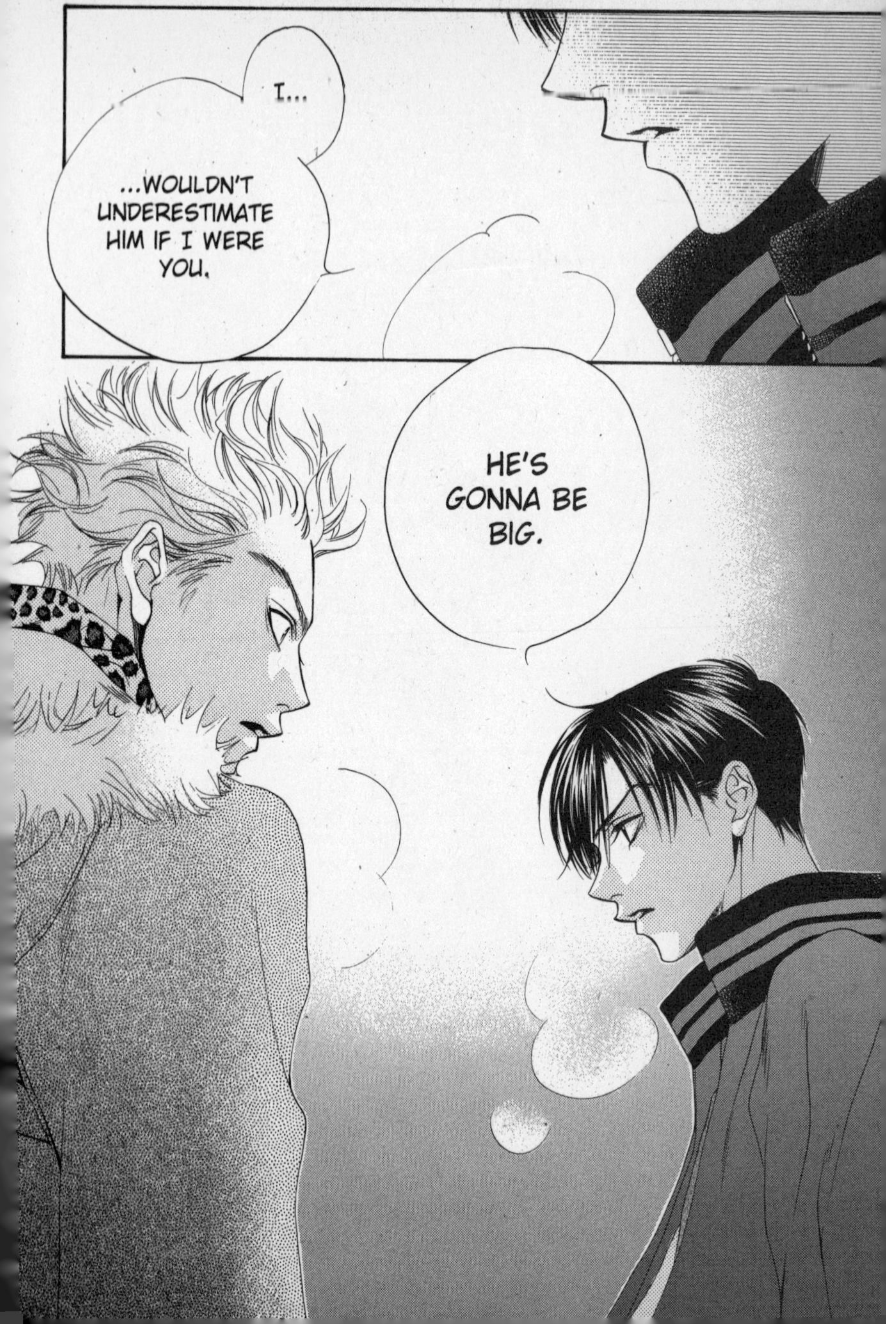
I...
...WOULDN'T UNDERESTIMATE HIM IF I WERE YOU.
HE'S GONNA BE BIG.

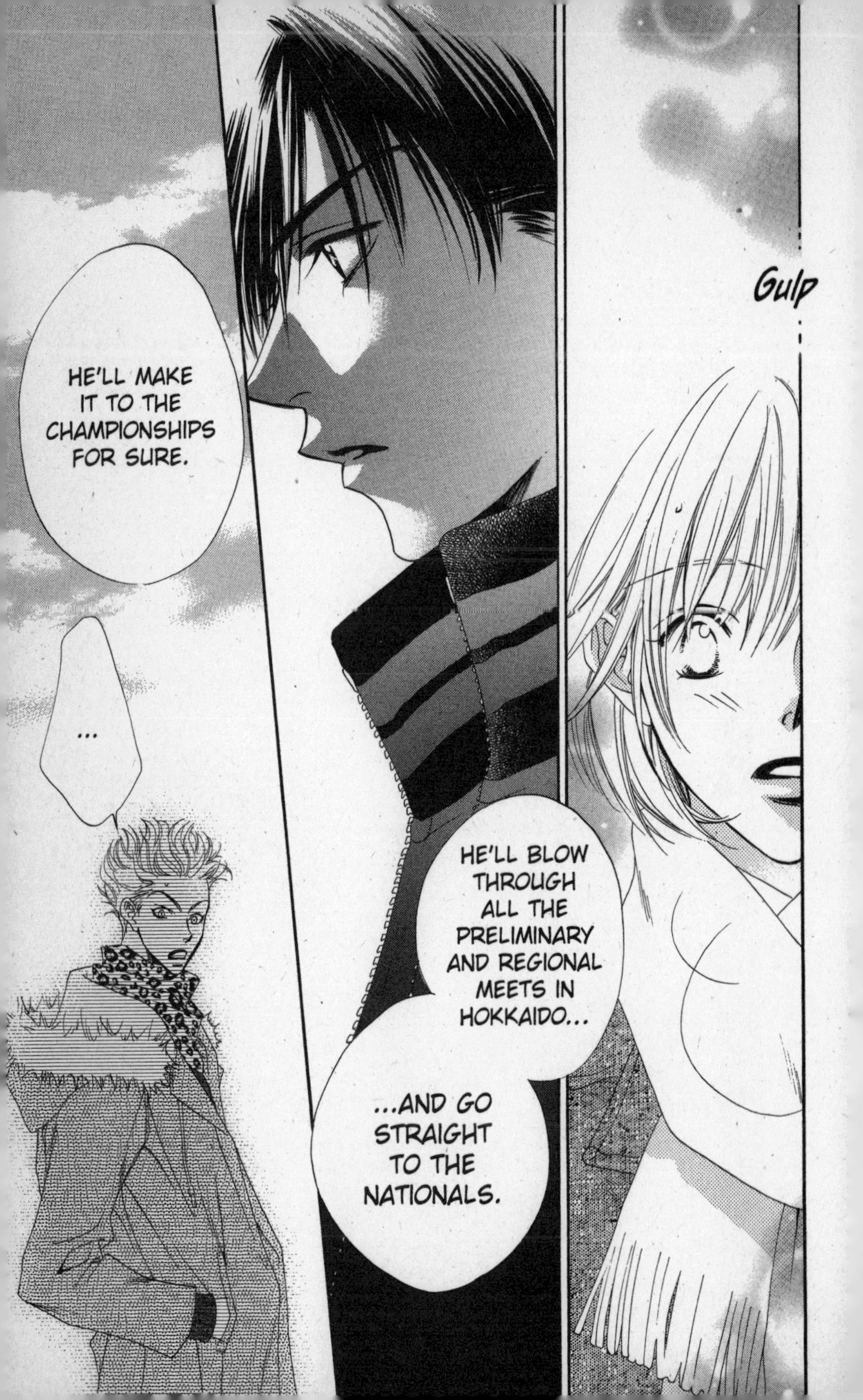
Gulp
HE'LL BLOW THROUGH ALL THE PRELIMINARY AND REGIONAL MEETS IN HOKKAIDO...
...AND GO STRAIGHT TO THE NATIONALS.
HE'LL MAKE IT TO THE CHAMPIONSHIPS FOR SURE.
...

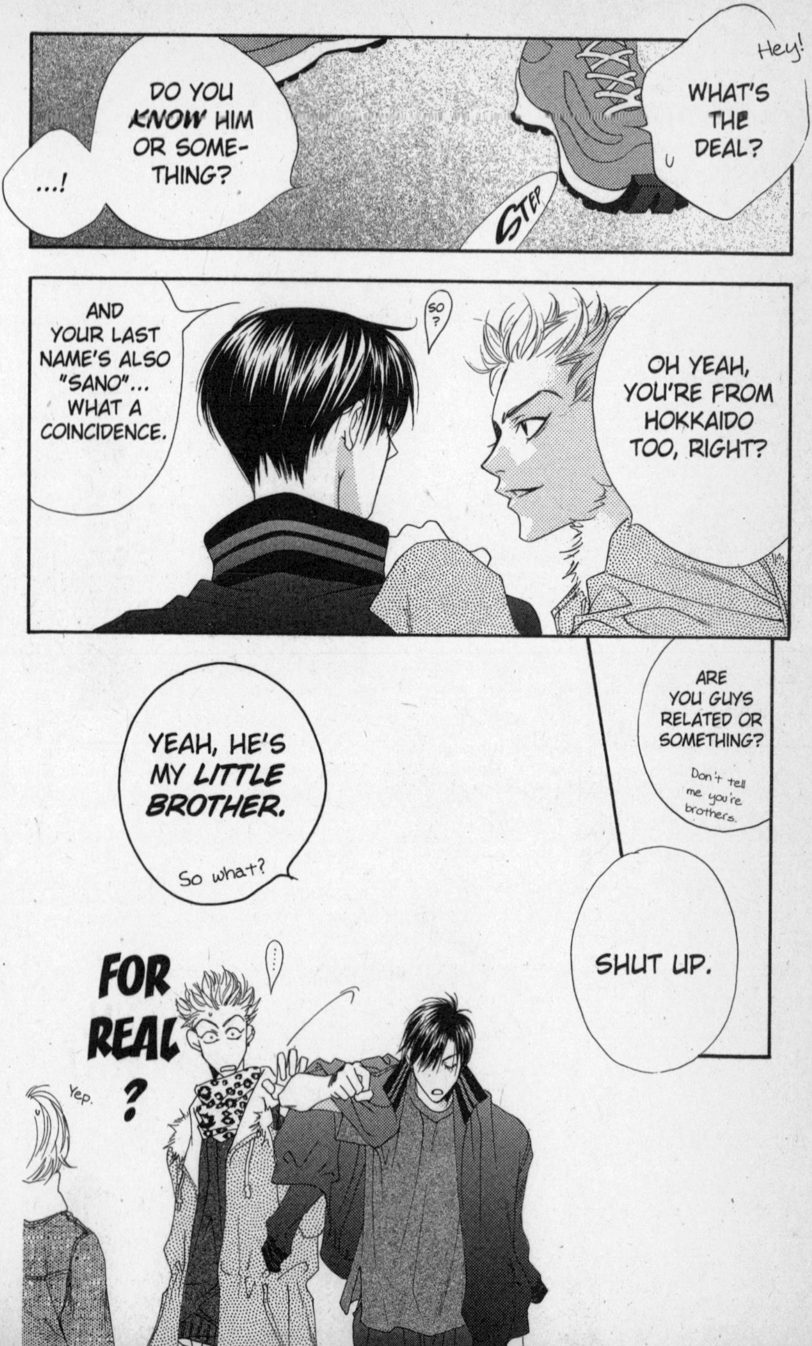
Hey!
WHAT'S THE DEAL?
STEP
DO YOU KNOW HIM OR SOME-THING?
...!
OH YEAH, YOU'RE FROM HOKKAIDO TOO, RIGHT?
SO?
AND YOUR LAST NAME'S ALSO "SANO"... WHAT A COINCIDENCE.
ARE YOU GUYS RELATED OR SOMETHING?
Don't tell me you're brothers.
YEAH, HE'S MY LITTLE BROTHER.
So what?
SHUT UP.
...
FOR REAL?
Yep.

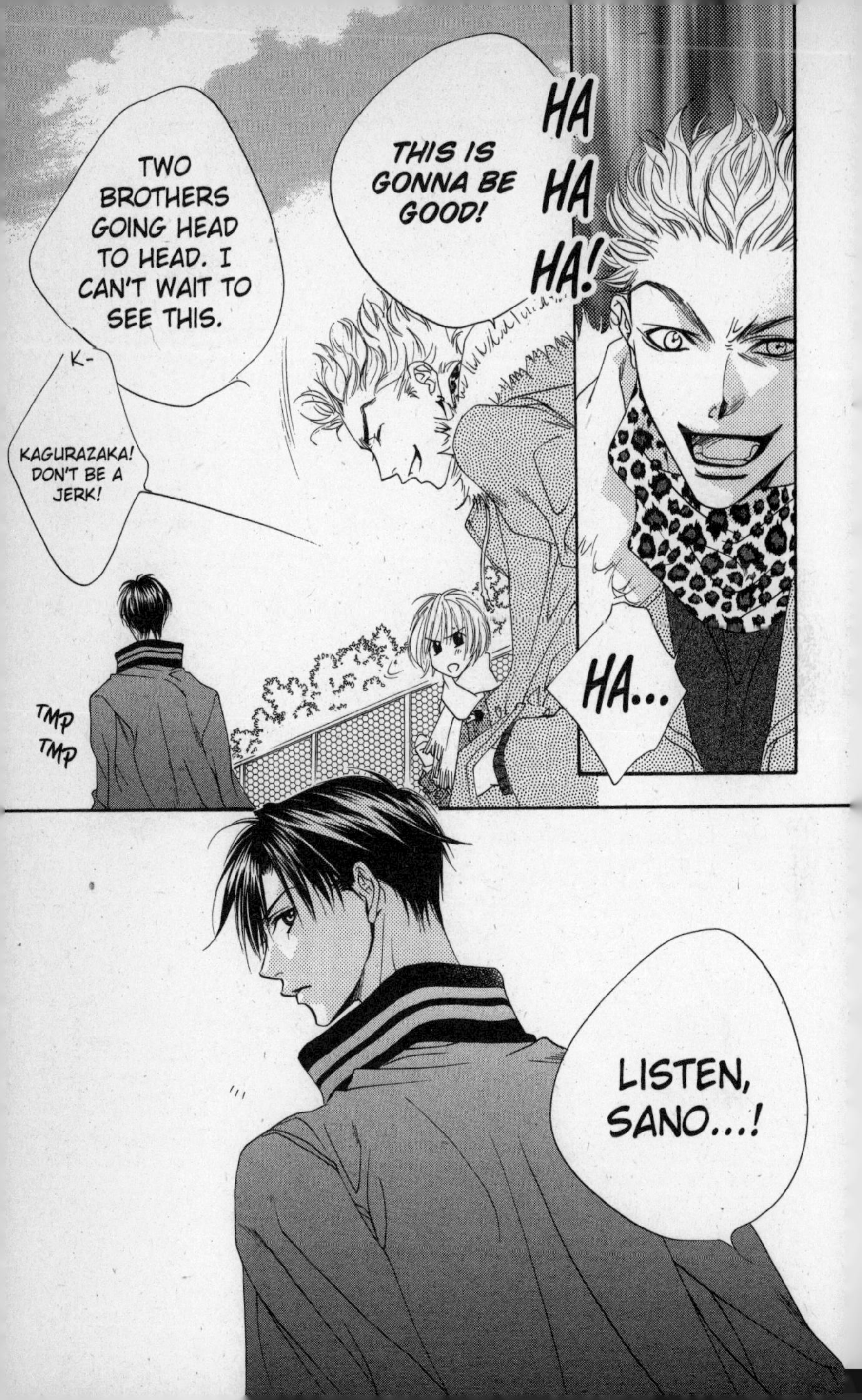
HA HA HA!
HA...
THIS IS GONNA BE GOOD!
TWO BROTHERS GOING HEAD TO HEAD. I CAN'T WAIT TO SEE THIS.
K-
KAGURAZAKA! DON'T BE A JERK!
TMP TMP
LISTEN, SANO...!

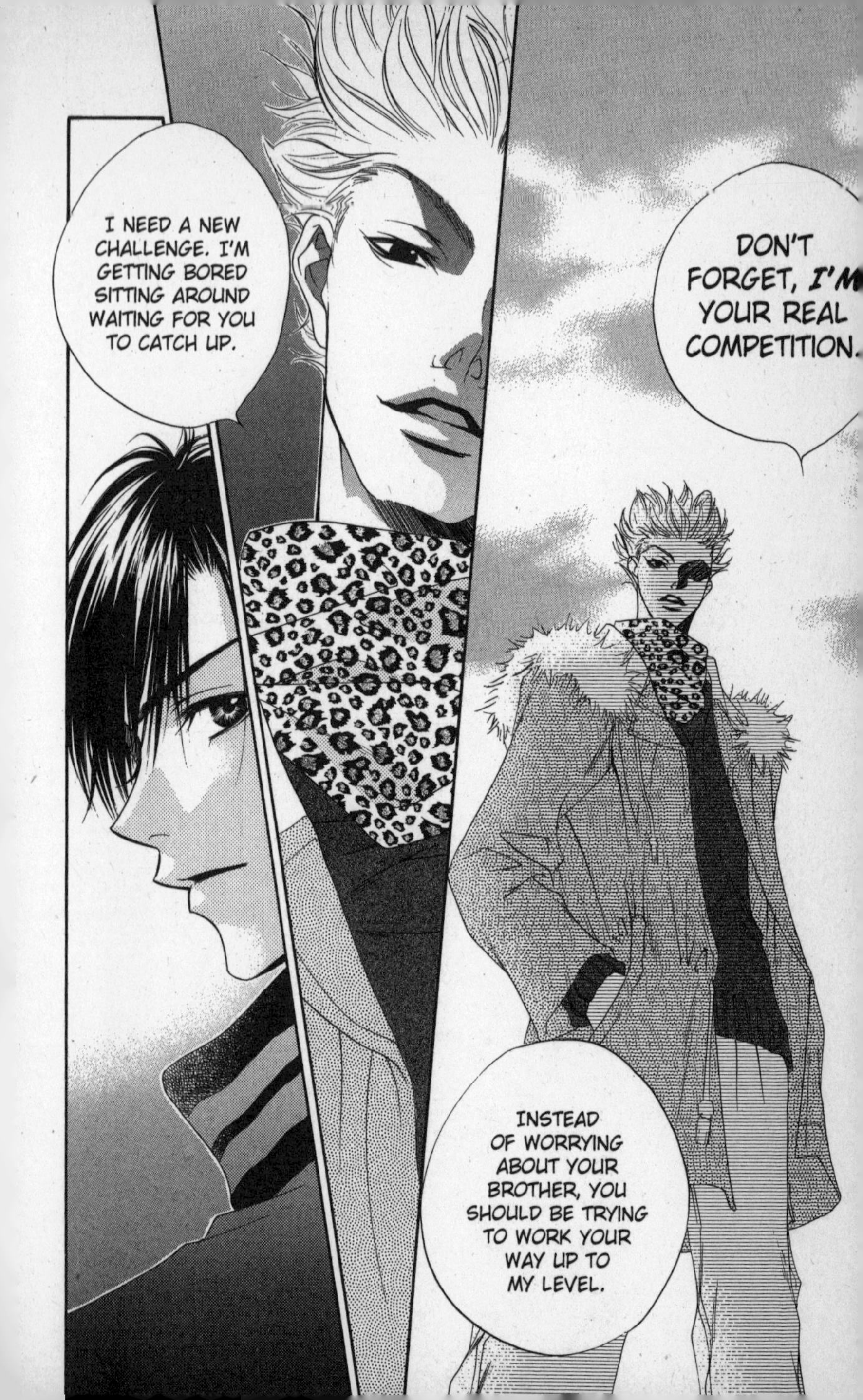
DON'T FORGET, I'M YOUR REAL COMPETITION.
INSTEAD OF WORRYING ABOUT YOUR BROTHER, YOU SHOULD BE TRYING TO WORK YOUR WAY UP TO MY LEVEL.
I NEED A NEW CHALLENGE. I'M GETTING BORED SITTING AROUND WAITING FOR YOU TO CATCH UP.

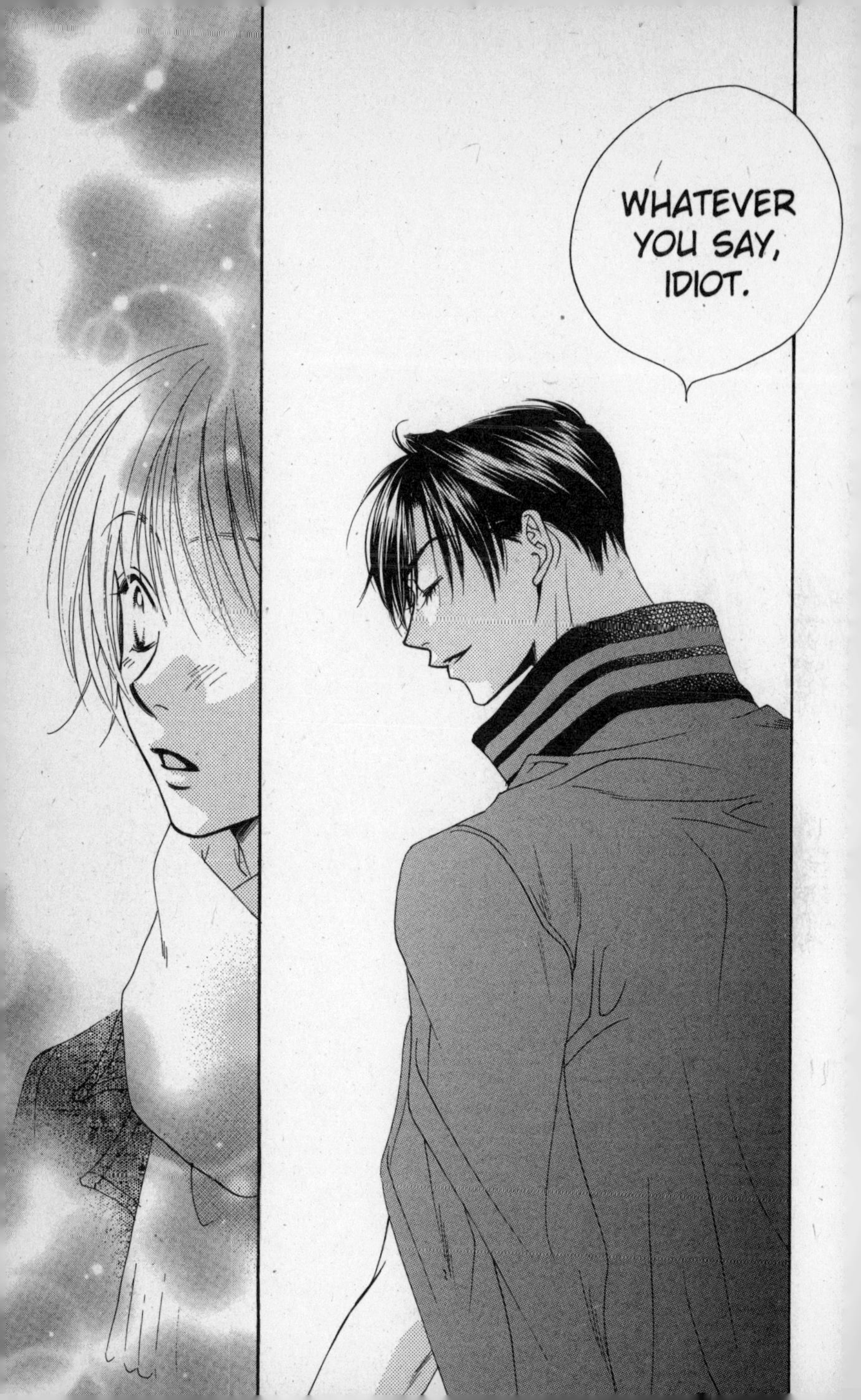
WHATEVER YOU SAY, IDIOT.

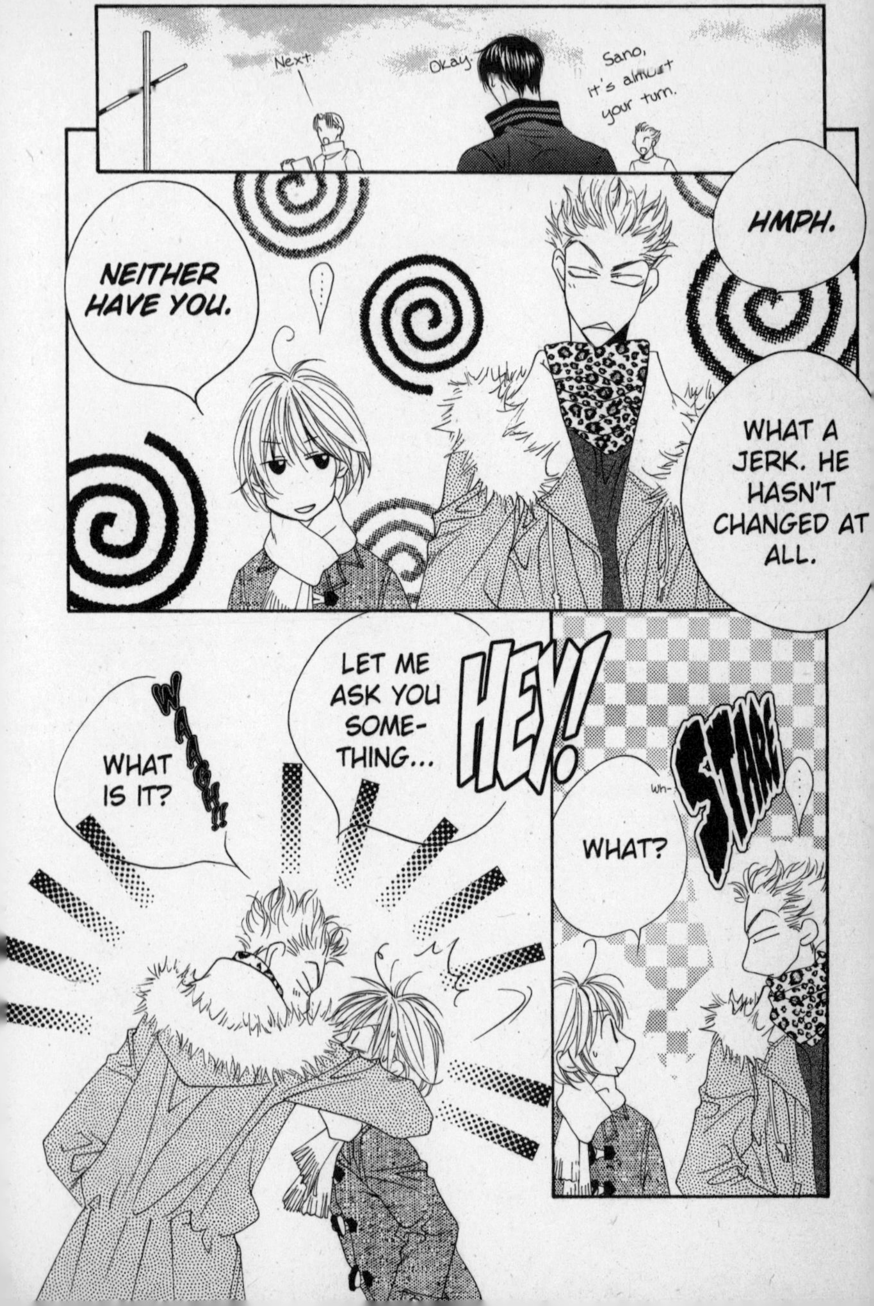
Sano, it's almost your turn.
Okay.
Next.
HMPH.
WHAT A JERK. HE HASN'T CHANGED AT ALL.
NEITHER HAVE YOU.
STARE
Wh-
WHAT?
HEY!
LET ME ASK YOU SOME-THING...
WAAAGH!!
WHAT IS IT?

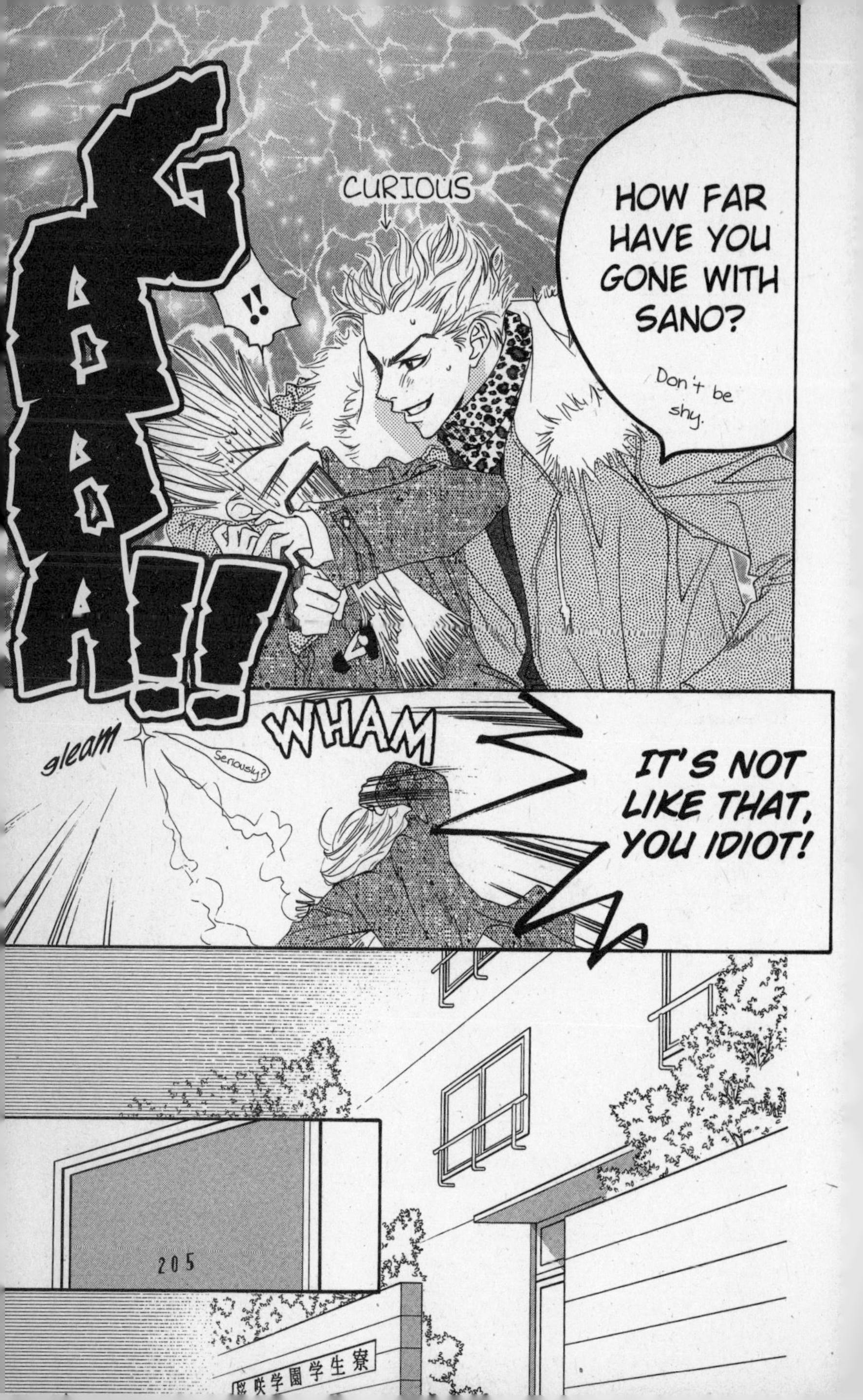
CURIOUS
HOW FAR HAVE YOU GONE WITH SANO?
Don't be shy.
!!
gleam
Seriously?
WHAM
IT'S NOT LIKE THAT, YOU IDIOT!
205
桜咲学園学生寮

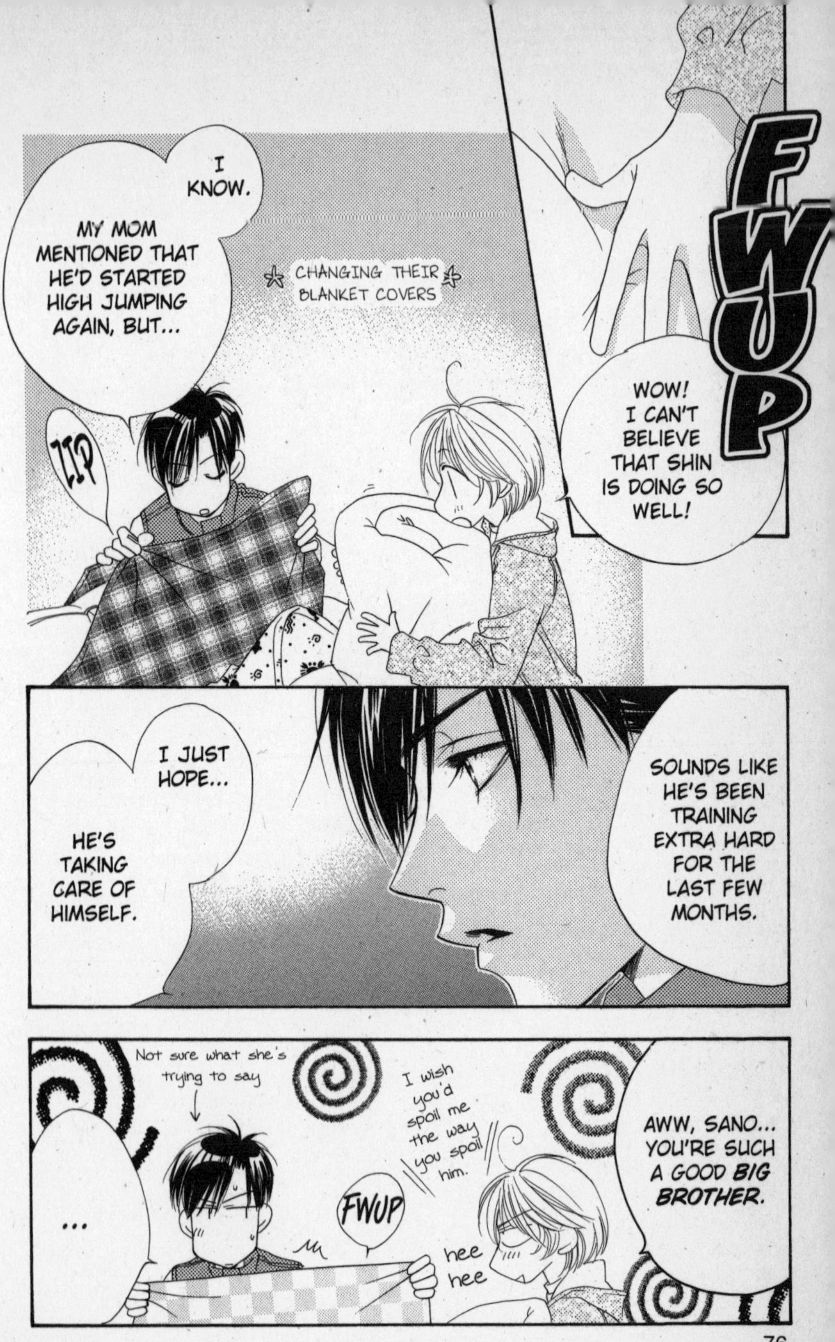
FWUP
WOW! I CAN'T BELIEVE THAT SHIN IS DOING SO WELL!
I KNOW.
MY MOM MENTIONED THAT HE'D STARTED HIGH JUMPING AGAIN, BUT...
CHANGING THEIR BLANKET COVERS
ZIP
SOUNDS LIKE HE'S BEEN TRAINING EXTRA HARD FOR THE LAST FEW MONTHS.
I JUST HOPE...
HE'S TAKING CARE OF HIMSELF.
AWW, SANO... YOU'RE SUCH A GOOD BIG BROTHER.
hee hee
I wish you'd spoil me the way you spoil him.
FWUP
Not sure what she's trying to say
...

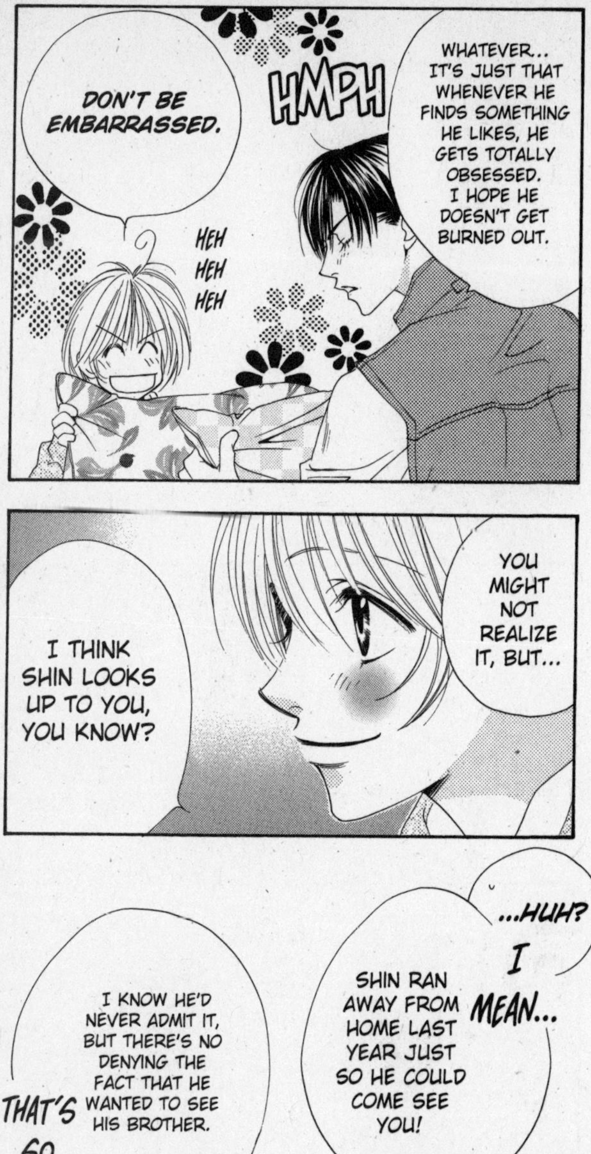
WHATEVER... IT'S JUST THAT WHENEVER HE FINDS SOMETHING HE LIKES, HE GETS TOTALLY OBSESSED. I HOPE HE DOESN'T GET BURNED OUT.
HMPH
DON'T BE EMBARRASSED.
HEH HEH HEH
YOU MIGHT NOT REALIZE IT, BUT...
I THINK SHIN LOOKS UP TO YOU, YOU KNOW?
...HUH?
I MEAN...
SHIN RAN AWAY FROM HOME LAST YEAR JUST SO HE COULD COME SEE YOU!
I KNOW HE'D NEVER ADMIT IT, BUT THERE'S NO DENYING THE FACT THAT HE WANTED TO SEE HIS BROTHER.
THAT'S SO CUTE.

RADIO SHOW 2 PART 2

I got more nervous this time than the first time I was on the radio. The producer told me that the first thing I should say on air was "Happy Birthday!" but the moment Kisaichi answered the phone, I totally forgot. I mentioned my radio appearance on my website, so I guess some of you probably listened to it. I had a really good time talking to Koyasu and Kisaichi. Right before I hung up the phone, Koyasu said, "Don't forget to bring cheesecake next time." Ha ha! If they ever invite me back, I'll definitely bring some.

At the time I had no idea that Kisaichi would be co-hosting the show. I only found out when they put me on...sorry.

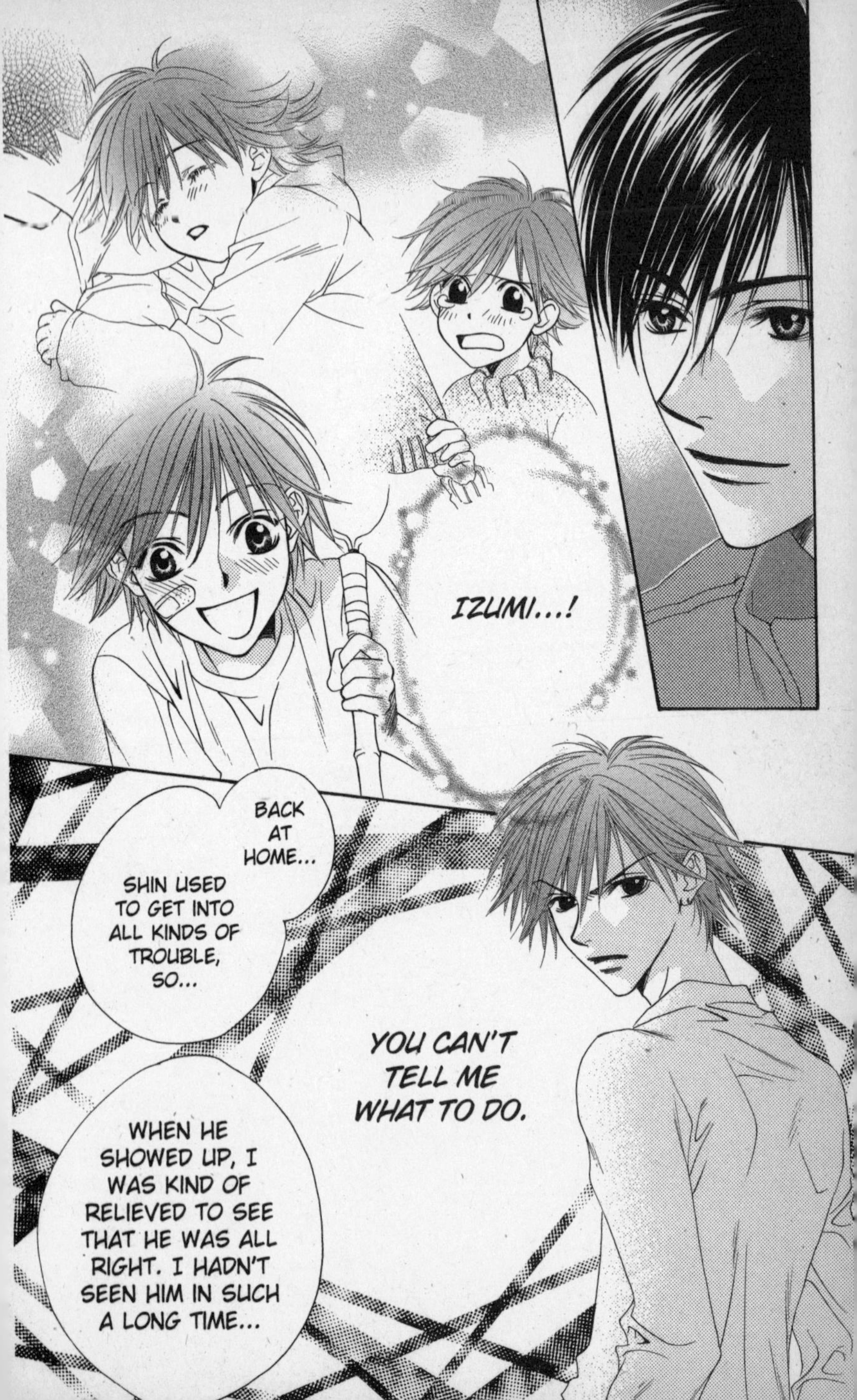
IZUMI...!
BACK AT HOME... SHIN USED TO GET INTO ALL KINDS OF TROUBLE, SO...
YOU CAN'T TELL ME WHAT TO DO.
WHEN HE SHOWED UP, I WAS KIND OF RELIEVED TO SEE THAT HE WAS ALL RIGHT. I HADN'T SEEN HIM IN SUCH A LONG TIME...

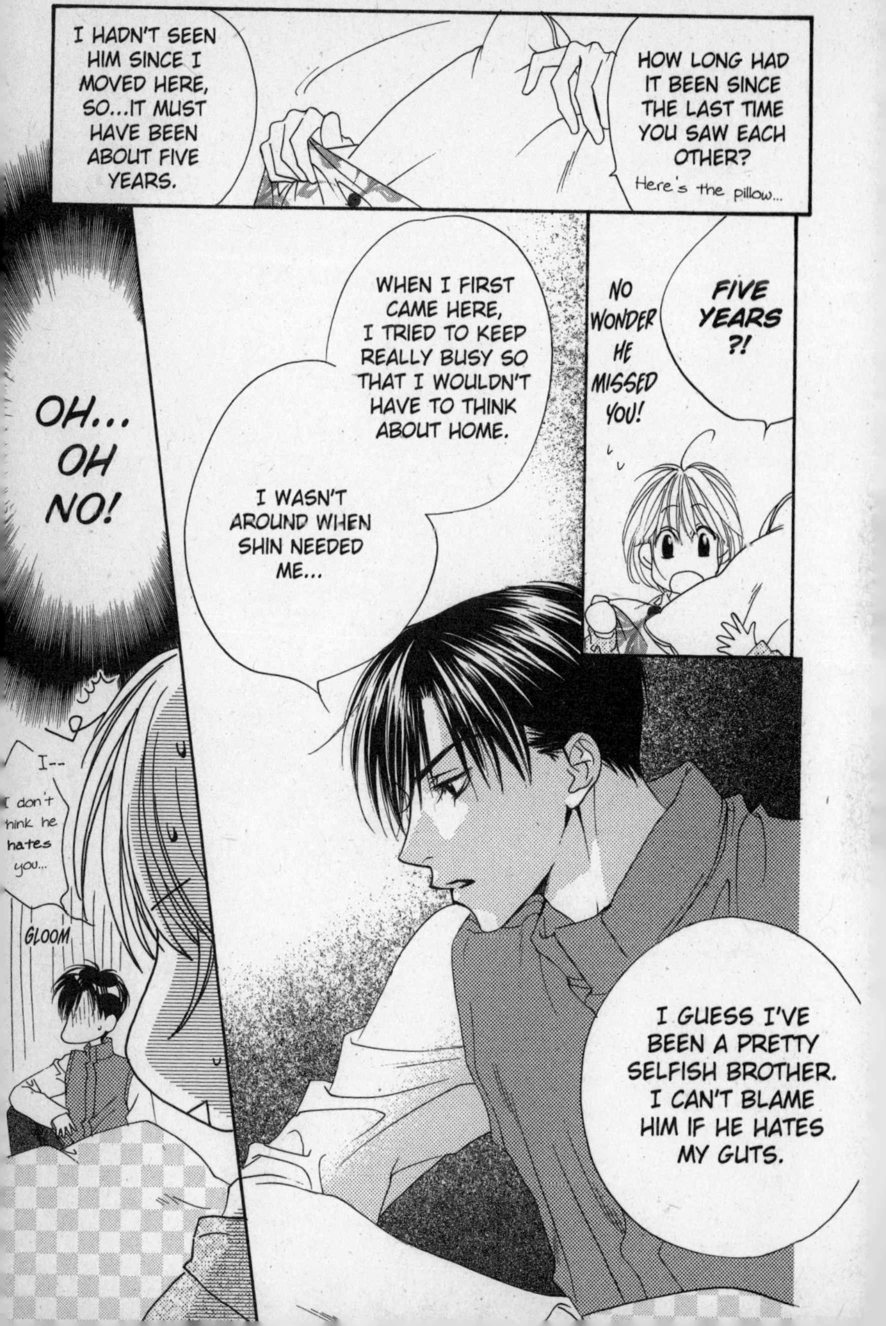
HOW LONG HAD IT BEEN SINCE THE LAST TIME YOU SAW EACH OTHER?
Here's the pillow...
I HADN'T SEEN HIM SINCE I MOVED HERE, SO...IT MUST HAVE BEEN ABOUT FIVE YEARS.
FIVE YEARS?!
NO WONDER HE MISSED YOU!
WHEN I FIRST CAME HERE, I TRIED TO KEEP REALLY BUSY SO THAT I WOULDN'T HAVE TO THINK ABOUT HOME.
I WASN'T AROUND WHEN SHIN NEEDED ME...
I GUESS I'VE BEEN A PRETTY SELFISH BROTHER. I CAN'T BLAME HIM IF HE HATES MY GUTS.
OH... OH NO!
I--
don't hink he hates you...
GLOOM

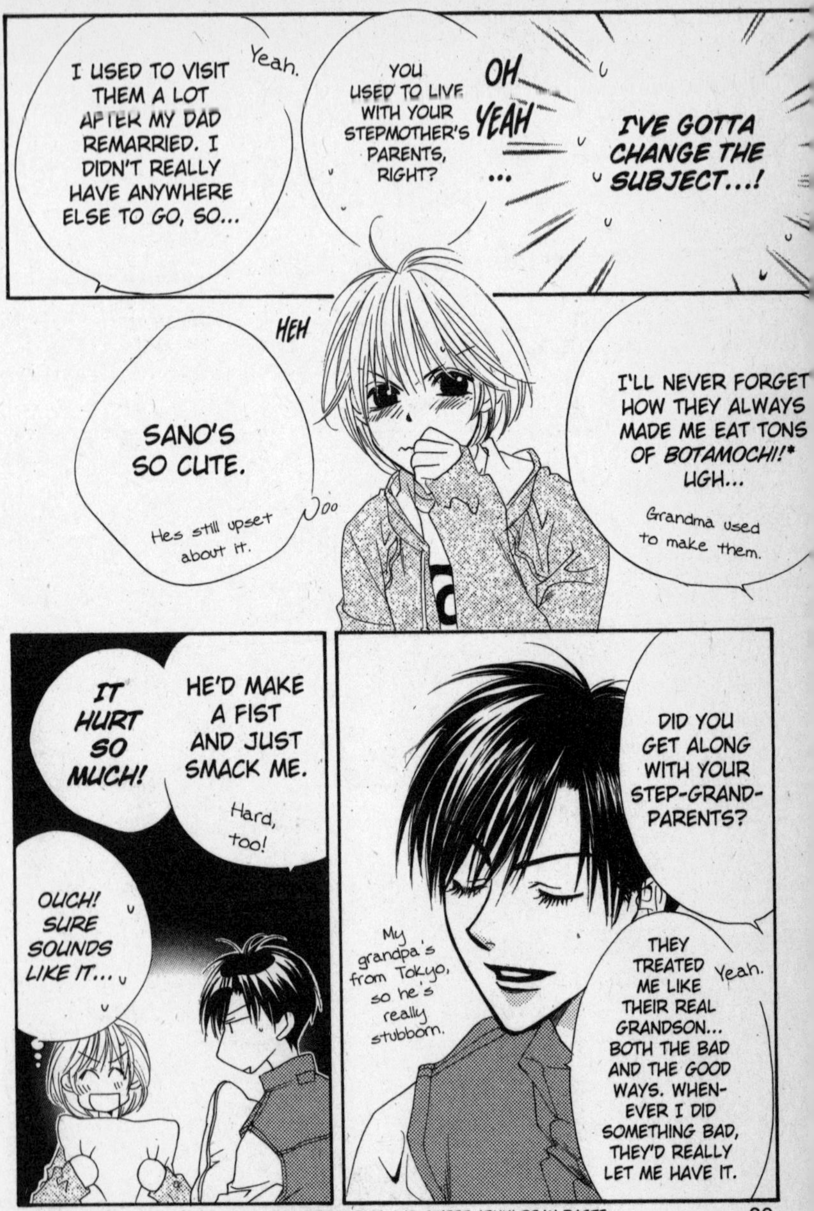
I'VE GOTTA CHANGE THE SUBJECT...!
OH YEAH ...
YOU USED TO LIVE WITH YOUR STEPMOTHER'S PARENTS, RIGHT?
Yeah.
I USED TO VISIT THEM A LOT AFTER MY DAD REMARRIED. I DIDN'T REALLY HAVE ANYWHERE ELSE TO GO, SO...
I'LL NEVER FORGET HOW THEY ALWAYS MADE ME EAT TONS OF BOTAMOCHI!* UGH...
Grandma used to make them.
HEH
SANO'S SO CUTE.
Noo
Hes still upset about it.
DID YOU GET ALONG WITH YOUR STEP-GRAND-PARENTS?
THEY TREATED ME LIKE THEIR REAL GRANDSON... BOTH THE BAD AND THE GOOD WAYS. WHEN-EVER I DID SOMETHING BAD, THEY'D REALLY LET ME HAVE IT.
Yeah.
My grandpa's from Tokyo, so he's really stubborn.
HE'D MAKE A FIST AND JUST SMACK ME.
Hard, too!
IT HURT SO MUCH!
OUCH! SURE SOUNDS LIKE IT...

*BOTAMOCHI=A DESSERT MADE WITH STICKY RICE AND SWEET AZUKI BEAN PASTE

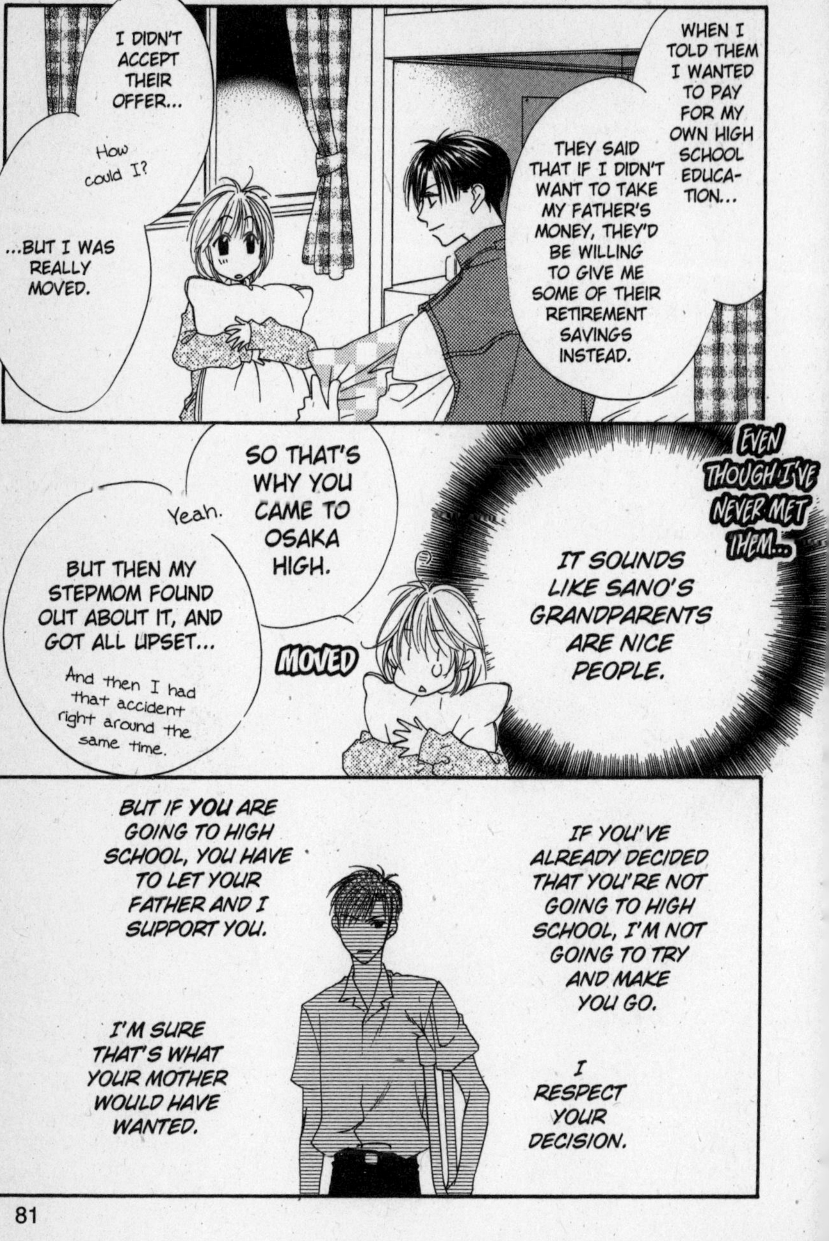
WHEN I TOLD THEM I WANTED TO PAY FOR MY OWN HIGH SCHOOL EDUCA-TION...
THEY SAID THAT IF I DIDN'T WANT TO TAKE MY FATHER'S MONEY, THEY'D BE WILLING TO GIVE ME SOME OF THEIR RETIREMENT SAVINGS INSTEAD.
I DIDN'T ACCEPT THEIR OFFER...
How could I?
...BUT I WAS REALLY MOVED.
EVEN THOUGH I'VE NEVER MET THEM...
IT SOUNDS LIKE SANO'S GRANDPARENTS ARE NICE PEOPLE.
MOVED
SO THAT'S WHY YOU CAME TO OSAKA HIGH.
Yeah.
BUT THEN MY STEPMOM FOUND OUT ABOUT IT, AND GOT ALL UPSET...
And then I had that accident right around the same time.
IF YOU'VE ALREADY DECIDED THAT YOU'RE NOT GOING TO HIGH SCHOOL, I'M NOT GOING TO TRY AND MAKE YOU GO.
I RESPECT YOUR DECISION.
BUT IF YOU ARE GOING TO HIGH SCHOOL, YOU HAVE TO LET YOUR FATHER AND I SUPPORT YOU.
I'M SURE THAT'S WHAT YOUR MOTHER WOULD HAVE WANTED.

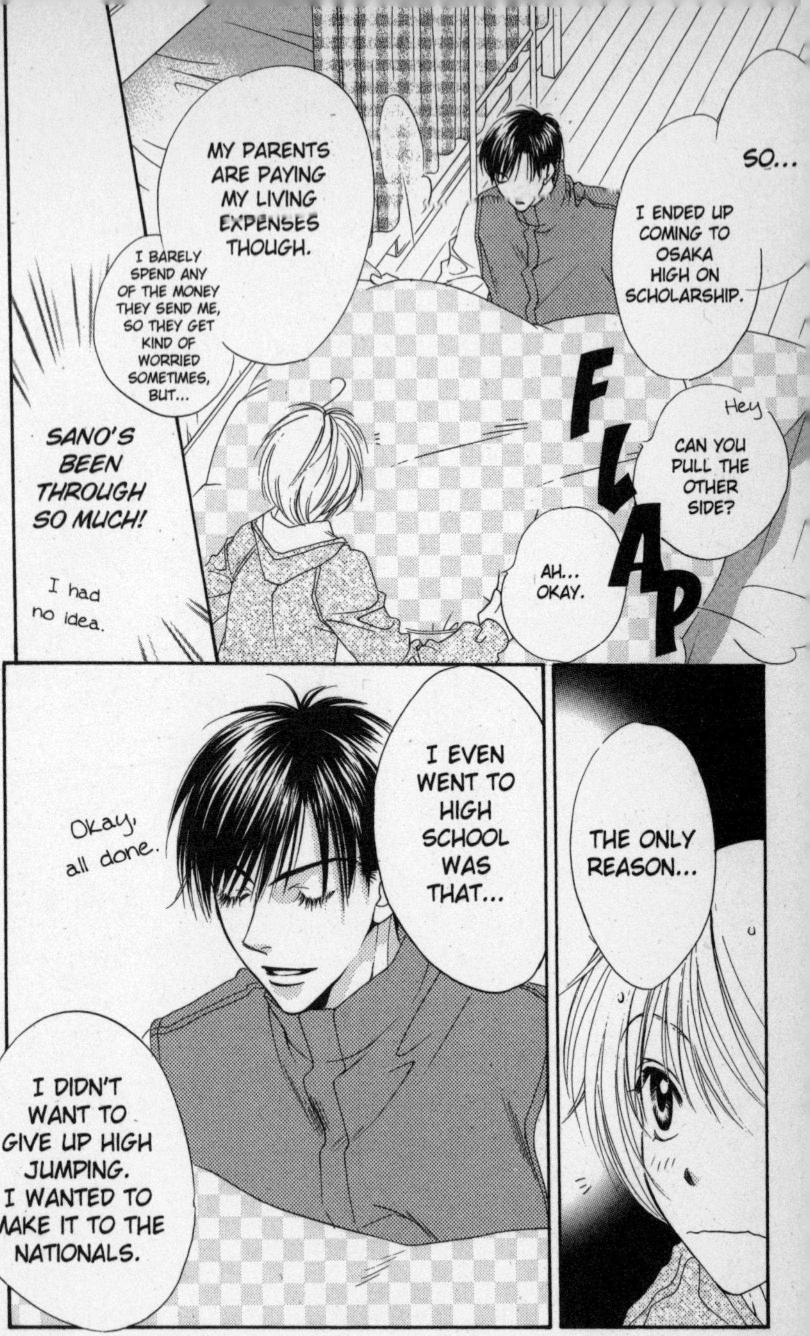
SO...
I ENDED UP COMING TO OSAKA HIGH ON SCHOLARSHIP.
MY PARENTS ARE PAYING MY LIVING EXPENSES THOUGH.
I BARELY SPEND ANY OF THE MONEY THEY SEND ME, SO THEY GET KIND OF WORRIED SOMETIMES, BUT...
Hey
CAN YOU PULL THE OTHER SIDE?
FLAP
AH... OKAY.
SANO'S BEEN THROUGH SO MUCH!
I had no idea.
THE ONLY REASON...
I EVEN WENT TO HIGH SCHOOL WAS THAT...
Okay, all done.
I DIDN'T WANT TO GIVE UP HIGH JUMPING. I WANTED TO MAKE IT TO THE NATIONALS.

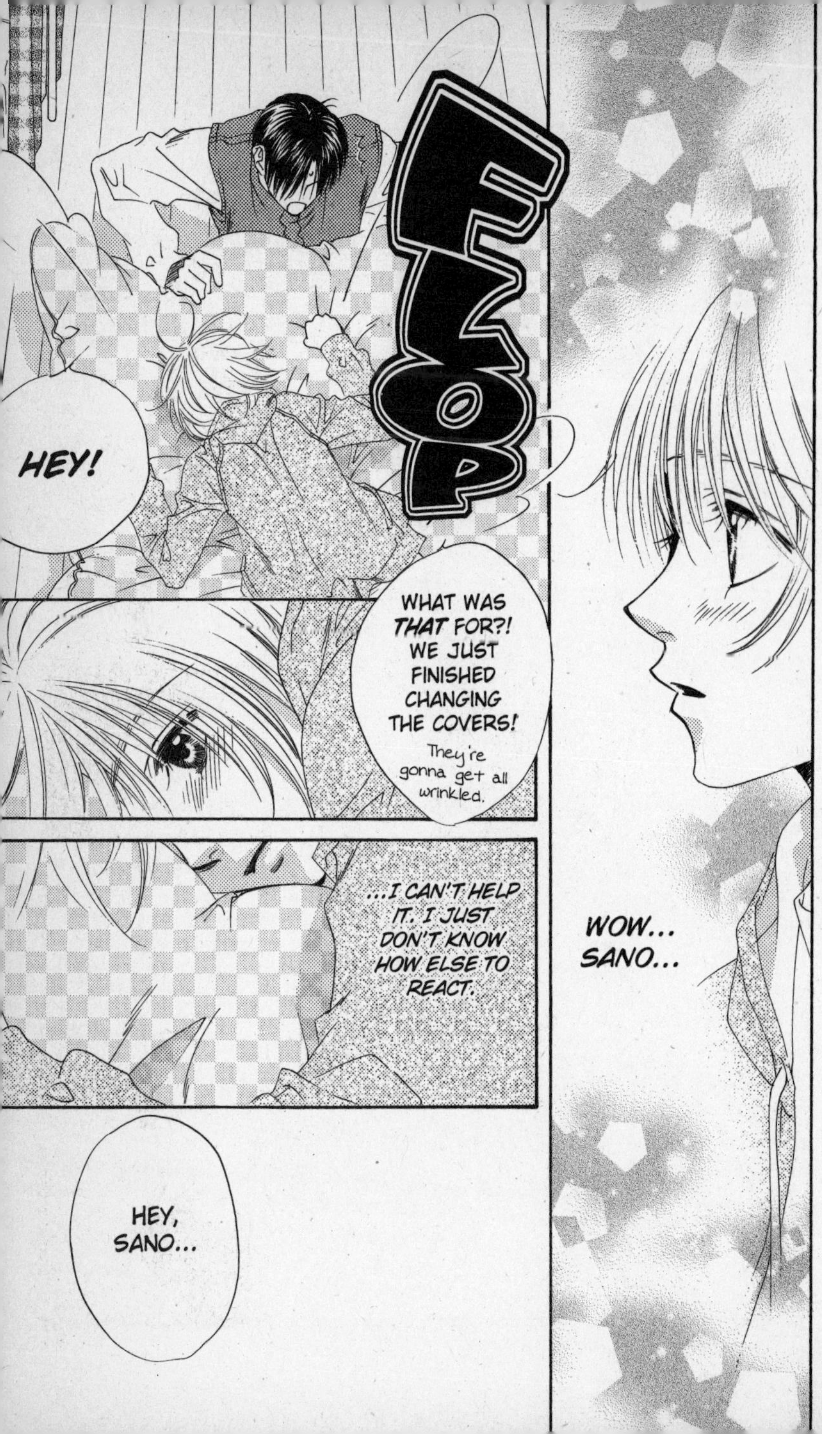
WOW... SANO...
FLOP
HEY!
WHAT WAS THAT FOR?! WE JUST FINISHED CHANGING THE COVERS!
They're gonna get all wrinkled.
...I CAN'T HELP IT. I JUST DON'T KNOW HOW ELSE TO REACT.
HEY, SANO...

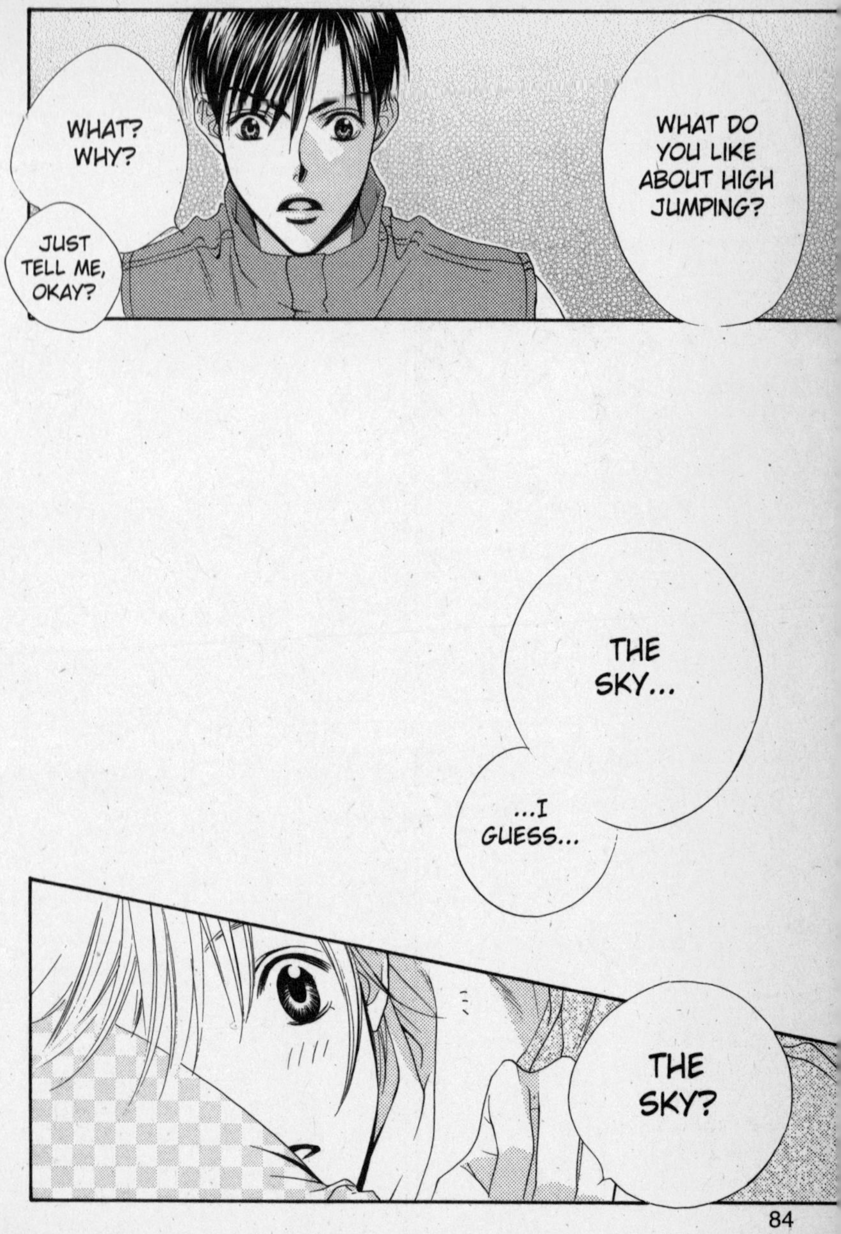
WHAT DO YOU LIKE ABOUT HIGH JUMPING?
WHAT? WHY?
JUST TELL ME, OKAY?
THE SKY...
...I GUESS...
THE SKY?

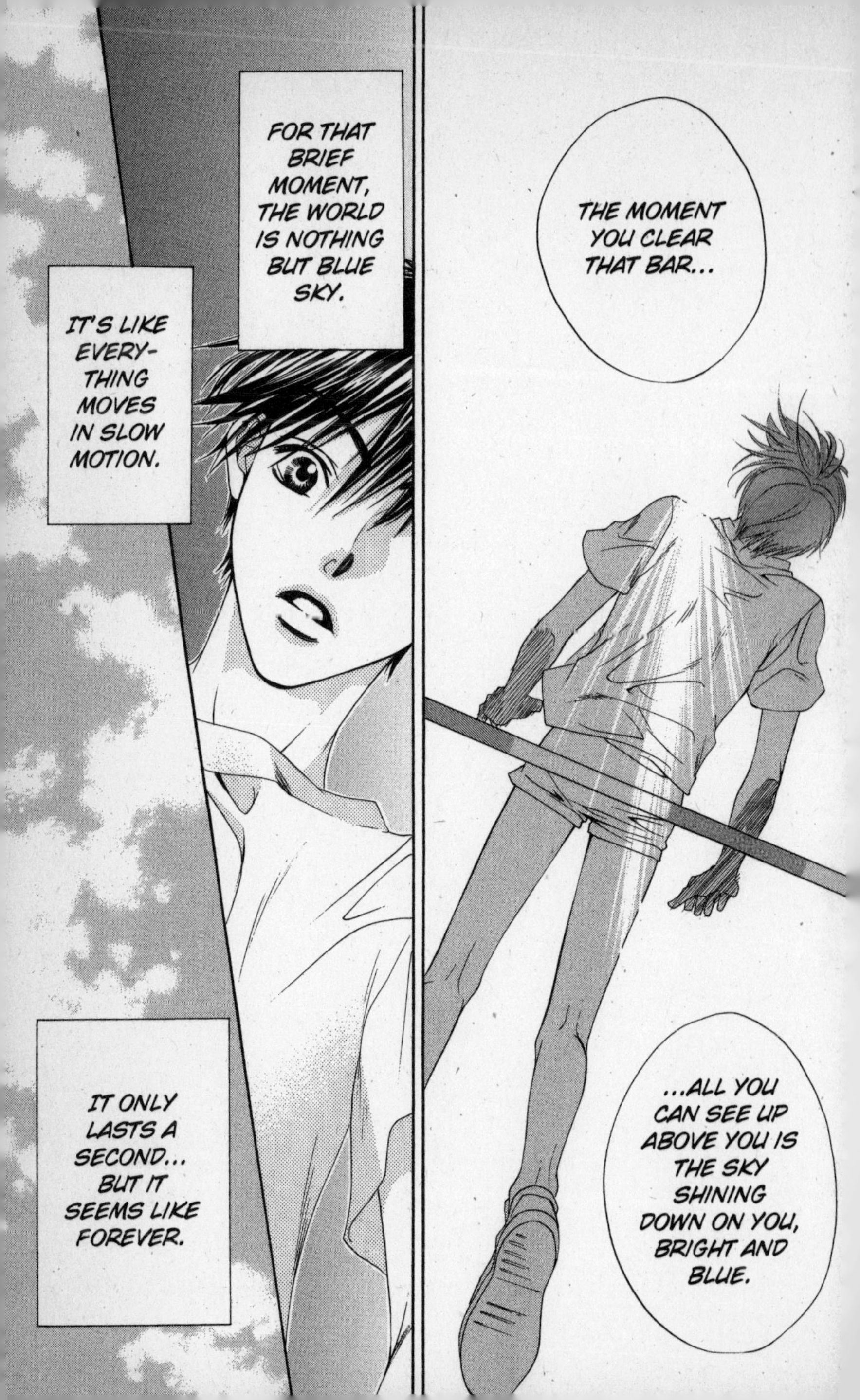
THE MOMENT YOU CLEAR THAT BAR...
...ALL YOU CAN SEE UP ABOVE YOU IS THE SKY SHINING DOWN ON YOU, BRIGHT AND BLUE.
FOR THAT BRIEF MOMENT, THE WORLD IS NOTHING BUT BLUE SKY.
IT'S LIKE EVERYTHING MOVES IN SLOW MOTION.
IT ONLY LASTS A SECOND... BUT IT SEEMS LIKE FOREVER.

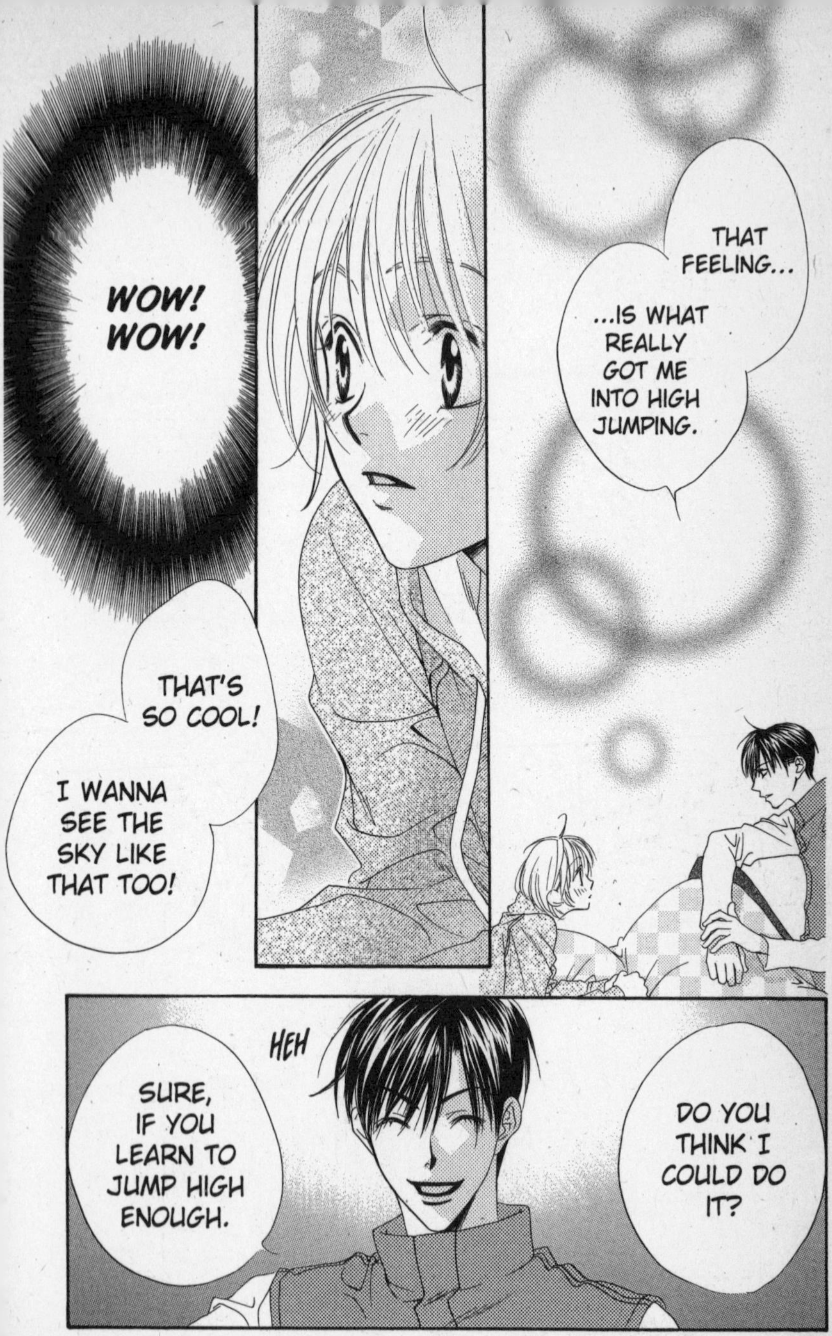
THAT FEELING...
...IS WHAT REALLY GOT ME INTO HIGH JUMPING.
WOW! WOW!
THAT'S SO COOL!
I WANNA SEE THE SKY LIKE THAT TOO!
DO YOU THINK I COULD DO IT?
HEH
SURE, IF YOU LEARN TO JUMP HIGH ENOUGH.

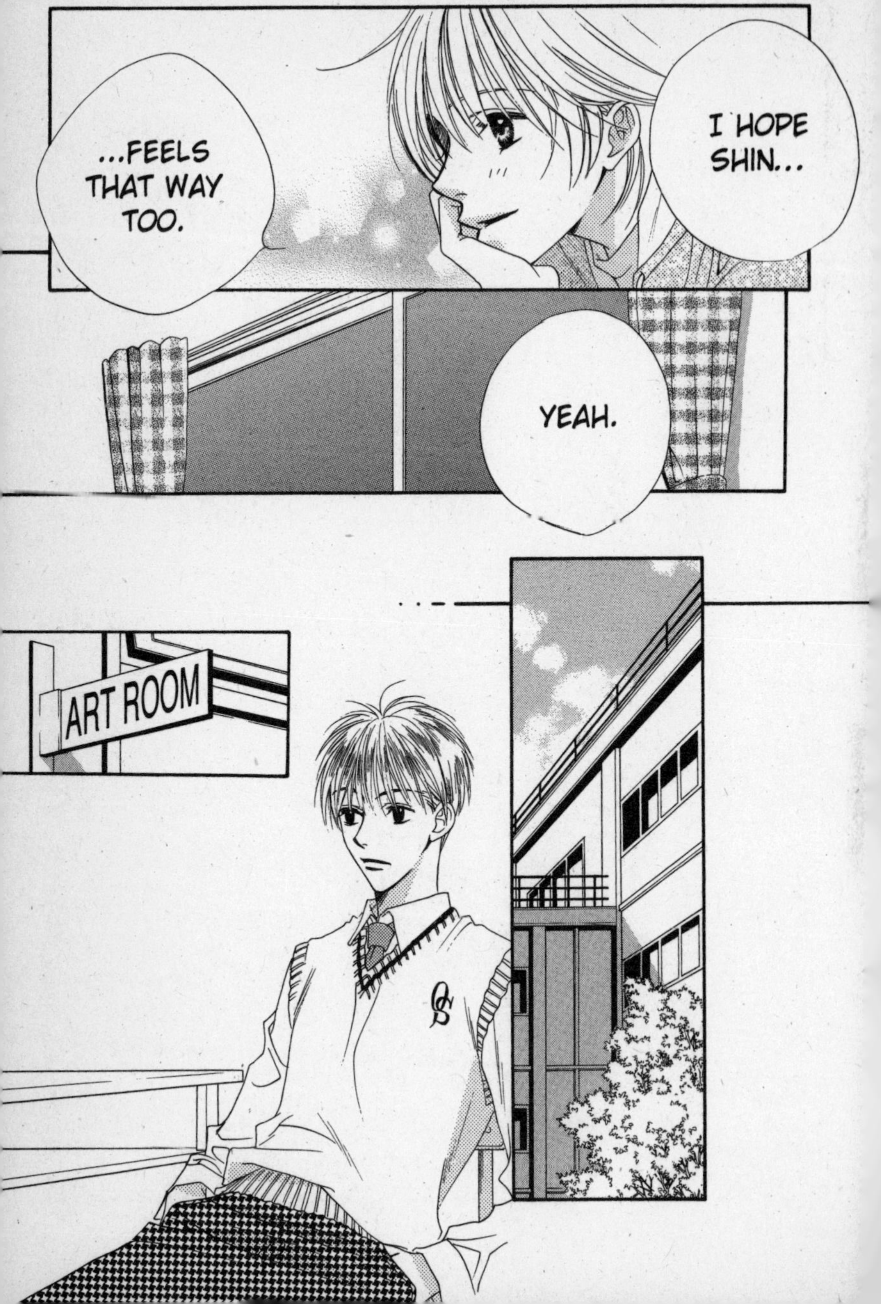
I HOPE SHIN...
...FEELS THAT WAY TOO.
YEAH.
ART ROOM

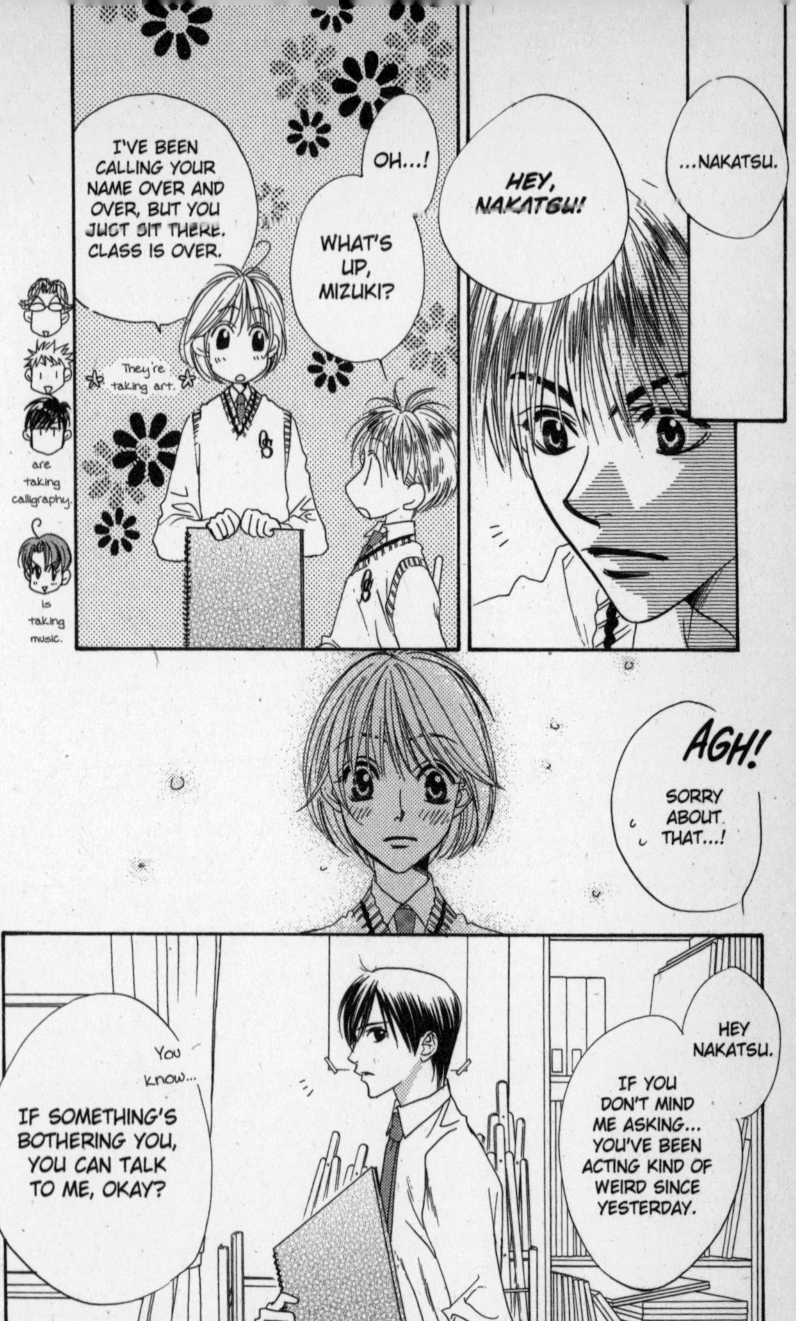
...NAKATSU.
HEY, NAKATSU!
OH...!
WHAT'S UP, MIZUKI?
I'VE BEEN CALLING YOUR NAME OVER AND OVER, BUT YOU JUST SIT THERE. CLASS IS OVER.
They're taking art.
are taking calligraphy.
is taking music.
AGH!
SORRY ABOUT THAT...!
HEY NAKATSU.
IF YOU DON'T MIND ME ASKING... YOU'VE BEEN ACTING KIND OF WEIRD SINCE YESTERDAY.
You know...
IF SOMETHING'S BOTHERING YOU, YOU CAN TALK TO ME, OKAY?

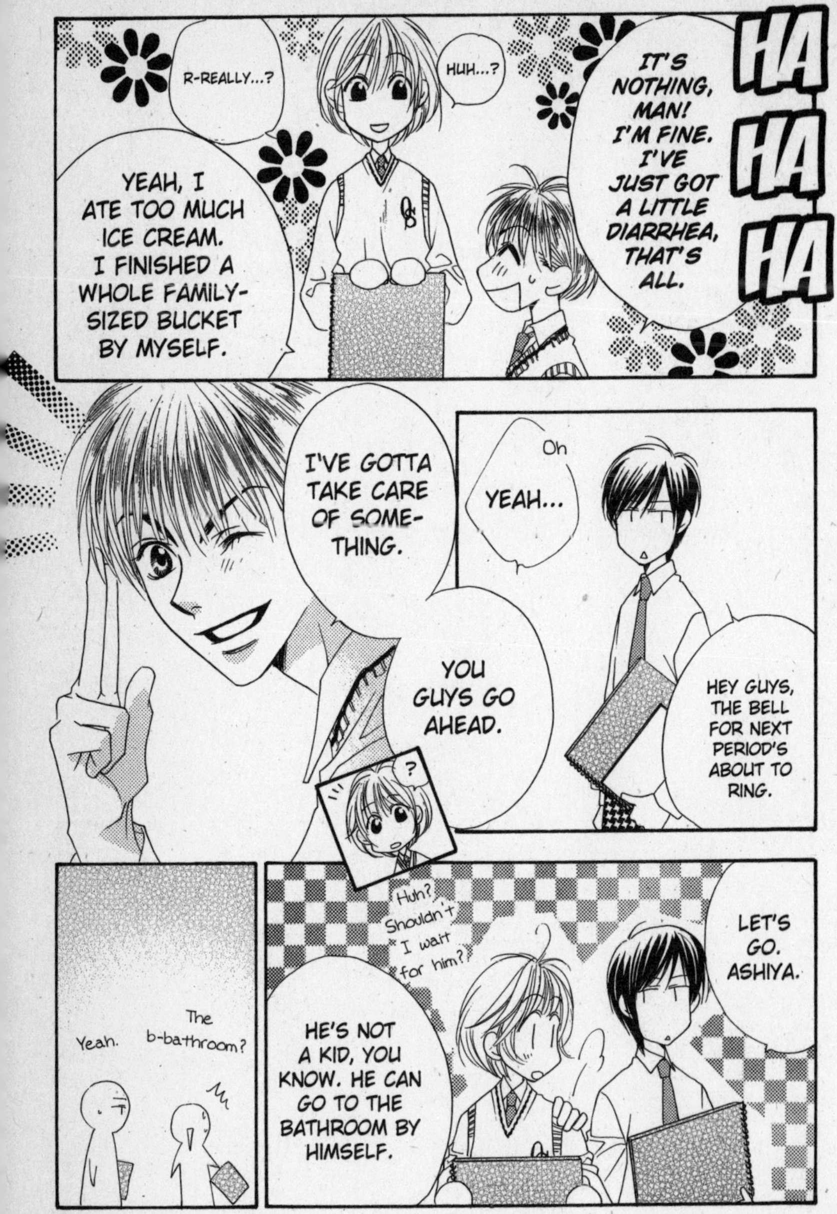
HA HA HA
IT'S NOTHING, MAN! I'M FINE. I'VE JUST GOT A LITTLE DIARRHEA, THAT'S ALL.
HUH...?
R-REALLY...?
YEAH, I ATE TOO MUCH ICE CREAM. I FINISHED A WHOLE FAMILY-SIZED BUCKET BY MYSELF.
HEY GUYS, THE BELL FOR NEXT PERIOD'S ABOUT TO RING.
Oh
YEAH...
I'VE GOTTA TAKE CARE OF SOME-THING.
YOU GUYS GO AHEAD.
?
LET'S GO. ASHIYA.
Huh? Shouldn't I wait for him?
HE'S NOT A KID, YOU KNOW. HE CAN GO TO THE BATHROOM BY HIMSELF.
The b-bathroom?
Yeah.

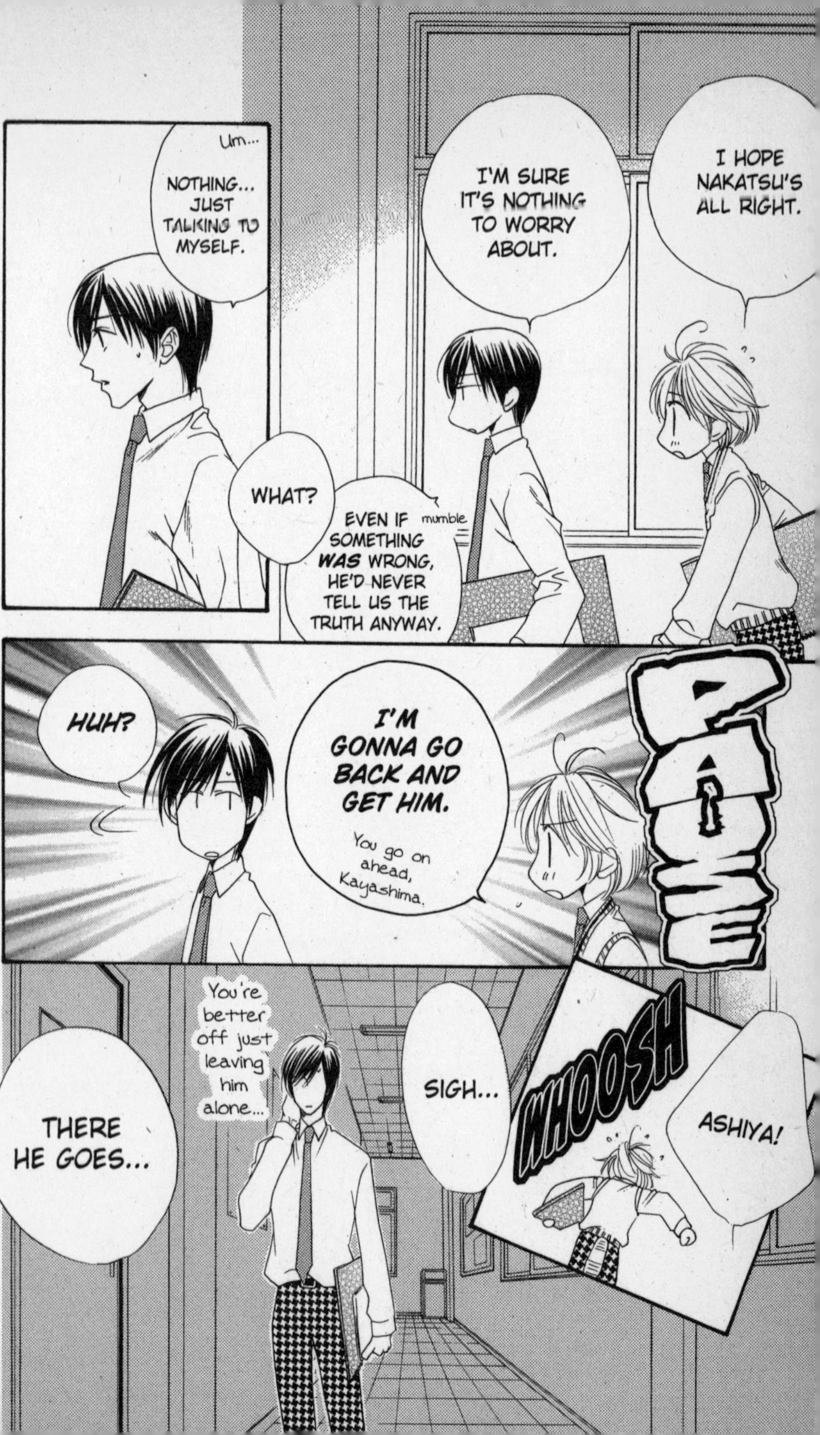
I HOPE NAKATSU'S ALL RIGHT.
I'M SURE IT'S NOTHING TO WORRY ABOUT.
EVEN IF SOMETHING WAS WRONG, HE'D NEVER TELL US THE TRUTH ANYWAY.
mumble
WHAT?
Um... NOTHING... JUST TALKING TO MYSELF.
I'M GONNA GO BACK AND GET HIM.
You go on ahead, Kayashima.
HUH?
ASHIYA!
WHOOSH
SIGH...
You're better off just leaving him alone...
THERE HE GOES...

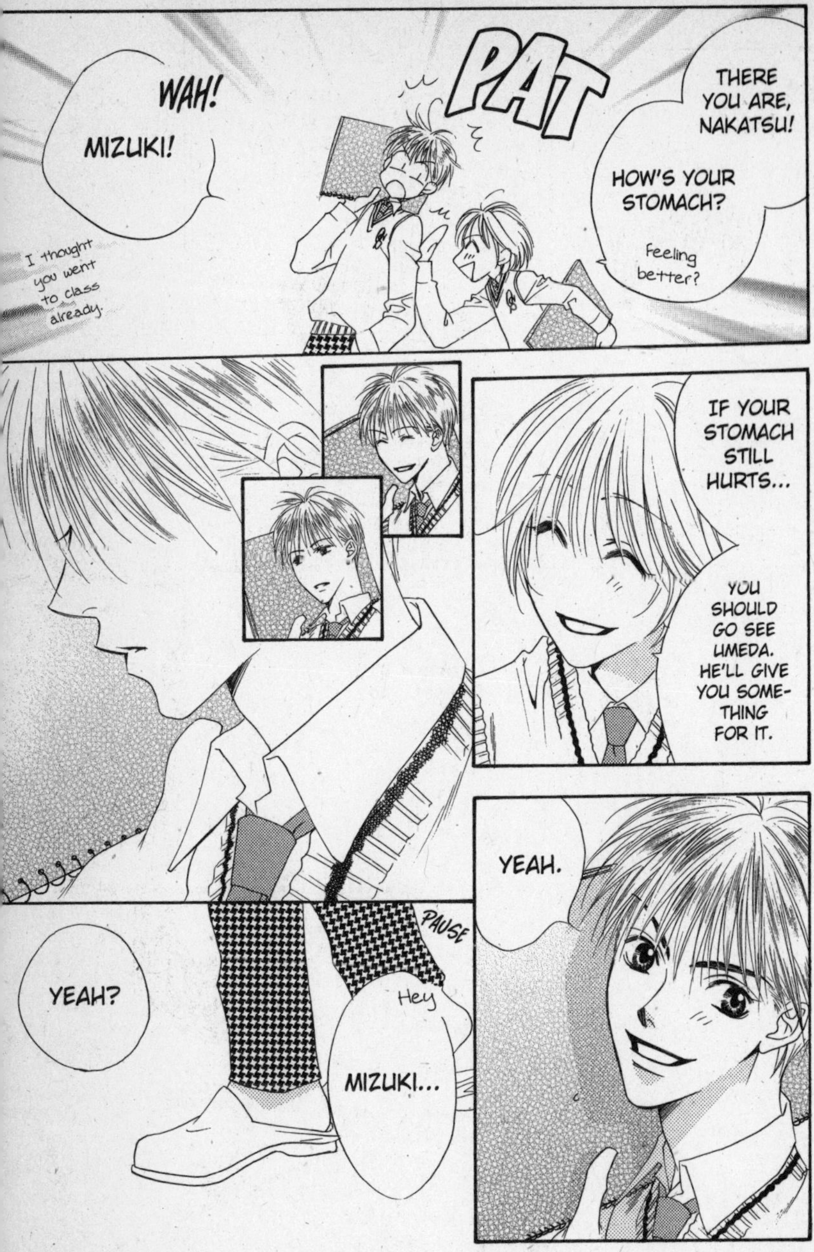
THERE YOU ARE, NAKATSU!
HOW'S YOUR STOMACH?
Feeling better?
PAT
WAH!
MIZUKI!
I thought you went to class already.
IF YOUR STOMACH STILL HURTS...
YOU SHOULD GO SEE UMEDA. HE'LL GIVE YOU SOME-THING FOR IT.
YEAH.
PAUSE
Hey
MIZUKI...
YEAH?

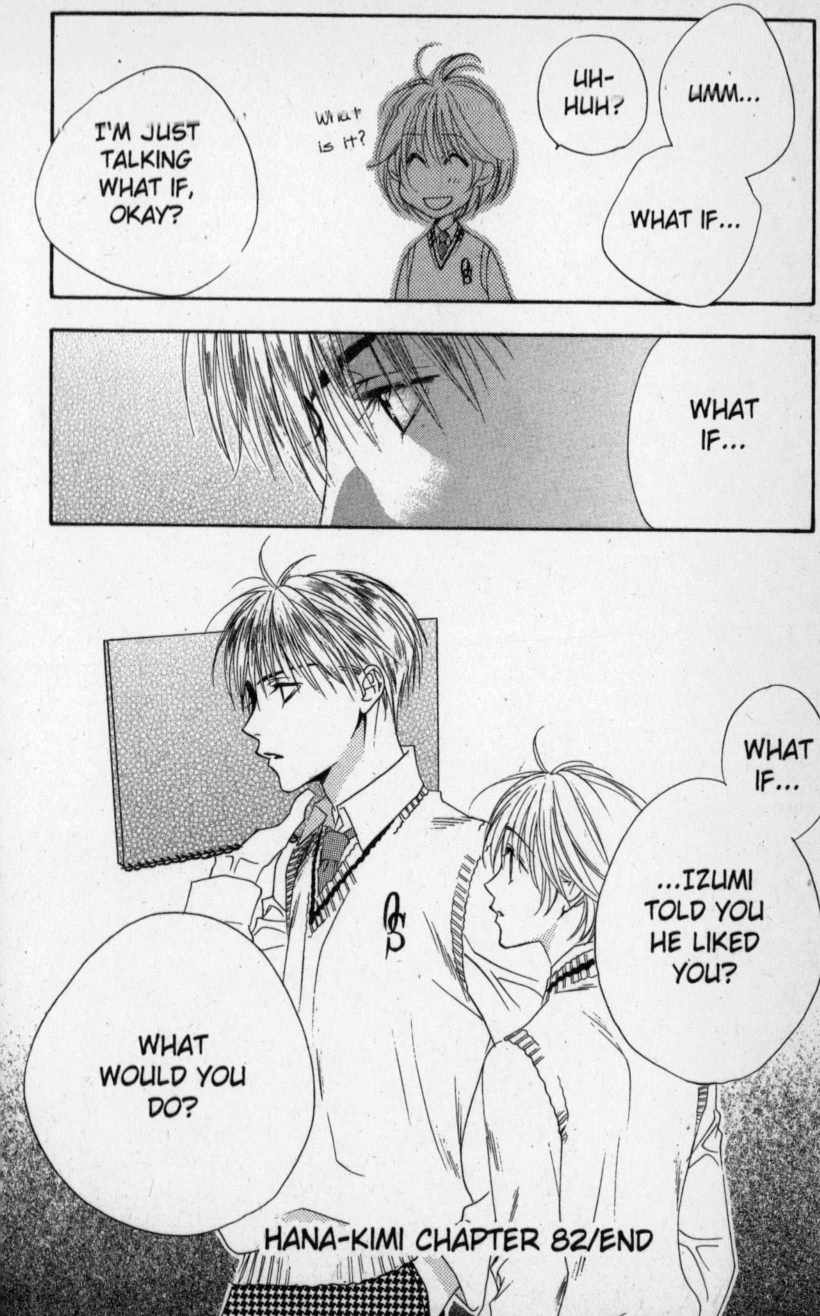
UMM... WHAT IF...
UH-HUH?
What is it?
I'M JUST TALKING WHAT IF, OKAY?
WHAT IF...
WHAT IF...
...IZUMI TOLD YOU HE LIKED YOU?
WHAT WOULD YOU DO?
HANA-KIMI CHAPTER 82/END

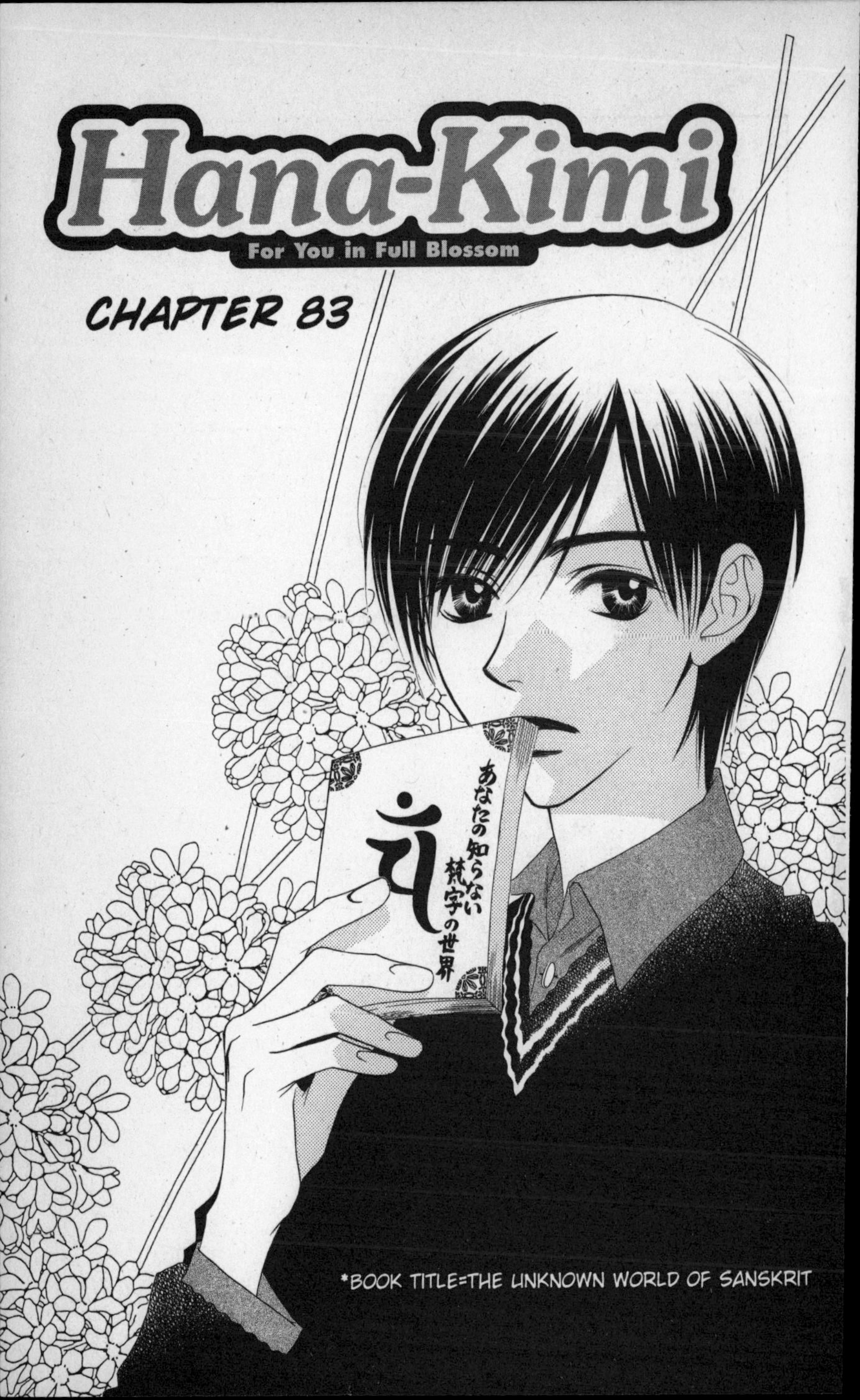
Hana-Kimi
For You in Full Blossom
CHAPTER 83
あなたの知らない梵字の世界
*BOOK TITLE=THE UNKNOWN WORLD OF SANSKRIT

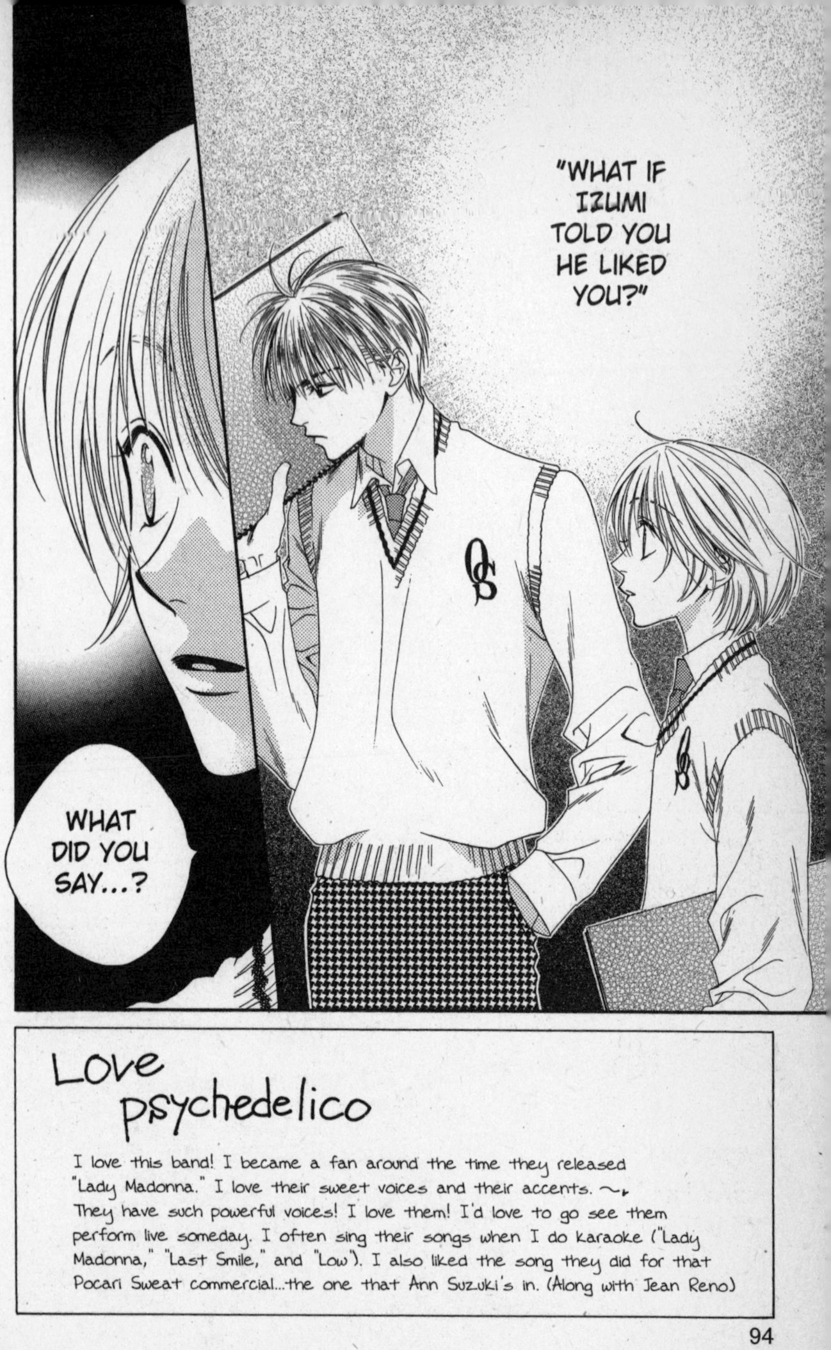
"WHAT IF IZUMI TOLD YOU HE LIKED YOU?"
WHAT DID YOU SAY...?

Love psychedelico

I love this band! I became a fan around the time they released "Lady Madonna." I love their sweet voices and their accents. ~ They have such powerful voices! I love them! I'd love to go see them perform live someday. I often sing their songs when I do karaoke ("Lady Madonna," "Last Smile," and "Low"). I also liked the song they did for that Pocari Sweat commercial...the one that Ann Suzuki's in. (Along with Jean Reno)

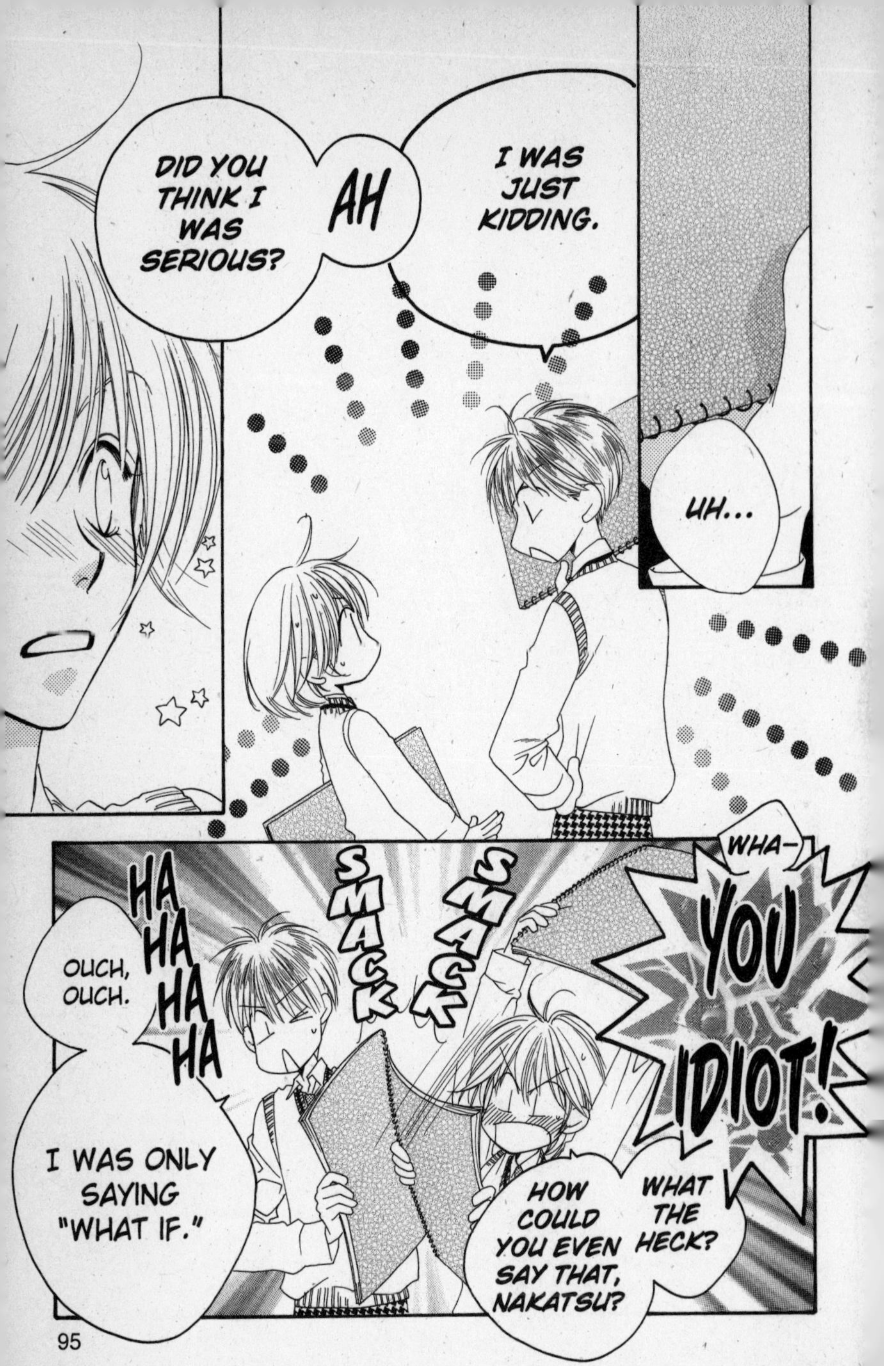
UH...
I WAS JUST KIDDING.
AH
DID YOU THINK I WAS SERIOUS?
WHA-
YOU IDIOT!
SMACK
SMACK
WHAT THE HECK?
HOW COULD YOU EVEN SAY THAT, NAKATSU?
HA HA HA HA
OUCH, OUCH.
I WAS ONLY SAYING "WHAT IF."

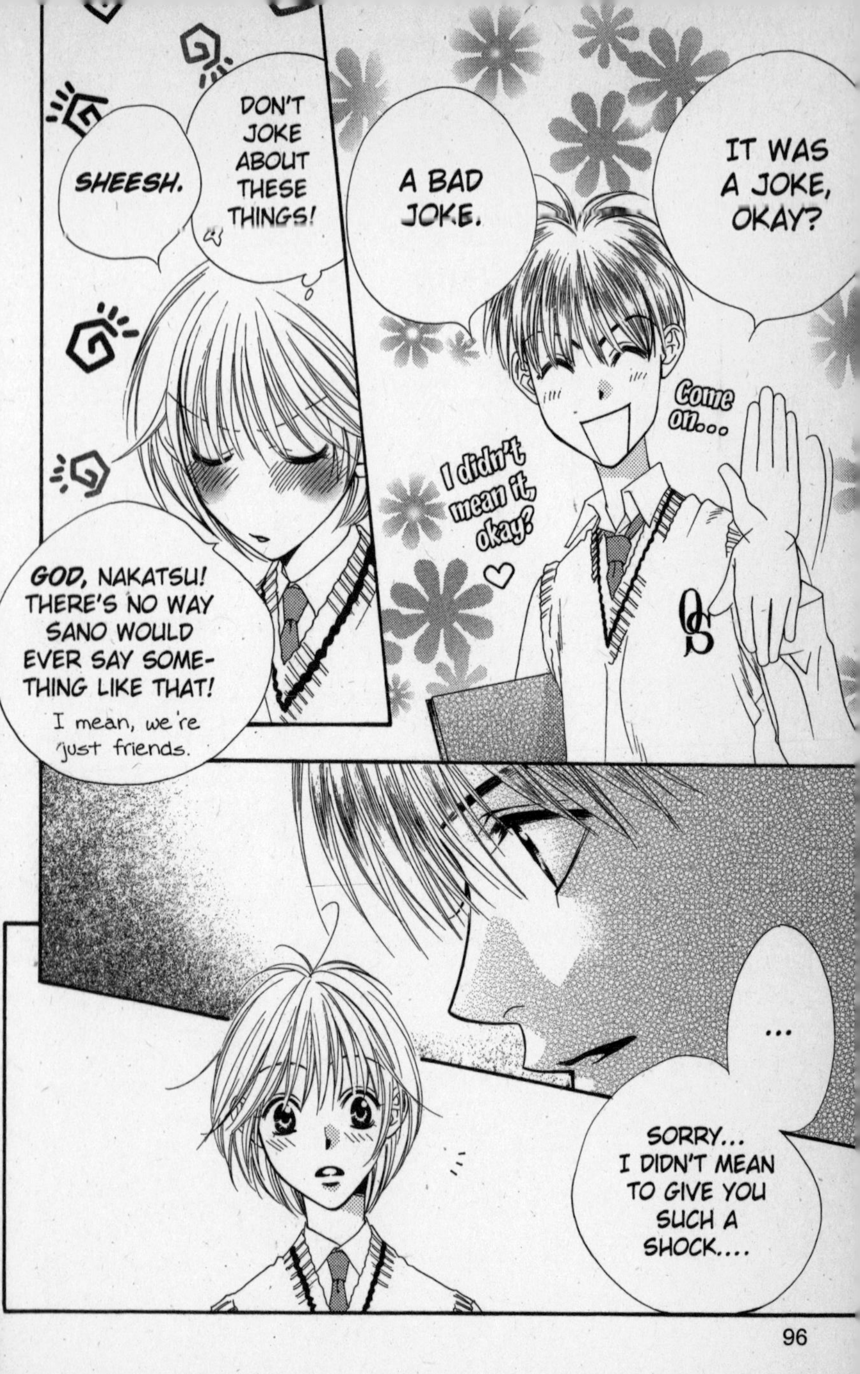
IT WAS A JOKE, OKAY?
A BAD JOKE.
Come on...
I didn't mean it, okay?
DON'T JOKE ABOUT THESE THINGS!
SHEESH.
GOD, NAKATSU! THERE'S NO WAY SANO WOULD EVER SAY SOME-THING LIKE THAT!
I mean, we're just friends.
...
SORRY... I DIDN'T MEAN TO GIVE YOU SUCH A SHOCK....

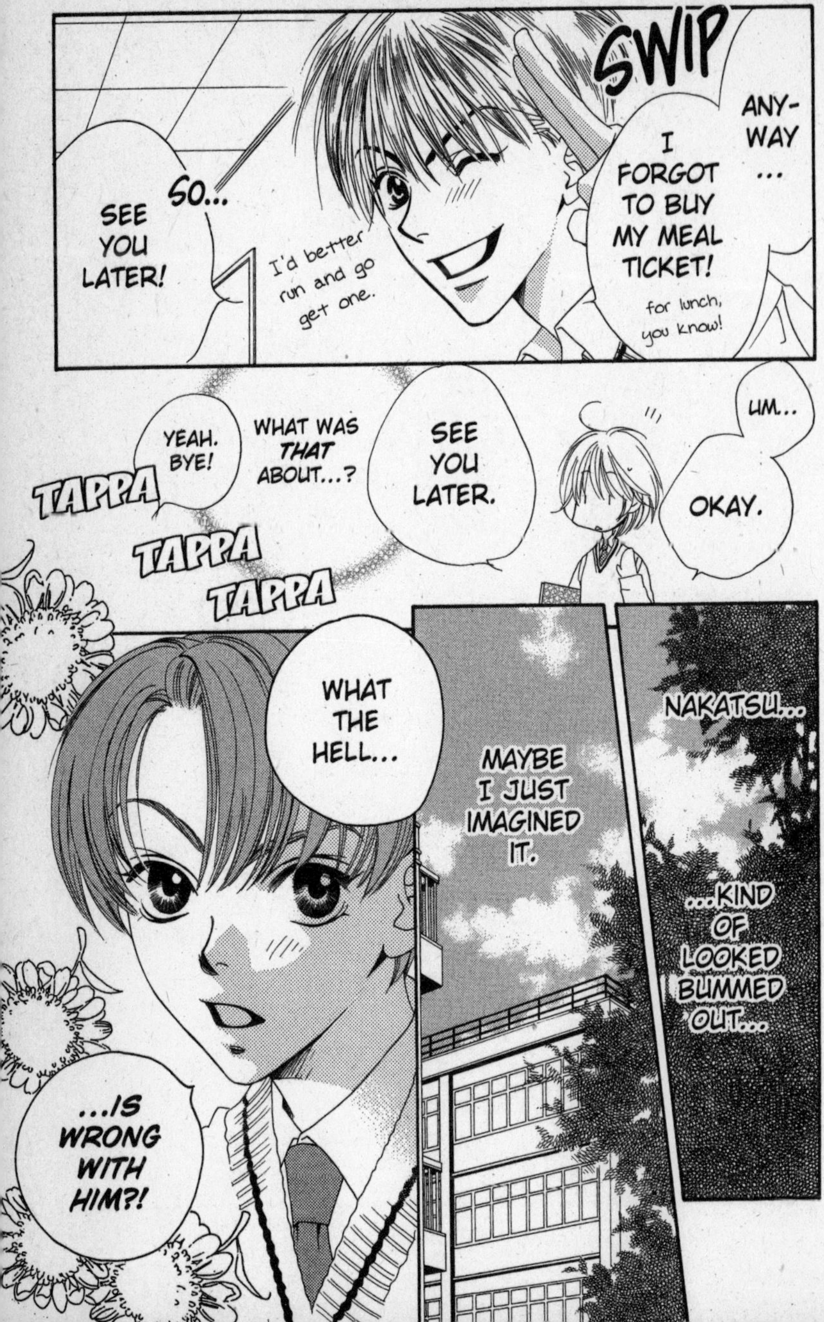
SWIP
ANY-WAY...
I FORGOT TO BUY MY MEAL TICKET!
for lunch, you know!
I'd better run and go get one.
SO...
SEE YOU LATER!
UM...
OKAY.
SEE YOU LATER.
WHAT WAS THAT ABOUT...?
YEAH. BYE!
TAPPA
TAPPA
TAPPA
NAKATSU...
...KIND OF LOOKED BUMMED OUT...
MAYBE I JUST IMAGINED IT.
WHAT THE HELL...
...IS WRONG WITH HIM?!

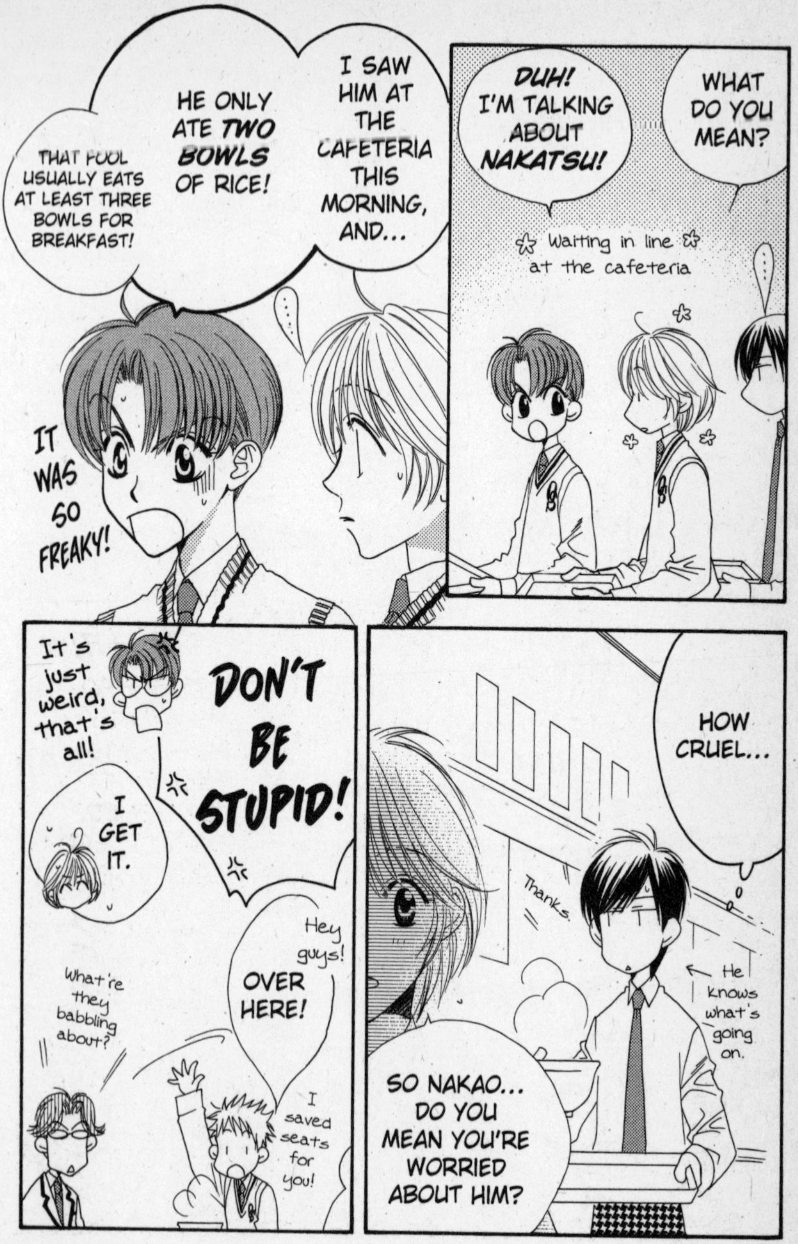
WHAT DO YOU MEAN?
DUH! I'M TALKING ABOUT NAKATSU!
Waiting in line at the cafeteria
I SAW HIM AT THE CAFETERIA THIS MORNING, AND...
HE ONLY ATE TWO BOWLS OF RICE!
THAT FOOL USUALLY EATS AT LEAST THREE BOWLS FOR BREAKFAST!
IT WAS SO FREAKY!
HOW CRUEL...
Thanks.
He knows what's going on.
SO NAKAO... DO YOU MEAN YOU'RE WORRIED ABOUT HIM?
DON'T BE STUPID!
It's just weird, that's all!
I GET IT.
Hey guys!
OVER HERE!
I saved seats for you!
What're they babbling about?

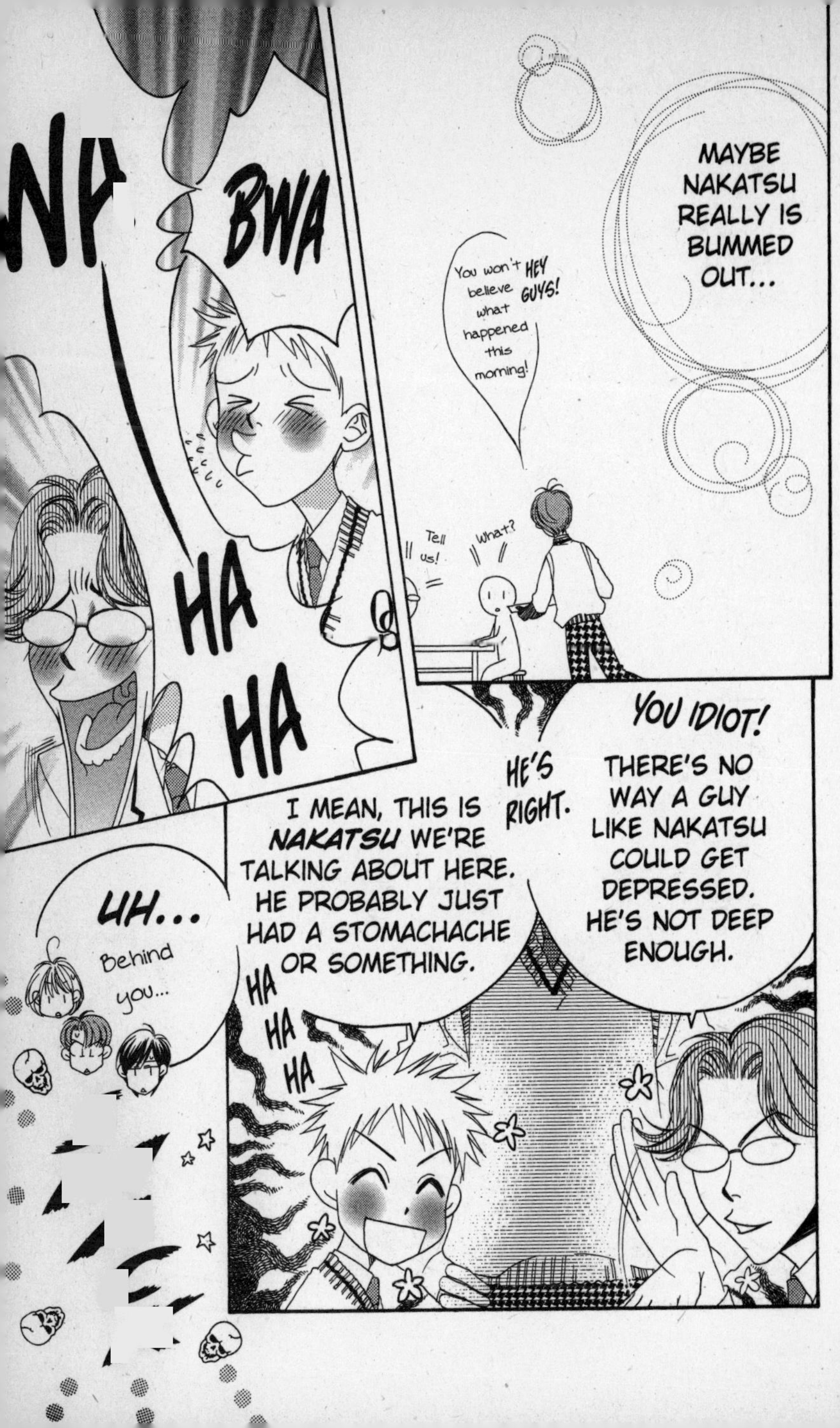
MAYBE NAKATSU REALLY IS BUMMED OUT...
HEY GUYS!
You won't believe what happened this morning!
What?
Tell us!
BWA
HA
HA
NA
YOU IDIOT!
THERE'S NO WAY A GUY LIKE NAKATSU COULD GET DEPRESSED. HE'S NOT DEEP ENOUGH.
HE'S RIGHT.
I MEAN, THIS IS NAKATSU WE'RE TALKING ABOUT HERE. HE PROBABLY JUST HAD A STOMACHACHE OR SOMETHING.
HA HA HA
UH...
Behind you...

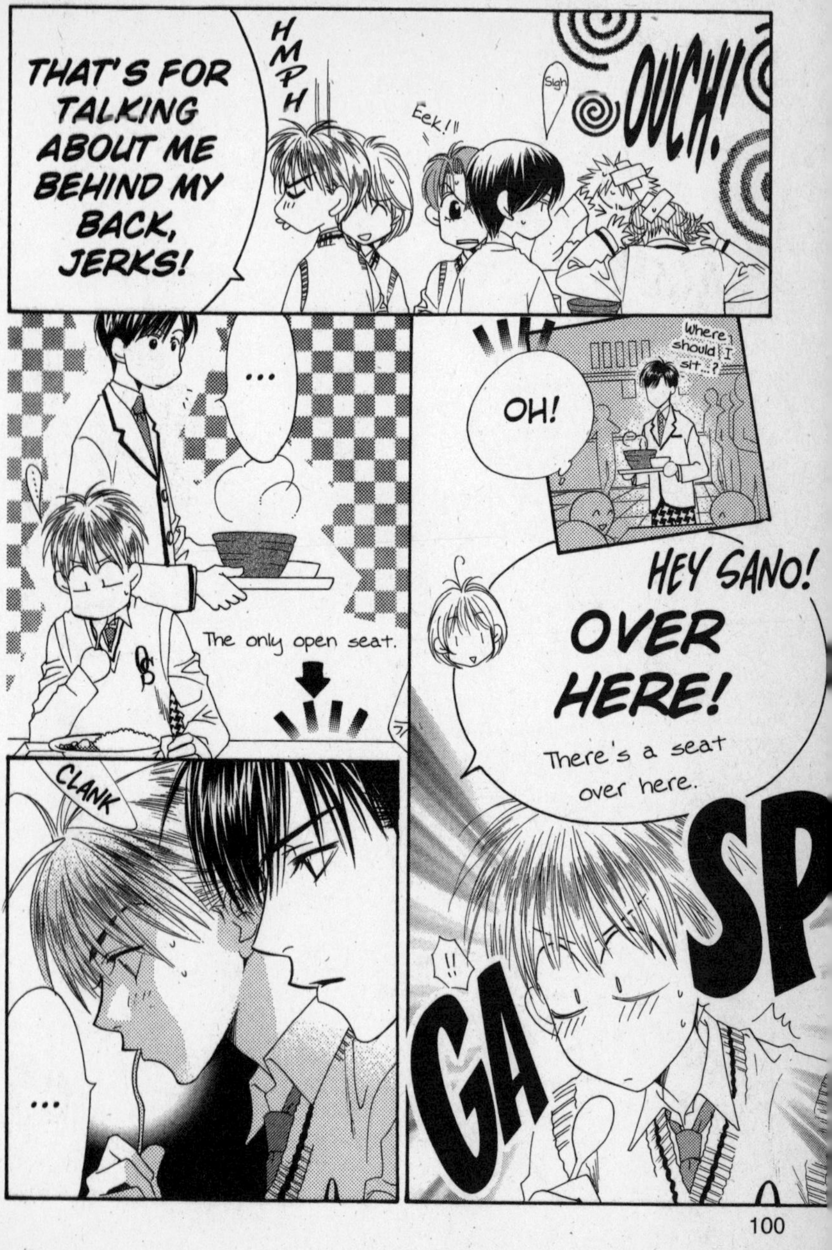
OUCH!
Sigh
Eek!!
HMPH
THAT'S FOR TALKING ABOUT ME BEHIND MY BACK, JERKS!
Where should I sit...?
OH!
HEY SANO!
OVER HERE!
There's a seat over here.
!!
GA
SP
...
The only open seat.
CLANK
...

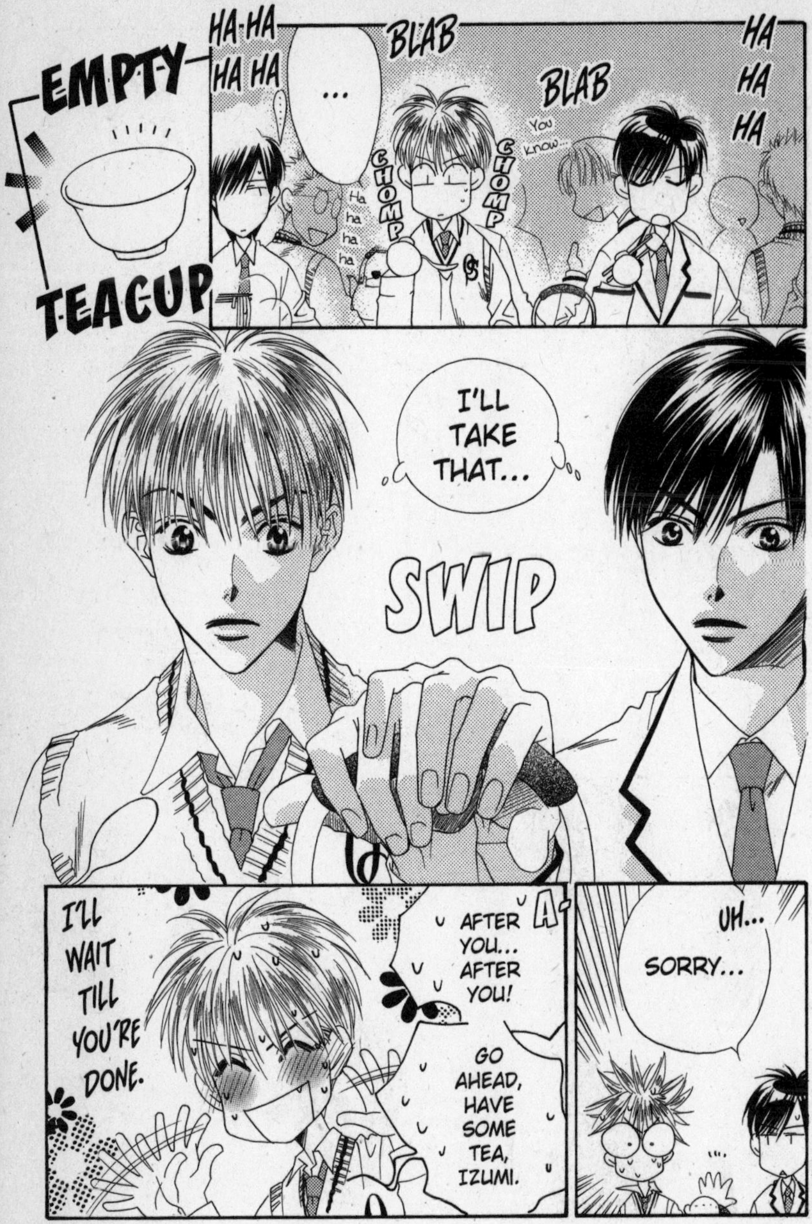
HA HA HA
BLAB
You know...
BLAB
CHOMP
CHOMP
...
Ha ha ha ha
HA-HA HA HA
EMPTY
TEACUP
I'LL TAKE THAT...
SWIP
UH...
SORRY...
A-
AFTER YOU... AFTER YOU!
GO AHEAD, HAVE SOME TEA, IZUMI.
I'LL WAIT TILL YOU'RE DONE.

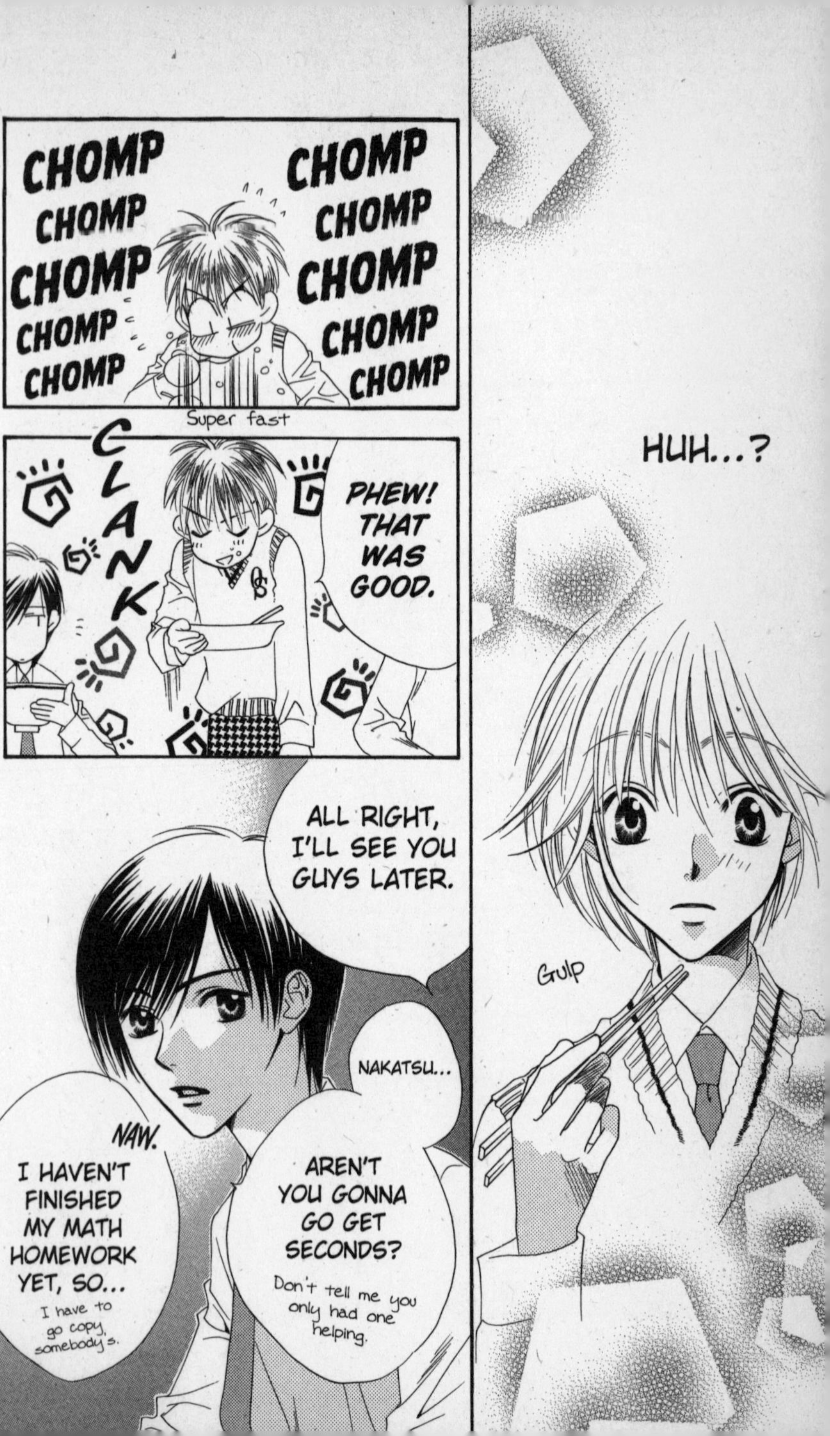
HUH...?
Gulp
CHOMP CHOMP CHOMP CHOMP CHOMP
CHOMP CHOMP CHOMP CHOMP CHOMP
Super fast
PHEW! THAT WAS GOOD.
CLANK
ALL RIGHT, I'LL SEE YOU GUYS LATER.
NAKATSU...
ARE'NT YOU GONNA GO GET SECONDS?
Don't tell me you only had one helping.
NAW.
I HAVEN'T FINISHED MY MATH HOMEWORK YET, SO...
I have to go copy somebody's.

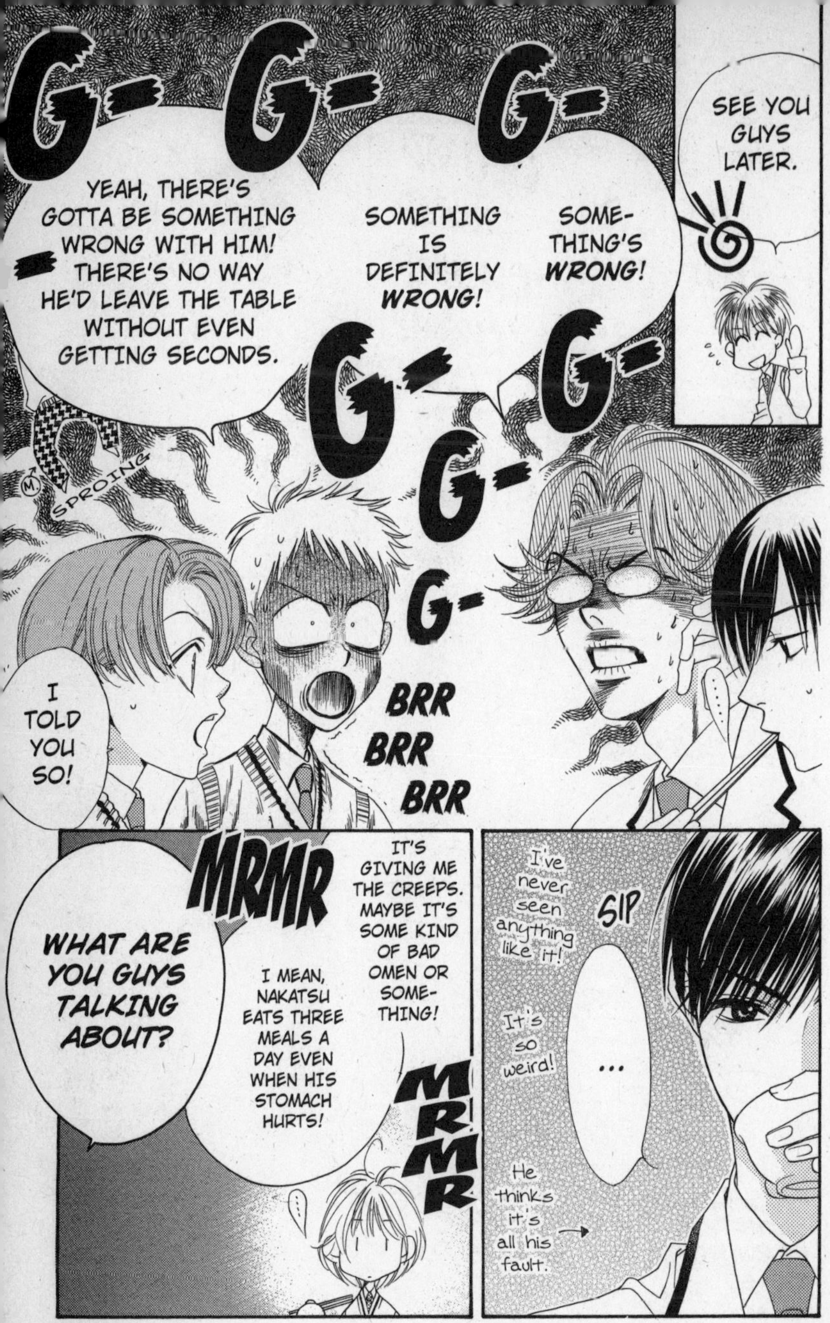
SEE YOU GUYS LATER.
G- G- G-
SOME-THING'S WRONG!
SOMETHING IS DEFINITELY WRONG!
YEAH, THERE'S GOTTA BE SOMETHING WRONG WITH HIM! THERE'S NO WAY HE'D LEAVE THE TABLE WITHOUT EVEN GETTING SECONDS.
G- G- G- G-
M.
SPROING
BRR BRR BRR
I TOLD YOU SO!
I've never seen anything like it!
SIP
It's so weird!
...
He thinks it's all his fault.
IT'S GIVING ME THE CREEPS. MAYBE IT'S SOME KIND OF BAD OMEN OR SOME-THING!
MRMR
I MEAN, NAKATSU EATS THREE MEALS A DAY EVEN WHEN HIS STOMACH HURTS!
WHAT ARE YOU GUYS TALKING ABOUT?
MRMR
...

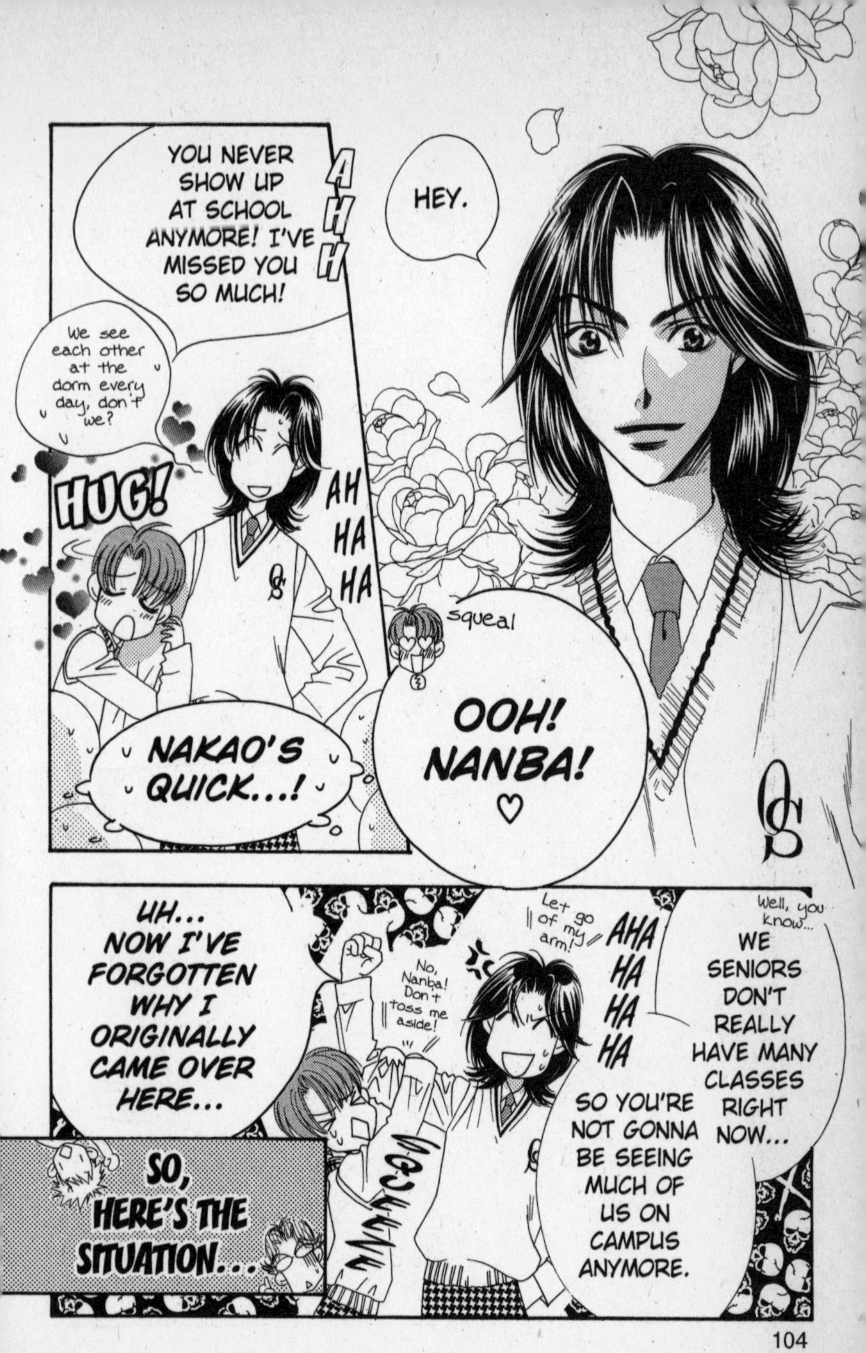
HEY.
OOH! NANBA! ♡
squeal
AHHH
YOU NEVER SHOW UP AT SCHOOL ANYMORE! I'VE MISSED YOU SO MUCH!
We see each other at the dorm every day, don't we?
HUG!
AH HA HA HA
NAKAO'S QUICK...!
Well, you know...
WE SENIORS DON'T REALLY HAVE MANY CLASSES RIGHT NOW...
AHA HA HA HA
Let go of my arm!
SO YOU'RE NOT GONNA BE SEEING MUCH OF US ON CAMPUS ANYMORE.
No, Nanba! Don't toss me aside!
UH... NOW I'VE FORGOTTEN WHY I ORIGINALLY CAME OVER HERE...
SO, HERE'S THE SITUATION...

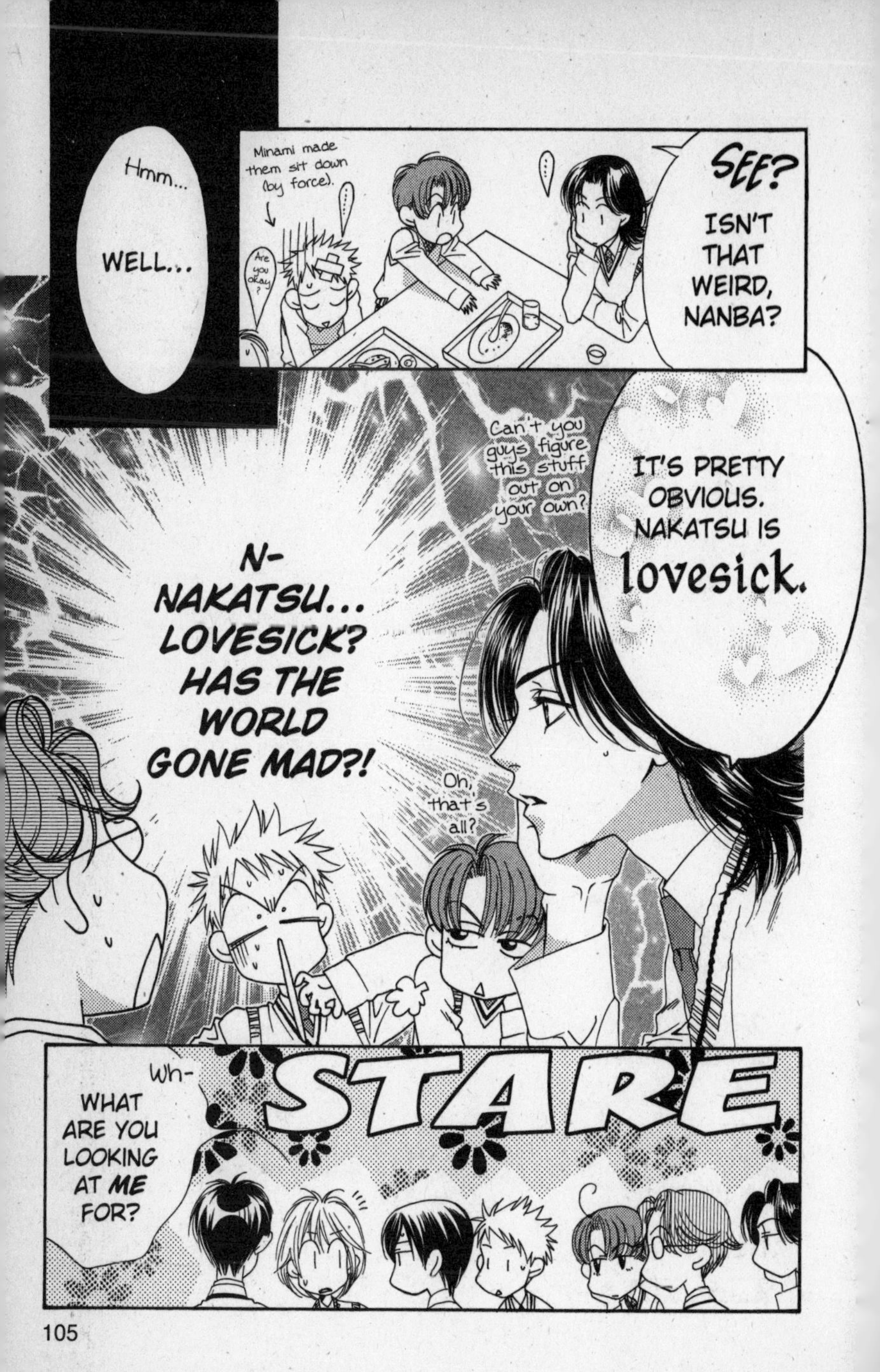
SEE? ISN'T THAT WEIRD, NANBA?
Minami made them sit down (by force).
Are you okay?
Hmm... WELL...
IT'S PRETTY OBVIOUS. NAKATSU IS lovesick.
Can't you guys figure this stuff out on your own?
N-NAKATSU... LOVESICK? HAS THE WORLD GONE MAD?!
Oh, that's all?
STARE
Wh- WHAT ARE YOU LOOKING AT ME FOR?

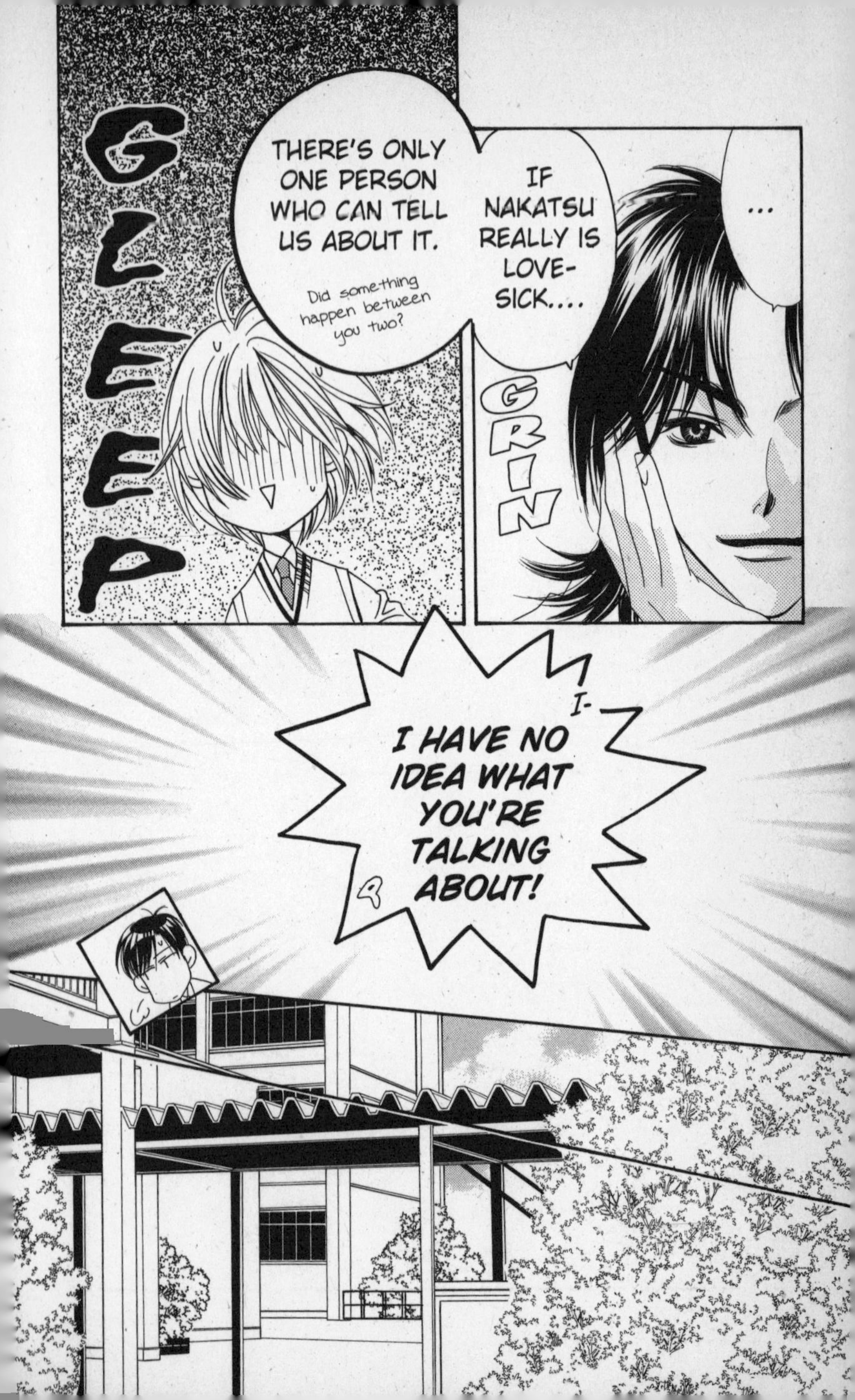
...
IF NAKATSU REALLY IS LOVE-SICK....
GRIN
THERE'S ONLY ONE PERSON WHO CAN TELL US ABOUT IT.
Did something happen between you two?
GLEEP
I- I HAVE NO IDEA WHAT YOU'RE TALKING ABOUT!

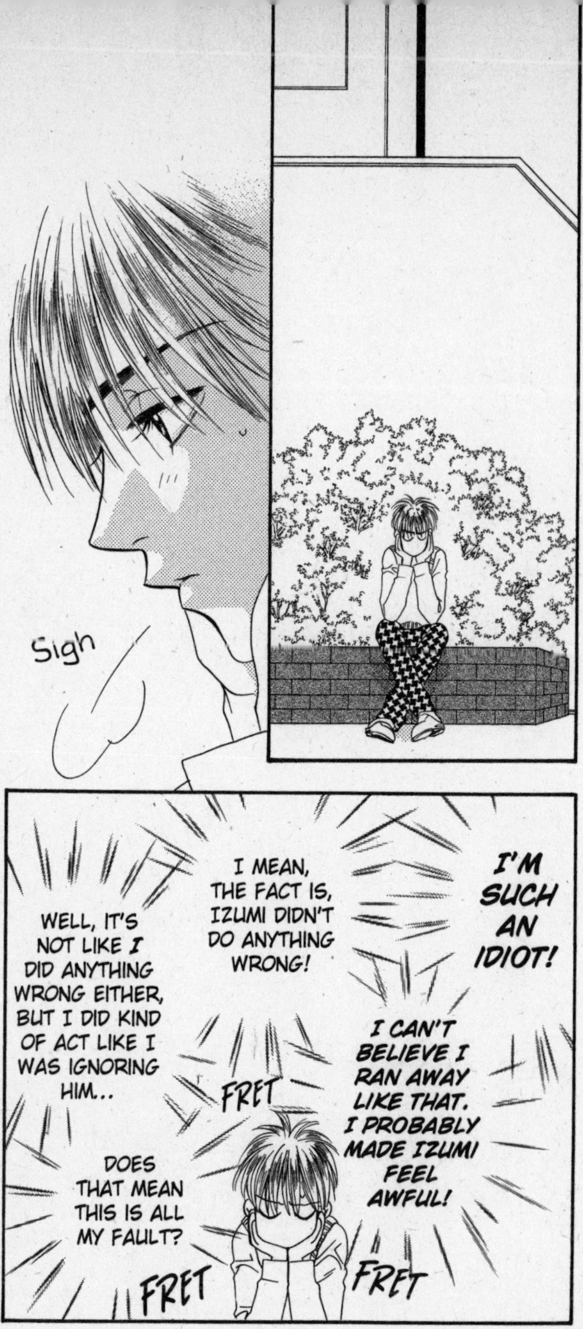
Sigh
I'M SUCH AN IDIOT!
I MEAN, THE FACT IS, IZUMI DIDN'T DO ANYTHING WRONG!
WELL, IT'S NOT LIKE *I* DID ANYTHING WRONG EITHER, BUT I DID KIND OF ACT LIKE I WAS IGNORING HIM...
I CAN'T BELIEVE I RAN AWAY LIKE THAT. I PROBABLY MADE IZUMI FEEL AWFUL!
FRET
DOES THAT MEAN THIS IS ALL MY FAULT?
FRET
FRET

Homepage

Ever since I made that announcement about my official webpage in volume 14 (www.wild-vanilla.com), many of you have been visiting my site. I'm so happy! Gradually, I've been increasing the site content. Here's some of what you'll find... "Behind the Scenes" tidbits, Wallpaper Downloads, and Himejima's guide to Character Birthdays. There's also a really fun Hana-Kimi novel written by screenwriter Yoshikazu Kuwashima, who my friend introduced me to. Plus you'll get to see some of the prettiest illustrations of Mizuki created by illustrator Shinji Katakura. It's becoming a really cool website! Yay!

-- June 2001

About the diary on my site... I'm such a lazy writer, but I really do put my heart into it.

The Webmaster

One of the shojo manga-related websites posted a comment saying, "The diary is filled with cool, in-depth insights on manga subculture"! Ha ha!

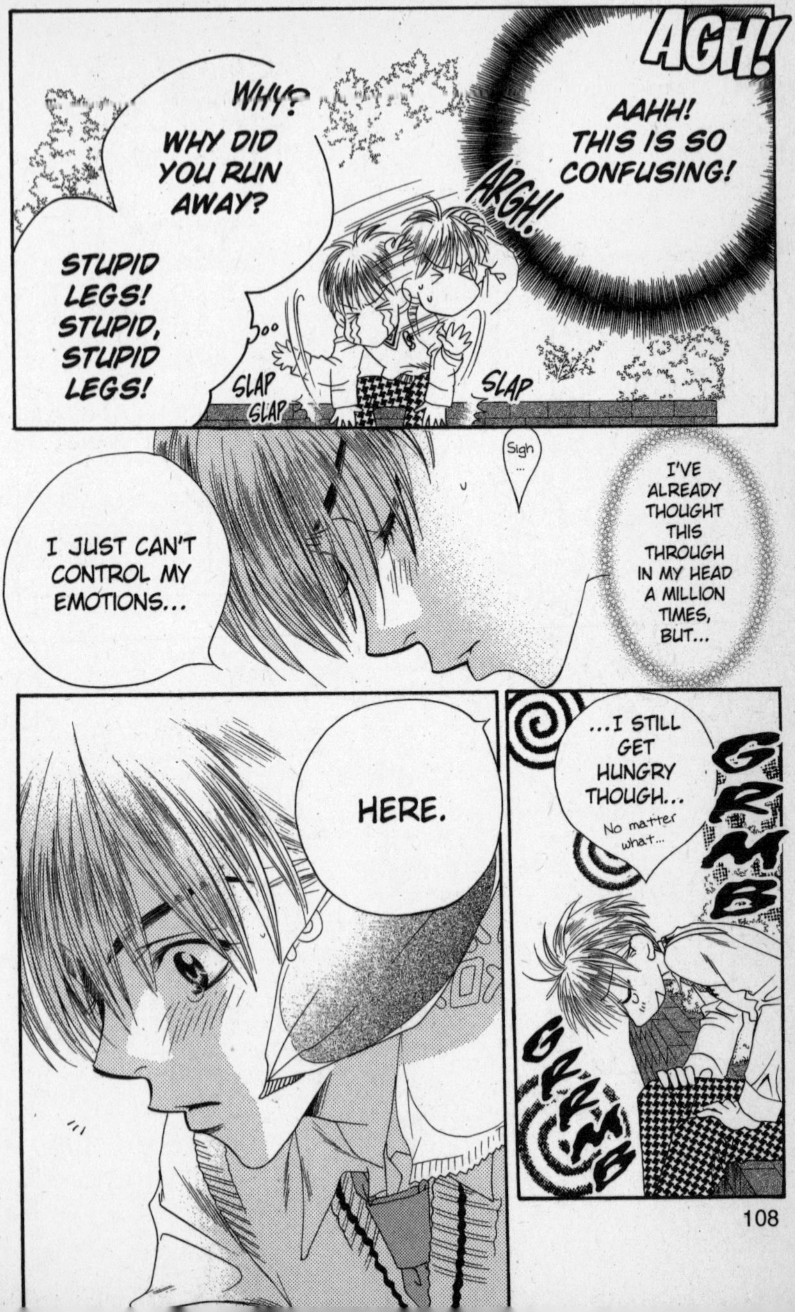
AGH!
AAHH! THIS IS SO CONFUSING!
ARGH!
WHY? WHY DID YOU RUN AWAY?
STUPID LEGS! STUPID, STUPID LEGS!
SLAP
SLAP SLAP
Sigh...
I'VE ALREADY THOUGHT THIS THROUGH IN MY HEAD A MILLION TIMES, BUT...
I JUST CAN'T CONTROL MY EMOTIONS...
...I STILL GET HUNGRY THOUGH...
No matter what...
GRMB
GRMB
HERE.

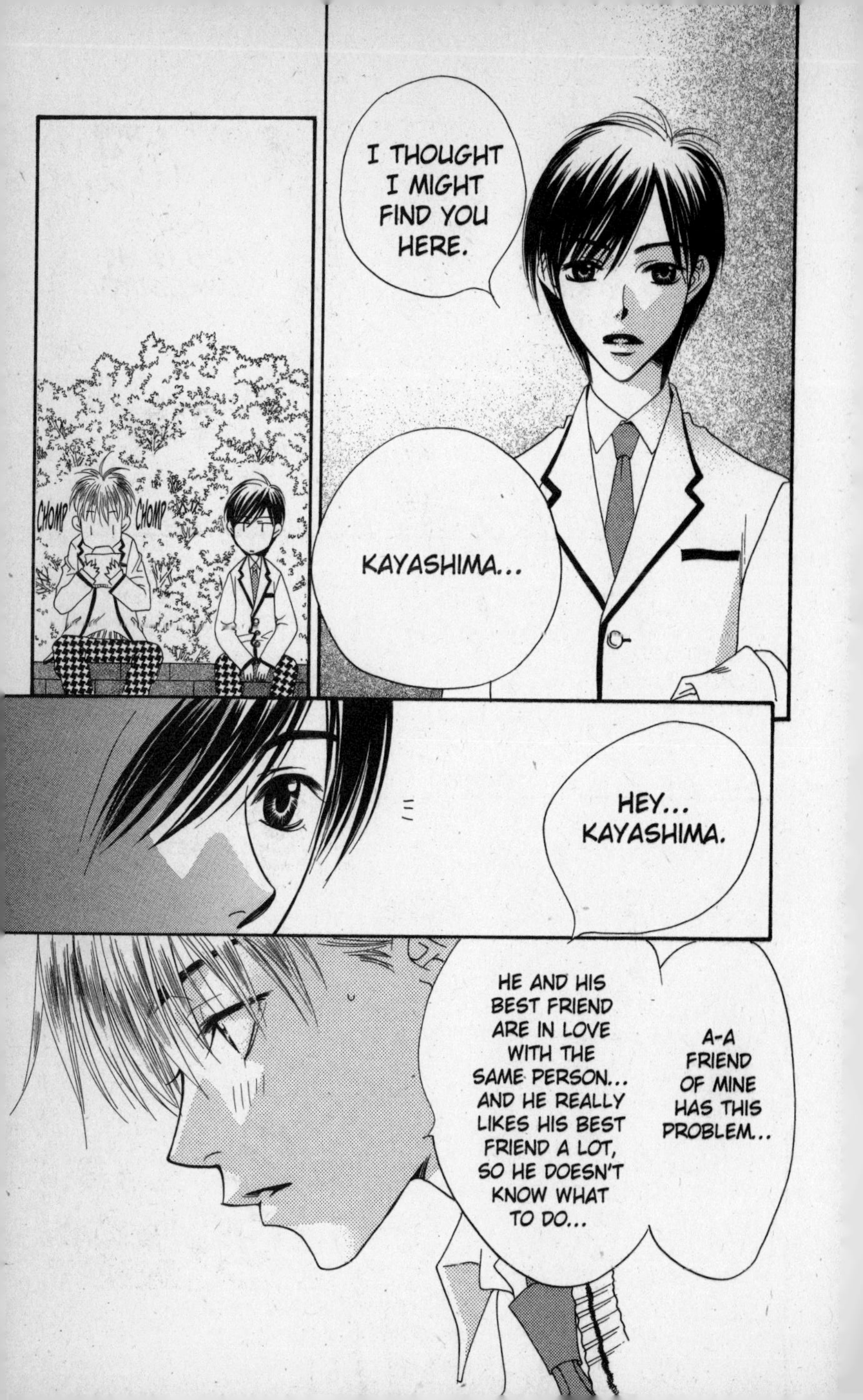
I THOUGHT I MIGHT FIND YOU HERE.
KAYASHIMA...
CHOMP
CHOMP
HEY... KAYASHIMA.
A-A FRIEND OF MINE HAS THIS PROBLEM...
HE AND HIS BEST FRIEND ARE IN LOVE WITH THE SAME PERSON... AND HE REALLY LIKES HIS BEST FRIEND A LOT, SO HE DOESN'T KNOW WHAT TO DO...

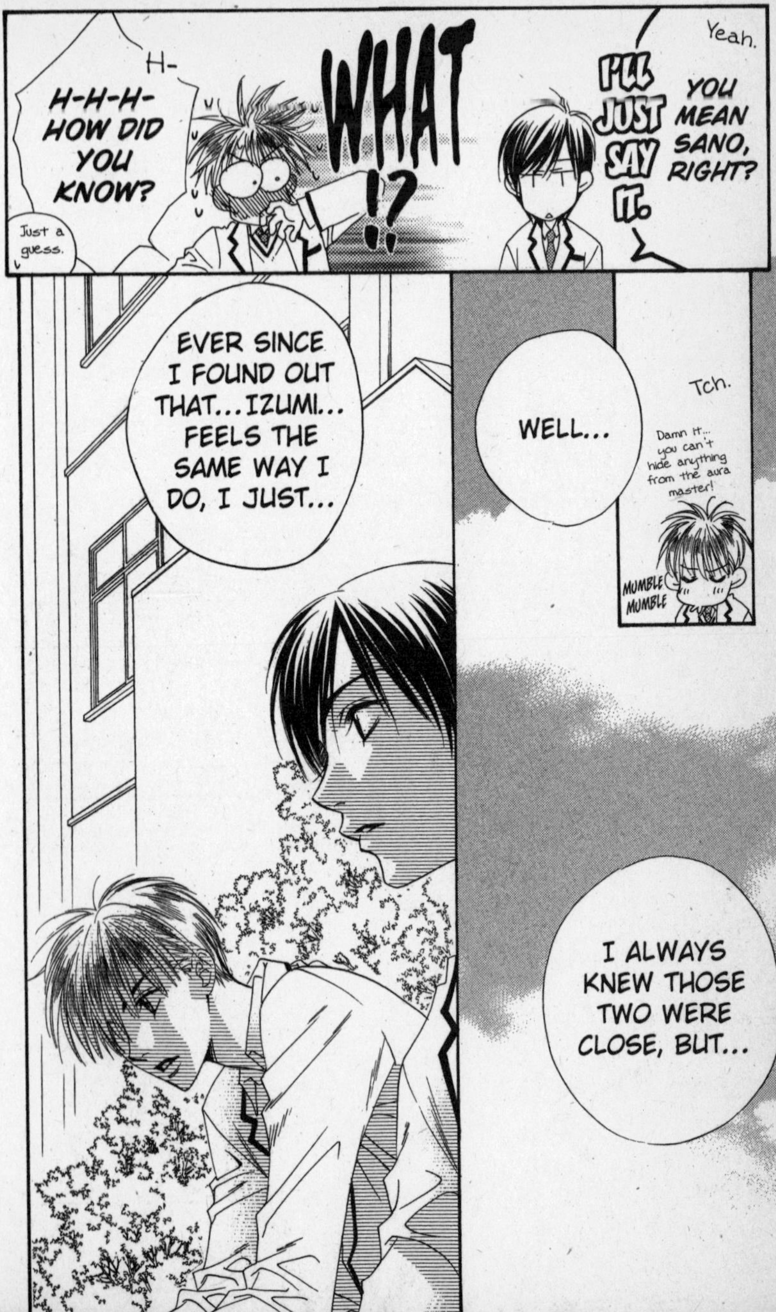
Yeah.
YOU MEAN SANO, RIGHT?
I'LL JUST SAY IT.
WHAT!?
H-
H-H-H-HOW DID YOU KNOW?
Just a guess.
Tch.
Damn it... you can't hide anything from the aura master!
MUMBLE MUMBLE
WELL...
I ALWAYS KNEW THOSE TWO WERE CLOSE, BUT...
EVER SINCE I FOUND OUT THAT...IZUMI... FEELS THE SAME WAY I DO, I JUST...

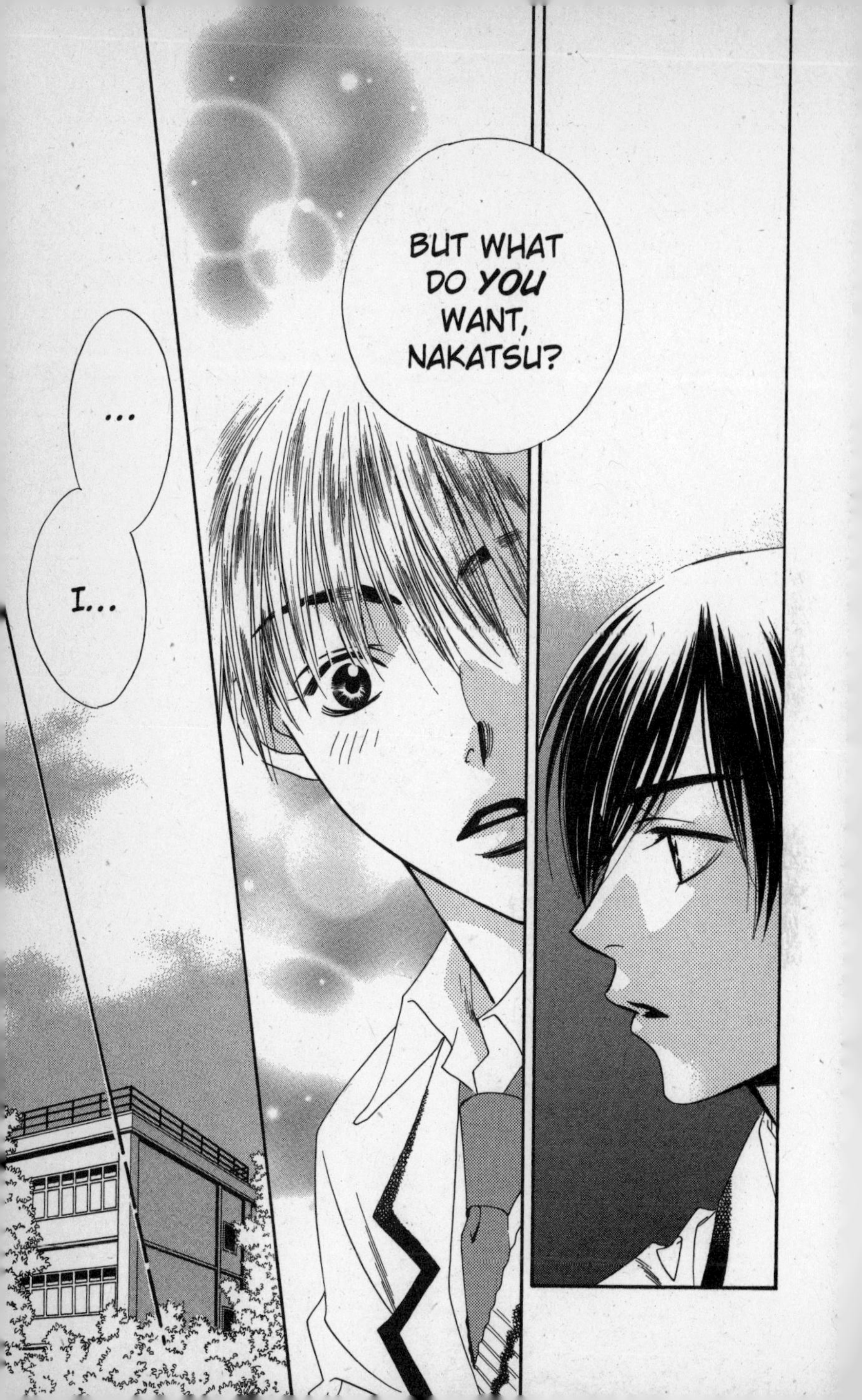
BUT WHAT DO *YOU* WANT, NAKATSU?
...
I...

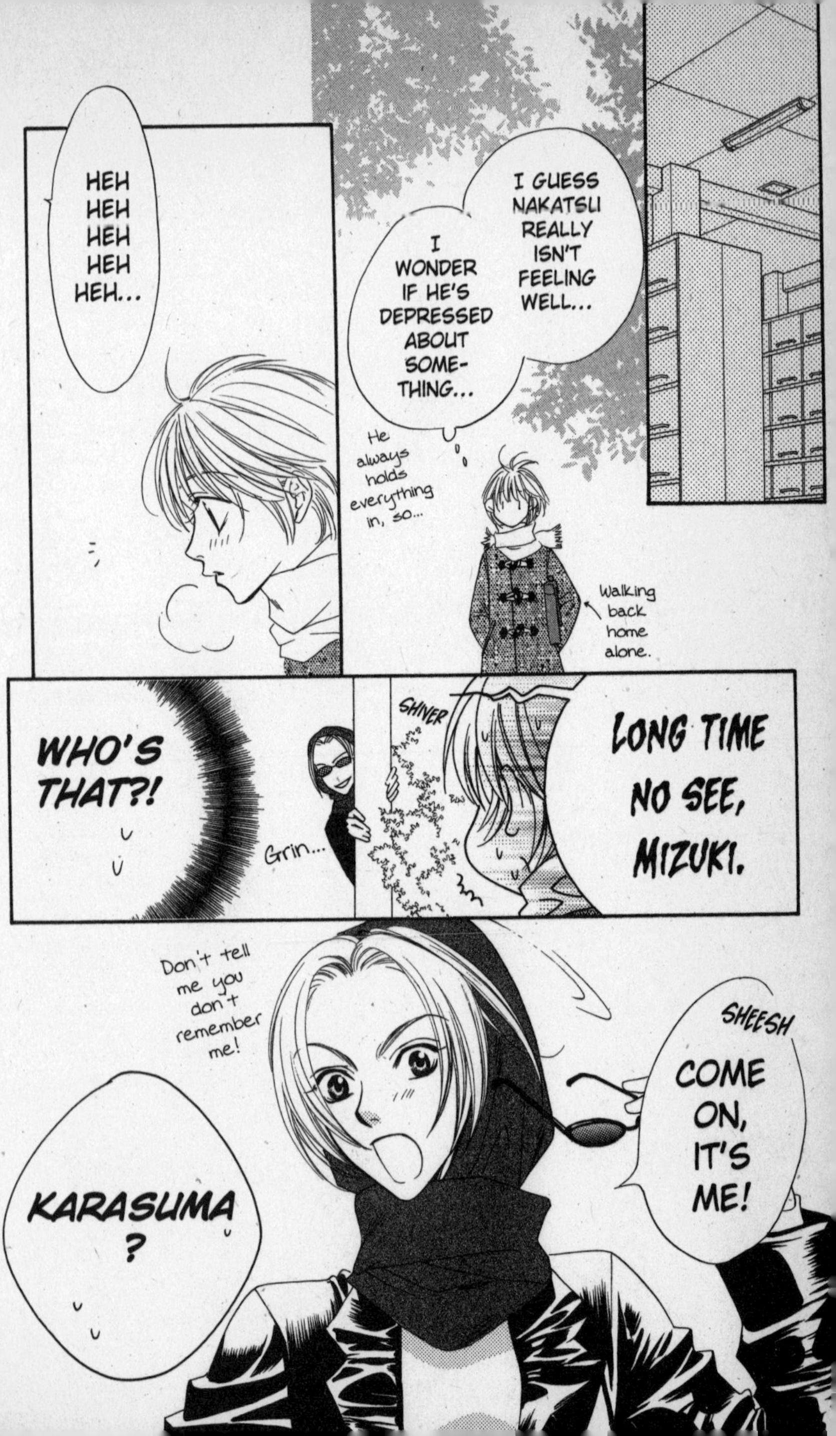
I GUESS NAKATSU REALLY ISN'T FEELING WELL...
I WONDER IF HE'S DEPRESSED ABOUT SOMETHING...
He always holds everything in, so...
Walking back home alone.
HEH HEH HEH HEH HEH...
LONG TIME NO SEE, MIZUKI.
SHIVER
Grin...
WHO'S THAT?!
SHEESH
COME ON, IT'S ME!
Don't tell me you don't remember me!
KARASUMA?

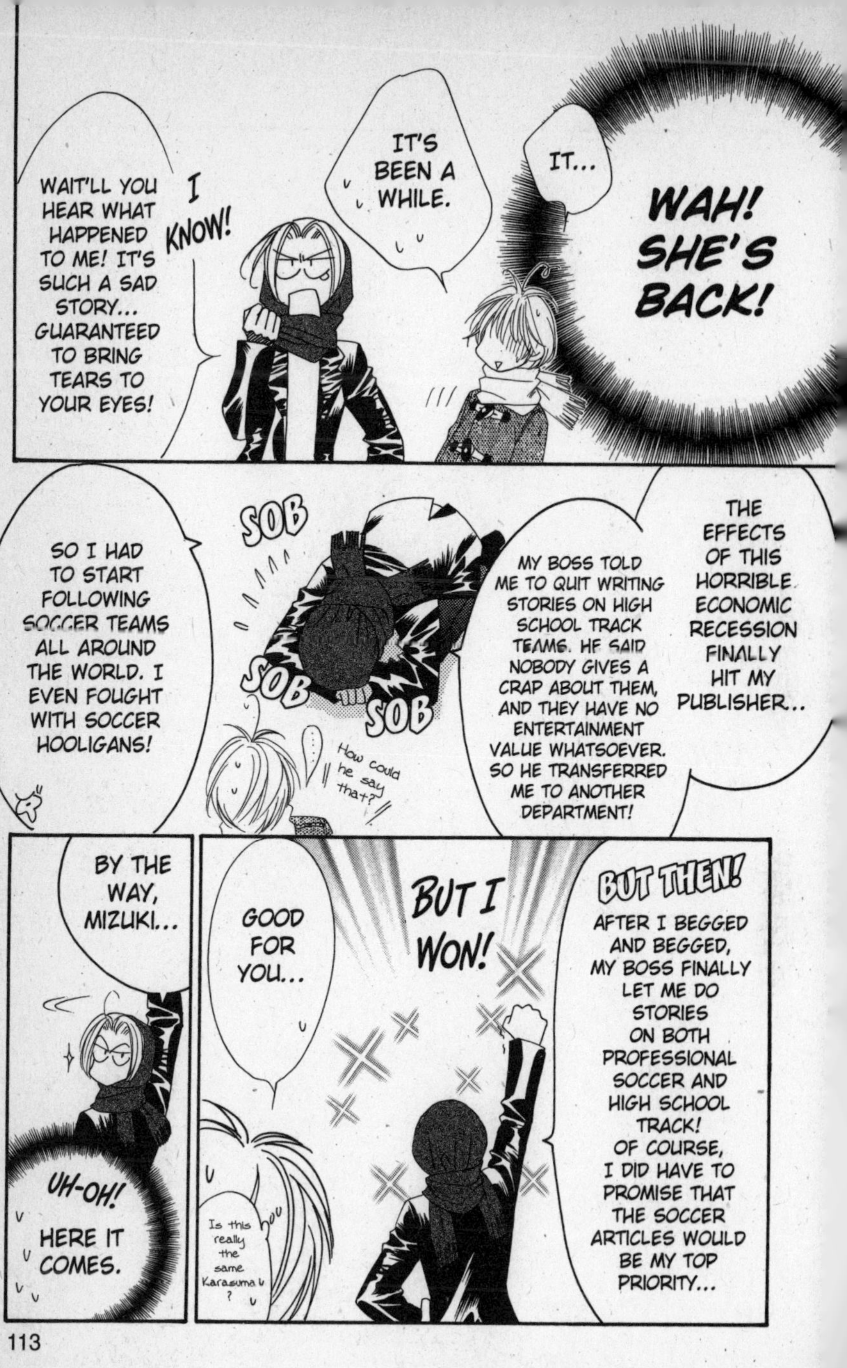
WAH! SHE'S BACK!
IT...
IT'S BEEN A WHILE.
I KNOW!
WAIT'LL YOU HEAR WHAT HAPPENED TO ME! IT'S SUCH A SAD STORY... GUARANTEED TO BRING TEARS TO YOUR EYES!
THE EFFECTS OF THIS HORRIBLE ECONOMIC RECESSION FINALLY HIT MY PUBLISHER...
MY BOSS TOLD ME TO QUIT WRITING STORIES ON HIGH SCHOOL TRACK TEAMS. HE SAID NOBODY GIVES A CRAP ABOUT THEM, AND THEY HAVE NO ENTERTAINMENT VALUE WHATSOEVER. SO HE TRANSFERRED ME TO ANOTHER DEPARTMENT!
SOB
SOB
SOB
How could he say that?
SO I HAD TO START FOLLOWING SOCCER TEAMS ALL AROUND THE WORLD. I EVEN FOUGHT WITH SOCCER HOOLIGANS!
BUT THEN!
AFTER I BEGGED AND BEGGED, MY BOSS FINALLY LET ME DO STORIES ON BOTH PROFESSIONAL SOCCER AND HIGH SCHOOL TRACK! OF COURSE, I DID HAVE TO PROMISE THAT THE SOCCER ARTICLES WOULD BE MY TOP PRIORITY...
BUT I WON!
GOOD FOR YOU...
Is this really the same Karasuma?
BY THE WAY, MIZUKI...
UH-OH! HERE IT COMES.

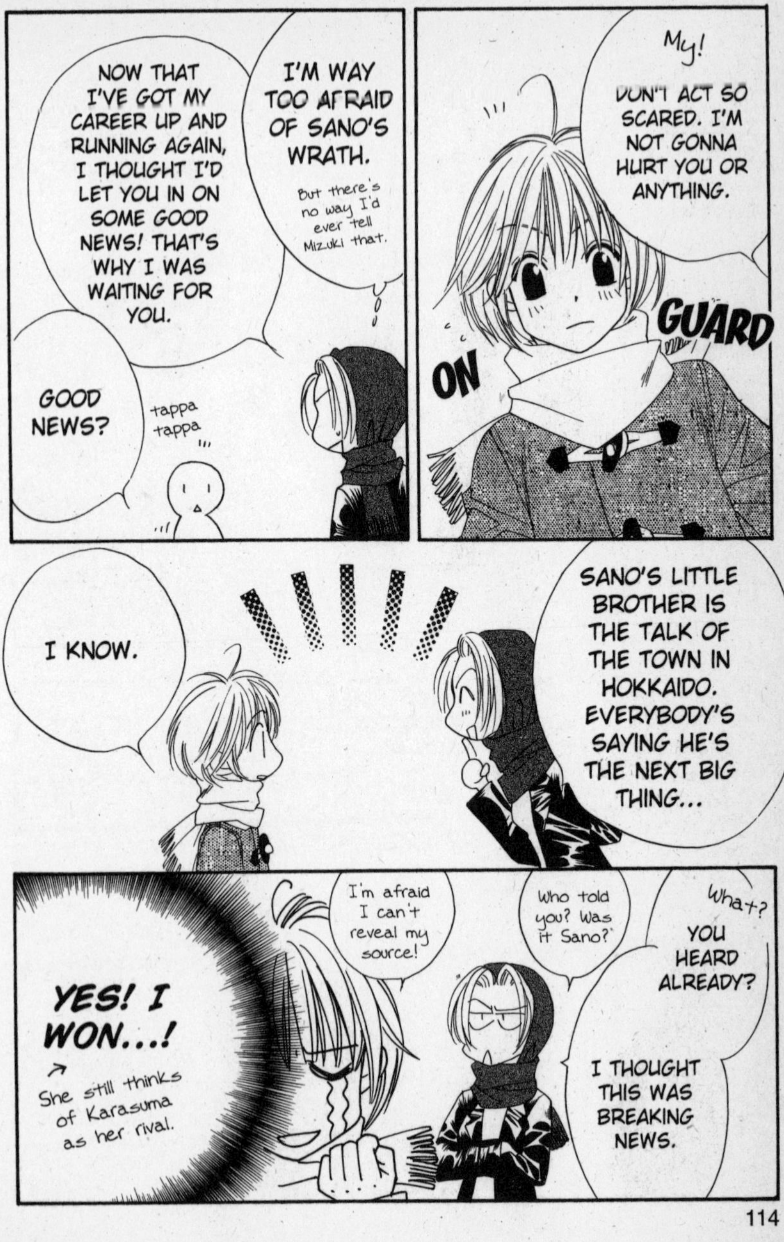
My!
DON'T ACT SO SCARED. I'M NOT GONNA HURT YOU OR ANYTHING.
ON GUARD
I'M WAY TOO AFRAID OF SANO'S WRATH.
But there's no way I'd ever tell Mizuki that.
NOW THAT I'VE GOT MY CAREER UP AND RUNNING AGAIN, I THOUGHT I'D LET YOU IN ON SOME GOOD NEWS! THAT'S WHY I WAS WAITING FOR YOU.
GOOD NEWS?
tappa tappa
SANO'S LITTLE BROTHER IS THE TALK OF THE TOWN IN HOKKAIDO. EVERYBODY'S SAYING HE'S THE NEXT BIG THING...
I KNOW.
What? YOU HEARD ALREADY?
I THOUGHT THIS WAS BREAKING NEWS.
Who told you? Was it Sano?
I'm afraid I can't reveal my source!
YES! I WON...!
She still thinks of Karasuma as her rival.

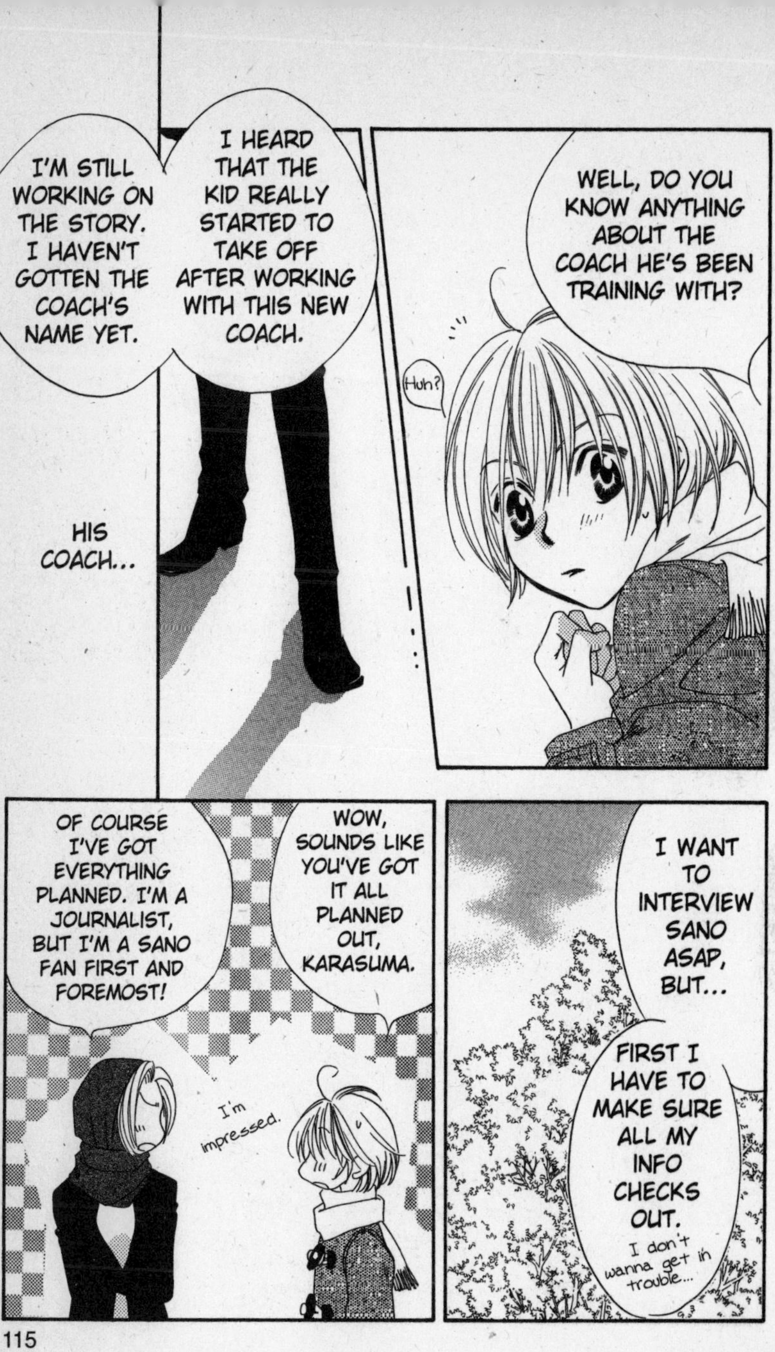
WELL, DO YOU KNOW ANYTHING ABOUT THE COACH HE'S BEEN TRAINING WITH?
Huh?
I HEARD THAT THE KID REALLY STARTED TO TAKE OFF AFTER WORKING WITH THIS NEW COACH.
I'M STILL WORKING ON THE STORY. I HAVEN'T GOTTEN THE COACH'S NAME YET.
HIS COACH...
I WANT TO INTERVIEW SANO ASAP, BUT...
FIRST I HAVE TO MAKE SURE ALL MY INFO CHECKS OUT.
I don't wanna get in trouble...
WOW, SOUNDS LIKE YOU'VE GOT IT ALL PLANNED OUT, KARASUMA.
I'm impressed.
OF COURSE I'VE GOT EVERYTHING PLANNED. I'M A JOURNALIST, BUT I'M A SANO FAN FIRST AND FOREMOST!

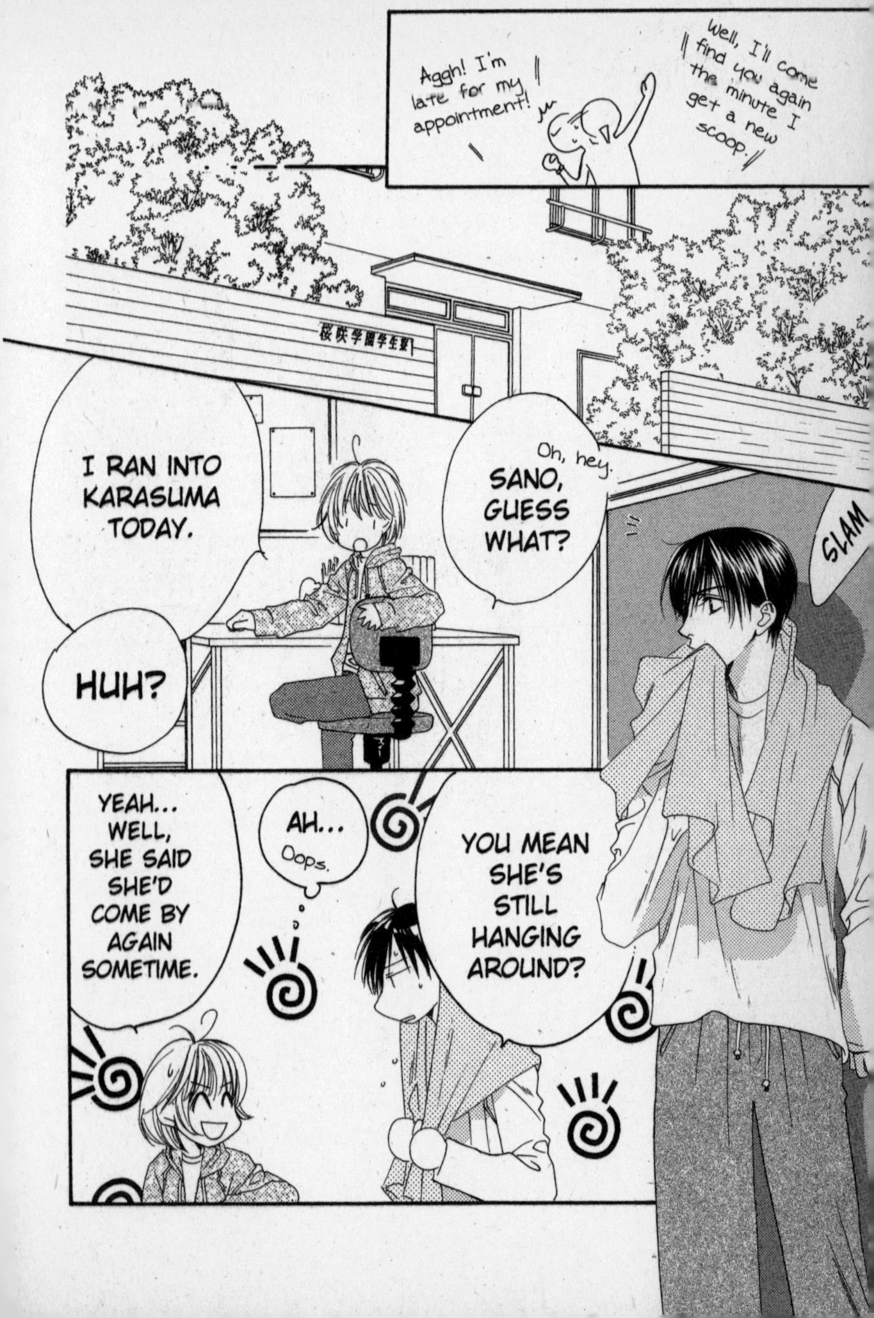
Well, I'll come find you again the minute I get a new scoop.
Aggh! I'm late for my appointment!
桜咲学園学生寮
SLAM
Oh, hey.
SANO, GUESS WHAT?
I RAN INTO KARASUMA TODAY.
HUH?
YOU MEAN SHE'S STILL HANGING AROUND?
AH... Oops.
YEAH... WELL, SHE SAID SHE'D COME BY AGAIN SOMETIME.

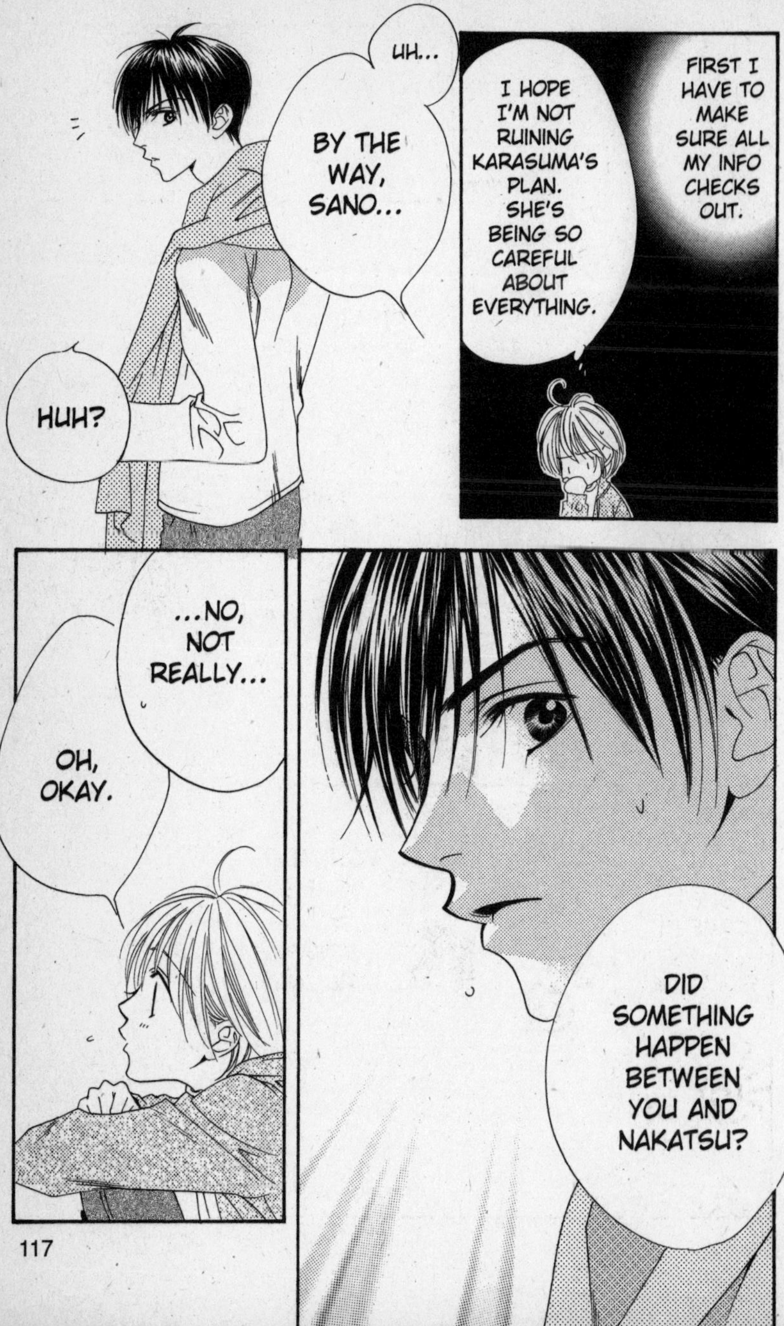
FIRST I HAVE TO MAKE SURE ALL MY INFO CHECKS OUT.
I HOPE I'M NOT RUINING KARASUMA'S PLAN. SHE'S BEING SO CAREFUL ABOUT EVERYTHING.
UH...
BY THE WAY, SANO...
HUH?
DID SOMETHING HAPPEN BETWEEN YOU AND NAKATSU?
...NO, NOT REALLY...
OH, OKAY.

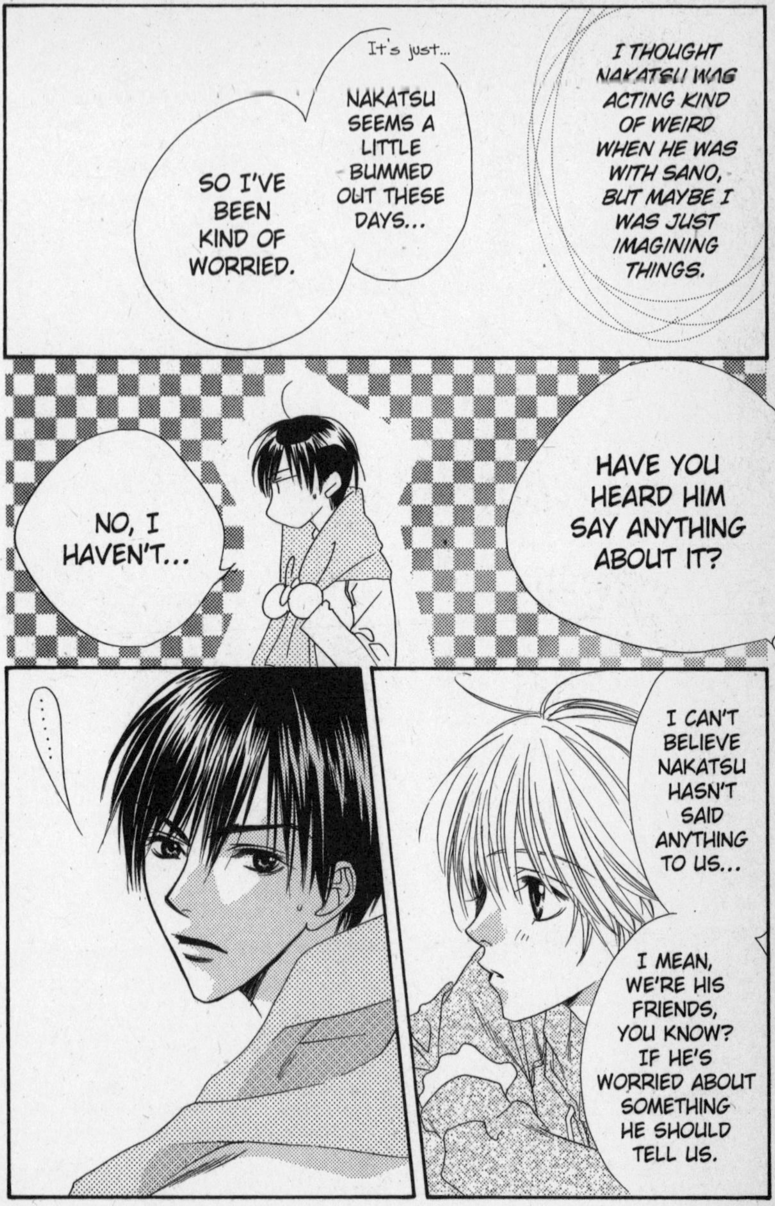
I THOUGHT NAKATSU WAS ACTING KIND OF WEIRD WHEN HE WAS WITH SANO, BUT MAYBE I WAS JUST IMAGINING THINGS.
It's just...
NAKATSU SEEMS A LITTLE BUMMED OUT THESE DAYS...
SO I'VE BEEN KIND OF WORRIED.
HAVE YOU HEARD HIM SAY ANYTHING ABOUT IT?
NO, I HAVEN'T...
I CAN'T BELIEVE NAKATSU HASN'T SAID ANYTHING TO US...
I MEAN, WE'RE HIS FRIENDS, YOU KNOW? IF HE'S WORRIED ABOUT SOMETHING HE SHOULD TELL US.
......

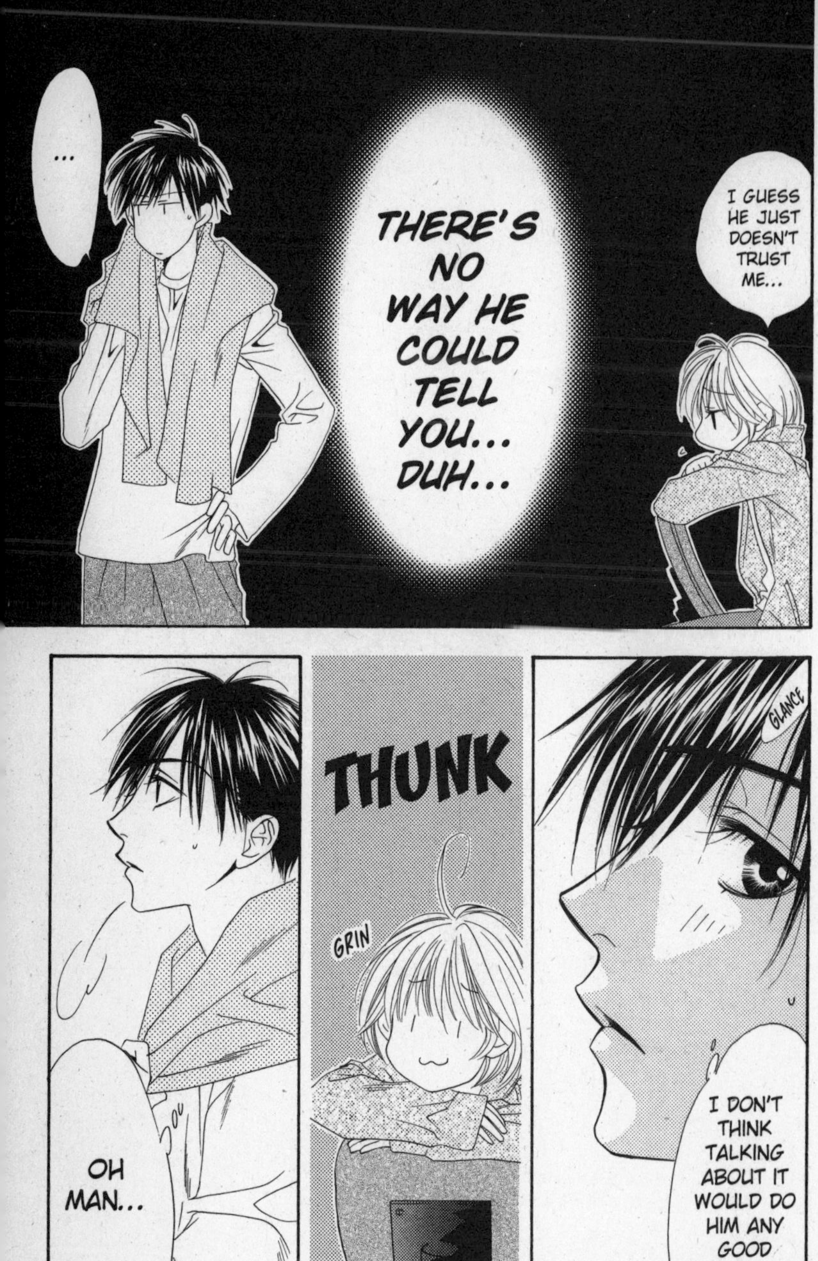
I GUESS HE JUST DOESN'T TRUST ME...
THERE'S NO WAY HE COULD TELL YOU... DUH...
...
GLANCE
I DON'T THINK TALKING ABOUT IT WOULD DO HIM ANY GOOD ANYWAY...
THUNK
GRIN
OH MAN...

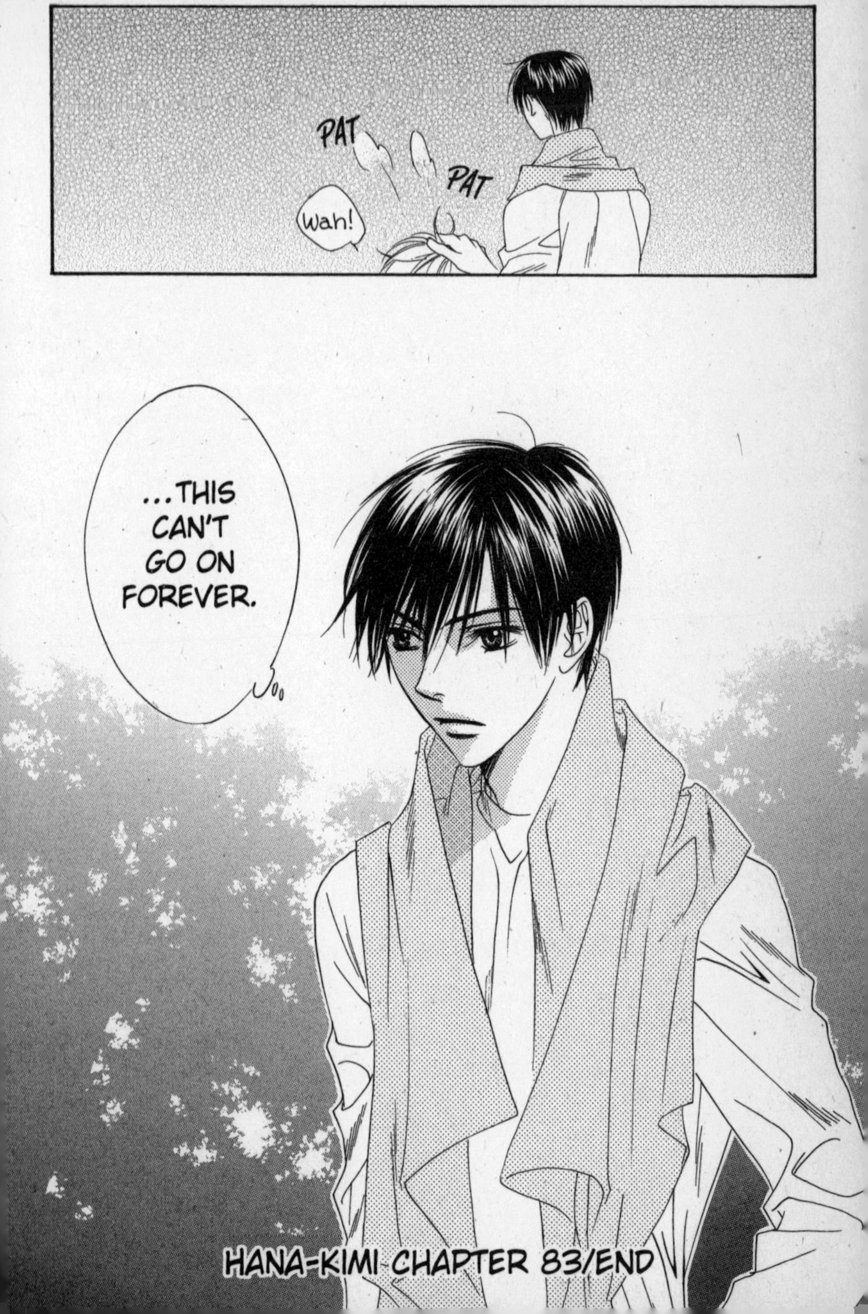
PAT
PAT
Wah!
...THIS CAN'T GO ON FOREVER.
HANA-KIMI CHAPTER 83/END

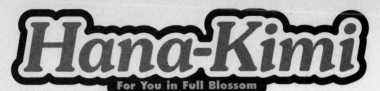

Hana-Kimi

For You in Full Blossom

CHAPTER 84

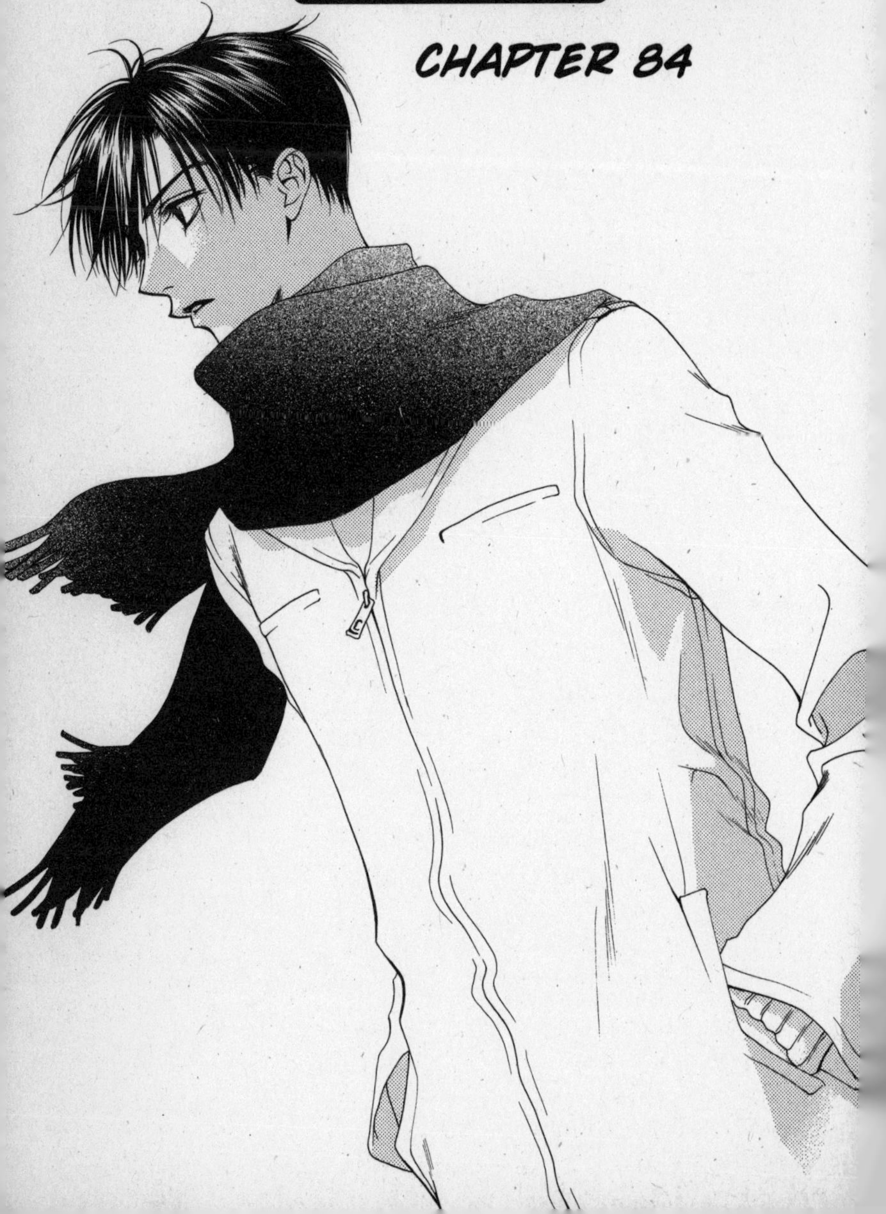

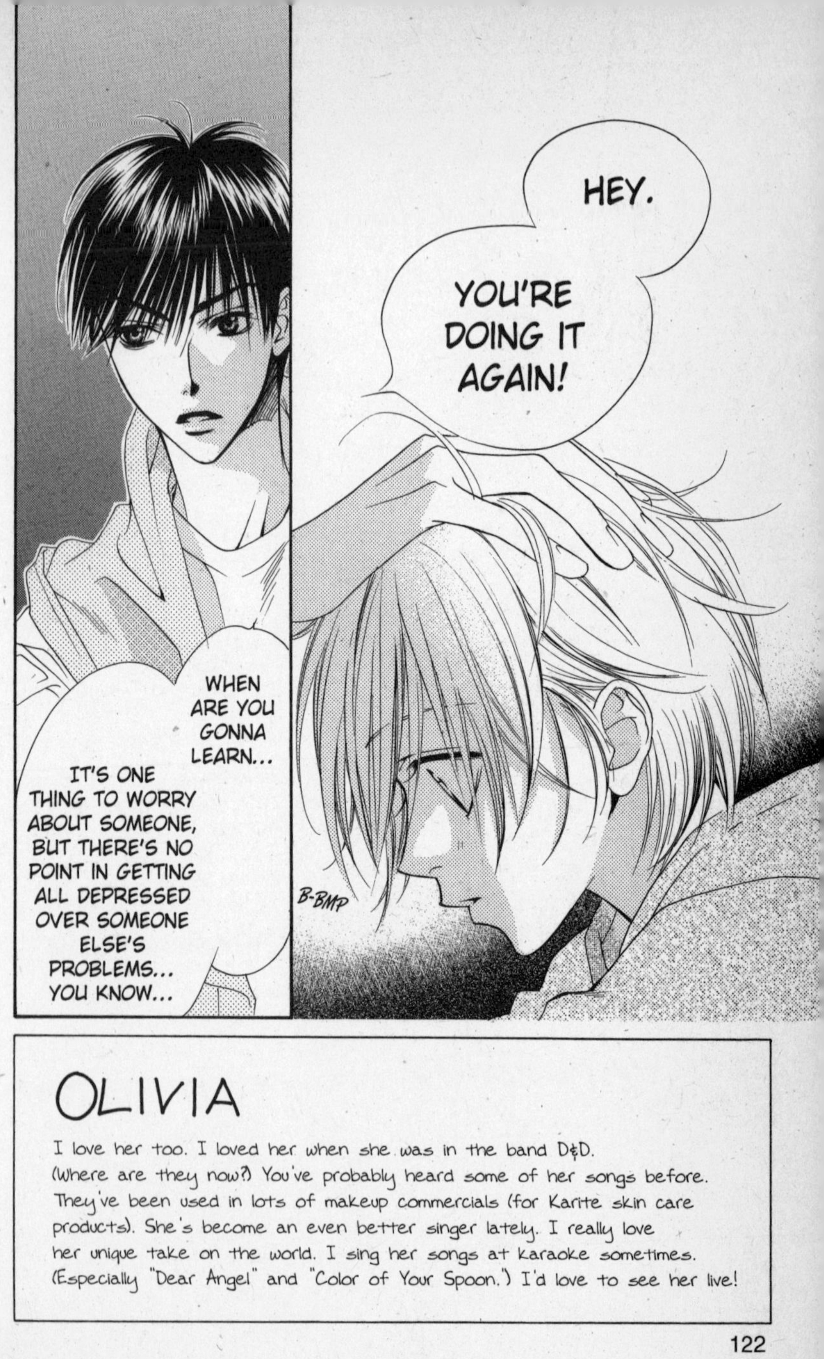
HEY.
YOU'RE DOING IT AGAIN!
B-BMP
WHEN ARE YOU GONNA LEARN...
IT'S ONE THING TO WORRY ABOUT SOMEONE, BUT THERE'S NO POINT IN GETTING ALL DEPRESSED OVER SOMEONE ELSE'S PROBLEMS... YOU KNOW...

OLIVIA

I love her too. I loved her when she was in the band D&D. (Where are they now?) You've probably heard some of her songs before. They've been used in lots of makeup commercials (for Karite skin care products). She's become an even better singer lately. I really love her unique take on the world. I sing her songs at karaoke sometimes. (Especially "Dear Angel" and "Color of Your Spoon.") I'd love to see her live!

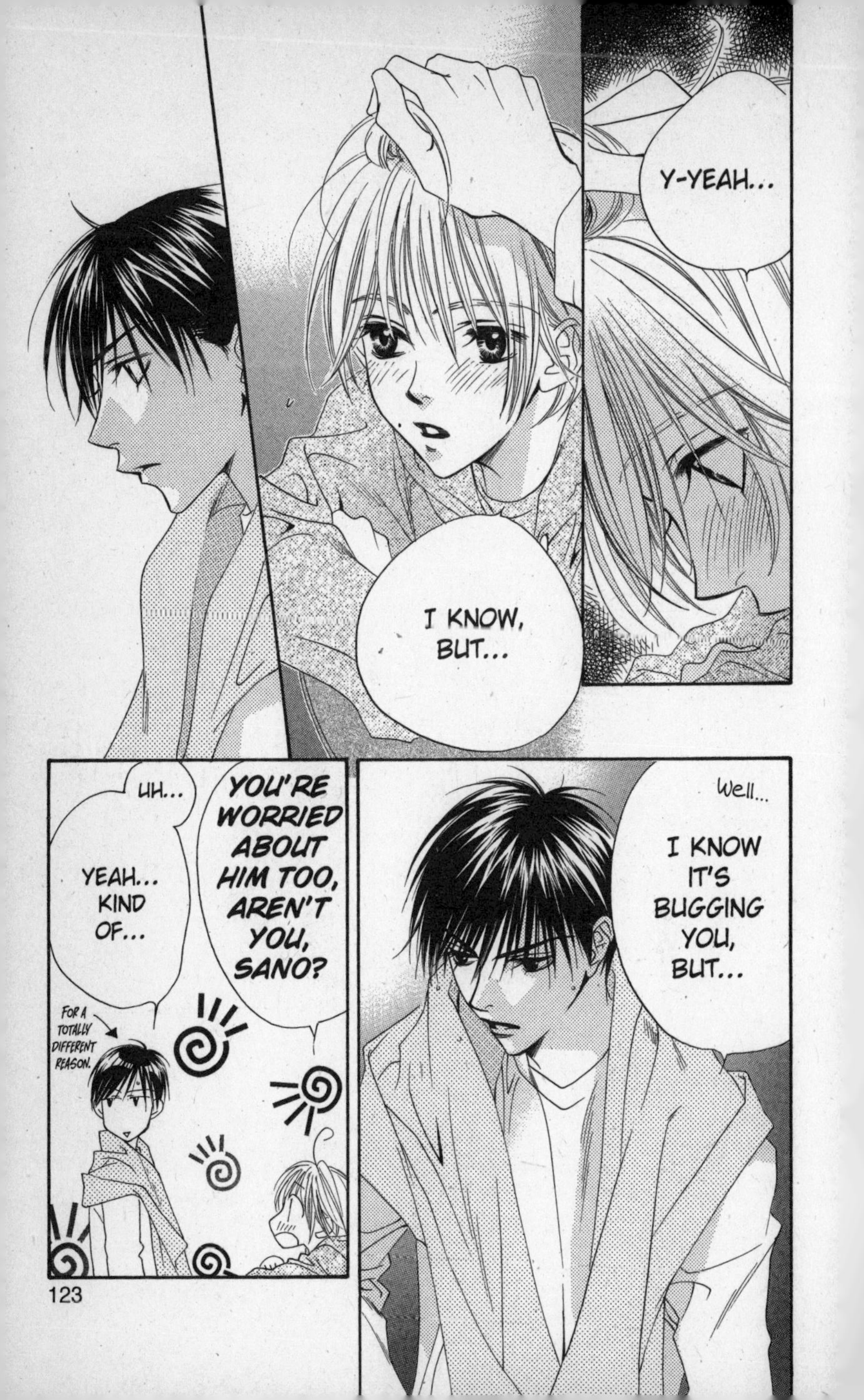
Y-YEAH...
I KNOW, BUT...
Well... I KNOW IT'S BUGGING YOU, BUT...
YOU'RE WORRIED ABOUT HIM TOO, AREN'T YOU, SANO?
UH... YEAH... KIND OF...
FOR A TOTALLY DIFFERENT REASON.

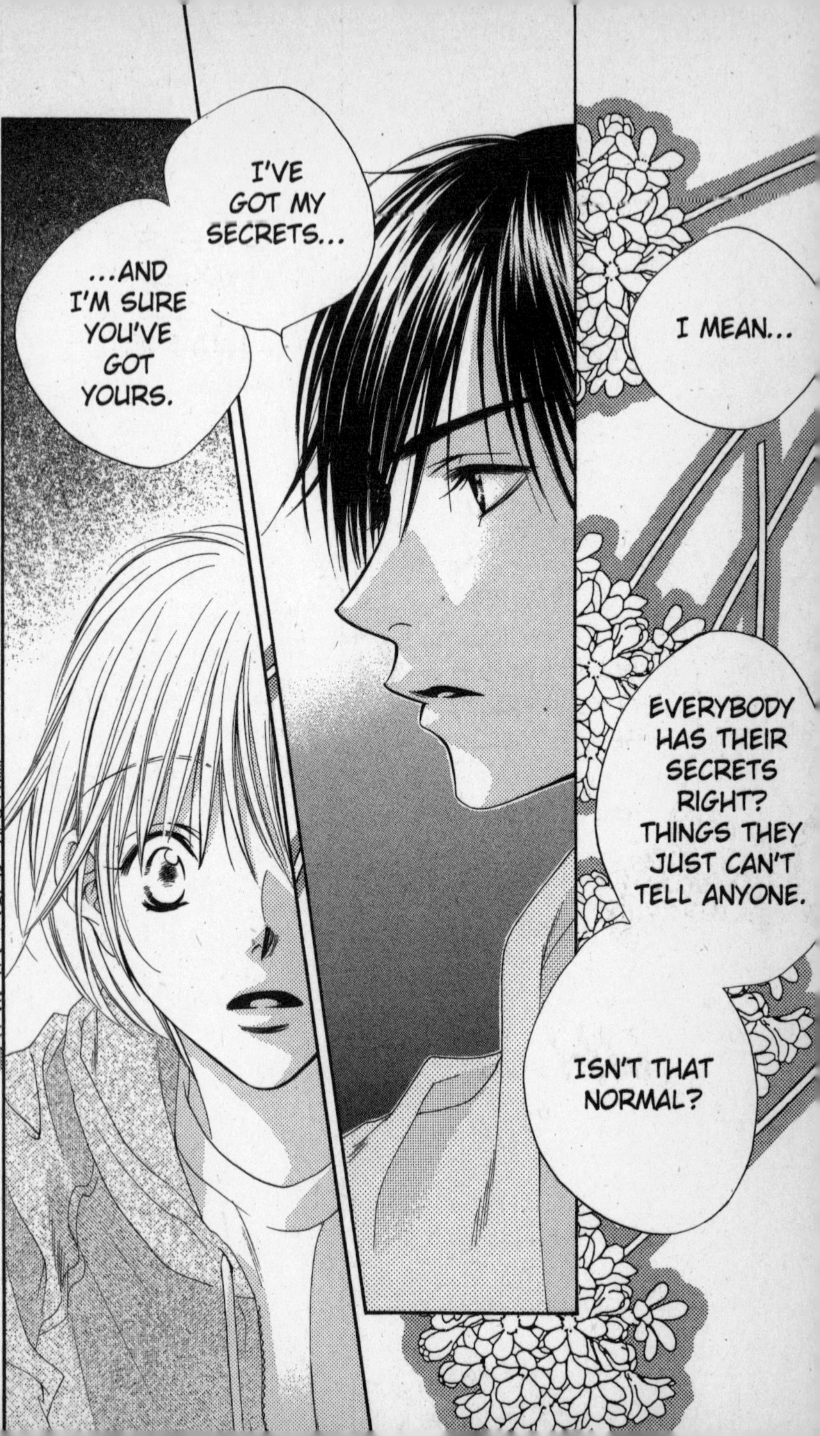
I'VE GOT MY SECRETS...
...AND I'M SURE YOU'VE GOT YOURS.
I MEAN...
EVERYBODY HAS THEIR SECRETS RIGHT? THINGS THEY JUST CAN'T TELL ANYONE.
ISN'T THAT NORMAL?

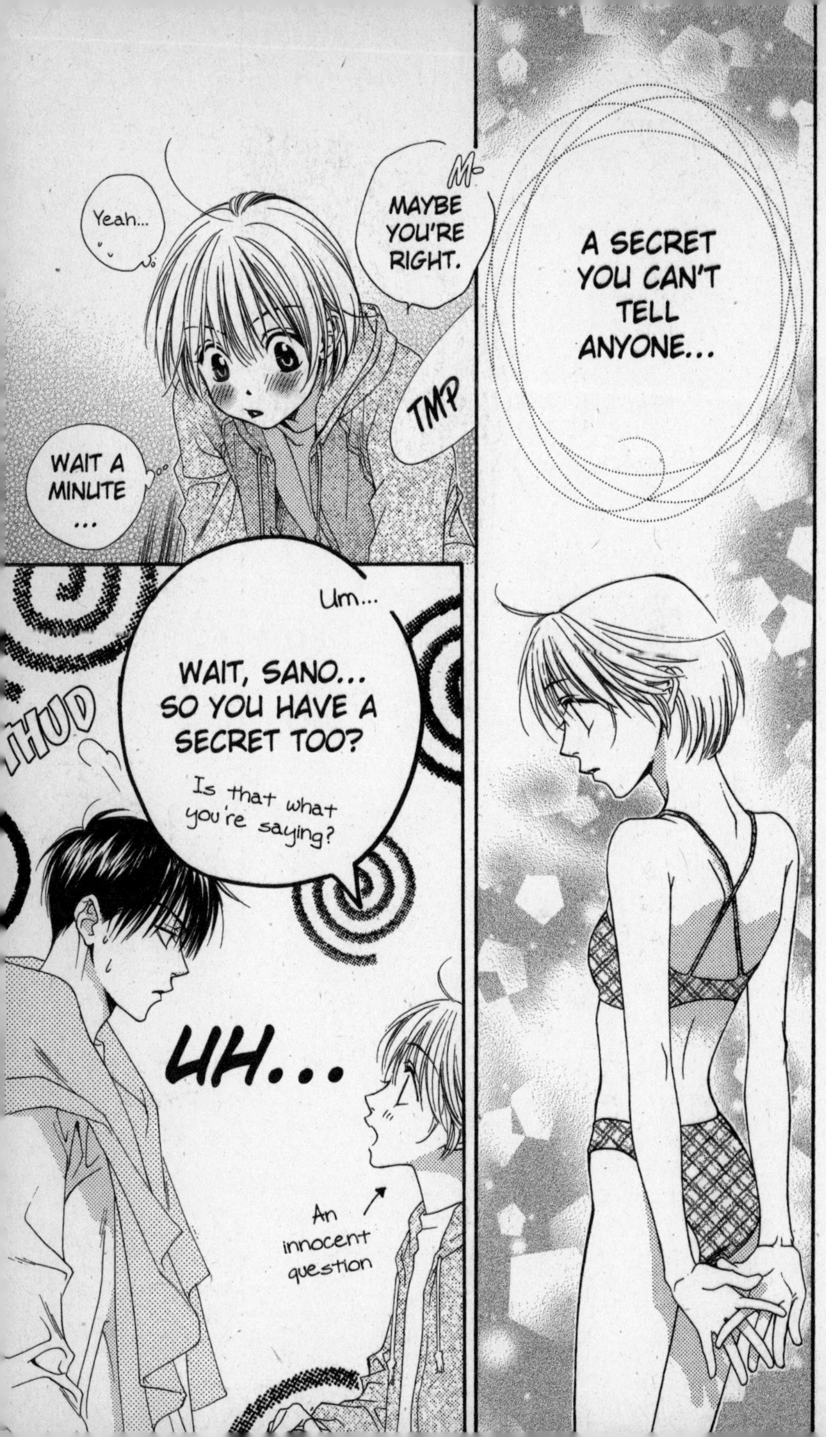
A SECRET YOU CAN'T TELL ANYONE...
M-
MAYBE YOU'RE RIGHT.
TMP
Yeah...
WAIT A MINUTE ...
Um...
WAIT, SANO... SO YOU HAVE A SECRET TOO?
Is that what you're saying?
THUD
UH...
An innocent question

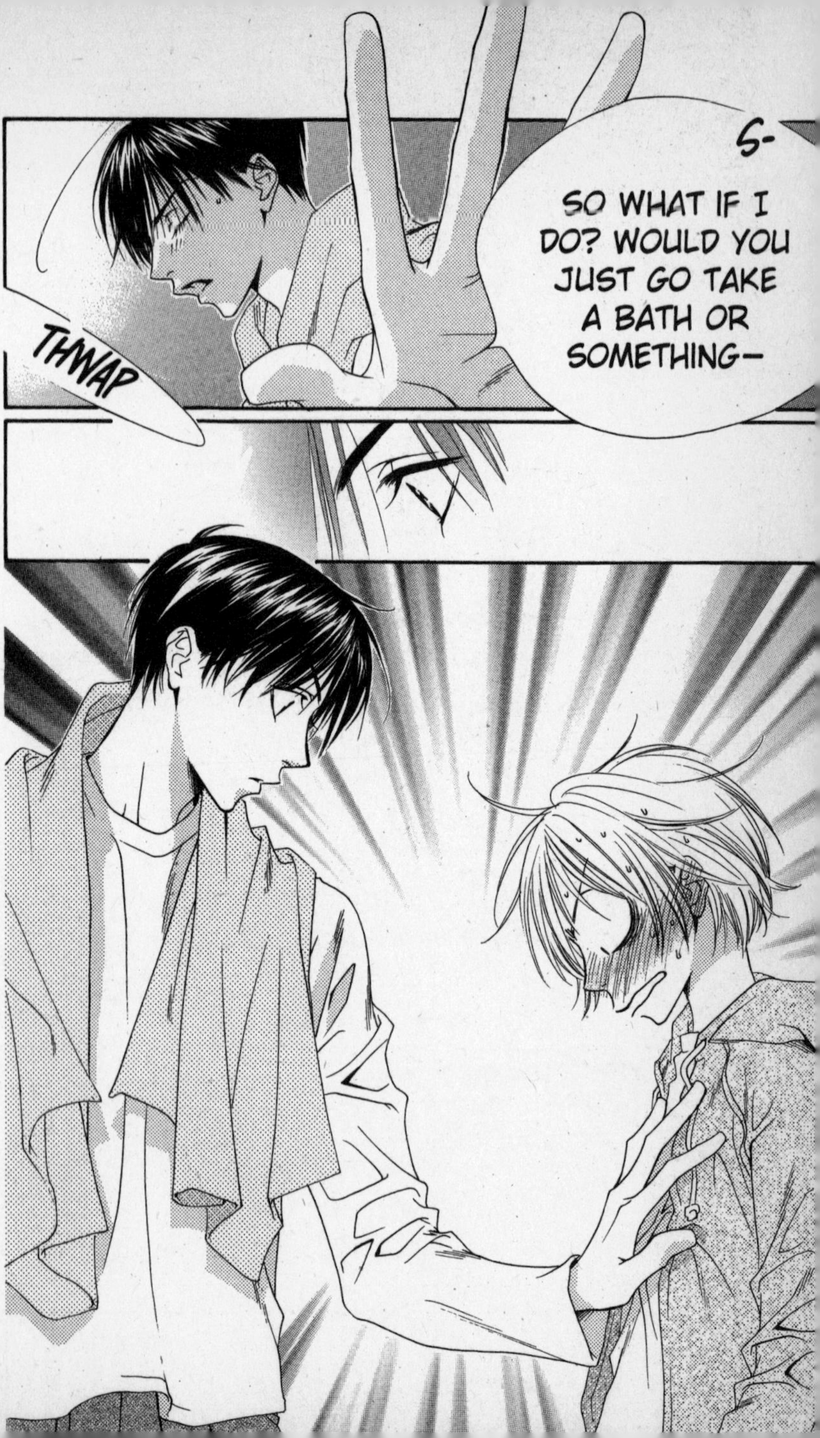
S-
SO WHAT IF I DO? WOULD YOU JUST GO TAKE A BATH OR SOMETHING-
THWAP

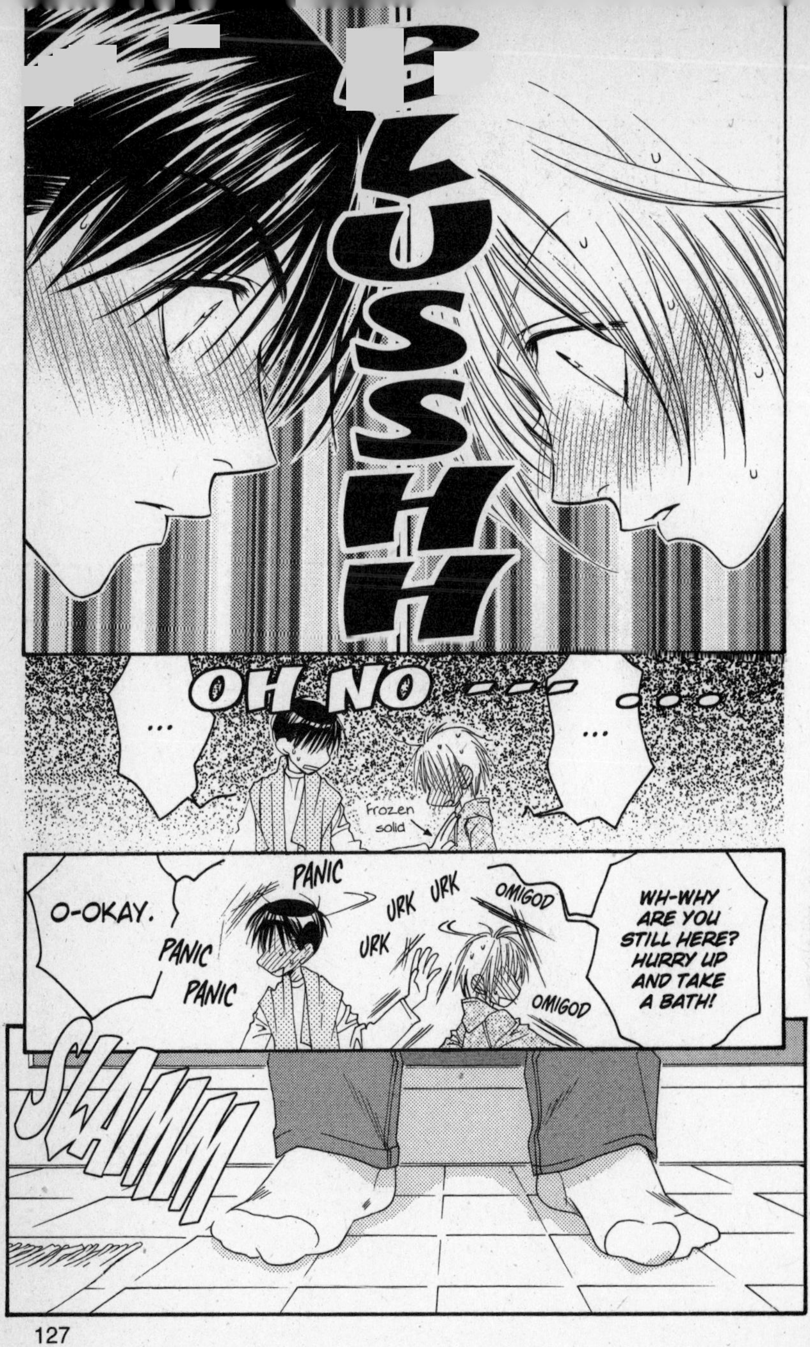
BLUSHH
...
OH NO --- ...
...
Frozen solid
WH-WHY ARE YOU STILL HERE? HURRY UP AND TAKE A BATH!
OMIGOD
OMIGOD
URK URK
URK
PANIC
O-OKAY.
PANIC
PANIC
SLAMM

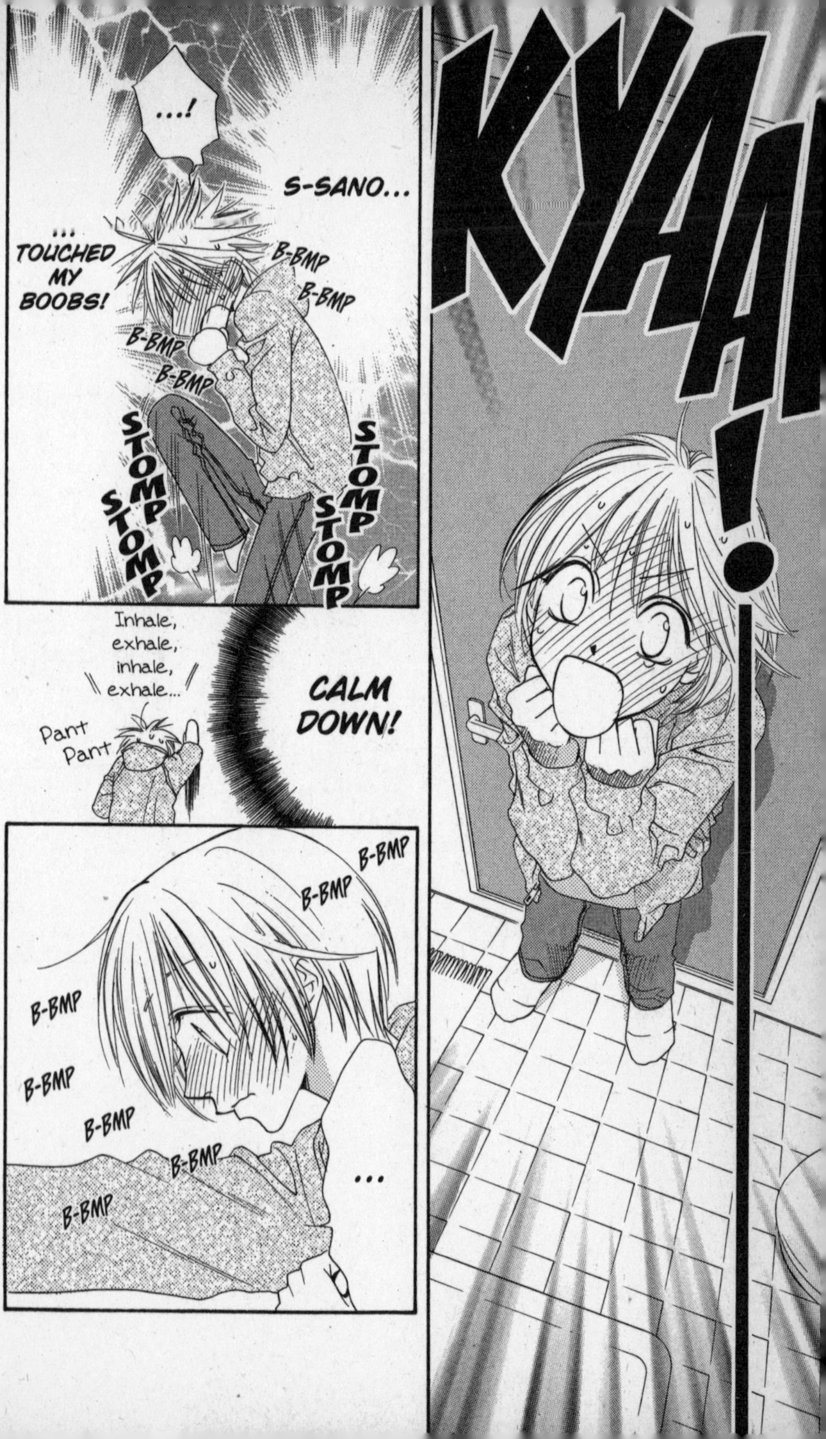
KYA
!
...!
S-SANO...
...TOUCHED MY BOOBS!
B-BMP
B-BMP
B-BMP
B-BMP
STOMP
STOMP
STOMP
STOMP
CALM DOWN!
Inhale, exhale, inhale, exhale...
Pant Pant
B-BMP
B-BMP
...
B-BMP
B-BMP
B-BMP
B-BMP
B-BMP

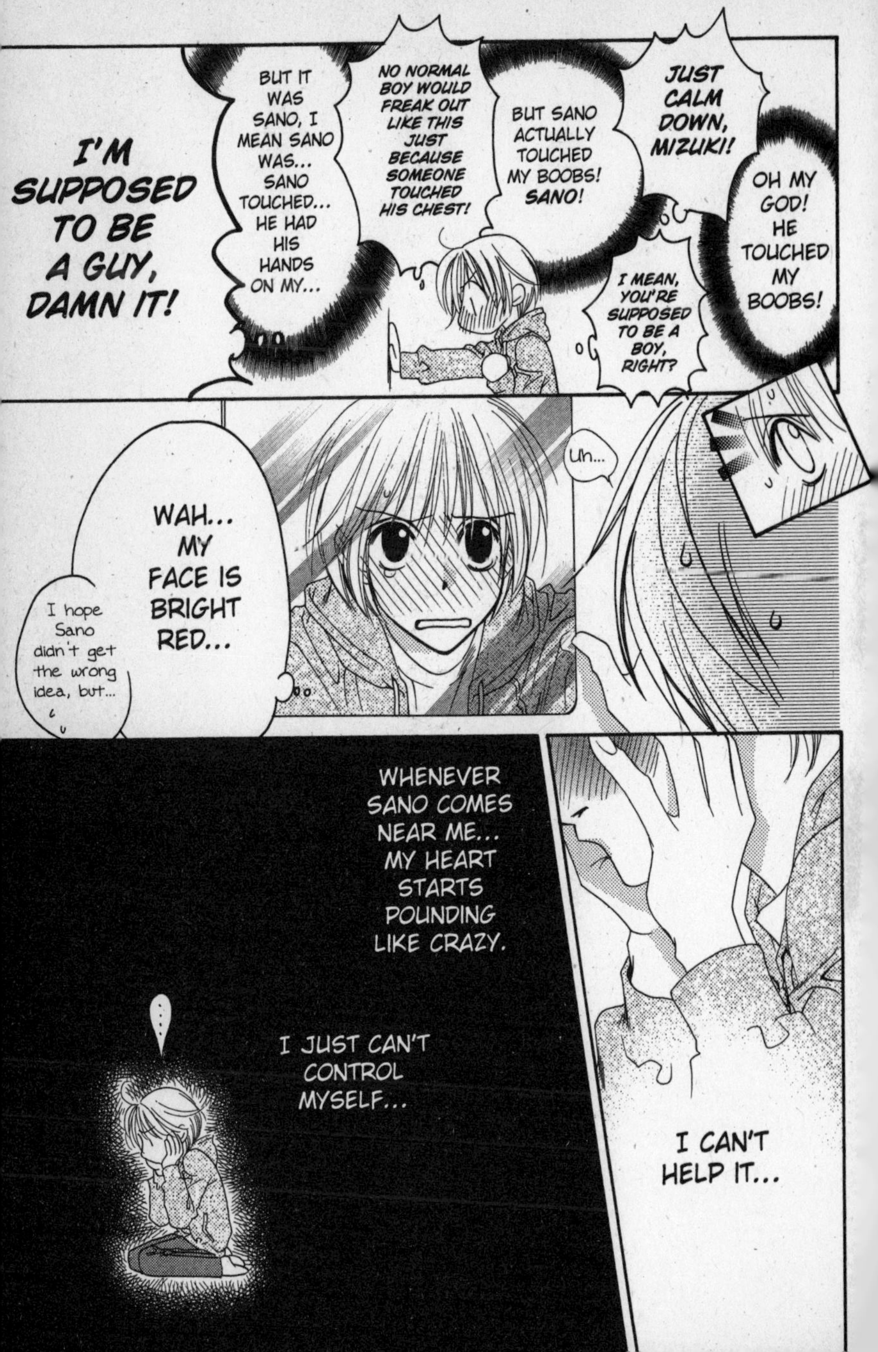
OH MY GOD! HE TOUCHED MY BOOBS!
JUST CALM DOWN, MIZUKI!
I MEAN, YOU'RE SUPPOSED TO BE A BOY, RIGHT?
BUT SANO ACTUALLY TOUCHED MY BOOBS! SANO!
NO NORMAL BOY WOULD FREAK OUT LIKE THIS JUST BECAUSE SOMEONE TOUCHED HIS CHEST!
BUT IT WAS SANO, I MEAN SANO WAS... SANO TOUCHED... HE HAD HIS HANDS ON MY...
I'M SUPPOSED TO BE A GUY, DAMN IT!
Uh...
WAH... MY FACE IS BRIGHT RED...
I hope Sano didn't get the wrong idea, but...
WHENEVER SANO COMES NEAR ME... MY HEART STARTS POUNDING LIKE CRAZY.
I JUST CAN'T CONTROL MYSELF...
I CAN'T HELP IT...

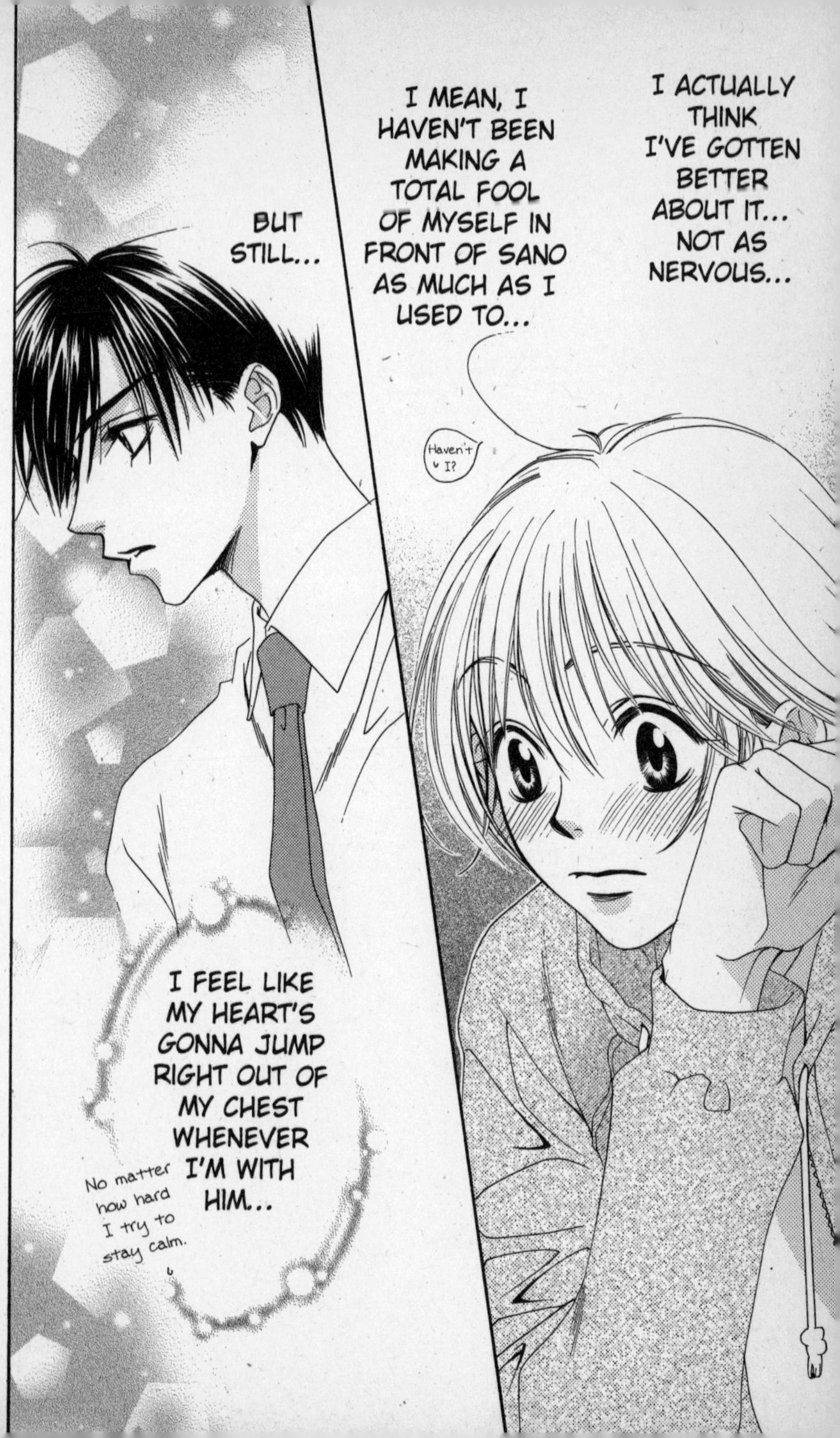
I ACTUALLY THINK I'VE GOTTEN BETTER ABOUT IT... NOT AS NERVOUS...
I MEAN, I HAVEN'T BEEN MAKING A TOTAL FOOL OF MYSELF IN FRONT OF SANO AS MUCH AS I USED TO...
Haven't I?
BUT STILL...
I FEEL LIKE MY HEART'S GONNA JUMP RIGHT OUT OF MY CHEST WHENEVER I'M WITH HIM...
No matter how hard I try to stay calm.

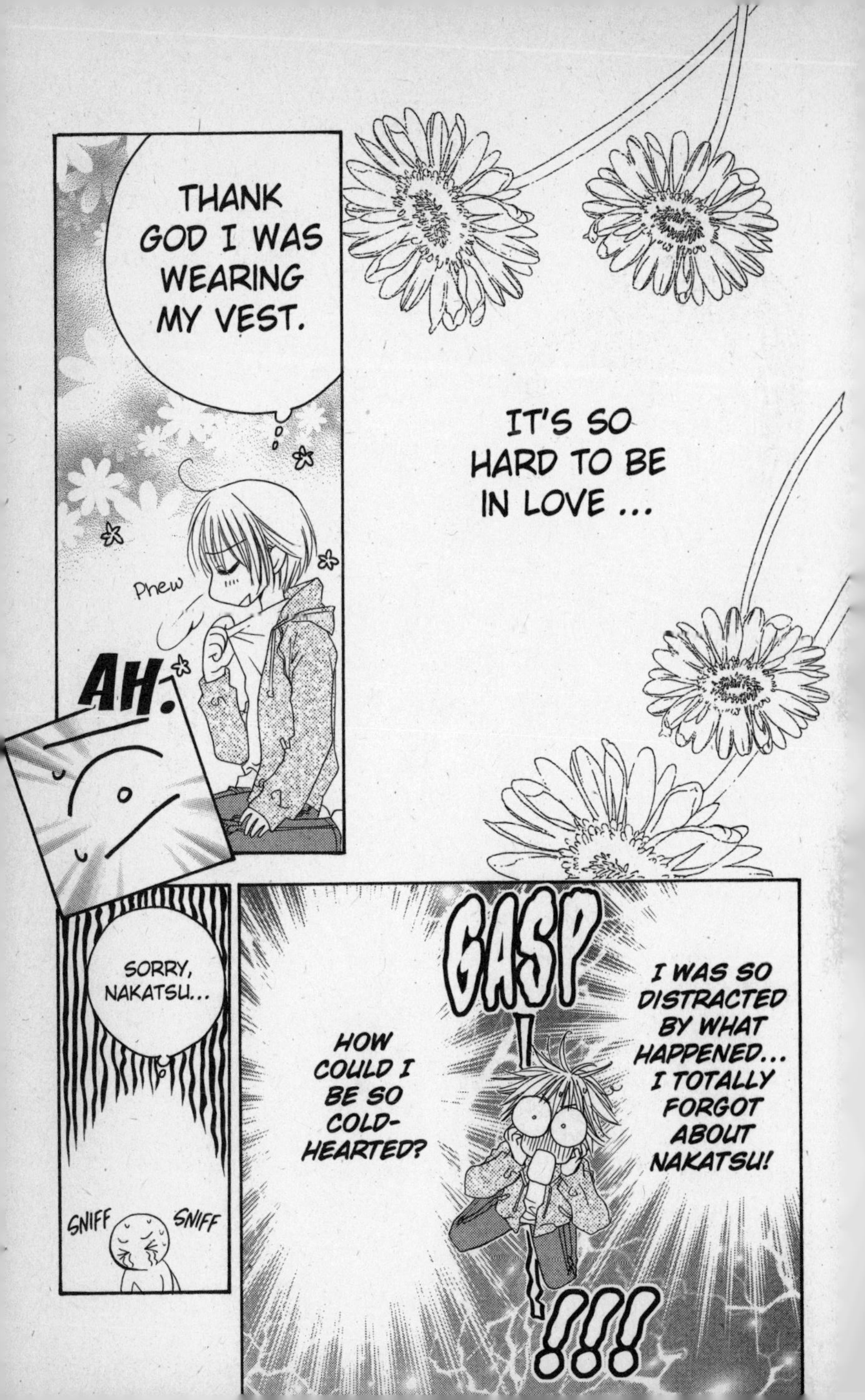
IT'S SO HARD TO BE IN LOVE ...
THANK GOD I WAS WEARING MY VEST.
Phew
AH.
GASP
I WAS SO DISTRACTED BY WHAT HAPPENED... I TOTALLY FORGOT ABOUT NAKATSU!
HOW COULD I BE SO COLD-HEARTED?
!!!
SORRY, NAKATSU...
SNIFF
SNIFF

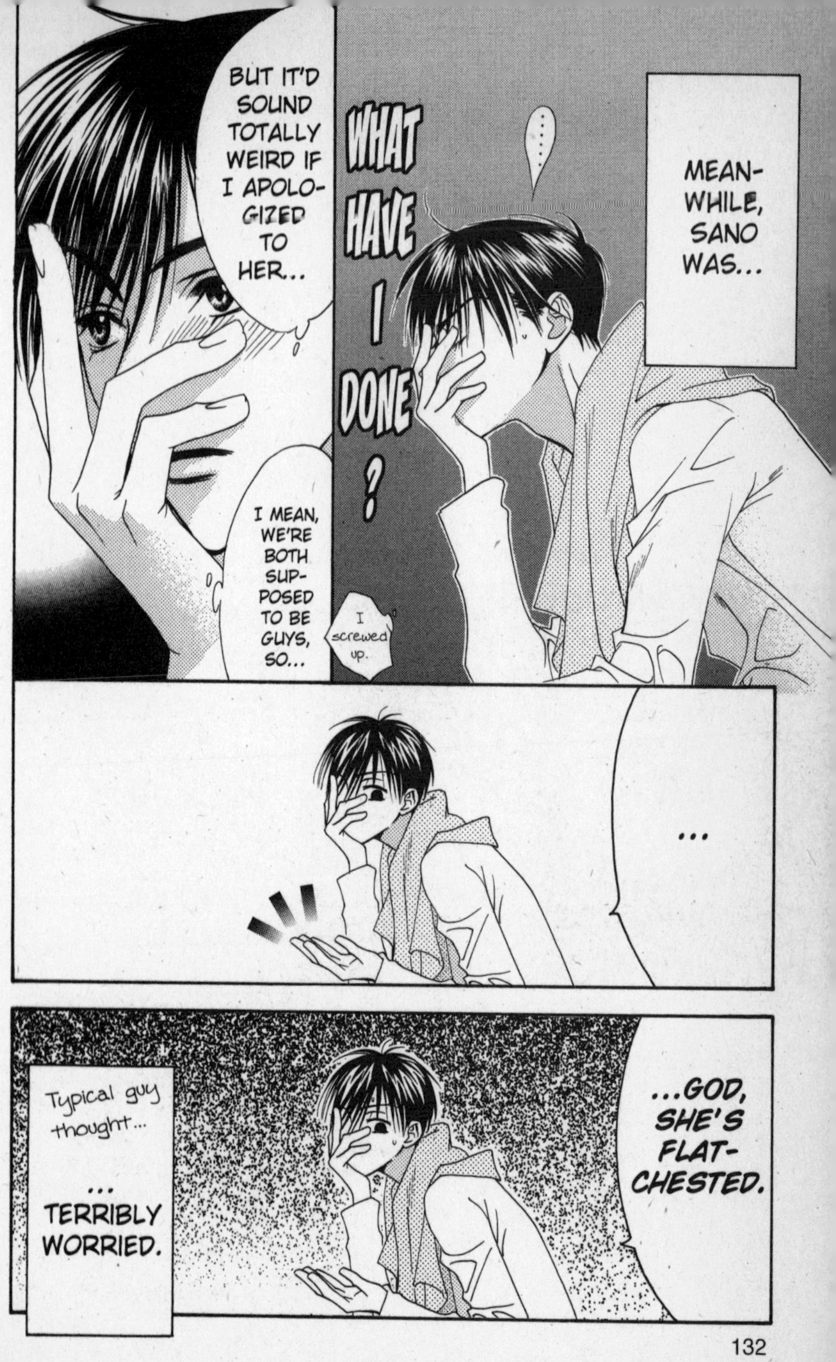
MEAN-WHILE, SANO WAS...
!
WHAT HAVE I DONE?
I screwed up.
BUT IT'D SOUND TOTALLY WEIRD IF I APOLOGIZED TO HER...
I MEAN, WE'RE BOTH SUPPOSED TO BE GUYS, SO...
...
...GOD, SHE'S FLAT-CHESTED.
Typical guy thought...
... TERRIBLY WORRIED.

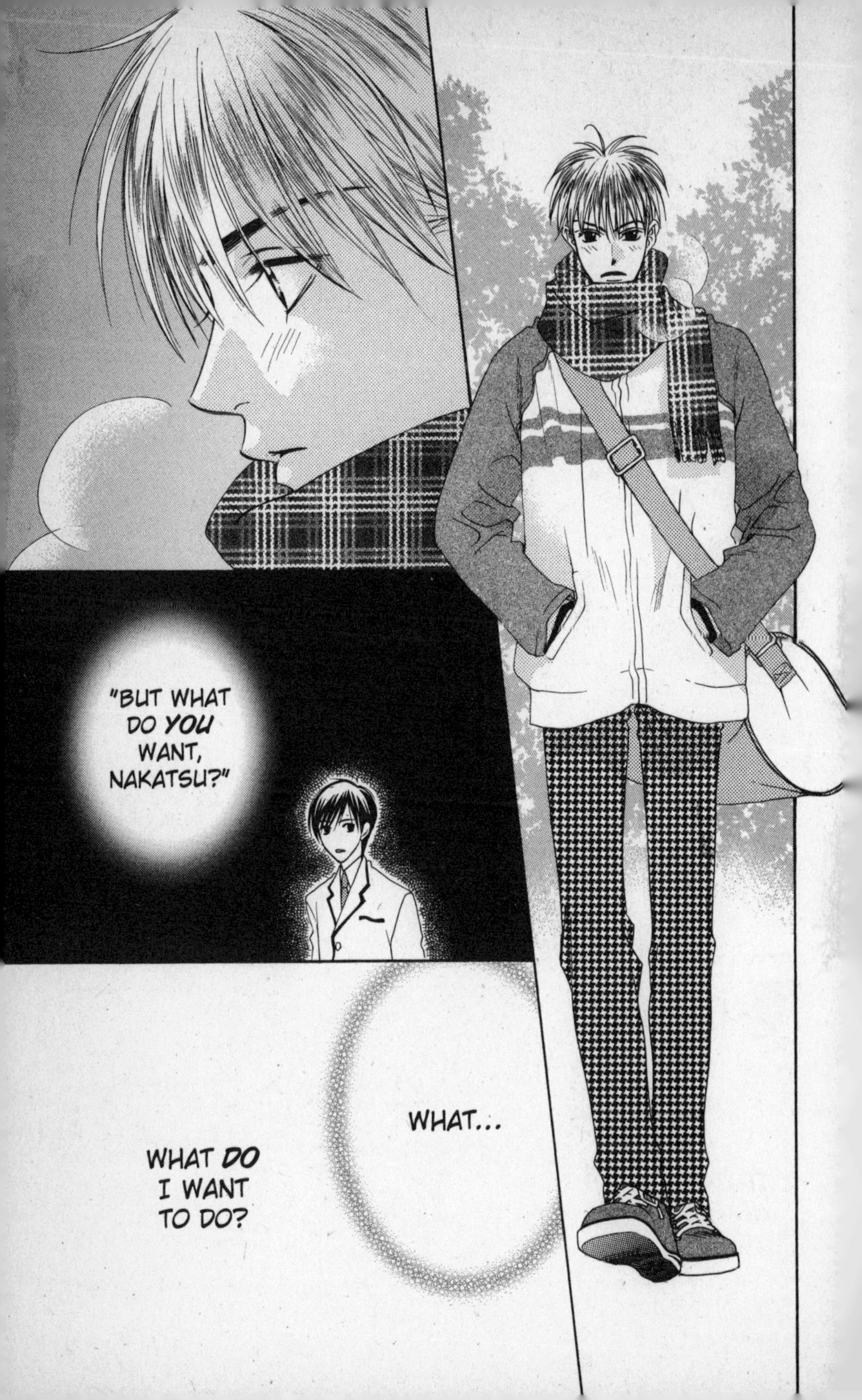
"BUT WHAT DO *YOU* WANT, NAKATSU?"
WHAT...
WHAT *DO* I WANT TO DO?

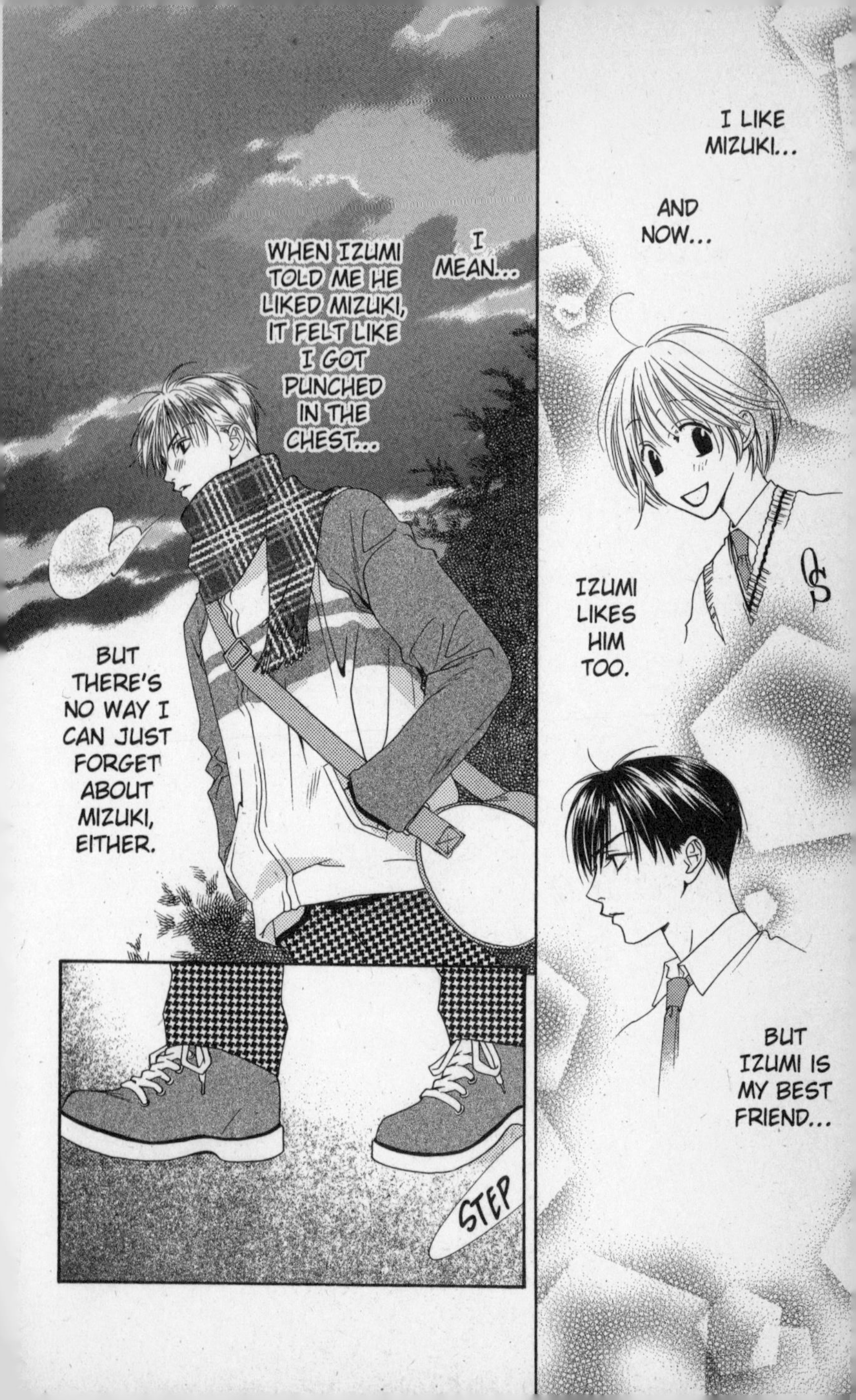
I LIKE MIZUKI...
AND NOW...
IZUMI LIKES HIM TOO.
BUT IZUMI IS MY BEST FRIEND...
I MEAN...
WHEN IZUMI TOLD ME HE LIKED MIZUKI, IT FELT LIKE I GOT PUNCHED IN THE CHEST...
BUT THERE'S NO WAY I CAN JUST FORGET ABOUT MIZUKI, EITHER.
STEP

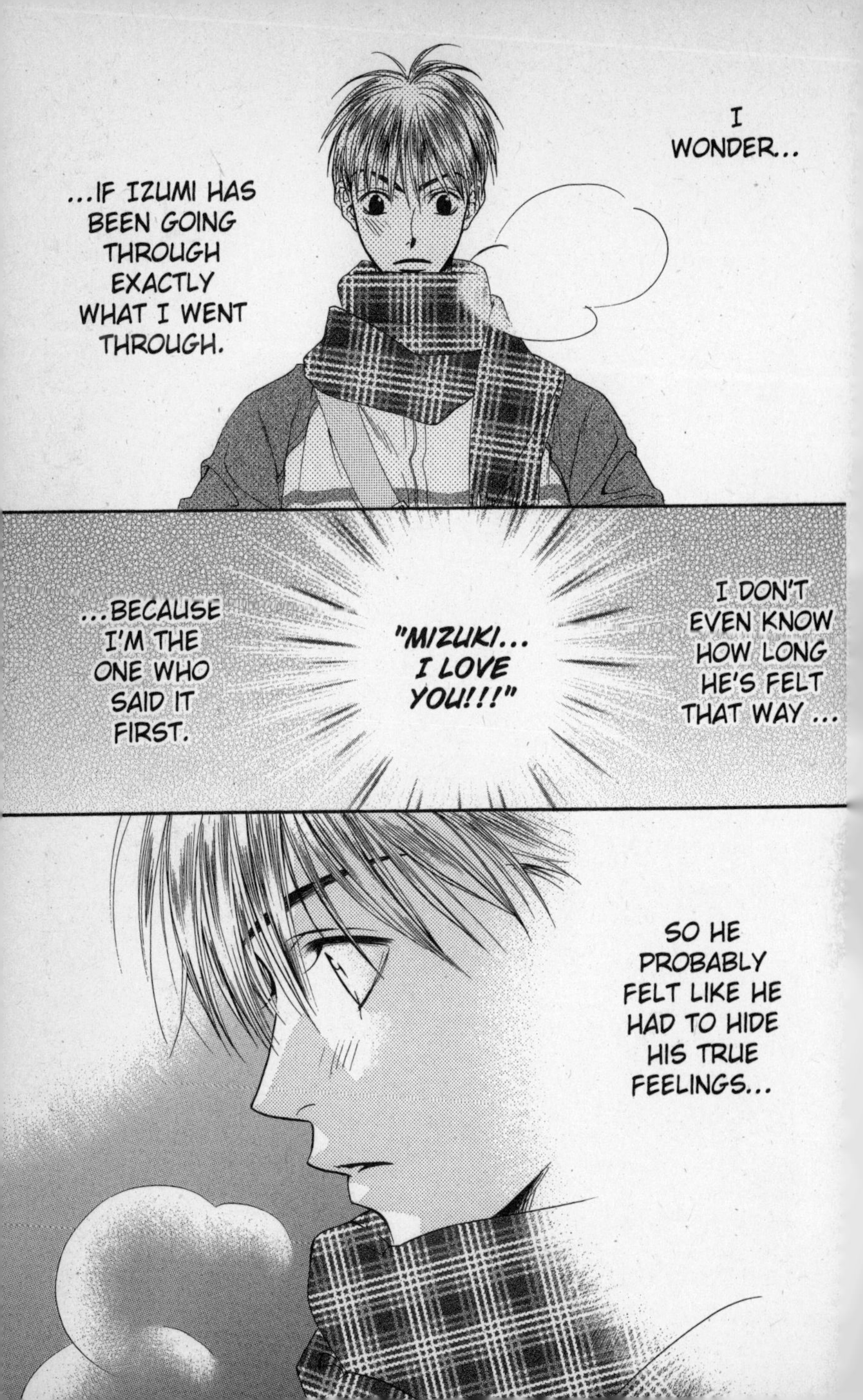
I WONDER...
...IF IZUMI HAS BEEN GOING THROUGH EXACTLY WHAT I WENT THROUGH.
I DON'T EVEN KNOW HOW LONG HE'S FELT THAT WAY...
"MIZUKI... I LOVE YOU!!!"
...BECAUSE I'M THE ONE WHO SAID IT FIRST.
SO HE PROBABLY FELT LIKE HE HAD TO HIDE HIS TRUE FEELINGS...

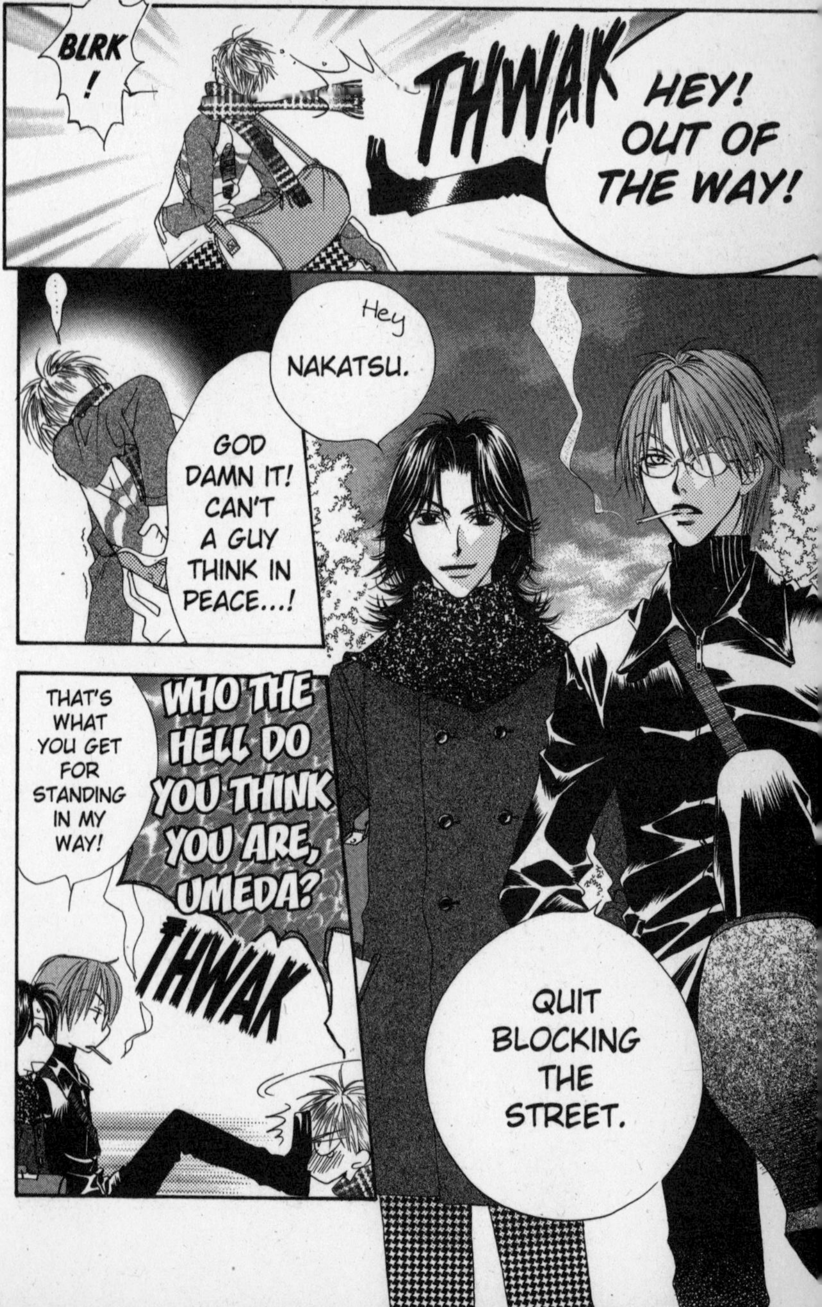
HEY! OUT OF THE WAY!
THWAK
BLRK !
Hey
NAKATSU.
QUIT BLOCKING THE STREET.
GOD DAMN IT! CAN'T A GUY THINK IN PEACE...!
WHO THE HELL DO YOU THINK YOU ARE, UMEDA?
THAT'S WHAT YOU GET FOR STANDING IN MY WAY!
THWAK

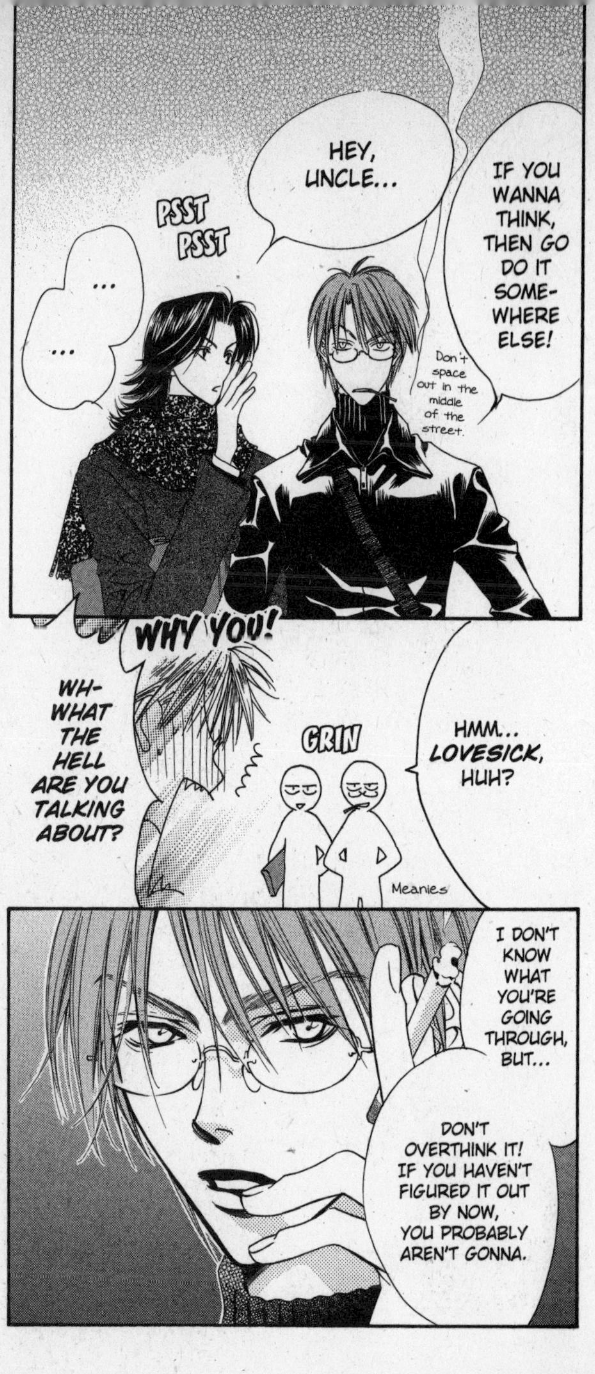
IF YOU WANNA THINK, THEN GO DO IT SOME-WHERE ELSE!
Don't space out in the middle of the street.
HEY, UNCLE...
PSST PSST
... ...
HMM... *LOVESICK*, HUH?
GRIN
WHY YOU!
WH-WHAT THE HELL ARE YOU TALKING ABOUT?
Meanies
I DON'T KNOW WHAT YOU'RE GOING THROUGH, BUT...
DON'T OVERTHINK IT! IF YOU HAVEN'T FIGURED IT OUT BY NOW, YOU PROBABLY AREN'T GONNA.

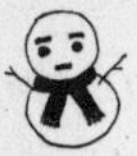

SNOWBALL FIGHT

It started snowing really hard right around the time I was working on Chapter 83 (or was it Chapter 82?), and when I looked out the window the next day, the whole neighborhood was covered in snow. "Ah, I wish I could have a snowball fight!" That's what I thought the moment I saw all that snow piled up. Seriously. But since my deadline was just a few days away, my assistants and I tried to focus on our work...but ten minutes later, we saw a neighborhood dog running around in the snow. The dog looked so happy that we couldn't help ourselves. "Let's go outside, everyone! We need a half-hour snow break!" We put on our coats, headed outside and started a huge snowball fight. We even made a snowman. We all agreed never to tell my editor about it. To this day, my editor still has absolutely no clue about what we did.

There's a huge parking lot next to the apartment where my office is. It's the perfect place.

The dog looked so happy in the snow, just like Yujiro. (We were happy too)

Actually, I guess I just gave away our secret.

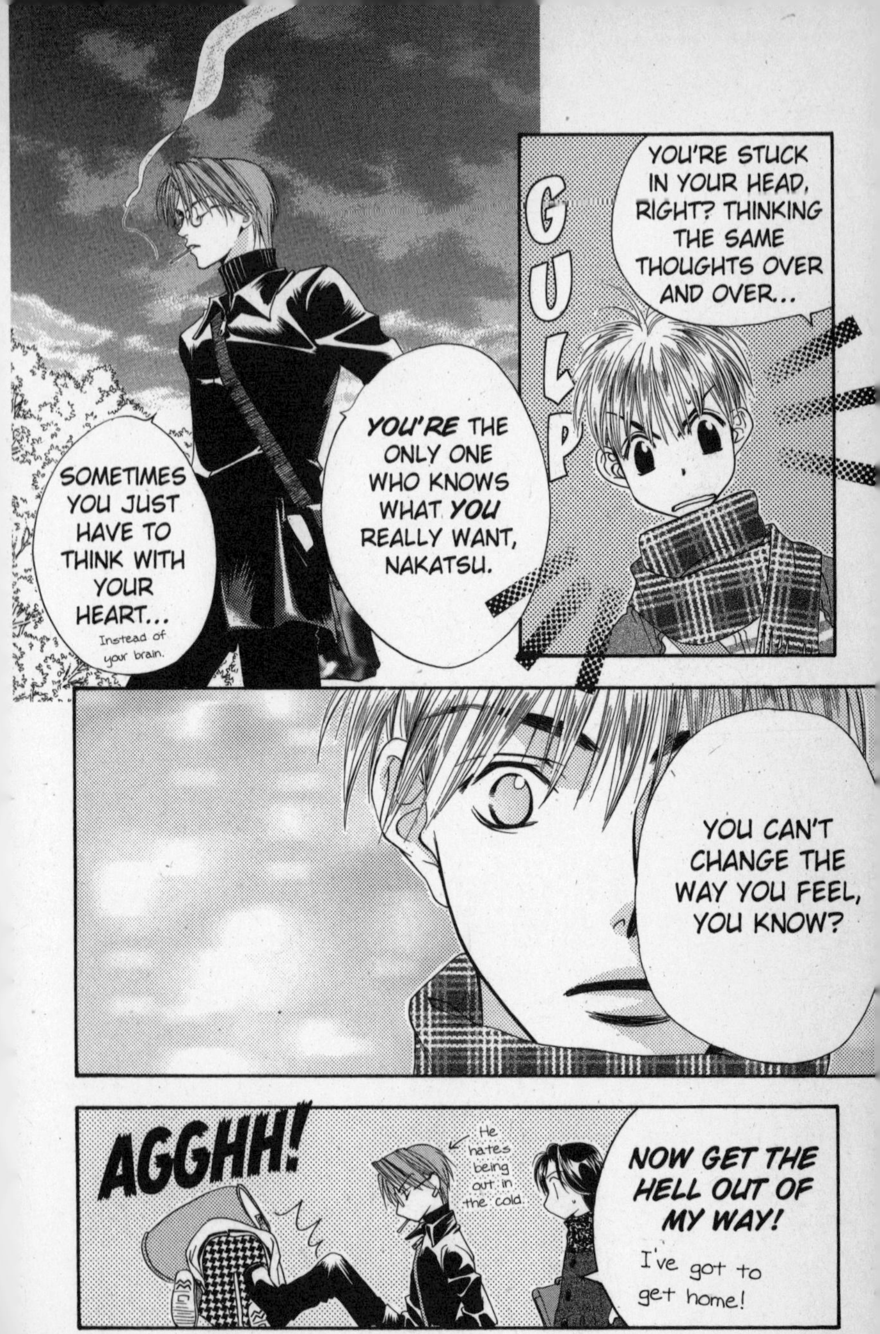
YOU'RE STUCK IN YOUR HEAD, RIGHT? THINKING THE SAME THOUGHTS OVER AND OVER...
GULP
YOU'RE THE ONLY ONE WHO KNOWS WHAT YOU REALLY WANT, NAKATSU.
SOMETIMES YOU JUST HAVE TO THINK WITH YOUR HEART...
Instead of your brain.
YOU CAN'T CHANGE THE WAY YOU FEEL, YOU KNOW?
NOW GET THE HELL OUT OF MY WAY!
I've got to get home!
He hates being out in the cold.
AGGHH!

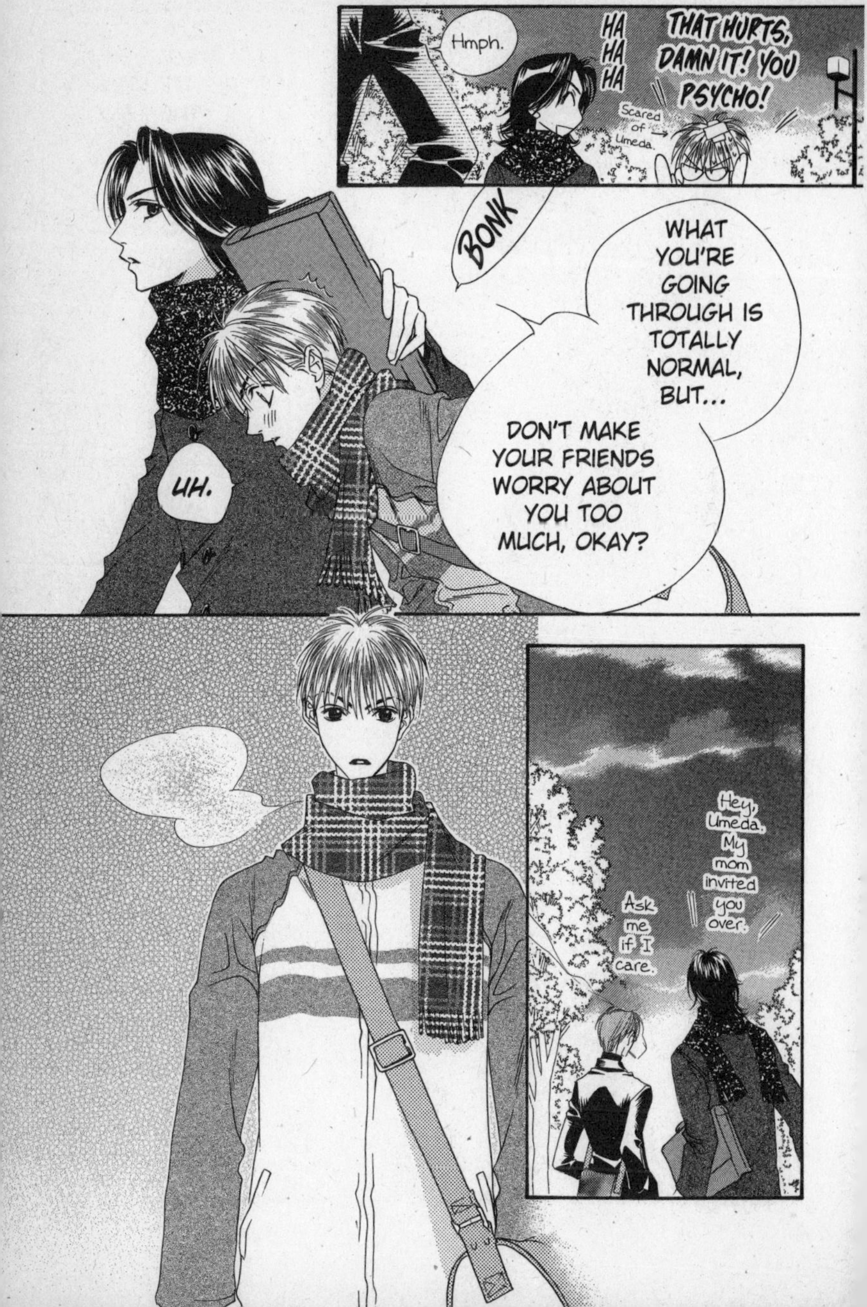
THAT HURTS, DAMN IT! YOU PSYCHO!
HA HA HA
Scared of → Umeda.
Hmph.
BONK
WHAT YOU'RE GOING THROUGH IS TOTALLY NORMAL, BUT...
DON'T MAKE YOUR FRIENDS WORRY ABOUT YOU TOO MUCH, OKAY?
UH.
Hey, Umeda. My mom invited you over.
Ask me if I care.

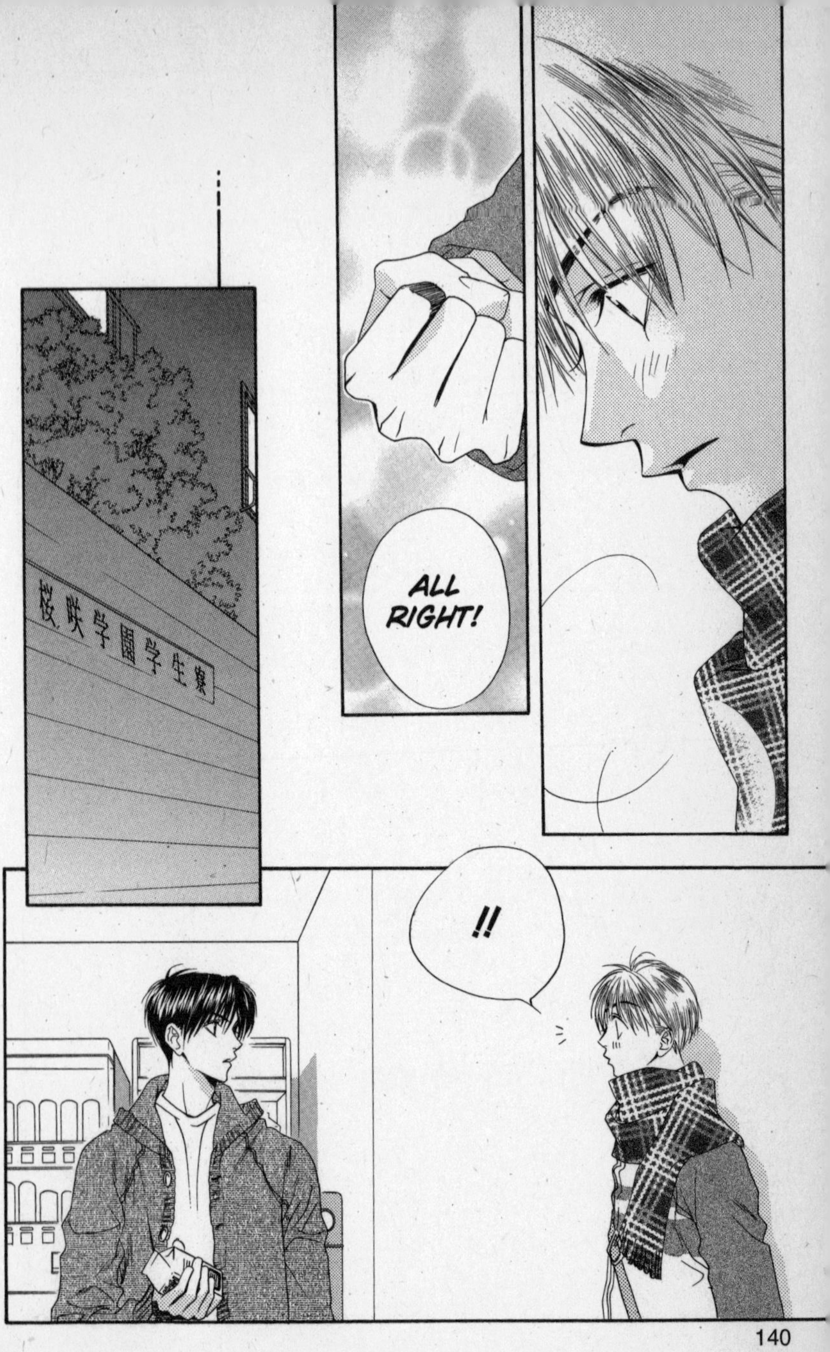
ALL RIGHT!
桜咲学園学生寮
!!

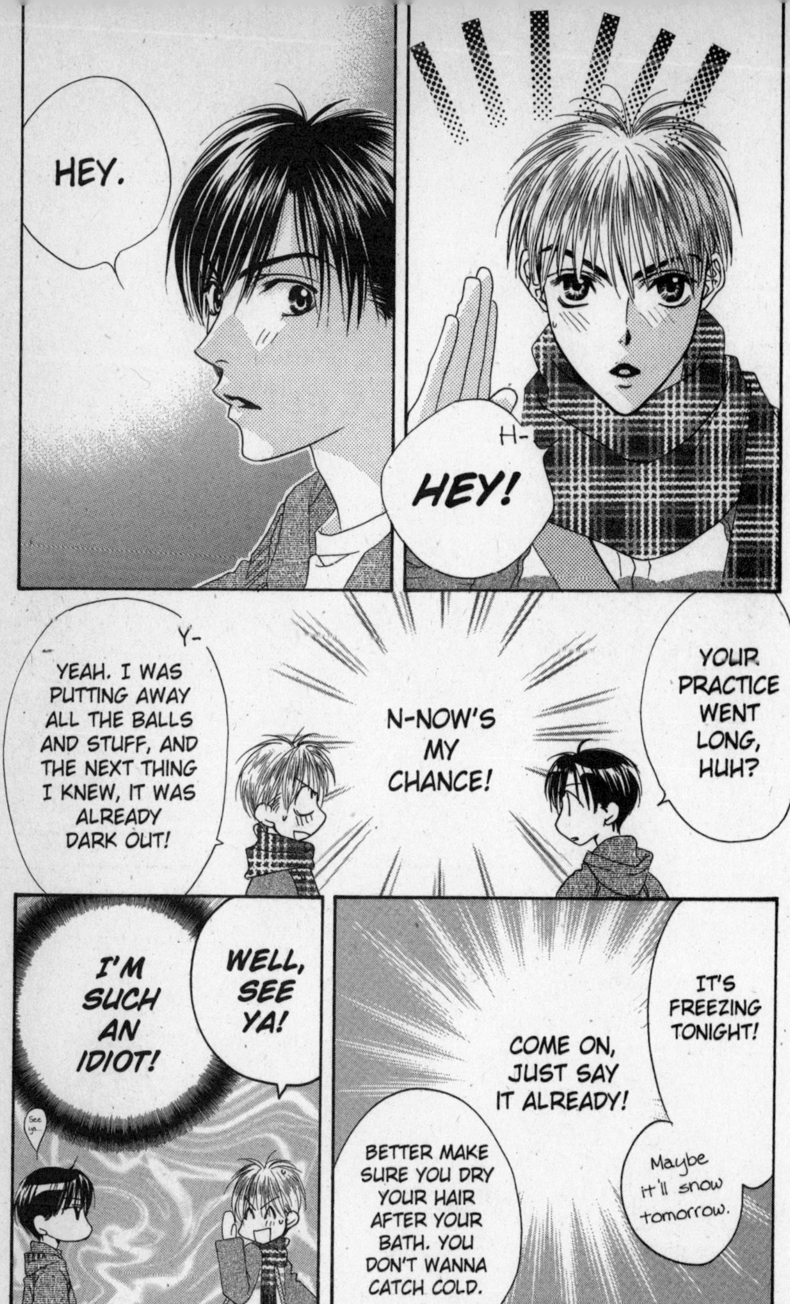
H-
HEY!
HEY.
YOUR PRACTICE WENT LONG, HUH?
N-NOW'S MY CHANCE!
Y- YEAH. I WAS PUTTING AWAY ALL THE BALLS AND STUFF, AND THE NEXT THING I KNEW, IT WAS ALREADY DARK OUT!
IT'S FREEZING TONIGHT!
COME ON, JUST SAY IT ALREADY!
Maybe it'll snow tomorrow.
BETTER MAKE SURE YOU DRY YOUR HAIR AFTER YOUR BATH. YOU DON'T WANNA CATCH COLD.
WELL, SEE YA!
I'M SUCH AN IDIOT!
See ya...

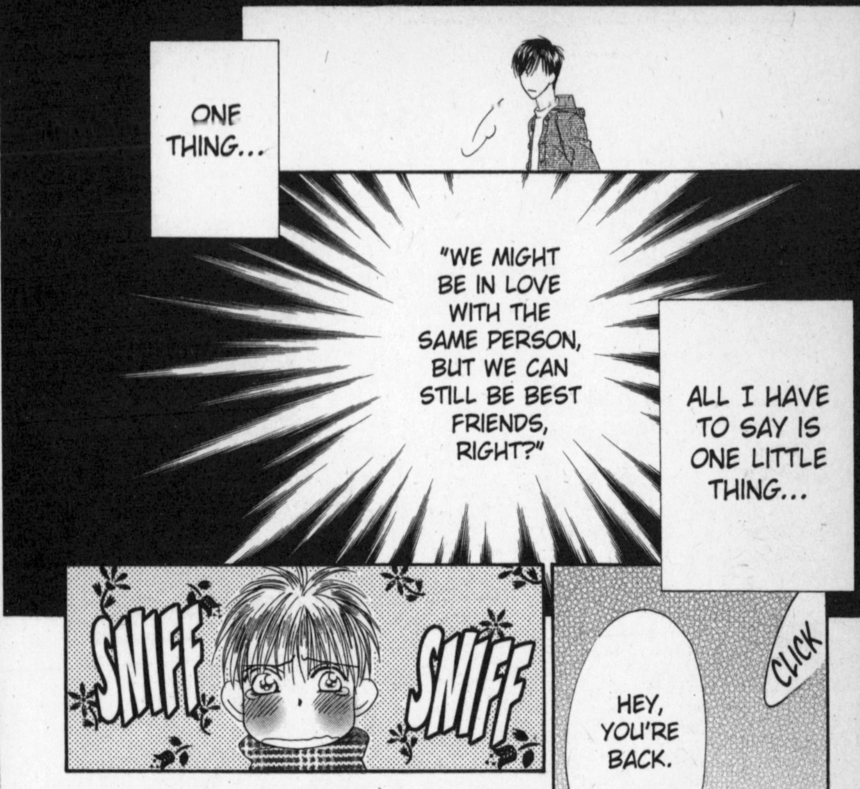
ONE THING...
ALL I HAVE TO SAY IS ONE LITTLE THING...
"WE MIGHT BE IN LOVE WITH THE SAME PERSON, BUT WE CAN STILL BE BEST FRIENDS, RIGHT?"
CLICK
HEY, YOU'RE BACK.
SNIFF
SNIFF
WAHHHH
I'M SUCH A WUSS!
What's wrong?

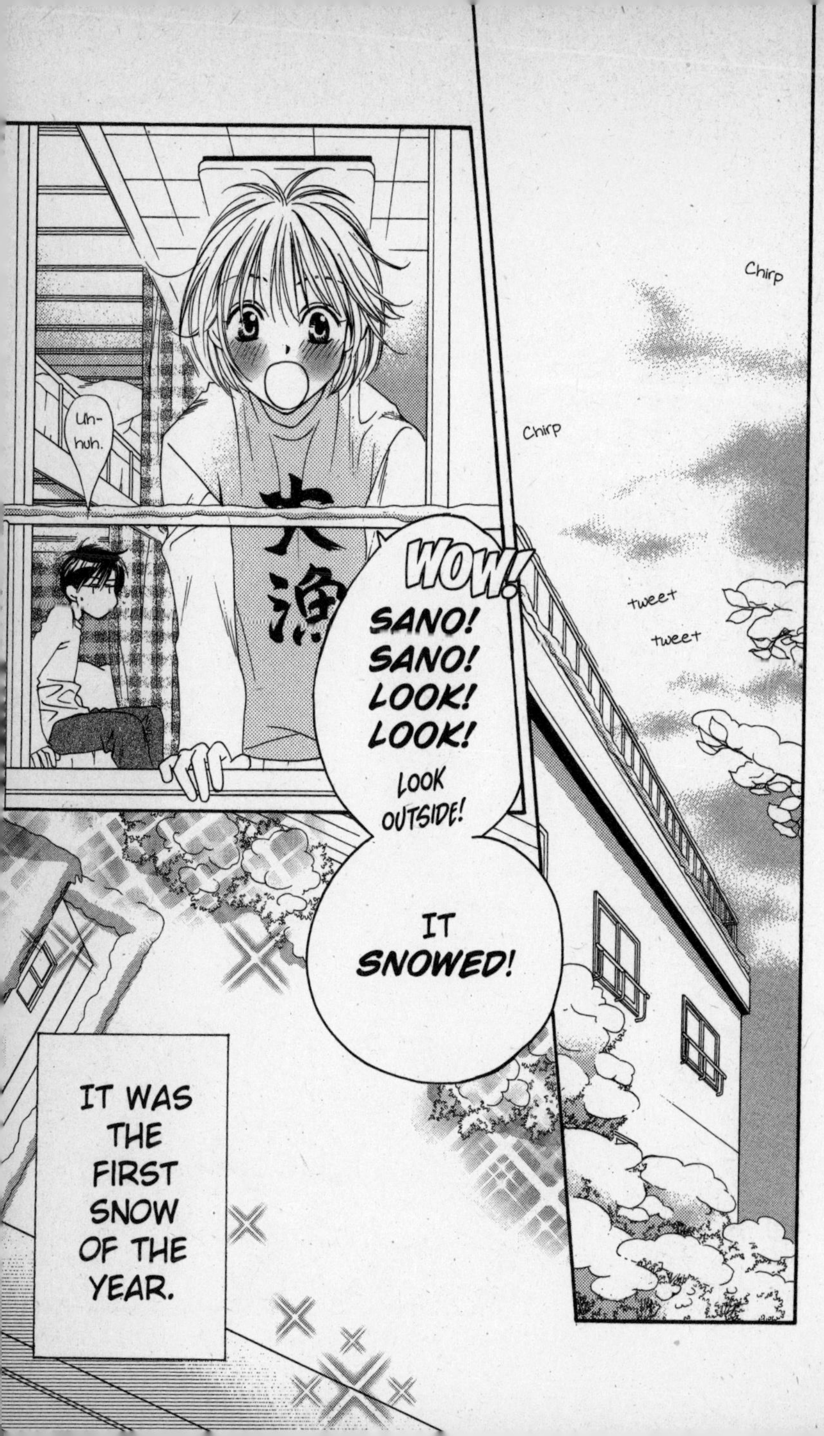

Chirp
Chirp
tweet
tweet
WOW! SANO! SANO! LOOK! LOOK! LOOK OUTSIDE!
IT SNOWED!
Uh-huh.
IT WAS THE FIRST SNOW OF THE YEAR.

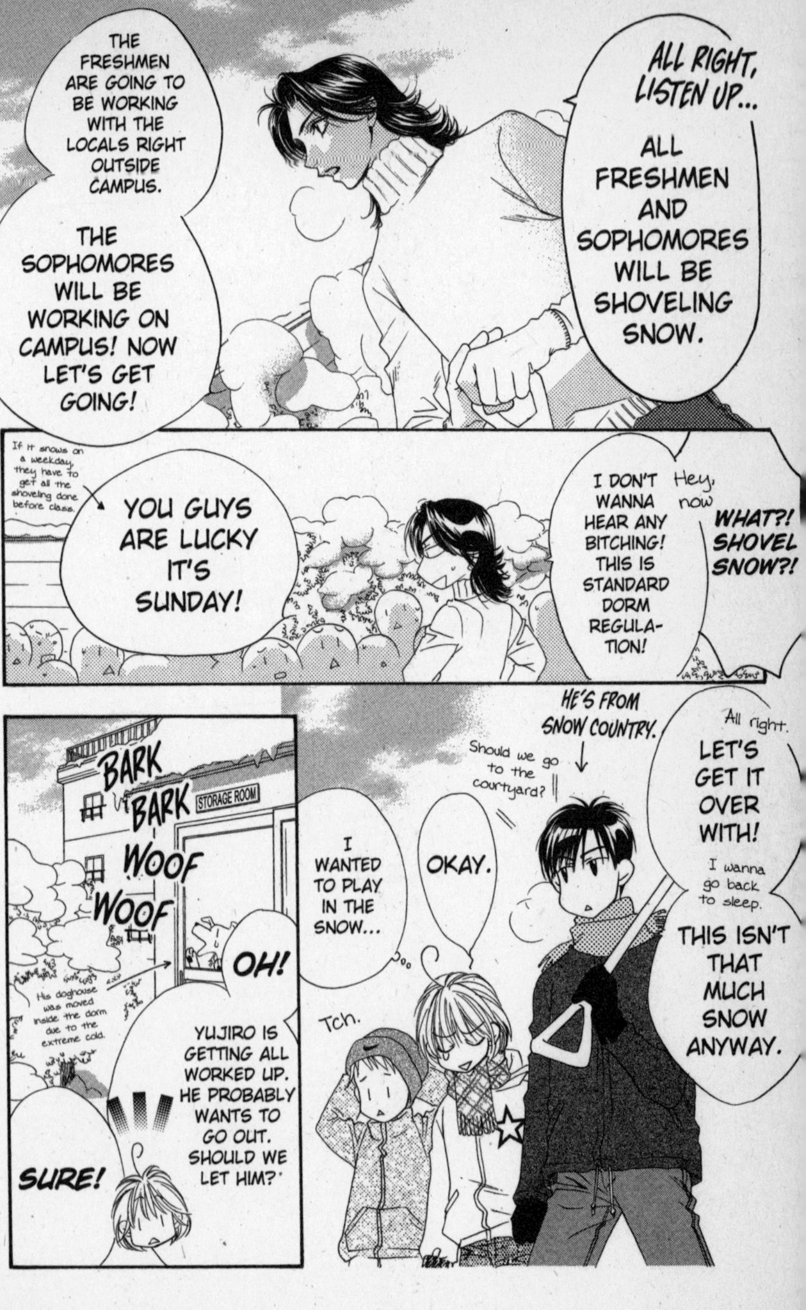
ALL RIGHT, LISTEN UP...
ALL FRESHMEN AND SOPHOMORES WILL BE SHOVELING SNOW.
THE FRESHMEN ARE GOING TO BE WORKING WITH THE LOCALS RIGHT OUTSIDE CAMPUS.
THE SOPHOMORES WILL BE WORKING ON CAMPUS! NOW LET'S GET GOING!
WHAT?! SHOVEL SNOW?!
Hey, now
I DON'T WANNA HEAR ANY BITCHING! THIS IS STANDARD DORM REGULA-TION!
YOU GUYS ARE LUCKY IT'S SUNDAY!
If it snows on a weekday, they have to get all the shoveling done before class.
All right.
LET'S GET IT OVER WITH!
HE'S FROM SNOW COUNTRY.
I wanna go back to sleep.
THIS ISN'T THAT MUCH SNOW ANYWAY.
Should we go to the courtyard?
OKAY.
I WANTED TO PLAY IN THE SNOW...
Tch.
BARK
BARK
STORAGE ROOM
WOOF
WOOF
OH!
YUJIRO IS GETTING ALL WORKED UP. HE PROBABLY WANTS TO GO OUT. SHOULD WE LET HIM?
His doghouse was moved inside the dorm due to the extreme cold.
SURE!

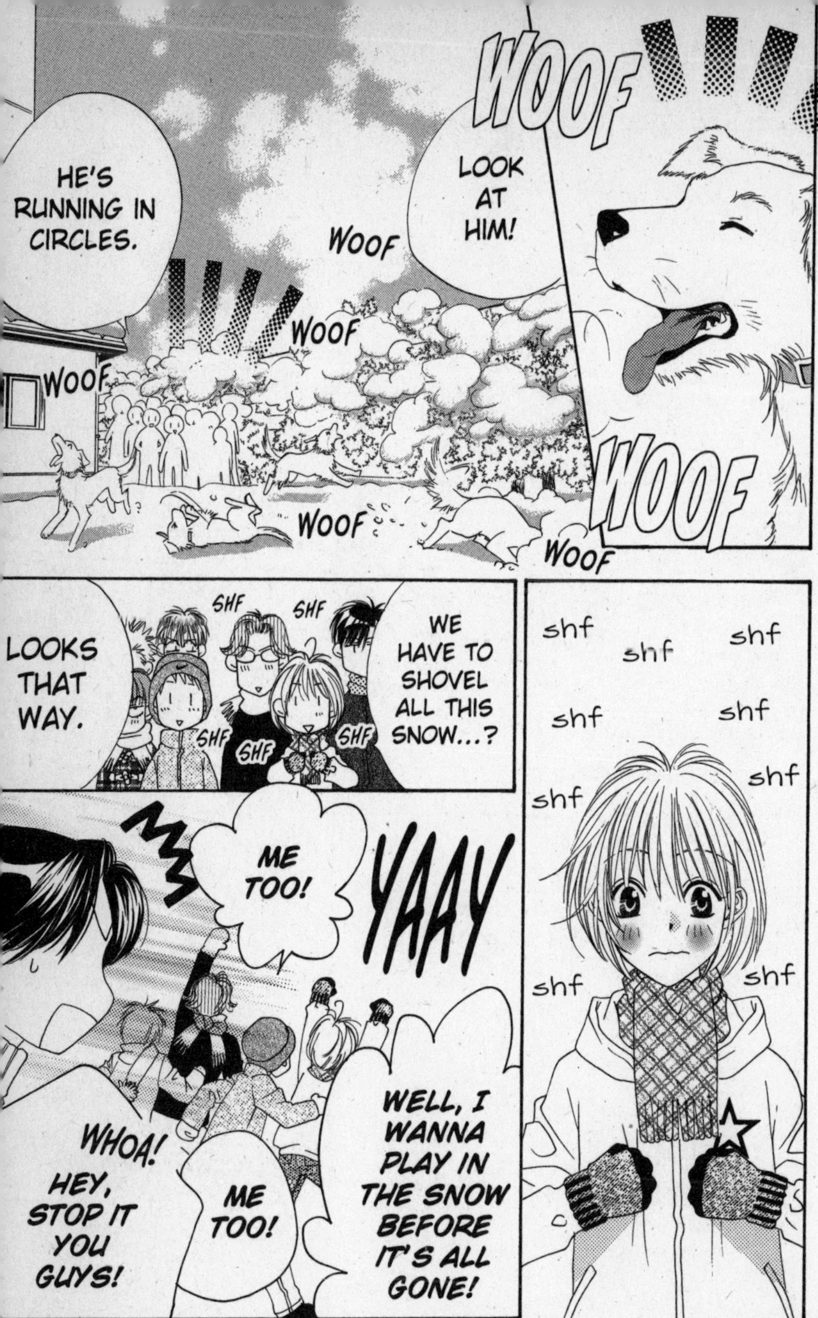
WOOF
WOOF
LOOK AT HIM!
WOOF
HE'S RUNNING IN CIRCLES.
WOOF
WOOF
WOOF
WOOF
shf
shf
shf
shf
shf
shf
shf
shf
shf
WE HAVE TO SHOVEL ALL THIS SNOW...?
SHF
SHF
SHF
SHF
SHF
LOOKS THAT WAY.
YAAY
ME TOO!
WELL, I WANNA PLAY IN THE SNOW BEFORE IT'S ALL GONE!
ME TOO!
WHOA!
HEY, STOP IT YOU GUYS!

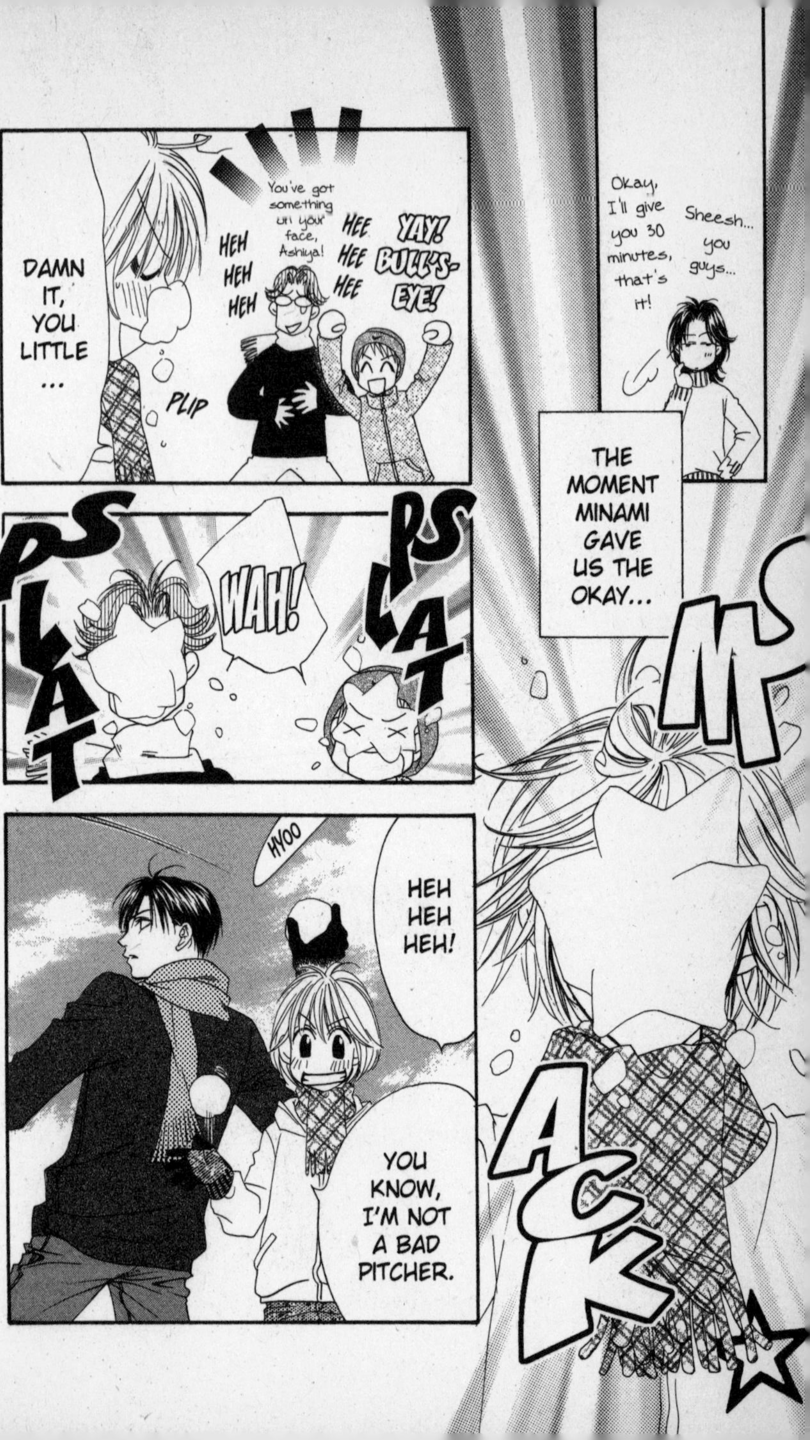

Okay, I'll give you 30 minutes, that's it!
Sheesh... you guys...
THE MOMENT MINAMI GAVE US THE OKAY...
M
ACK
DAMN IT, YOU LITTLE ...
PLIP
You've got something on your face, Ashiya!
HEH HEH HEH
HEE HEE HEE
YAY! BULL'S-EYE!
PSPLAT
WAH!
PSPLAT
KYOO
HEH HEH HEH!
YOU KNOW, I'M NOT A BAD PITCHER.

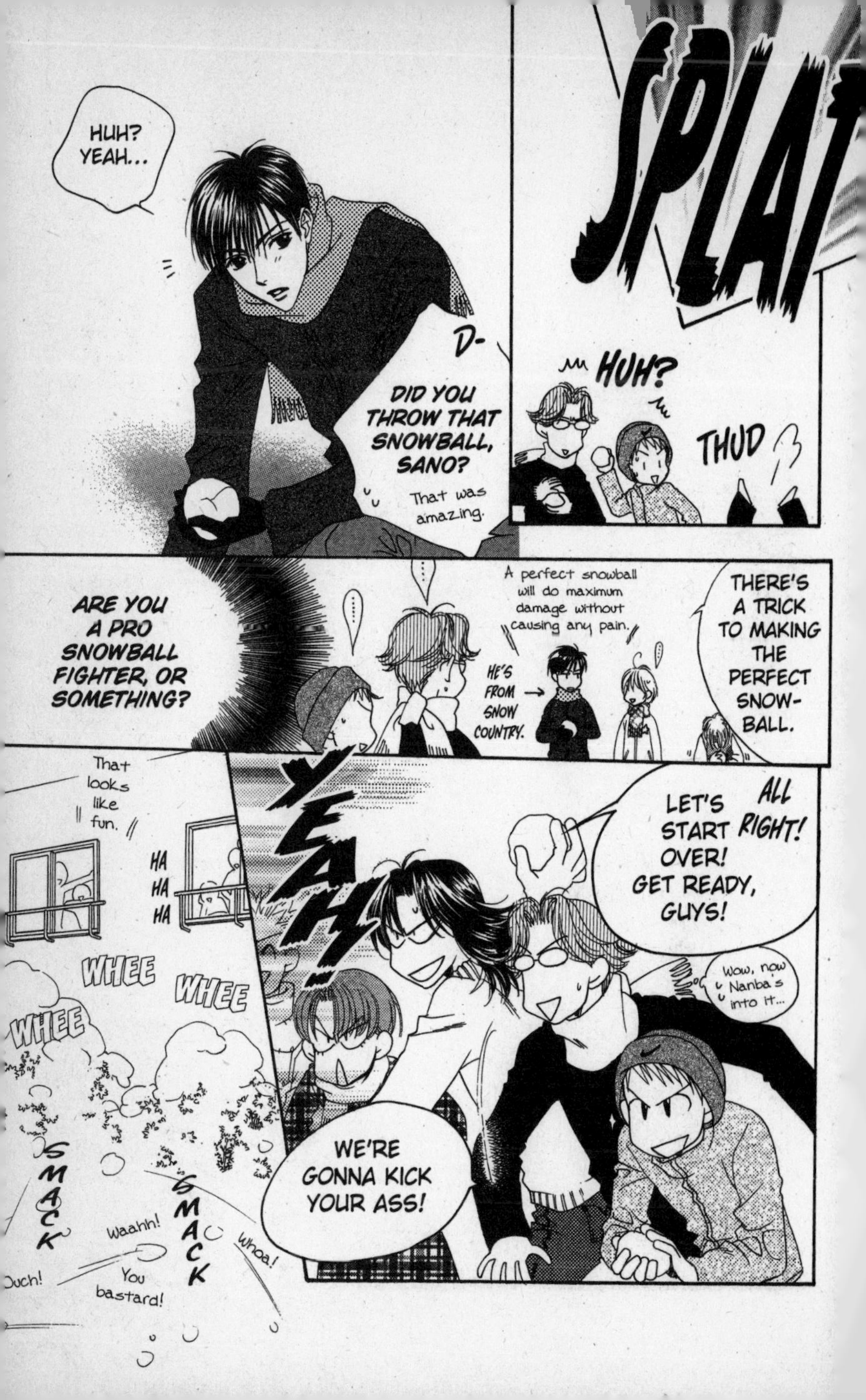
SPLAT
HUH?
THUD
D-
DID YOU THROW THAT SNOWBALL, SANO?
That was amazing.
HUH? YEAH...
THERE'S A TRICK TO MAKING THE PERFECT SNOWBALL.
A perfect snowball will do maximum damage without causing any pain.
HE'S FROM SNOW COUNTRY.
ARE YOU A PRO SNOWBALL FIGHTER, OR SOMETHING?
ALL RIGHT!
LET'S START OVER! GET READY, GUYS!
Wow, now Nanba's into it...
YEAH!
WE'RE GONNA KICK YOUR ASS!
That looks like fun.
HA HA HA
WHEE
WHEE
WHEE
SMACK
SMACK
Whoa!
Waahh!
You bastard!
Ouch!

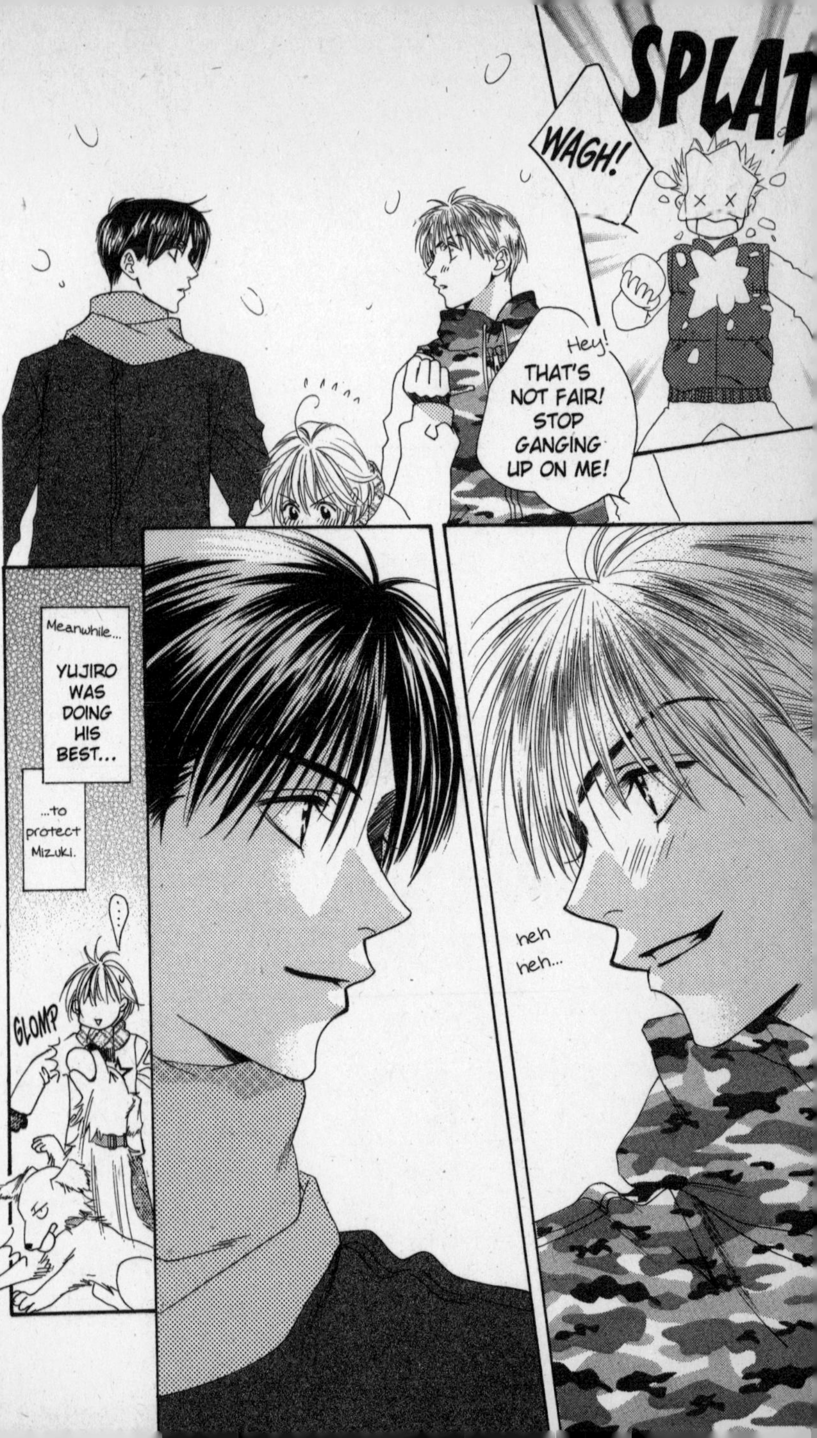
SPLAT
WAGH!
Hey!
THAT'S NOT FAIR! STOP GANGING UP ON ME!
heh heh...
Meanwhile...
YUJIRO WAS DOING HIS BEST...
...to protect Mizuki.
...
GLOMP

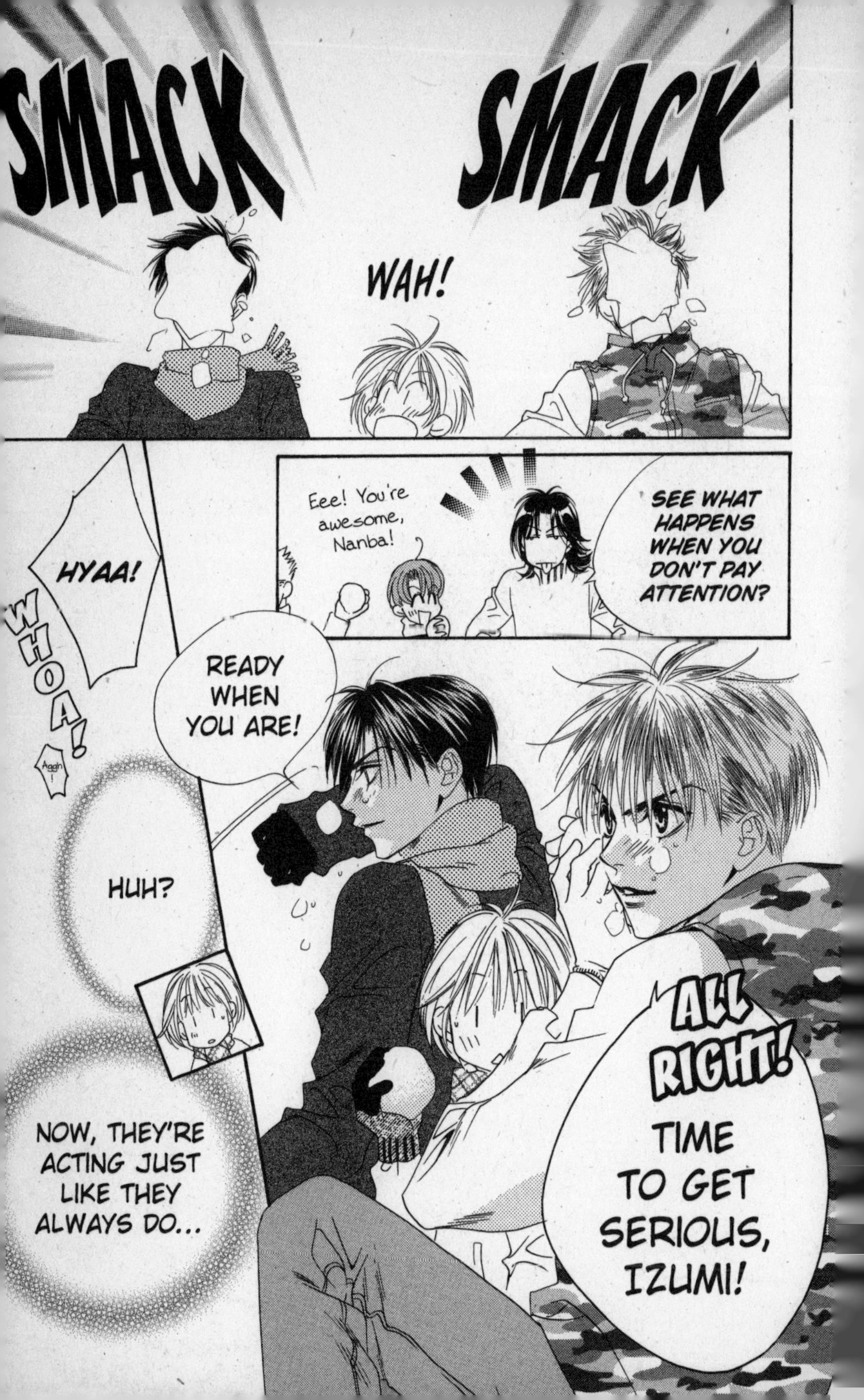
SMACK
WAH!
SMACK
SEE WHAT HAPPENS WHEN YOU DON'T PAY ATTENTION?
Eee! You're awesome, Nanba!
HYAA!
WHOA!
Aggh!
ALL RIGHT!
TIME TO GET SERIOUS, IZUMI!
READY WHEN YOU ARE!
HUH?
NOW, THEY'RE ACTING JUST LIKE THEY ALWAYS DO...

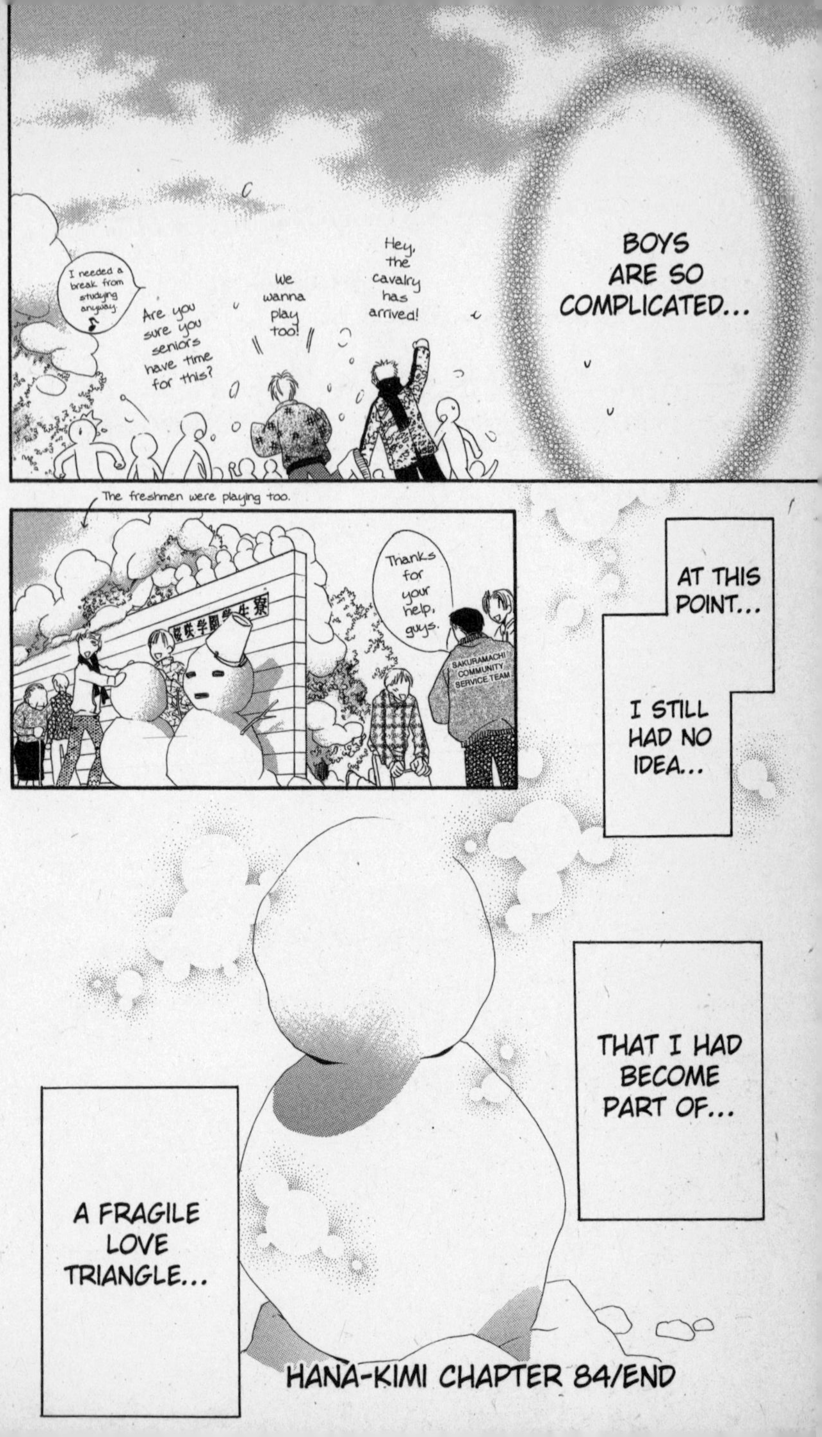
BOYS ARE SO COMPLICATED...
Hey, the cavalry has arrived!
We wanna play too!
Are you sure you seniors have time for this?
I needed a break from studying anyway.
AT THIS POINT...
I STILL HAD NO IDEA...
Thanks for your help, guys.
SAKURAMACHI COMMUNITY SERVICE TEAM
The freshmen were playing too.
THAT I HAD BECOME PART OF...
A FRAGILE LOVE TRIANGLE...
HANA-KIMI CHAPTER 84/END

Hana-Kimi

For You in Full Blossom

CHAPTER 85

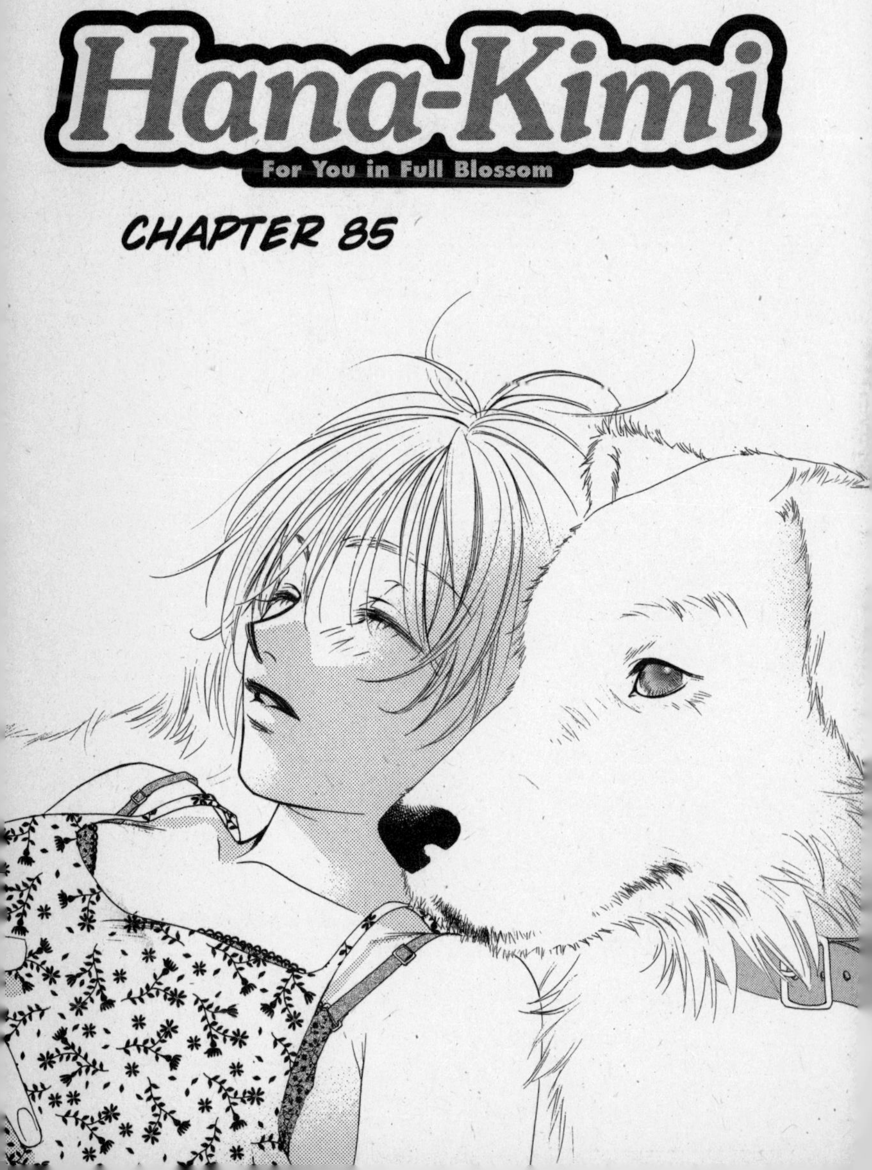

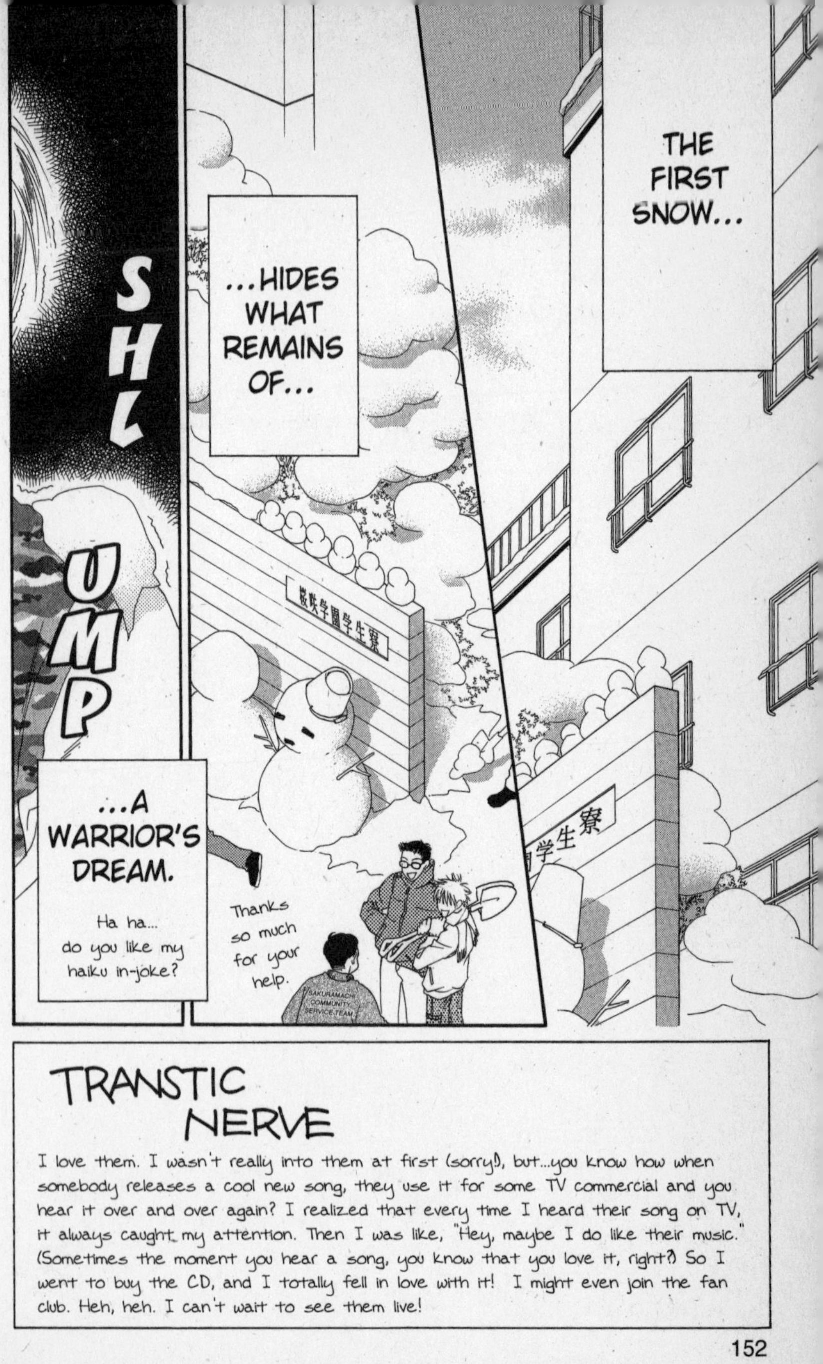
THE FIRST SNOW...
...HIDES WHAT REMAINS OF...
桜咲学園学生寮
学生寮
Thanks so much for your help.
SAKURAMACHI COMMUNITY SERVICE TEAM
SHLUMP
...A WARRIOR'S DREAM.
Ha ha... do you like my haiku in-joke?

TRANSTIC NERVE

I love them. I wasn't really into them at first (sorry!), but...you know how when somebody releases a cool new song, they use it for some TV commercial and you hear it over and over again? I realized that every time I heard their song on TV, it always caught my attention. Then I was like, "Hey, maybe I do like their music." (Sometimes the moment you hear a song, you know that you love it, right?) So I went to buy the CD, and I totally fell in love with it! I might even join the fan club. Heh, heh. I can't wait to see them live!

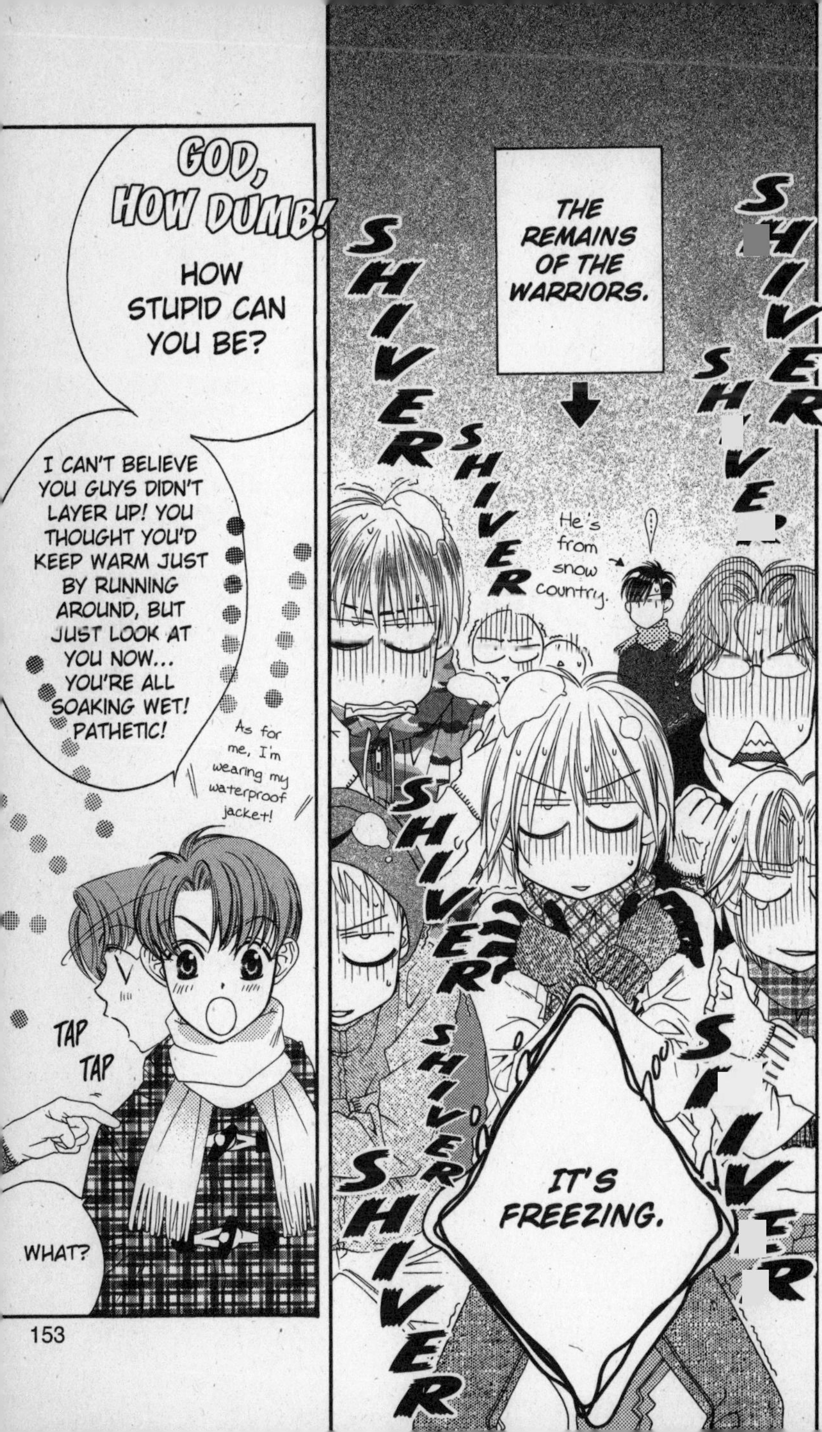
THE REMAINS OF THE WARRIORS.
SHIVER
SHIVER
SHIVER
SHIVER
He's from snow country.
SHIVER
SHIVER
SHIVER
SHIVER
IT'S FREEZING.
GOD, HOW DUMB!
HOW STUPID CAN YOU BE?
I CAN'T BELIEVE YOU GUYS DIDN'T LAYER UP! YOU THOUGHT YOU'D KEEP WARM JUST BY RUNNING AROUND, BUT JUST LOOK AT YOU NOW... YOU'RE ALL SOAKING WET! PATHETIC!
As for me, I'm wearing my waterproof jacket!
TAP TAP
WHAT?

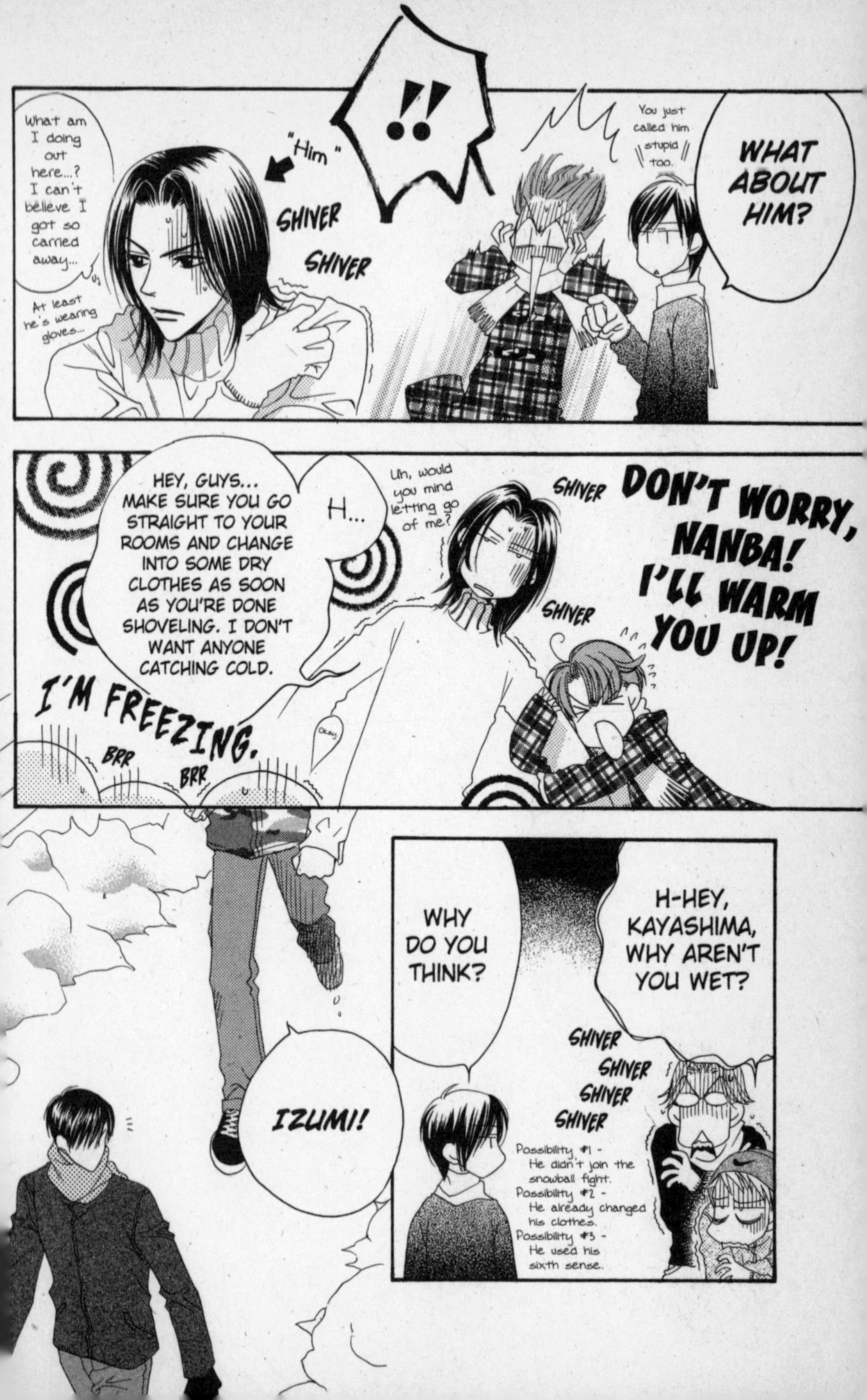
WHAT ABOUT HIM?
You just called him stupid too.
!!
"Him"
SHIVER
SHIVER
What am I doing out here...? I can't believe I got so carried away...
At least he's wearing gloves...
DON'T WORRY, NANBA! I'LL WARM YOU UP!
SHIVER
SHIVER
Uh, would you mind letting go of me?
H...
HEY, GUYS... MAKE SURE YOU GO STRAIGHT TO YOUR ROOMS AND CHANGE INTO SOME DRY CLOTHES AS SOON AS YOU'RE DONE SHOVELING. I DON'T WANT ANYONE CATCHING COLD.
I'M FREEZING.
Okay.
BRR
BRR
H-HEY, KAYASHIMA, WHY AREN'T YOU WET?
WHY DO YOU THINK?
SHIVER
SHIVER
SHIVER
SHIVER
Possibility #1 - He didn't join the snowball fight.
Possibility #2 - He already changed his clothes.
Possibility #3 - He used his sixth sense.
IZUMI!

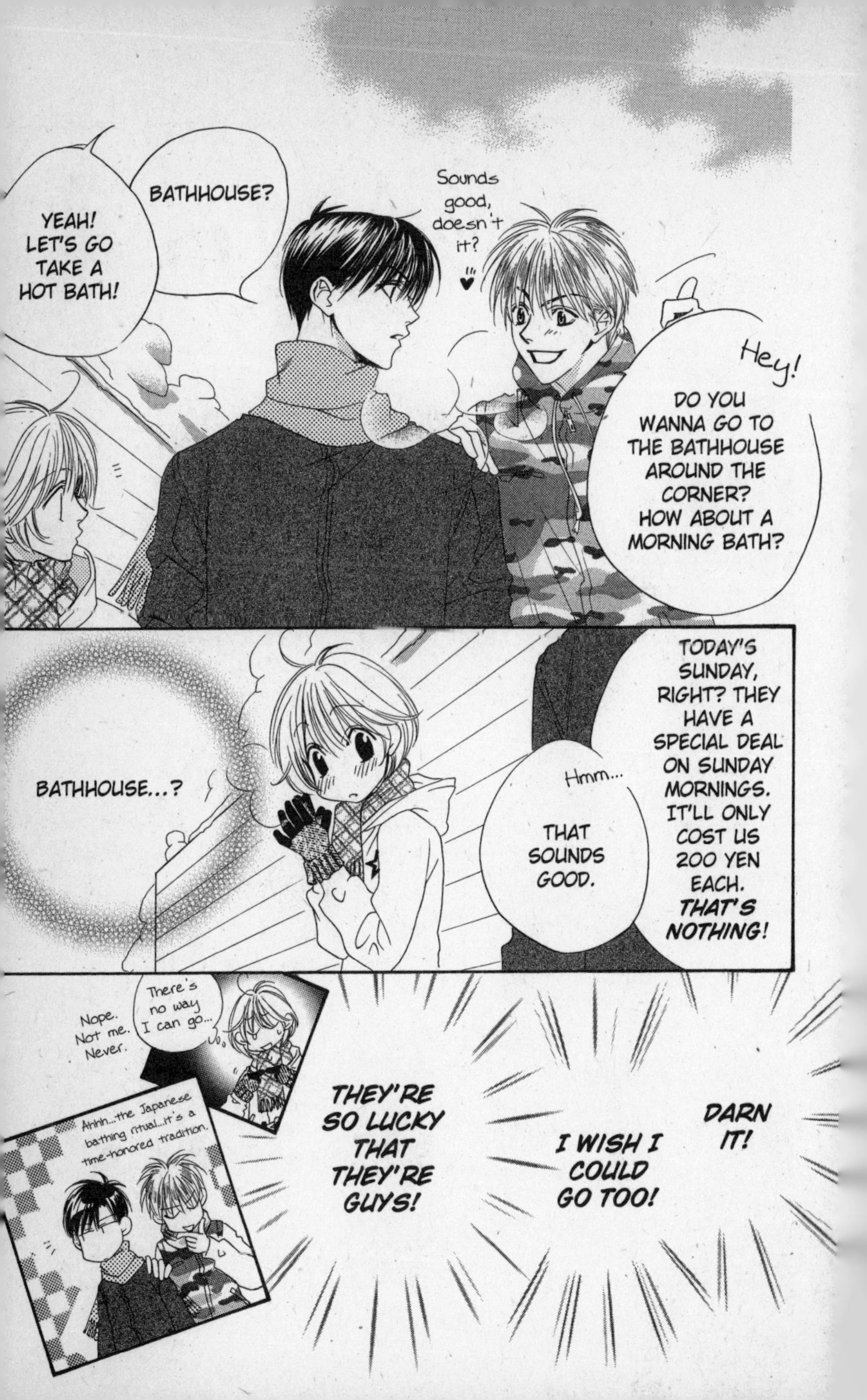
Hey! DO YOU WANNA GO TO THE BATHHOUSE AROUND THE CORNER? HOW ABOUT A MORNING BATH?
Sounds good, doesn't it?
BATHHOUSE?
YEAH! LET'S GO TAKE A HOT BATH!
TODAY'S SUNDAY, RIGHT? THEY HAVE A SPECIAL DEAL ON SUNDAY MORNINGS. IT'LL ONLY COST US 200 YEN EACH. THAT'S NOTHING!
Hmm... THAT SOUNDS GOOD.
BATHHOUSE...?
DARN IT!
I WISH I COULD GO TOO!
THEY'RE SO LUCKY THAT THEY'RE GUYS!
There's no way I can go...
Nope. Not me. Never.
Ahhh...the Japanese bathing ritual...it's a time-honored tradition.

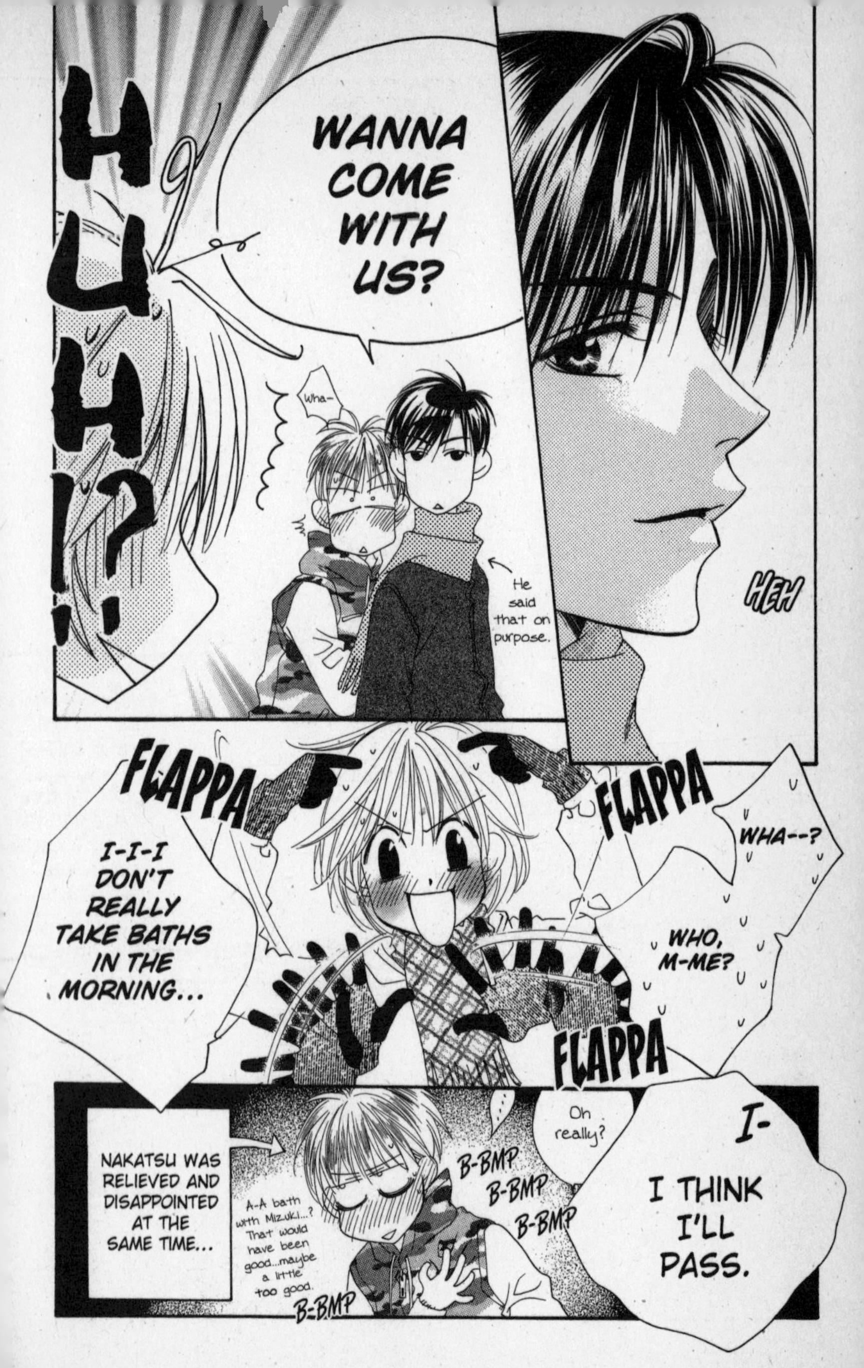
HEH
WANNA COME WITH US?
HUH!?
Wha-
He said that on purpose.
FLAPPA
WHA--?
WHO, M-ME?
FLAPPA
I-I-I DON'T REALLY TAKE BATHS IN THE MORNING...
FLAPPA
I- I THINK I'LL PASS.
Oh really?
B-BMP
B-BMP
B-BMP
A-A bath with Mizuki...? That would have been good...maybe a little too good.
NAKATSU WAS RELIEVED AND DISAPPOINTED AT THE SAME TIME...
B-BMP

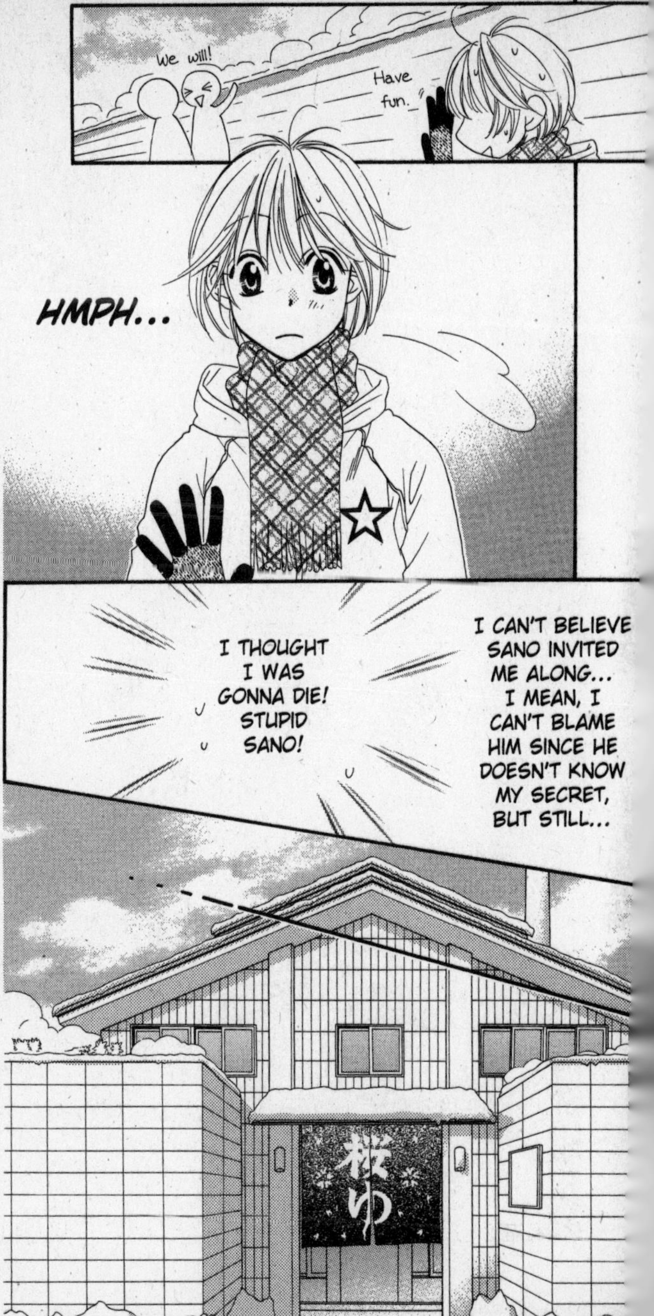
Have fun.
We will!
HMPH...
I CAN'T BELIEVE SANO INVITED ME ALONG... I MEAN, I CAN'T BLAME HIM SINCE HE DOESN'T KNOW MY SECRET, BUT STILL...
I THOUGHT I WAS GONNA DIE! STUPID SANO!

「See you」

La, la, la... This is the last quarter page for this volume. I want to thank all of you so much for your support! I get filled with positive energy whenever I read your letters and e-mails! A lot of times people write, "I'm not sure you'll actually read my letter..." but don't worry! I read all of them! See you in book 16! ～♪

--Hisaya Nakajo

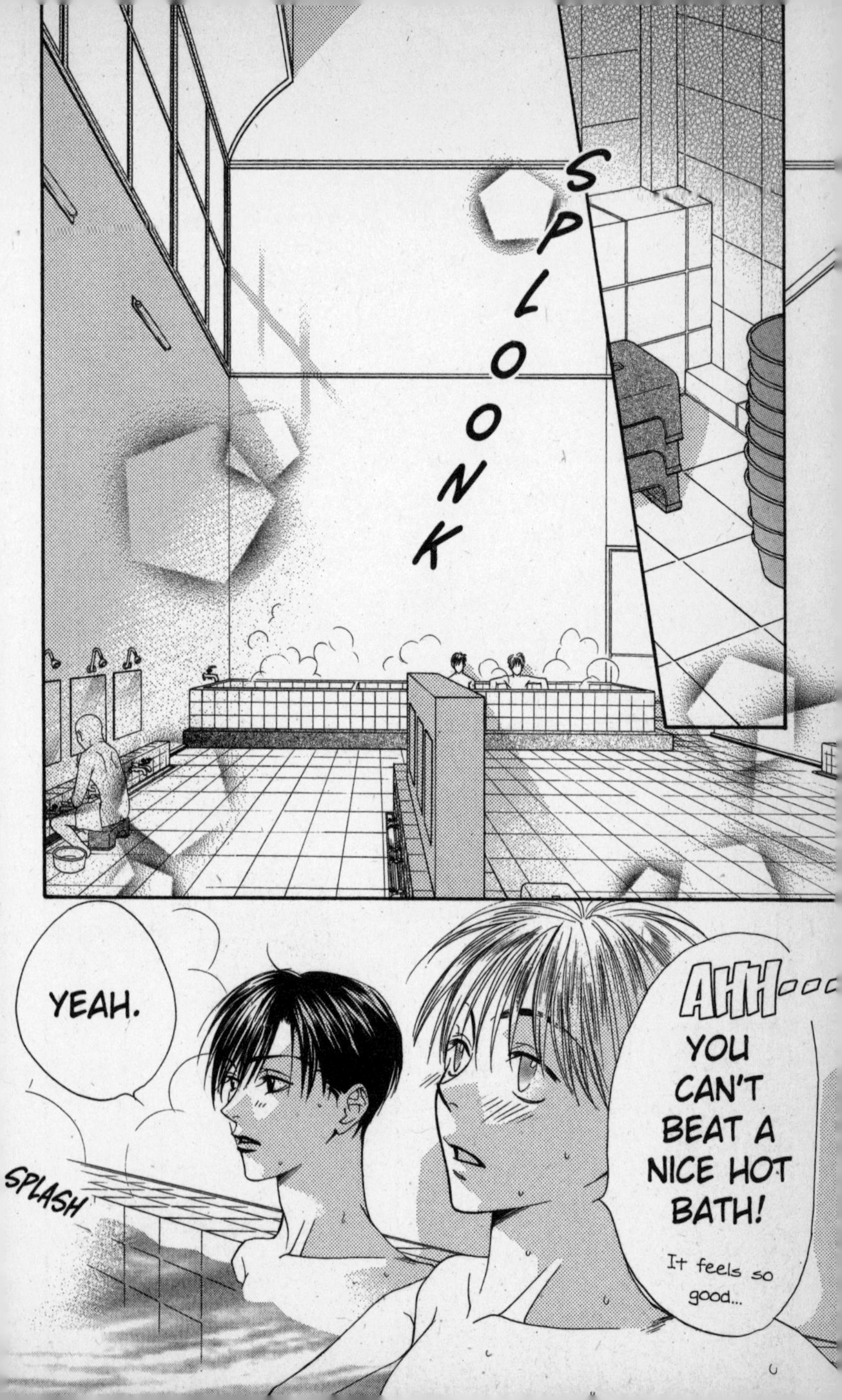
SPLOONK
AHH... YOU CAN'T BEAT A NICE HOT BATH!
It feels so good...
YEAH.
SPLASH

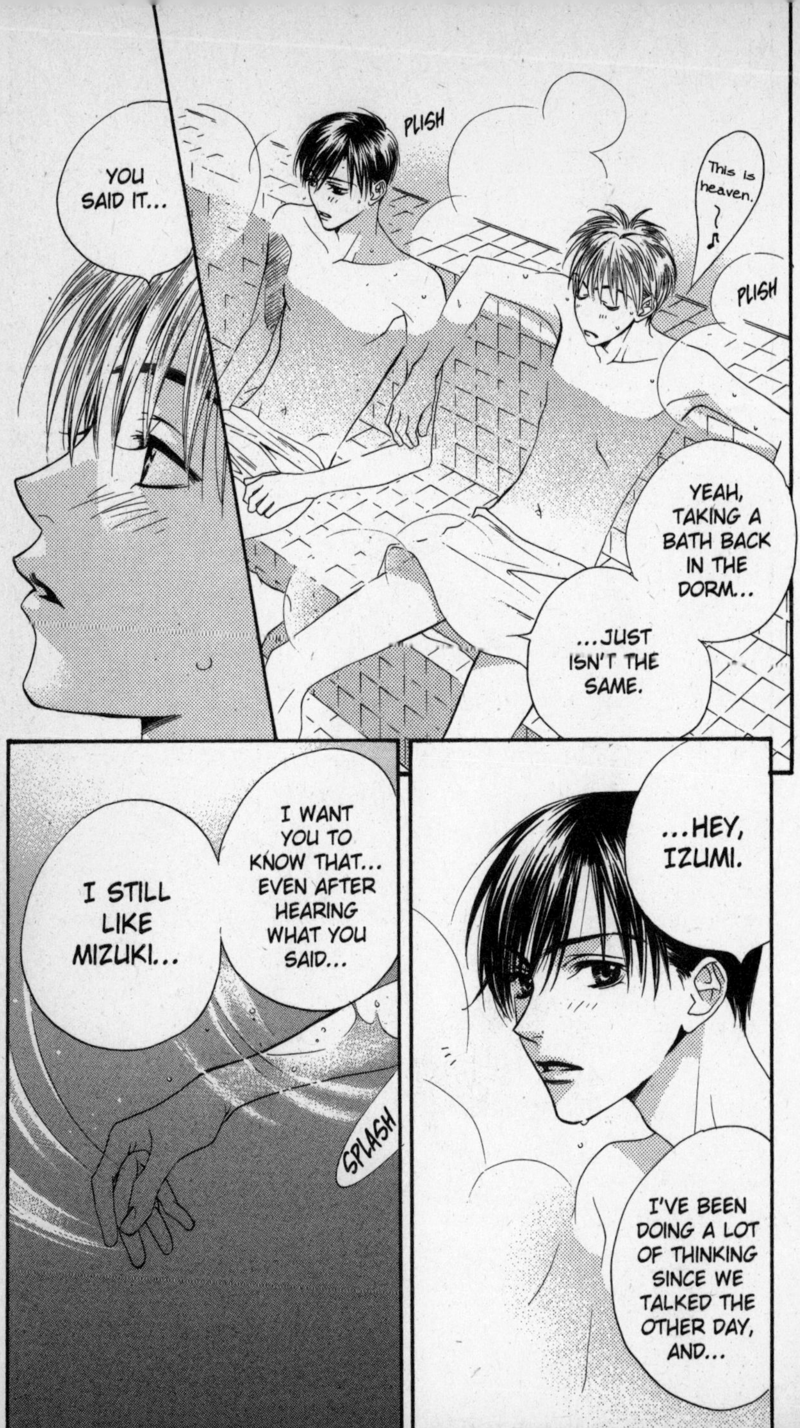
This is heaven. ♪
PLISH
PLISH
YEAH, TAKING A BATH BACK IN THE DORM...
...JUST ISN'T THE SAME.
YOU SAID IT...
...HEY, IZUMI.
I'VE BEEN DOING A LOT OF THINKING SINCE WE TALKED THE OTHER DAY, AND...
I WANT YOU TO KNOW THAT... EVEN AFTER HEARING WHAT YOU SAID...
I STILL LIKE MIZUKI...
SPLASH

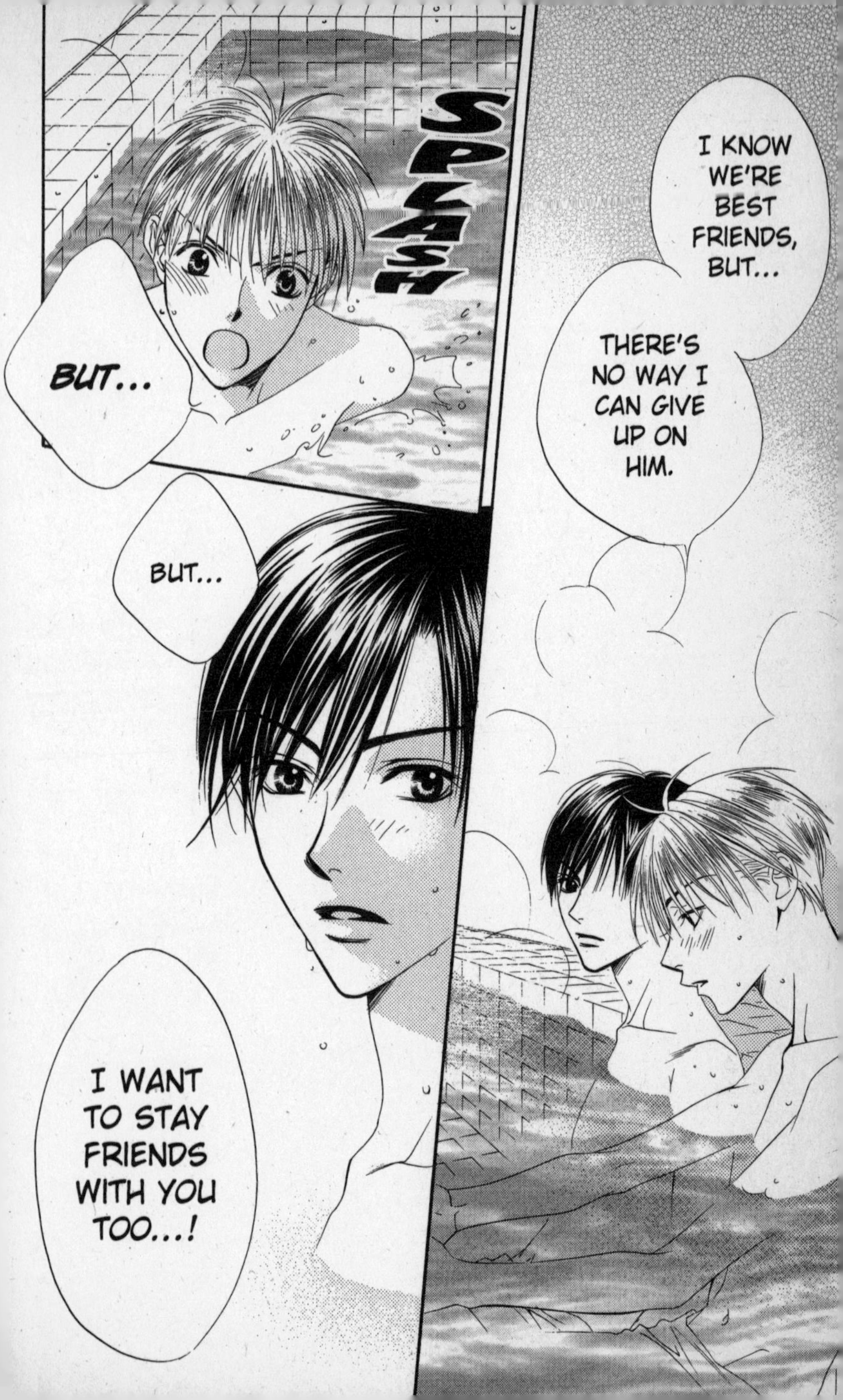
I KNOW WE'RE BEST FRIENDS, BUT...
THERE'S NO WAY I CAN GIVE UP ON HIM.
SPLASH
BUT...
BUT...
I WANT TO STAY FRIENDS WITH YOU TOO...!

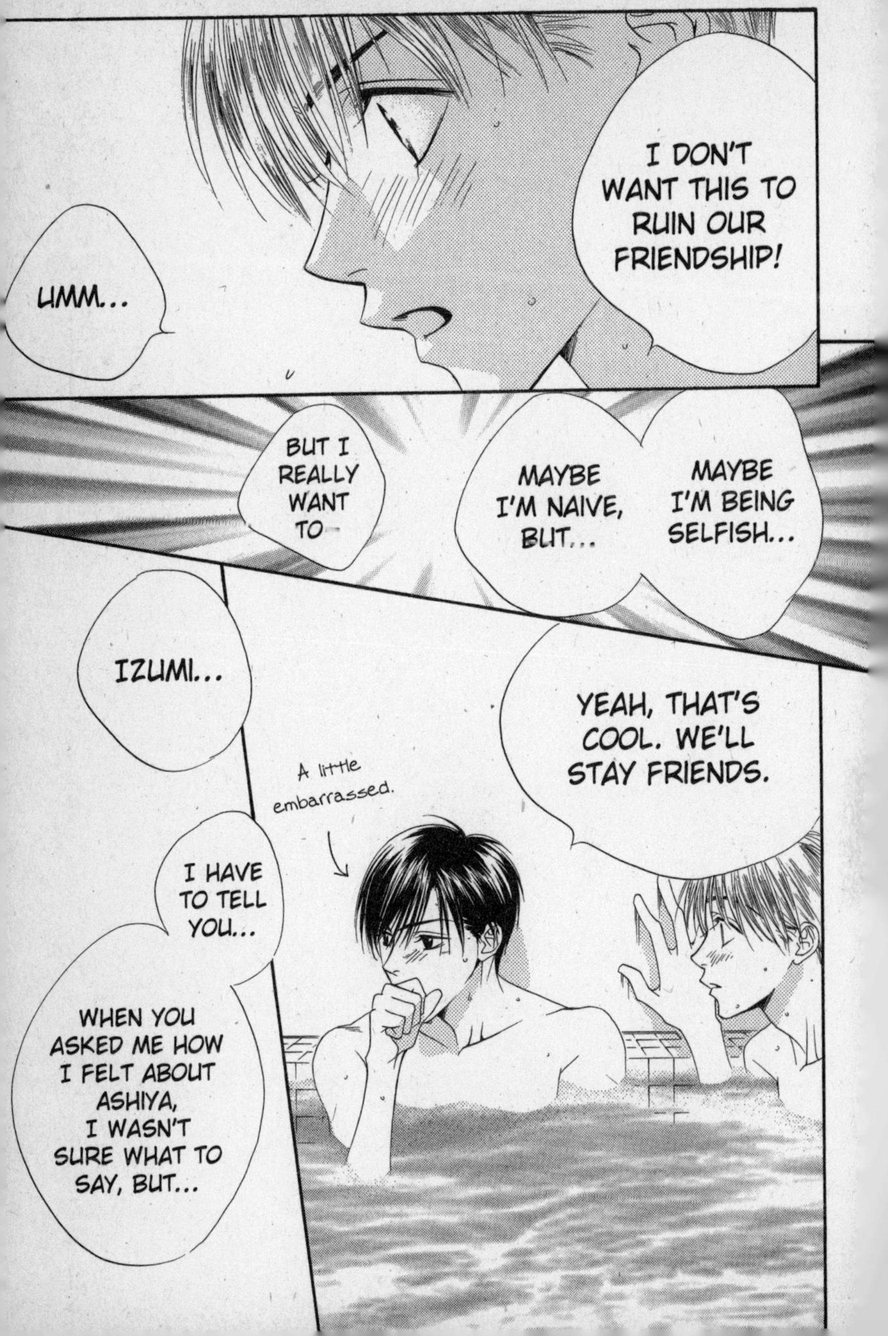
I DON'T WANT THIS TO RUIN OUR FRIENDSHIP!
UMM...
MAYBE I'M BEING SELFISH...
MAYBE I'M NAIVE, BUT...
BUT I REALLY WANT TO—
YEAH, THAT'S COOL. WE'LL STAY FRIENDS.
A little embarrassed.
IZUMI...
I HAVE TO TELL YOU...
WHEN YOU ASKED ME HOW I FELT ABOUT ASHIYA, I WASN'T SURE WHAT TO SAY, BUT...

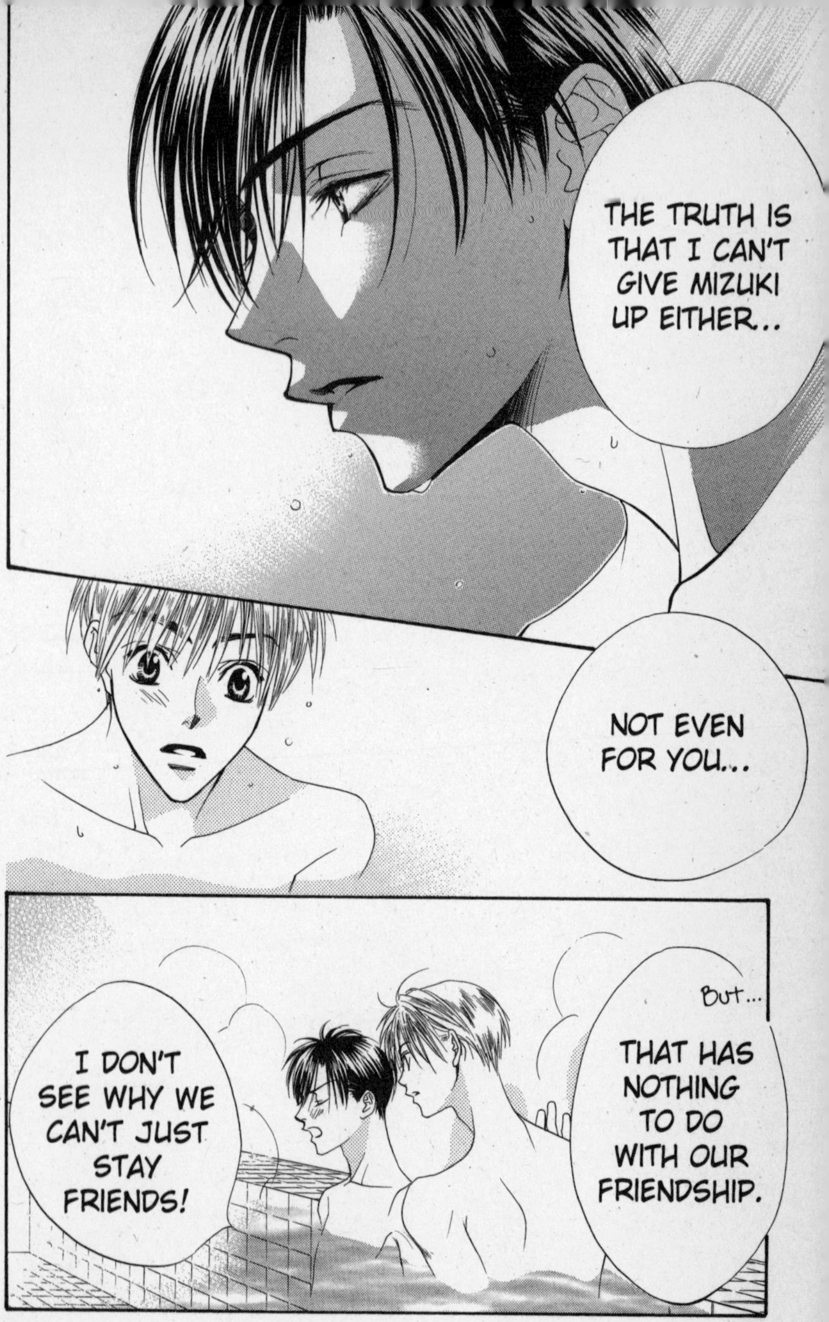
THE TRUTH IS THAT I CAN'T GIVE MIZUKI UP EITHER...
NOT EVEN FOR YOU...
But...
THAT HAS NOTHING TO DO WITH OUR FRIENDSHIP.
I DON'T SEE WHY WE CAN'T JUST STAY FRIENDS!

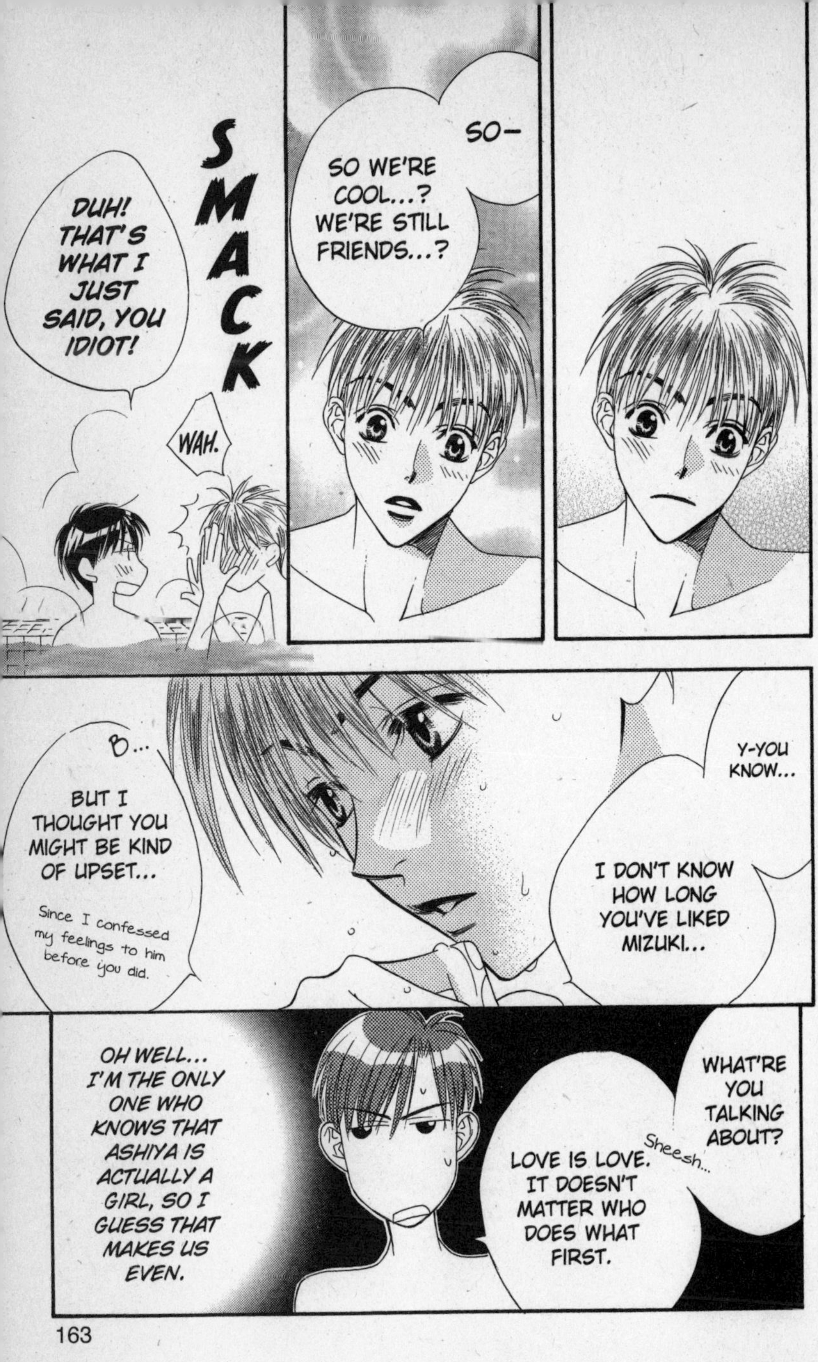
SO–
SO WE'RE COOL...? WE'RE STILL FRIENDS...?
SMACK
DUH! THAT'S WHAT I JUST SAID, YOU IDIOT!
WAH.
Y-YOU KNOW...
I DON'T KNOW HOW LONG YOU'VE LIKED MIZUKI...
B...
BUT I THOUGHT YOU MIGHT BE KIND OF UPSET...
Since I confessed my feelings to him before you did.
WHAT'RE YOU TALKING ABOUT?
Sheesh...
LOVE IS LOVE. IT DOESN'T MATTER WHO DOES WHAT FIRST.
OH WELL... I'M THE ONLY ONE WHO KNOWS THAT ASHIYA IS ACTUALLY A GIRL, SO I GUESS THAT MAKES US EVEN.

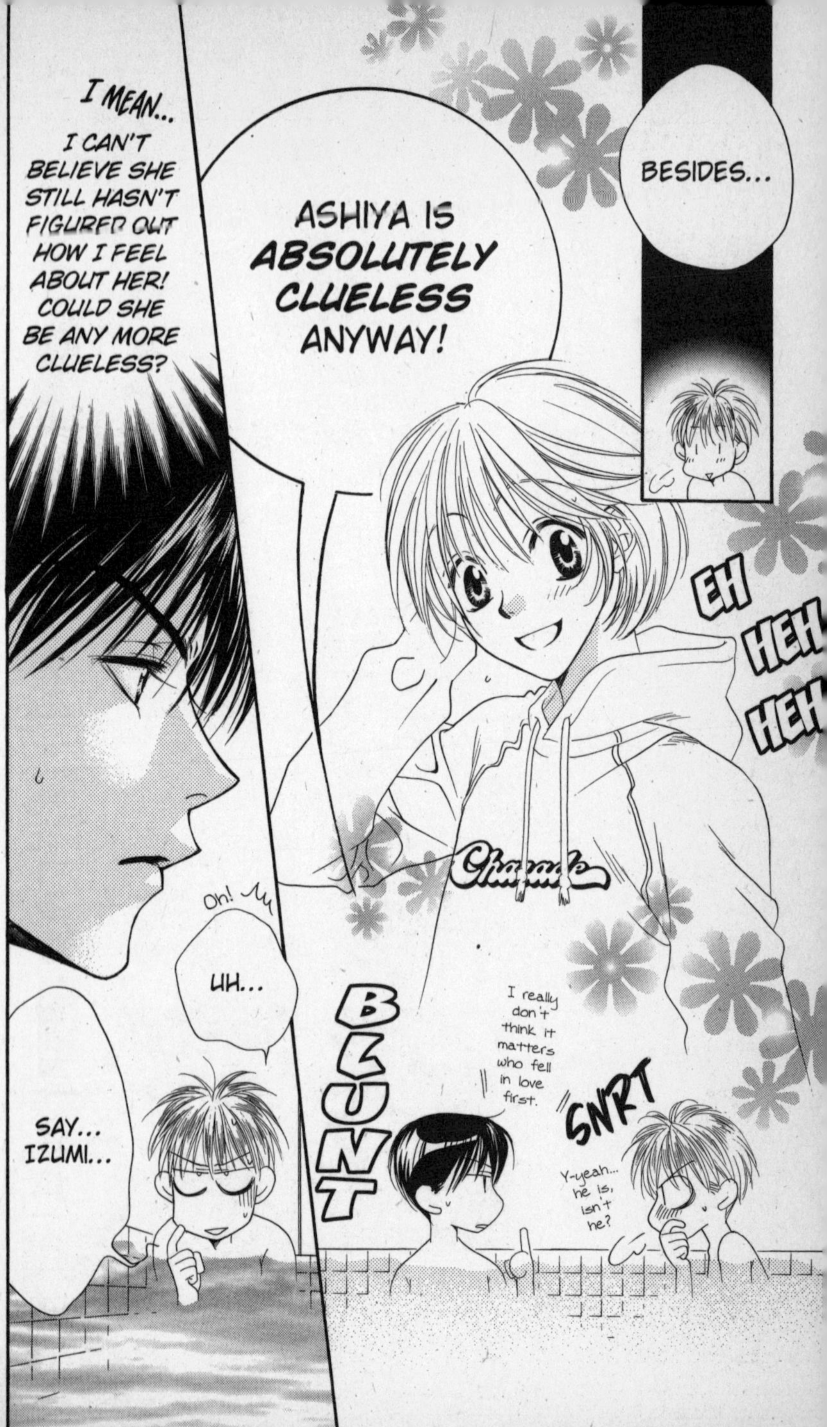
BESIDES...
ASHIYA IS ABSOLUTELY CLUELESS ANYWAY!
EH HEH HEH
I MEAN... I CAN'T BELIEVE SHE STILL HASN'T FIGURED OUT HOW I FEEL ABOUT HER! COULD SHE BE ANY MORE CLUELESS?
SNRT
Y-yeah... he is, isn't he?
I really don't think it matters who fell in love first.
BLUNT
Oh!
UH...
SAY... IZUMI...

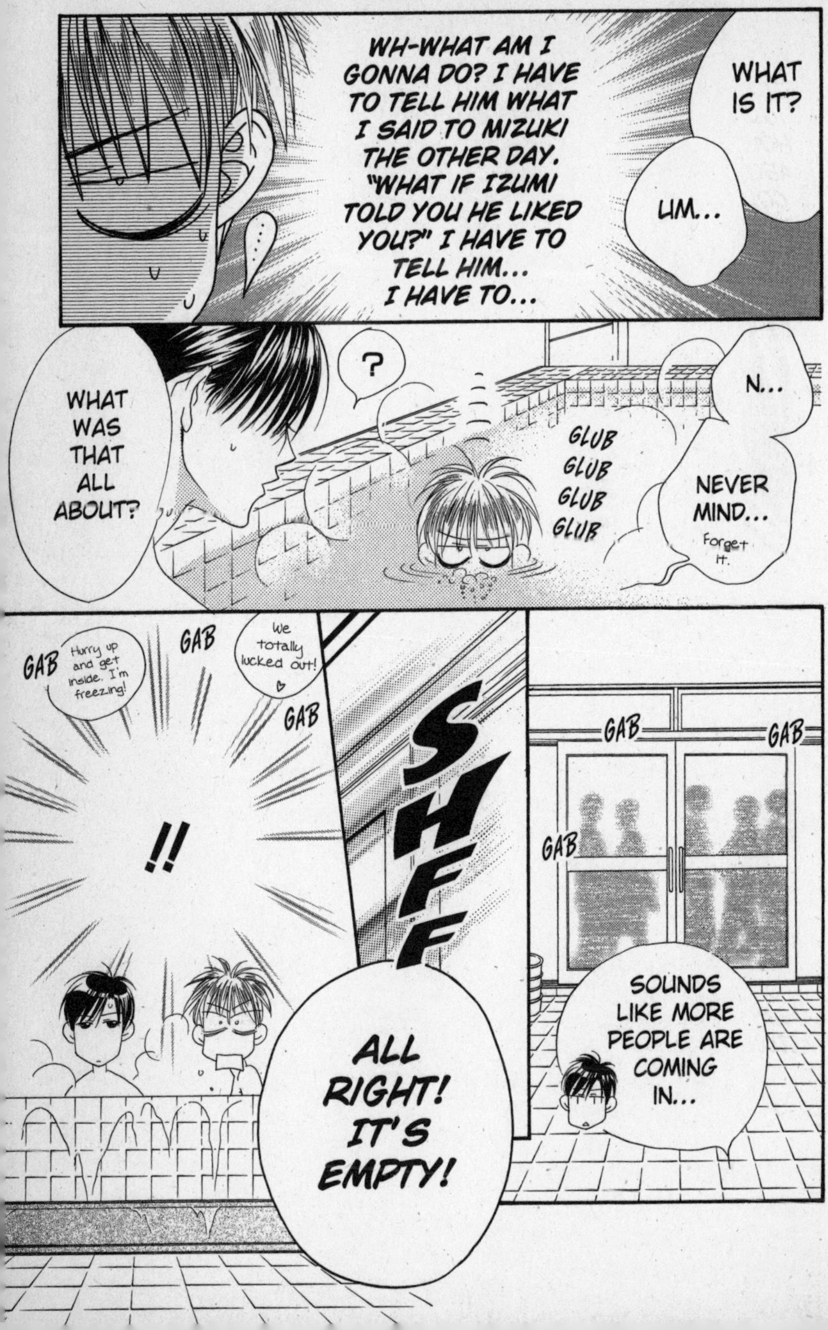
WHAT IS IT?
UM...
WH-WHAT AM I GONNA DO? I HAVE TO TELL HIM WHAT I SAID TO MIZUKI THE OTHER DAY. "WHAT IF IZUMI TOLD YOU HE LIKED YOU?" I HAVE TO TELL HIM... I HAVE TO...
N...
NEVER MIND... Forget it.
GLUB GLUB GLUB GLUB
?
WHAT WAS THAT ALL ABOUT?
GAB
GAB
GAB
SOUNDS LIKE MORE PEOPLE ARE COMING IN...
SHFF
ALL RIGHT! IT'S EMPTY!
GAB
We totally lucked out!
GAB
Hurry up and get inside. I'm freezing!
GAB
!!

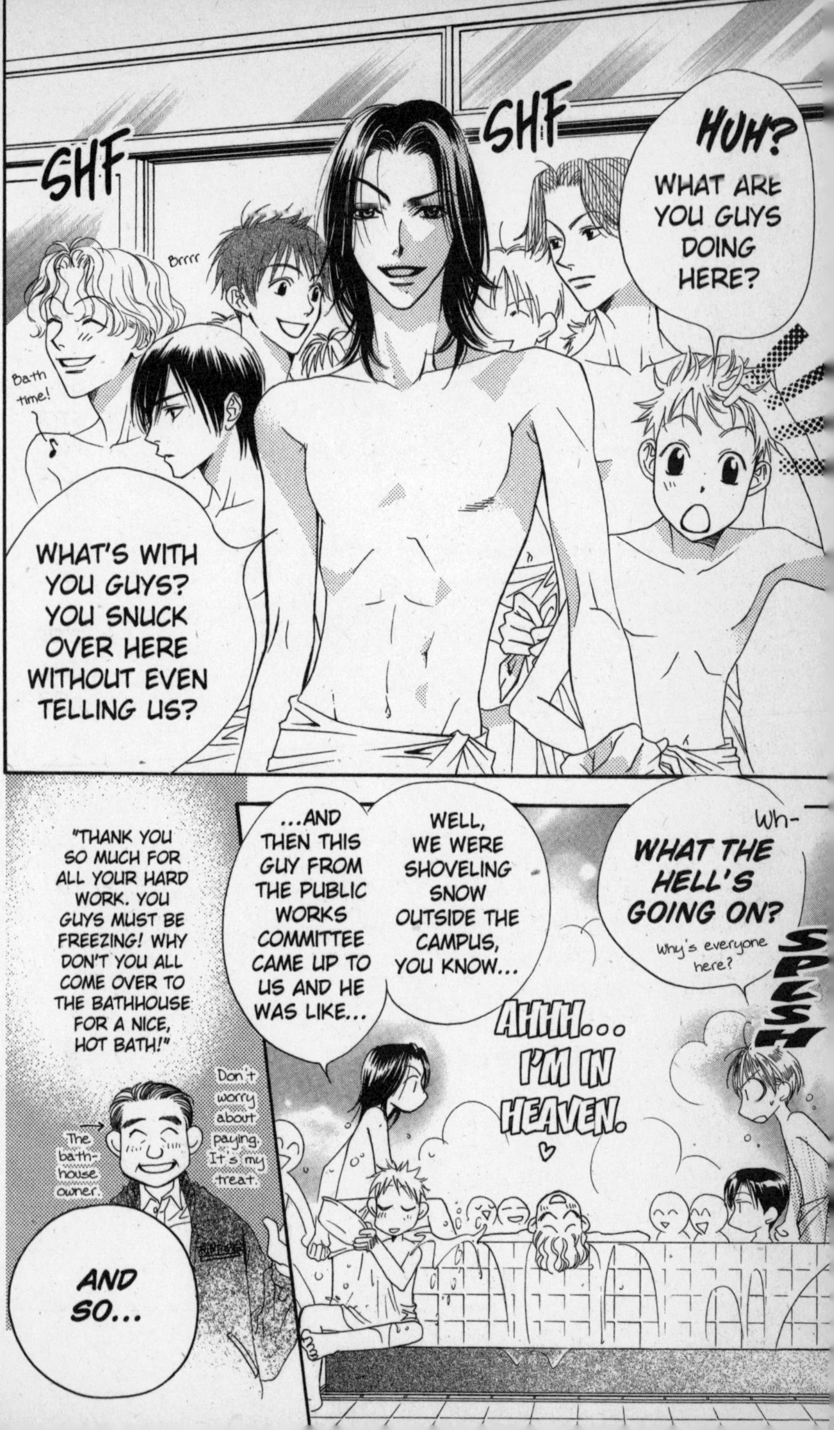
SHF
SHF
HUH? WHAT ARE YOU GUYS DOING HERE?
Brrrr
Bath time! ♪
WHAT'S WITH YOU GUYS? YOU SNUCK OVER HERE WITHOUT EVEN TELLING US?
Wh- WHAT THE HELL'S GOING ON?
Why's everyone here?
SPLSH
AHHH... I'M IN HEAVEN.
WELL, WE WERE SHOVELING SNOW OUTSIDE THE CAMPUS, YOU KNOW...
...AND THEN THIS GUY FROM THE PUBLIC WORKS COMMITTEE CAME UP TO US AND HE WAS LIKE...
"THANK YOU SO MUCH FOR ALL YOUR HARD WORK. YOU GUYS MUST BE FREEZING! WHY DON'T YOU ALL COME OVER TO THE BATHHOUSE FOR A NICE, HOT BATH!"
Don't worry about paying. It's my treat.
The bath-house owner.
AND SO...

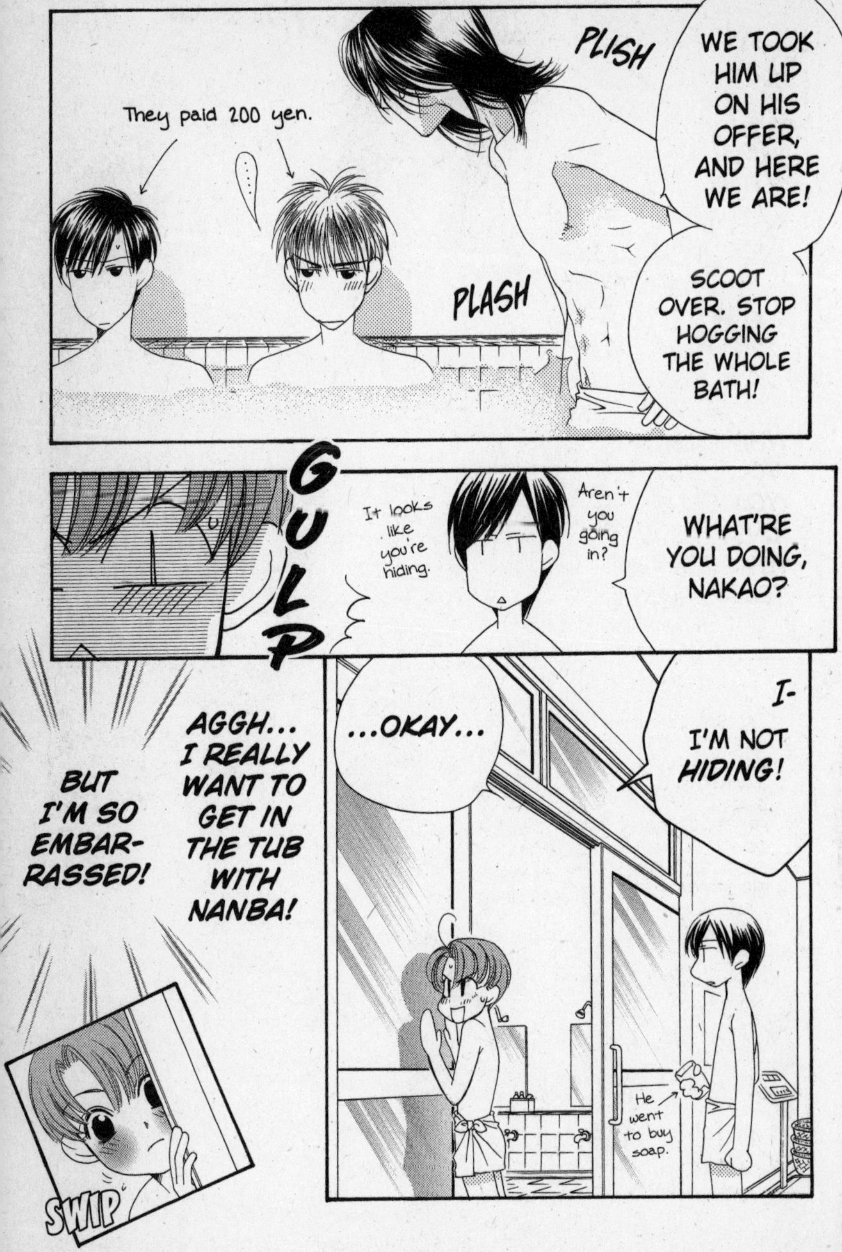
WE TOOK HIM UP ON HIS OFFER, AND HERE WE ARE!
PLISH
SCOOT OVER. STOP HOGGING THE WHOLE BATH!
PLASH
They paid 200 yen.
...
WHAT'RE YOU DOING, NAKAO?
Aren't you going in?
It looks like you're hiding.
GULP
I-
I'M NOT HIDING!
...OKAY...
He went to buy soap.
AGGH... I REALLY WANT TO GET IN THE TUB WITH NANBA!
BUT I'M SO EMBARRASSED!
SWIP

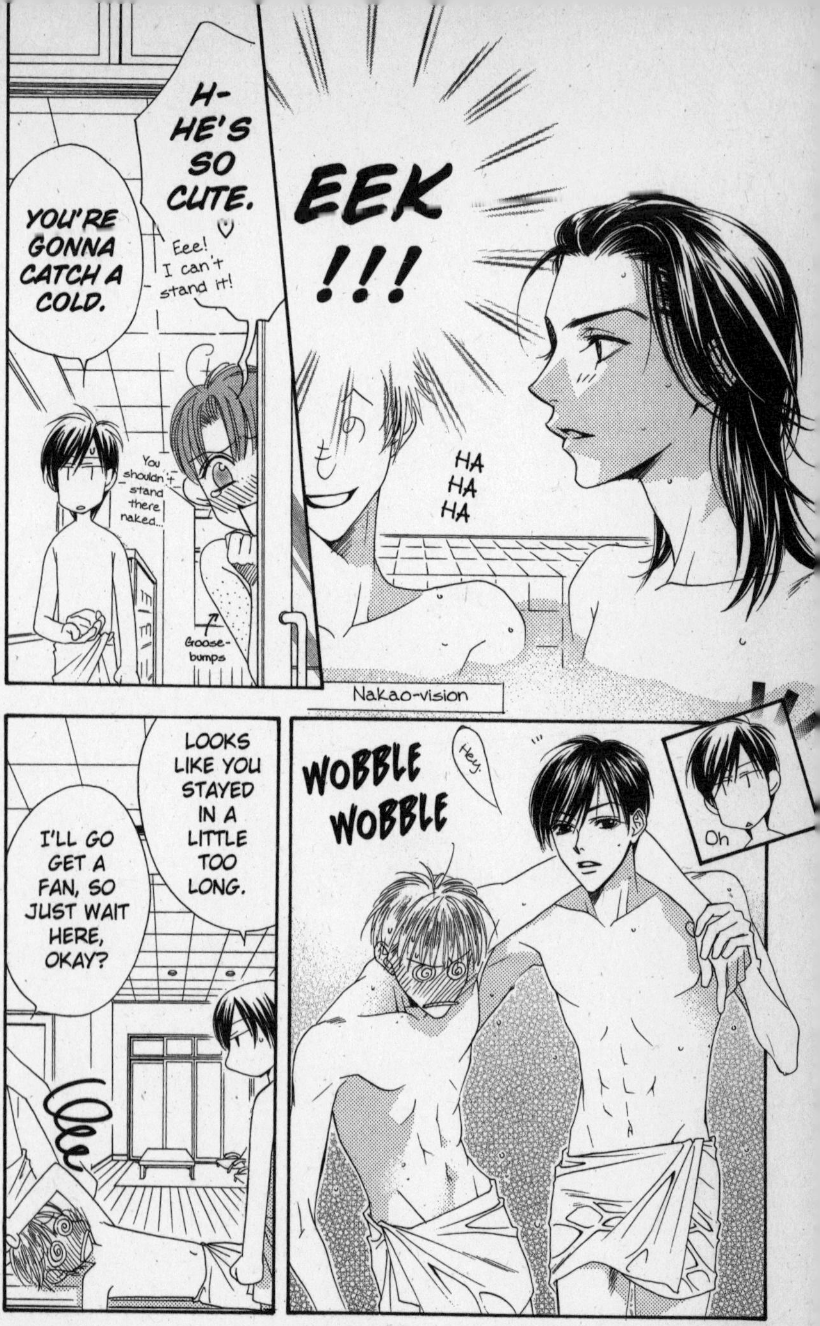
EEK !!!
HA HA HA
Nakao-vision
H- HE'S SO CUTE. ♡
Eee! I can't stand it!
YOU'RE GONNA CATCH A COLD.
You shouldn't stand there naked...
Goose-bumps
WOBBLE WOBBLE
Hey.
Oh
LOOKS LIKE YOU STAYED IN A LITTLE TOO LONG.
I'LL GO GET A FAN, SO JUST WAIT HERE, OKAY?

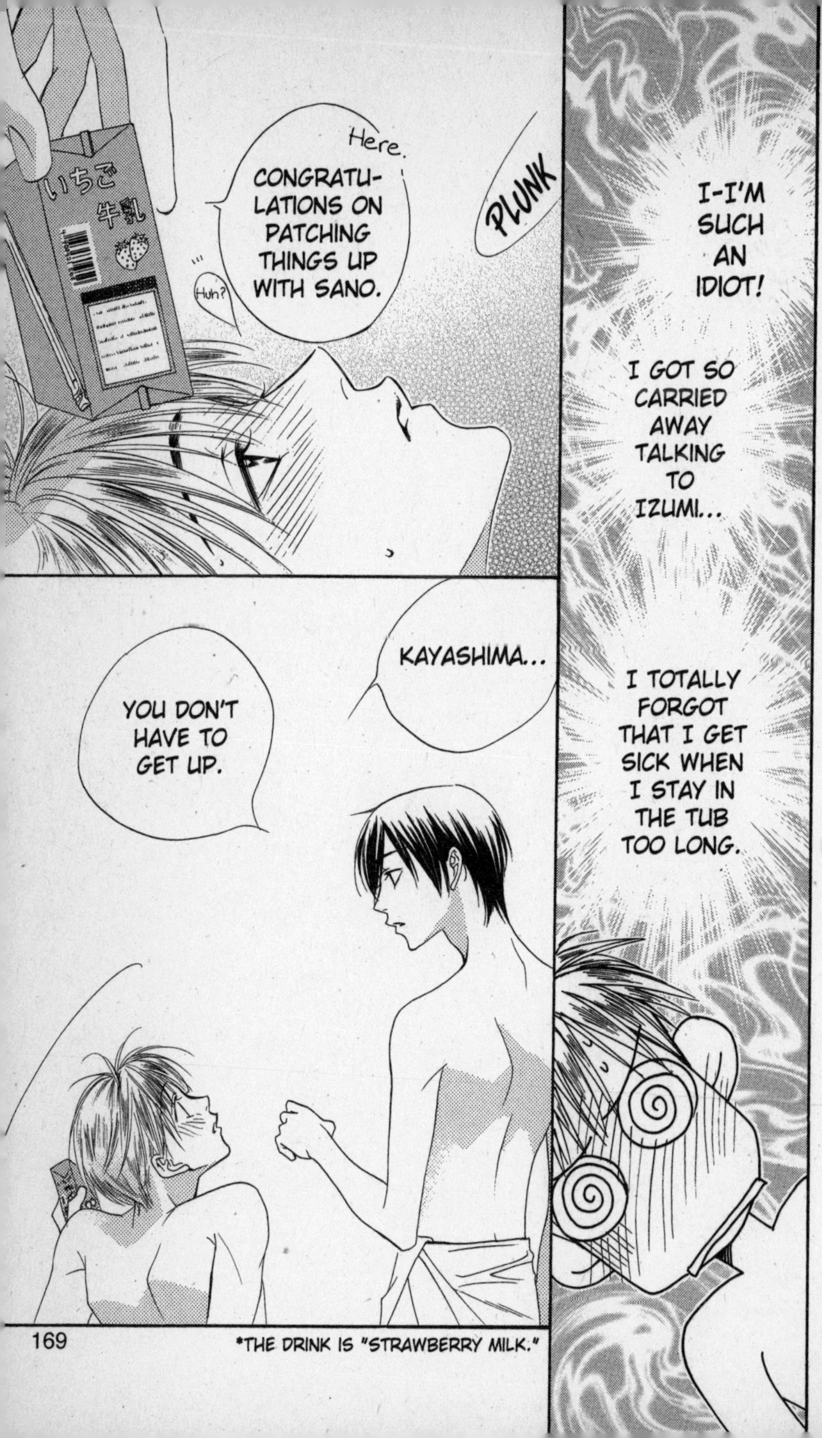
I-I'M SUCH AN IDIOT!
I GOT SO CARRIED AWAY TALKING TO IZUMI...
I TOTALLY FORGOT THAT I GET SICK WHEN I STAY IN THE TUB TOO LONG.
PLUNK
Here.
CONGRATU-LATIONS ON PATCHING THINGS UP WITH SANO.
いちご牛乳
Huh?
KAYASHIMA...
YOU DON'T HAVE TO GET UP.

*THE DRINK IS "STRAWBERRY MILK."

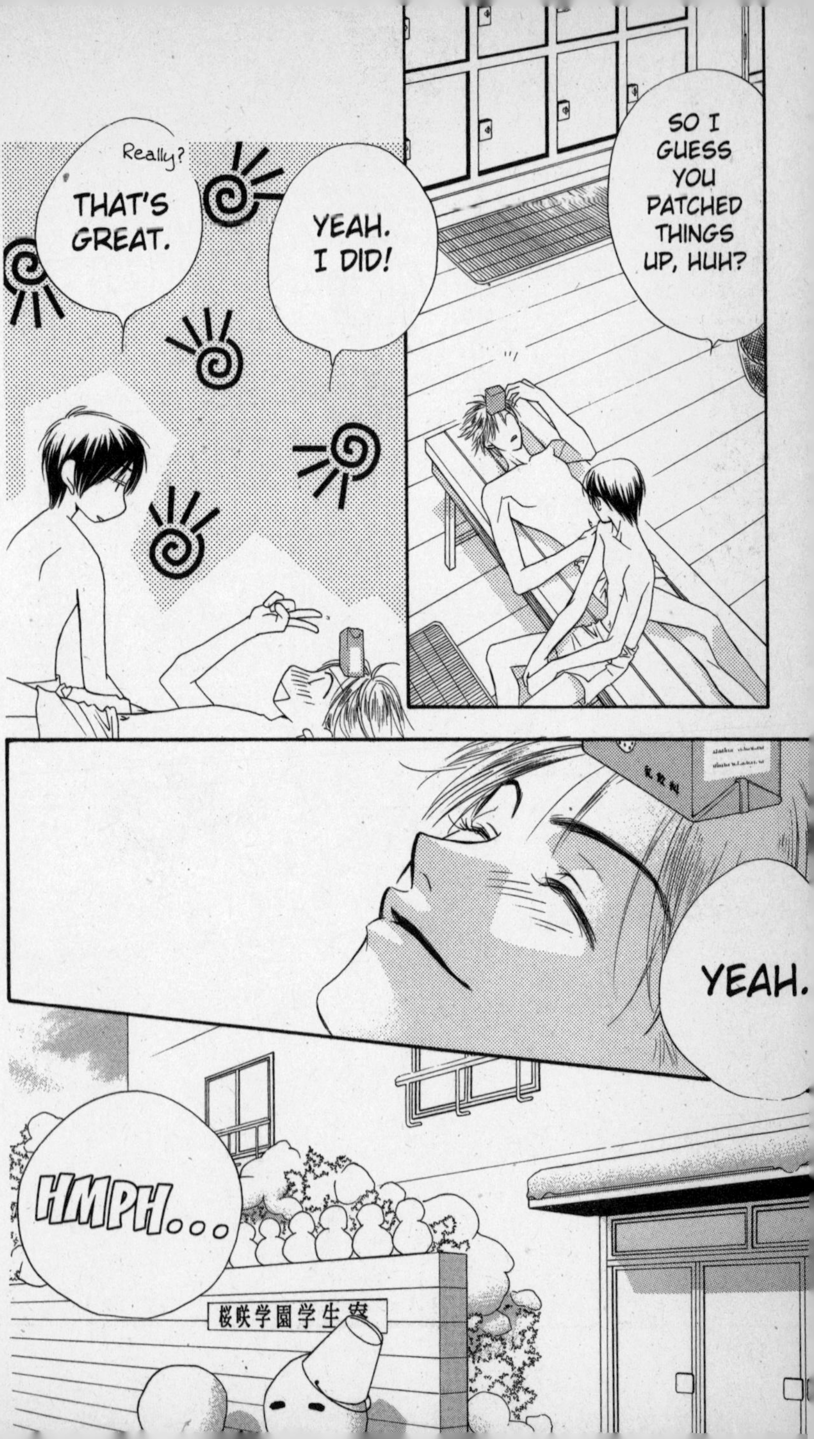
SO I GUESS YOU PATCHED THINGS UP, HUH?
YEAH. I DID!
Really?
THAT'S GREAT.
YEAH.
HMPH...
桜咲学園学生

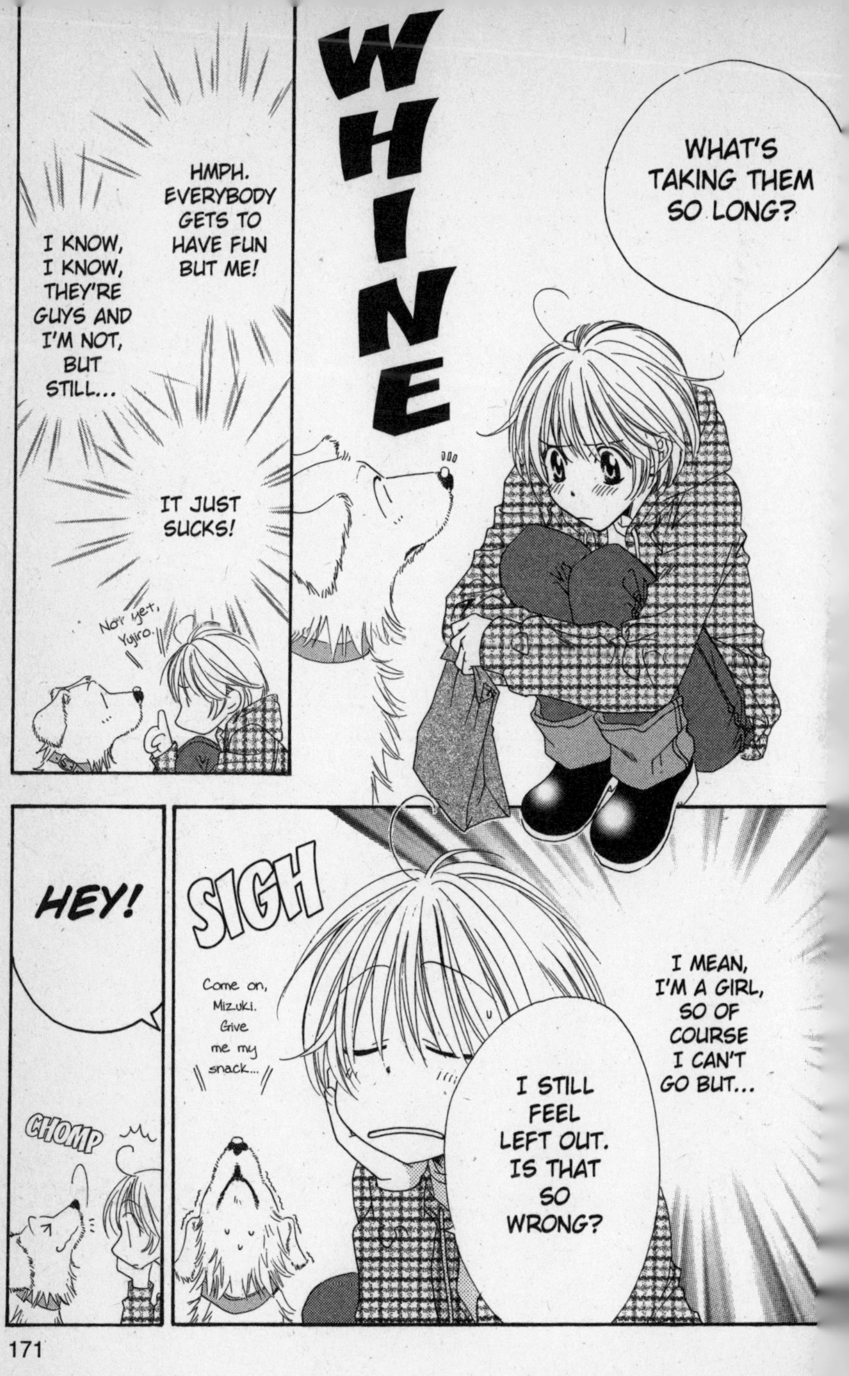
WHAT'S TAKING THEM SO LONG?
WHINE
HMPH. EVERYBODY GETS TO HAVE FUN BUT ME!
I KNOW, I KNOW, THEY'RE GUYS AND I'M NOT, BUT STILL...
IT JUST SUCKS!
Not yet, Yujiro.
SIGH
I MEAN, I'M A GIRL, SO OF COURSE I CAN'T GO BUT...
I STILL FEEL LEFT OUT. IS THAT SO WRONG?
Come on, Mizuki. Give me my snack...
HEY!
CHOMP

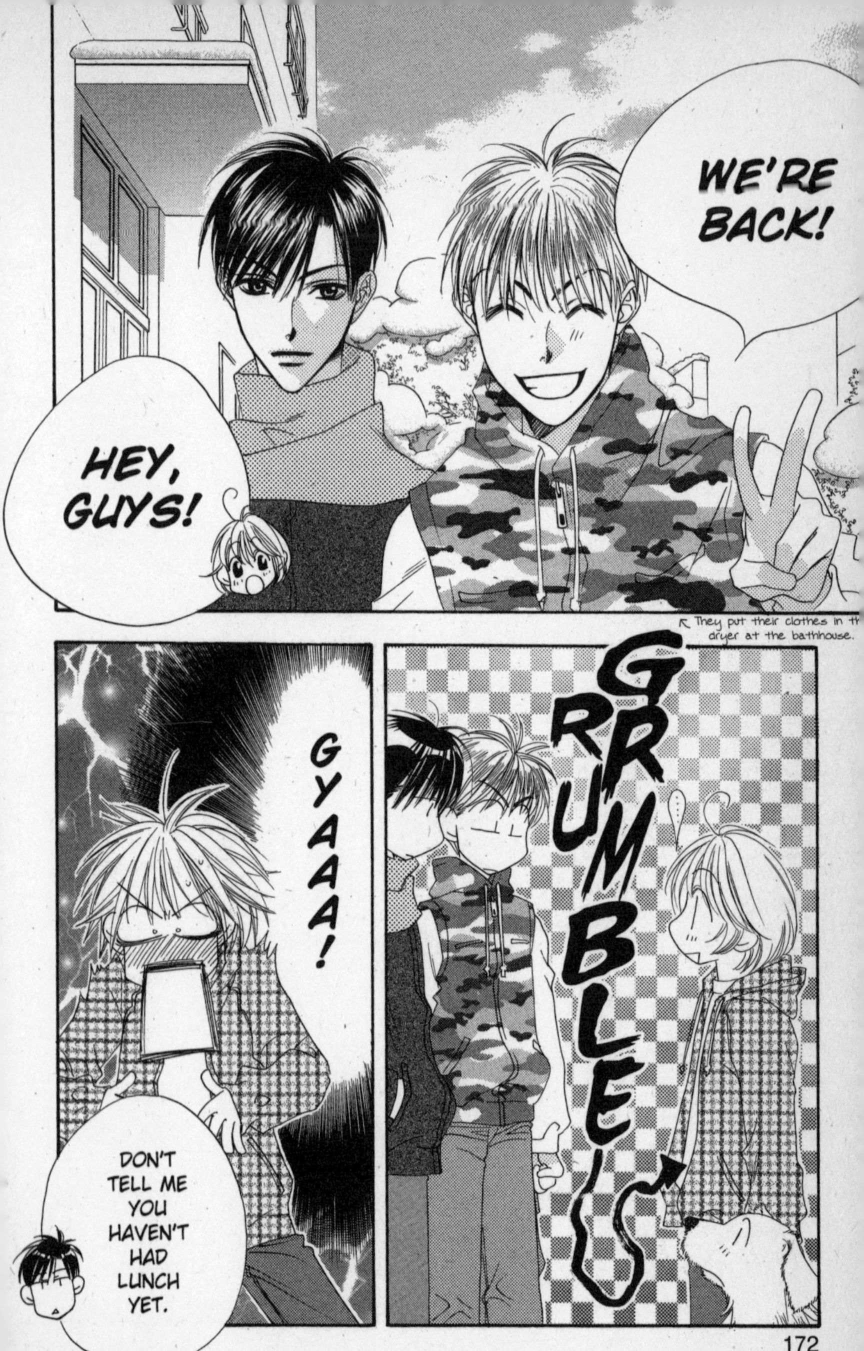
WE'RE BACK!
HEY, GUYS!
They put their clothes in th dryer at the bathhouse.
GRRUMBLE!
GYAAAA!
DON'T TELL ME YOU HAVEN'T HAD LUNCH YET.

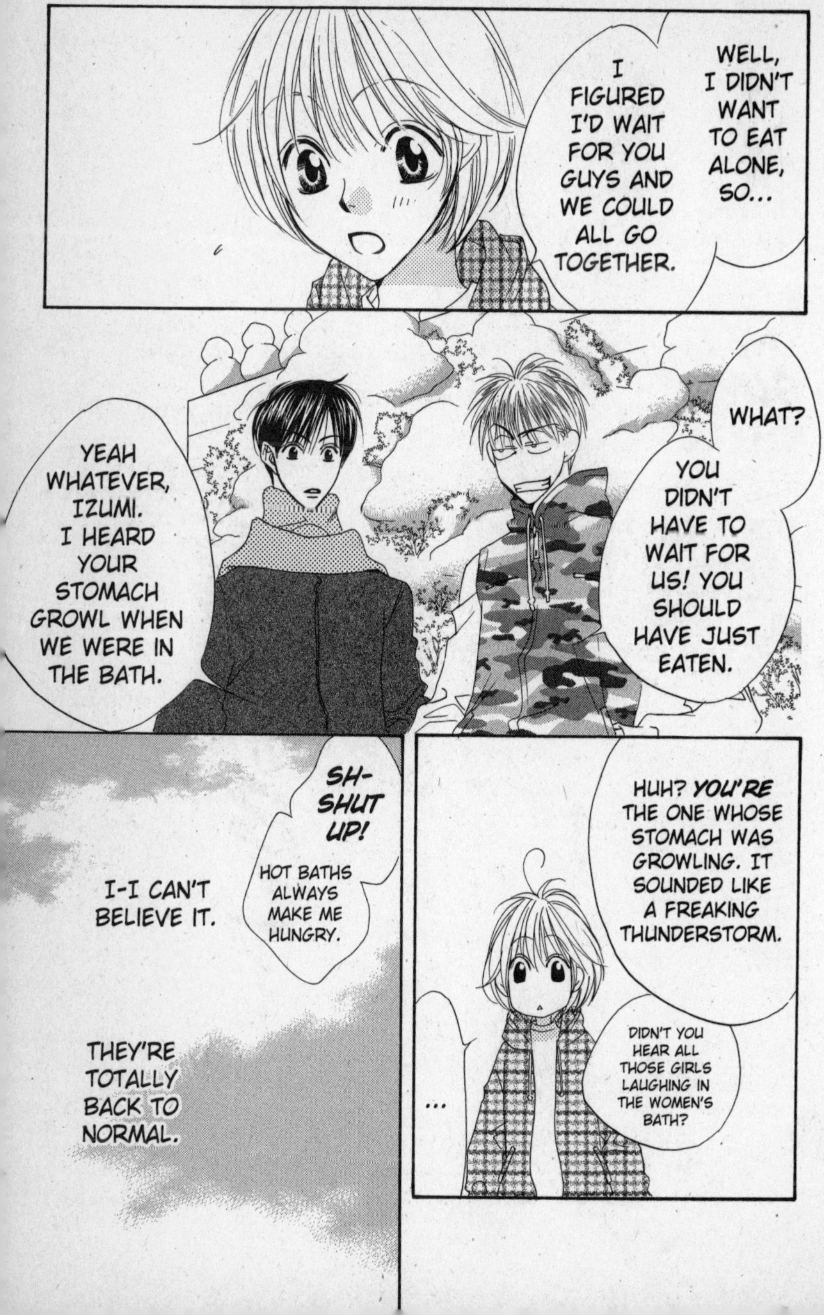
WELL, I DIDN'T WANT TO EAT ALONE, SO...
I FIGURED I'D WAIT FOR YOU GUYS AND WE COULD ALL GO TOGETHER.
WHAT?
YOU DIDN'T HAVE TO WAIT FOR US! YOU SHOULD HAVE JUST EATEN.
YEAH WHATEVER, IZUMI. I HEARD YOUR STOMACH GROWL WHEN WE WERE IN THE BATH.
HUH? *YOU'RE* THE ONE WHOSE STOMACH WAS GROWLING. IT SOUNDED LIKE A FREAKING THUNDERSTORM.
DIDN'T YOU HEAR ALL THOSE GIRLS LAUGHING IN THE WOMEN'S BATH?
...
SH-SHUT UP!
HOT BATHS ALWAYS MAKE ME HUNGRY.
I-I CAN'T BELIEVE IT.
THEY'RE TOTALLY BACK TO NORMAL.

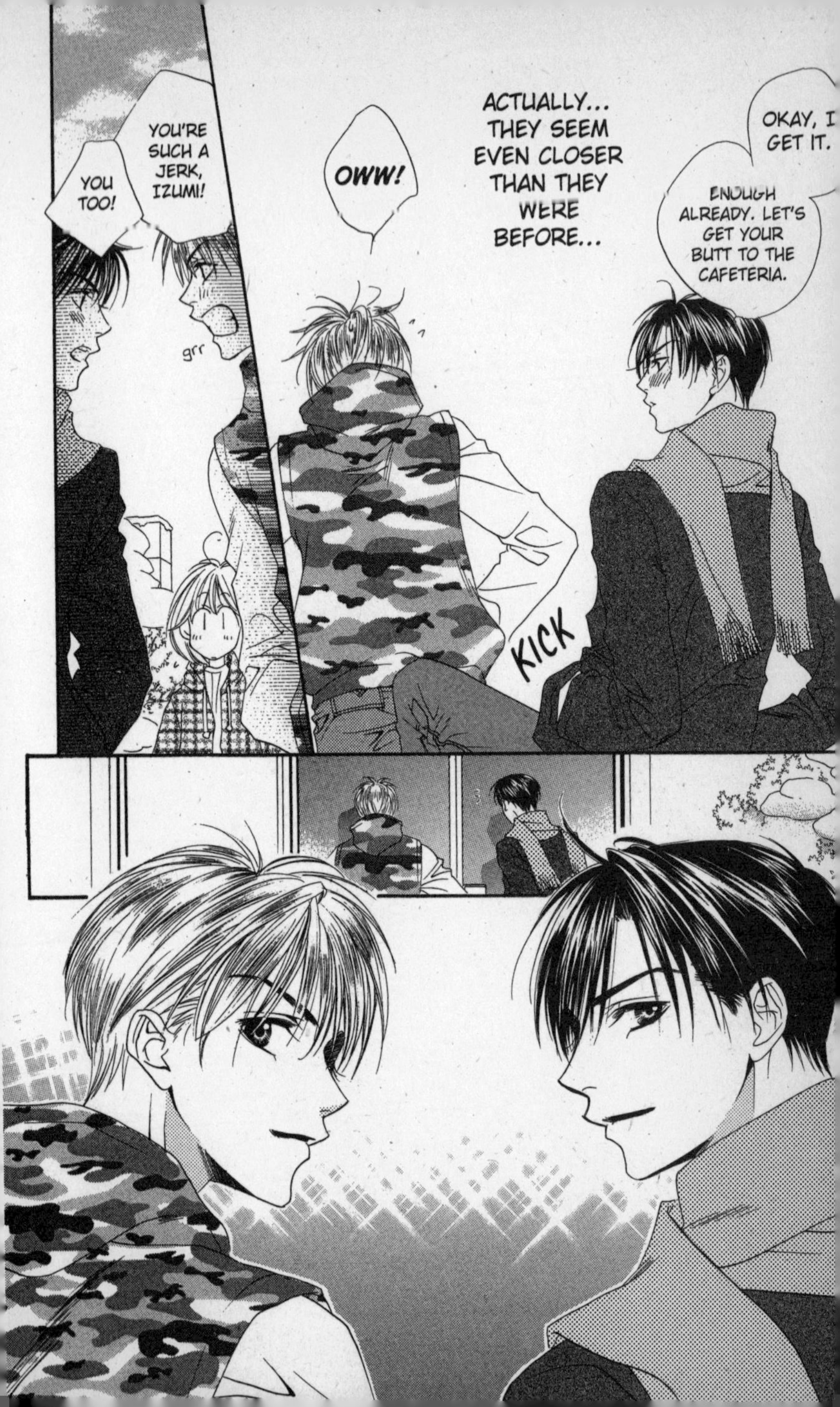
OKAY, I GET IT.
ENOUGH ALREADY. LET'S GET YOUR BUTT TO THE CAFETERIA.
KICK
ACTUALLY... THEY SEEM EVEN CLOSER THAN THEY WERE BEFORE...
OWW!
YOU'RE SUCH A JERK, IZUMI!
YOU TOO!
grr

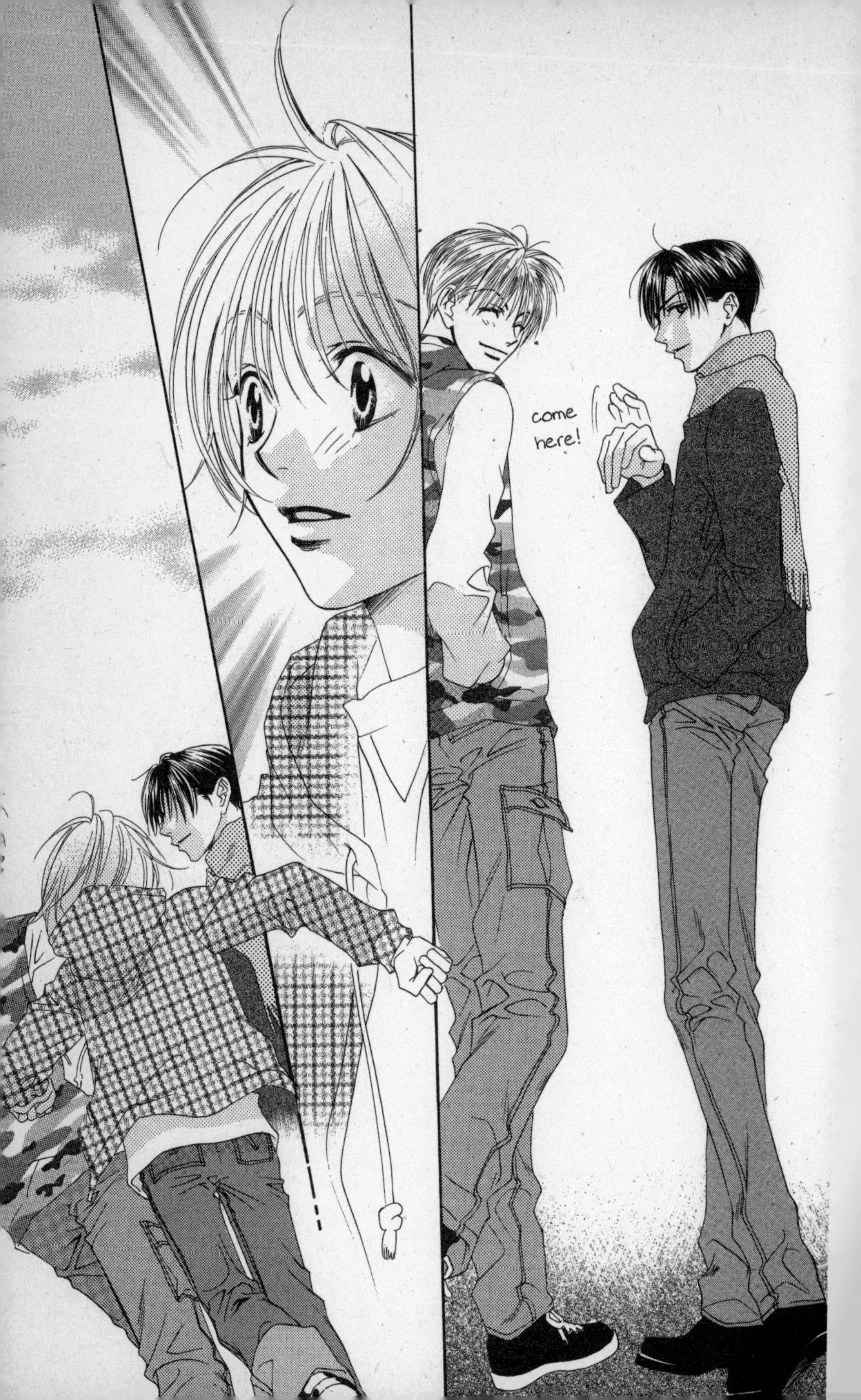
come here!

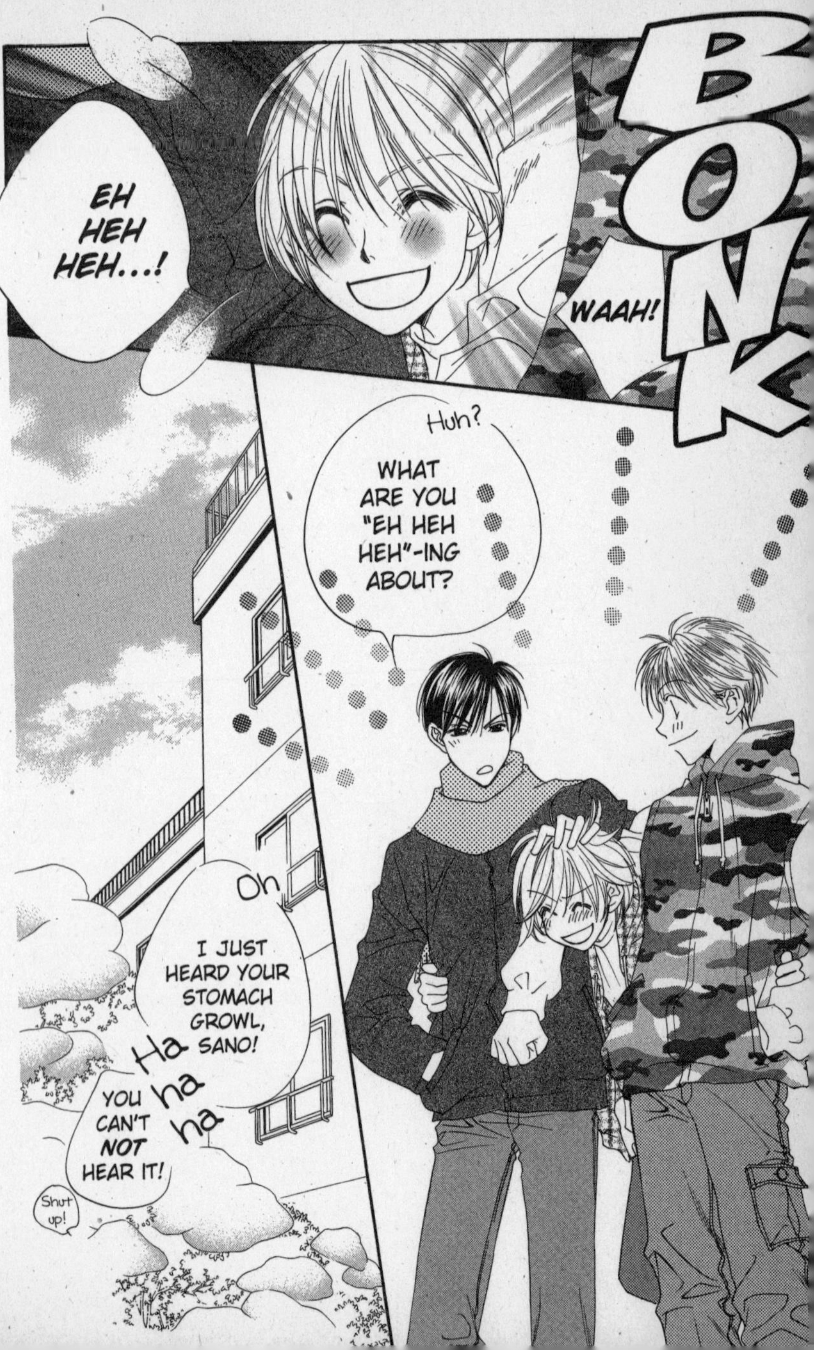
BONK
WAAH!
EH HEH HEH...!
Huh?
WHAT ARE YOU "EH HEH HEH"-ING ABOUT?
Oh
I JUST HEARD YOUR STOMACH GROWL, SANO!
Ha ha ha
YOU CAN'T NOT HEAR IT!
Shut up!

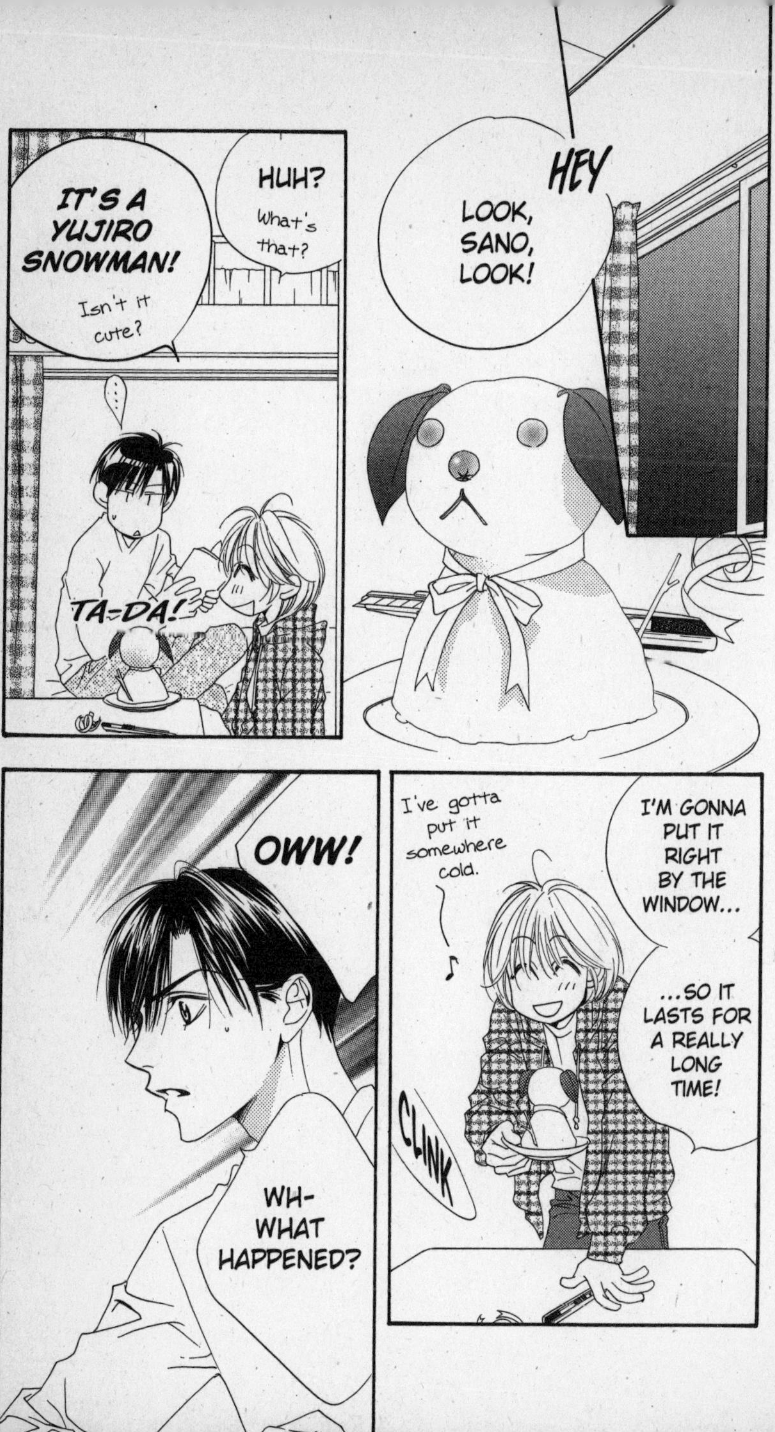
HEY
LOOK, SANO, LOOK!
HUH?
What's that?
IT'S A YUJIRO SNOWMAN!
Isn't it cute?
TA-DA!
I'M GONNA PUT IT RIGHT BY THE WINDOW...
I've gotta put it somewhere cold.
...SO IT LASTS FOR A REALLY LONG TIME!
CLINK
OWW!
WH-WHAT HAPPENED?

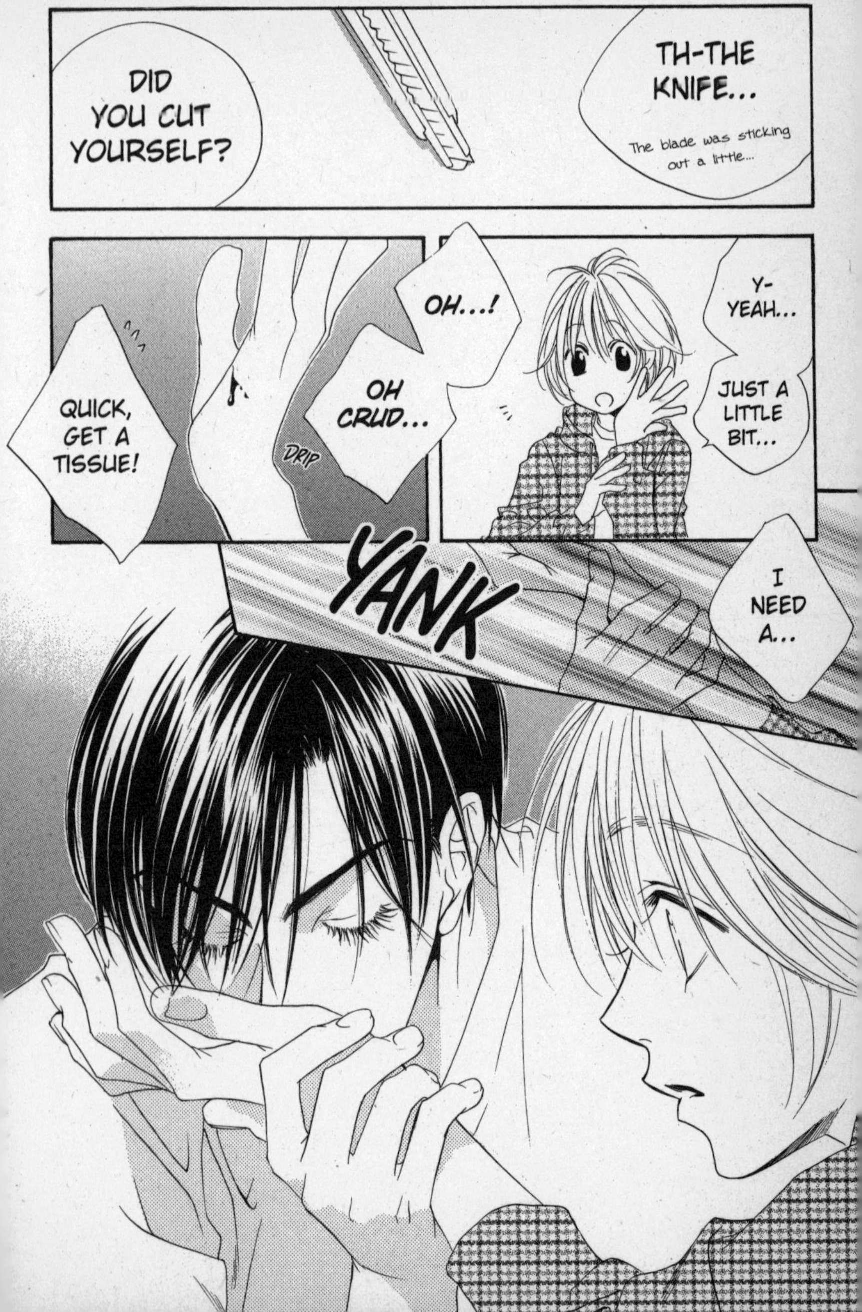
TH-THE KNIFE...
The blade was sticking out a little...
DID YOU CUT YOURSELF?
Y- YEAH...
JUST A LITTLE BIT...
OH...!
OH CRUD...
DRIP
QUICK, GET A TISSUE!
I NEED A...
YANK

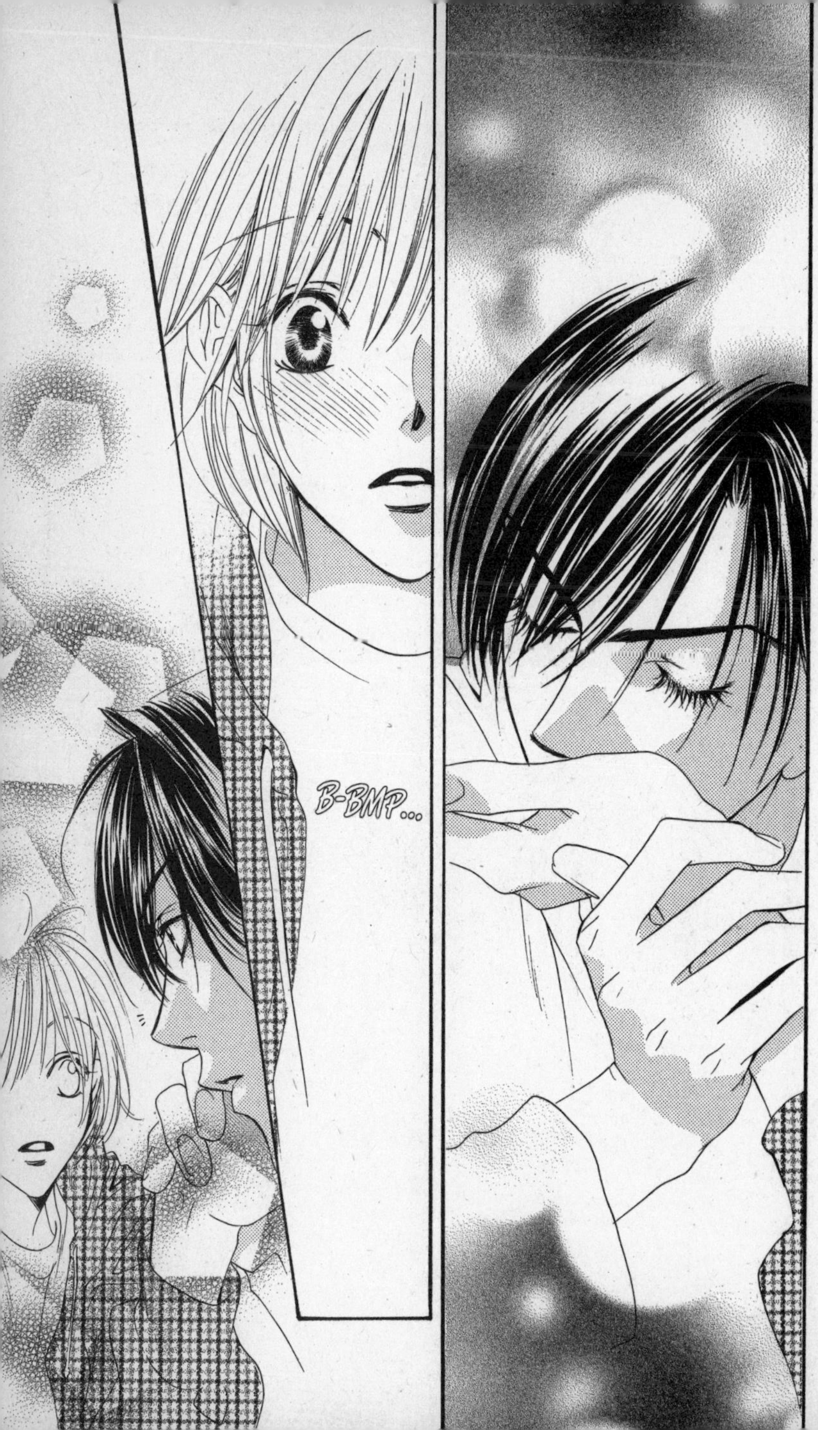
B-BMP...

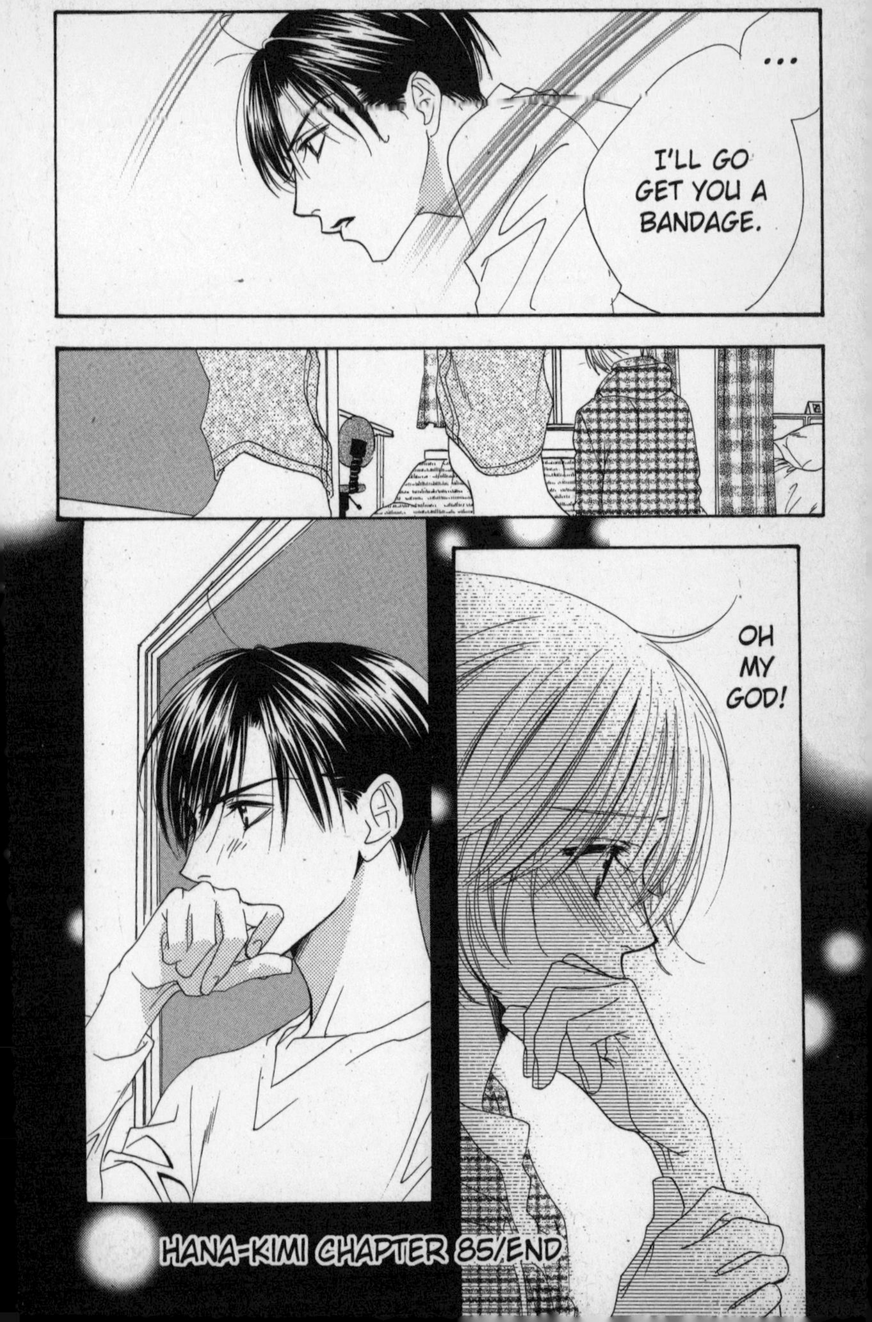
...
I'LL GO GET YOU A BANDAGE.
OH MY GOD!
HANA-KIMI CHAPTER 85/END

NAKAJO Q & A CORNER!

UM...I'D LIKE TO TAKE THIS OPPORTUNITY TO
ANSWER SOME FREQUENTLY ASKED QUESTIONS!
SO HERE'S THE Q&A! LET'S GO!

Q : WHAT'S YOUR BIRTHDAY, YOUR SIGN, ETC.?
A: DATE OF BIRTH: SEPTEMBER 12. BLOOD TYPE: B.
ASTROLOGICAL SIGN: VIRGO (YOU CAN ALSO FIND
THIS INFO IN BOOK 2, PAGE 9.)

Q: ARE YOU MALE OR A FEMALE?
A: I AM FEMALE. (LAUGHS)

Q: WHAT KIND OF DRAWING MATERIALS DO YOU USE?
A: THE ONLY KIND OF PEN I USE IS NIKKO'S "MARUPEN."
THE TYPE OF INK I USE IS CALLED "HOLBEIN." I ALWAYS
USE A BRAND NEW PEN TO DRAW HAIR AND EYES. WHEN THE
PENS START GETTING A LITTLE WORN, I USE THEM TO DRAW
THE BASE LINES OF THE CHARACTERS AND STUFF. WHEN THEY
GET REALLY OLD, I USE THEM TO DRAW THE WORD BALLOONS.
HOLBEIN INK IS WATERPROOF, SO IT'S SAFE EVEN WHEN
YOU ACCIDENTALLY SPILL WATER OVER IT. I'VE BEEN USING
IT SINCE BEFORE I GOT PUBLISHED. AS FAR AS PAPER GOES,
I USED TO ONLY USE THE SPECIAL "HANA TO YUME" PAPER
(UP TILL HANA-KIMI BOOK 12) BUT THEN I SWITCHED
TO AISHII BRAND PAPER.

Q: WHAT KIND OF MATERIALS DO YOU USE FOR COLOR
ILLUSTRATIONS? DO YOU USE COPIC MARKERS?
A: I ONLY USE DR. PH. MARTIN'S BRAND COLOR INK.
I DO USE COPICS WHEN I DO MY SIGNATURE. I'VE ALWAYS
COLORED ALL MY ILLUSTRATIONS BY HAND. I USE HOLBEIN
INK TO DRAW THE MAIN LINES, AND I USE CANSON BOARD
PAPER. (I USED TO USE CRESCENT PAPER TOO, BUT NOW
I ONLY USE CANSON BOARD.) FOR PAINTBRUSHES,
I USE WHITE SABLE. (THIS TYPE OF SYNTHETIC
BRUSH IS VERY SMOOTH AND EASY TO USE.)

NAKAJO Q & A CORNER!

Q: WHAT KIND OF MUSIC DO YOU LISTEN TO WHEN YOU WORK?
A: USUALLY WHEN I'M WORKING, I WATCH VARIETY SHOWS ON TV. ("SEKAI MARUMIE," "GAKKOU HE IKOU!," "UNBELIEVABLE!," "DENPA SHONEN," ETC.) SOMETIMES I WATCH DRAMAS OR ANIME, AND IF I HAVE NOTHING TO WATCH ON TV, I SWITCH ON MY DVD PLAYER, AND WATCH MOVIES AND ANIME THAT MY ASSISTANTS BRING OVER. ~♪ LATELY, I'VE BEEN WATCHING LIVE FOOTAGE OF THE NATIONAL CONGRESS MEETINGS, BUT MY ASSISTANTS CAN'T STAND IT. -:HA HA:-

Q: I HEARD YOU NAMED YOUR CHARACTERS AFTER NEIGHBORHOODS AND TRAIN STATIONS IN OSAKA. ANY PARTICULAR REASON?
A: THERE ARE LOTS OF INTERESTING-SOUNDING NEIGHBORHOOD AND STATION NAMES THAT MAKE GREAT CHARACTER NAMES. I THOUGHT IT MIGHT BE A FUN IDEA. I NAMED OSAKA HIGH SCHOOL AFTER A SLOGAN THAT GOES "OSAKA SAKASO" (MAY OSAKA BLOOM). THAT'S WHERE MY INSPIRATION CAME FROM. (I HAVEN'T USED THE NAME OF MY HOMETOWN YET.)

Q: WHAT ARE YOU DOING WHEN YOU'RE NOT WORKING ON "HANA TO YUME"?
A: I'VE GOT TONS OF COLOR ILLUSTRATION JOBS TO DO WHEN I'M NOT WORKING ON MY "HANA TO YUME" SERIES. (I'M EXAGGERATING.) I'M USUALLY WORKING ON THINGS LIKE "HANA TO YUME" COVERS, COLOR SPLASH PAGES, "THE HANA" COVERS, ART FOR GIVEAWAYS AND PROMOTIONS, ETC.

Q: I WANT TO BE A MANGA ARTIST IN THE FUTURE. HOW CAN I IMPROVE MY SKILLS? HOW CAN I LEARN TO DRAW CUTE BOYS? IF I BECOME A MANGA ARTIST, WILL YOU BE MY FRIEND?
A: OKAY! LET'S BE FRIENDS! THE BEST WAY TO IMPROVE YOUR SKILLS IS TO KEEP DRAWING AND KEEP SHOWING YOUR WORK TO YOUR FRIENDS. BUT TRY NOT TO GET TOO OBSESSED WITH DRAWING MANGA. DON'T FORGET TO ENJOY THE REAL WORLD TOO. WHEN YOU DRAW BOY CHARACTERS, TRY TO FIGURE OUT WHAT YOU LIKE ABOUT CERTAIN MALE CELEBRITIES OR CHARACTERS. YOU CAN LEARN A LOT THAT WAY. DON'T PUT TOO MUCH PRESSURE ON YOURSELF, AND REMEMBER TO ALWAYS KEEP DRAWING. IT'S IMPORTANT TO TRY TO FINISH EVERY PROJECT. THERE'S ALWAYS SOMETHING TO BE LEARNED. I WISH YOU ALL THE BEST! AH! LOOKS LIKE I'M RUNNING OUT OF SPACE. OKAY, I'LL SEE YOU IN THE NEXT NAKAJO Q & A! (WHEN'S THAT GONNA BE?)

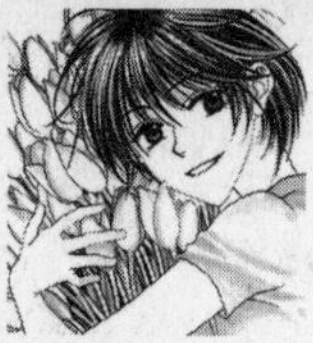

ABOUT THE AUTHOR

Hisaya Nakajo's manga series **Hanazakari no Kimitachi he** (For You in Full Blossom, casually known as **Hana-Kimi**) has been a hit since it first appeared in 1997 in the shôjo manga magazine **Hana to Yume** (Flowers and Dreams). In Japan, two **Hana-Kimi** art books and several "drama CDs" have been released. Her other manga series include **Missing Piece** (2 volumes) and **Yumemiru Happa** (The Dreaming Leaf, 1 volume).

Hisaya Nakajo's website:
www.wild-vanilla.com

CORRECTION AND APOLOGY

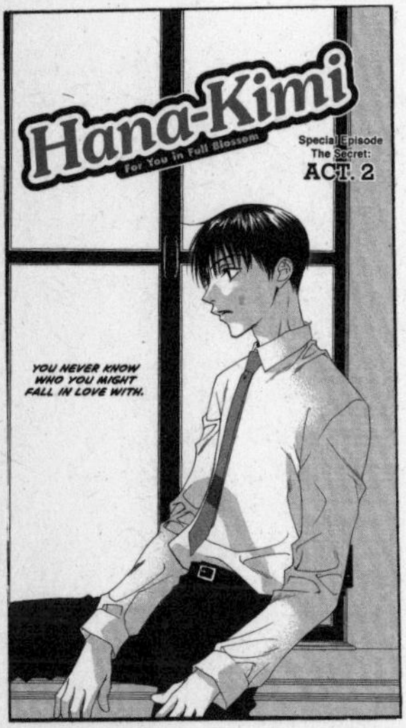
Hana-Kimi
For You in Full Blossom
Special Episode
The Secret:
ACT. 2
YOU NEVER KNOW WHO YOU MIGHT FALL IN LOVE WITH.

This is the page I was talking about. This is the correct version. In case you're thinking, "What?! nothing's different," that's because it was corrected in the second printing. (And in the first printing of the English edition -- The Editor) So you can only see the error in the first edition. Maybe it'll become a collector's item. If you happen to have the first edition, please get a pencil, and write the text in.

I found out that some text was missing from Chapter 78 of Volume 14. Specifically, it was a line of internal monologue from page 130, the opening page of the chapter. I didn't realize it was missing until long after the book was published. There was supposed to be a line of text like the one on the left, but somehow it was accidentally omitted during the publishing process. Apparently, they didn't see the text or didn't know it was supposed to be in the final print. I'm so sorry... The text was definitely meant to be there, but the readers didn't seem to have any problem following the story without it... (Aggh!) The truth is, page 129 and page 130 were supposed to match, so it wasn't quite right without the text. I'm so sorry if it was confusing! I'll be more careful next time!

--Hisaya Nakajo

IN THE NEXT VOLUME ...

Sano's little brother Shin returns...but this time he's Sano's rival! Shin has become a rising star of the high jump, and he's determined to prove himself by beating his older brother. But that's not the only blood on the track...the one coaching Shin is their father! Between Sano, Shin and Kagurazaka, who will be the new rising star?

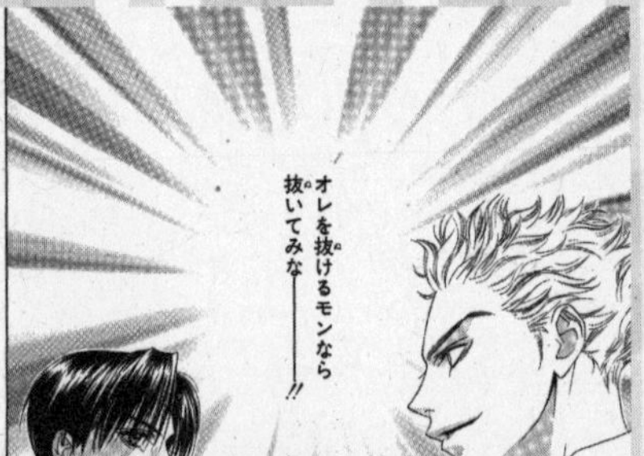
オレを抜けるモンなら
抜いてみな――――!!

COMING FEBRUARY 2007!

What happens when the hottest guy in school is a girl?!?

Find out in the popular manga series!

With original artwork by series creator Hisaya Nakajo, your favorite characters come to life in this art book!

Hana-Kimi™

GET THE COMPLETE
FUSHIGI YÛGI COLLECTION

www.viz.com
store.viz.com   © 1992 Yuu WATASE/Shogakukan Inc.

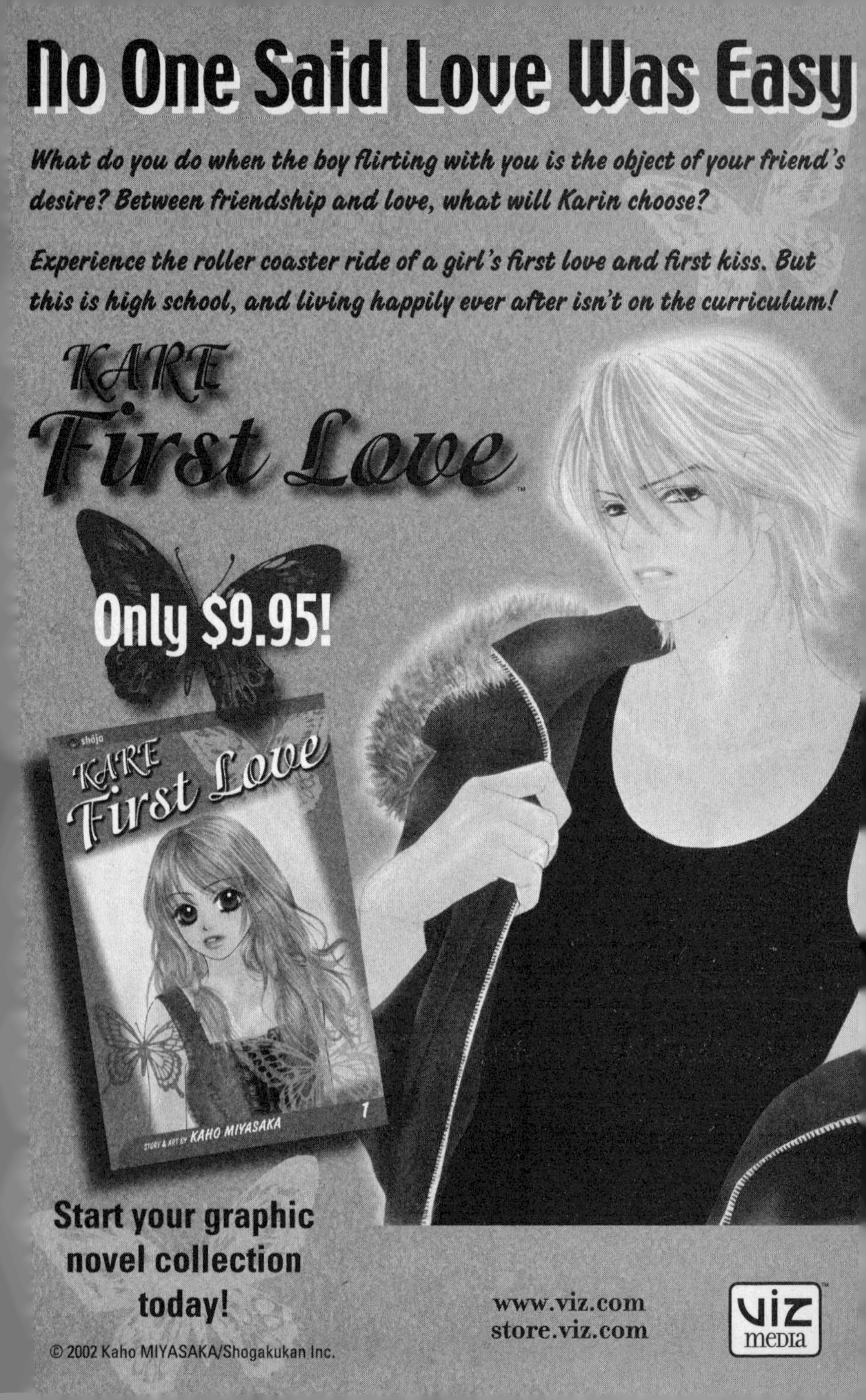
No One Said Love Was Easy
What do you do when the boy flirting with you is the object of your friend's desire? Between friendship and love, what will Karin choose?
Experience the roller coaster ride of a girl's first love and first kiss. But this is high school, and living happily ever after isn't on the curriculum!
KARE First Love™
Only $9.95!
shōjo
KARE First Love
1
STORY & ART BY KAHO MIYASAKA
Start your graphic novel collection today!
www.viz.com
store.viz.com
viz media
© 2002 Kaho MIYASAKA/Shogakukan Inc.